Unattainable Bride Russia

Unattainable Bride Russia

GENDERING NATION, STATE, AND INTELLIGENTSIA
IN RUSSIAN INTELLECTUAL CULTURE

Ellen Rutten

NORTHWESTERN UNIVERSITY PRESS / EVANSTON, ILLINOIS

Northwestern University Press
www.nupress.northwestern.edu

Copyright © 2010 by Northwestern University Press.
Published 2010. All rights reserved.

Printed in the United States of America

10 9 8 7 6 5 4 3 2 1

ISBN 978-0-8101-2869-9

   The Library of Congress has cataloged the original, hardcover edition as follows:
Rutten, Ellen, 1975–
    Unattainable bride Russia : gendering nation, state, and intelligentsia in
    Russian intellectual culture / Ellen Rutten.
        p. cm. — (Studies in Russian literature and theory)
    Includes bibliographical references and index.
    ISBN 978-0-8101-2656-5 (cloth : alk. paper)
    1. Russian literature—History and criticism. 2. Russia—In literature. 3. Femi-
ninity in literature. 4. Gender identity in literature. 5. Russia—Intellectual life.
I. Title. II. Series: Studies in Russian literature and theory.
PG2951.R88 2010
891.7093522—dc22

                                                                    2009049635

♾ The paper used in this publication meets the minimum requirements of the
American National Standard for Information Sciences—Permanence of Paper for
Printed Library Materials, ANSI Z39.48-1992.

Contents

Acknowledgments

If a panoramic view of twentieth-century Russian intellectual thought were possible, then its range of symbolic representations of Russia as unattainable bride would certainly strike the eye. The "bride Russia" of Nikolai Berdiaev's philosophy, the equation of Russia with Lara in *Doctor Zhivago,* Vladimir Sorokin's consummately Russian heroines: in their depiction of Russia, several twentieth-century literary, philosophical, political, and journalistic texts take recourse to the metaphor of an unattainable female beloved or bride-to-be.

By and large, such bridal metaphors can be linked with an underlying sociopolitical tension that has its roots in the nineteenth century. They are traceable to what could be labeled a "crisis of identity" within the Russian intellectual elite. From the early nineteenth century onward, Russian aristocratic—and later nonaristocratic as well—intellectuals were haunted by a growing sense of alienation from both the Russian state and the common people. Although thoroughly westernized themselves, they tended to criticize the Russian state retrospectively, from the reign of Peter I on, as a foreign Western entity that had estranged itself from "genuine" Russian culture. This ambivalent attitude toward both the regime and the West coincided with their increasing distance from Russia's native culture and population. Intellectual discourse revolved around the wish to bridge this distance and to create a new society that would be no less egalitarian than authentically Russian. That the dream of this "more Russian" society sprang from Romantic ideals of *Western* rather than Russian origin mattered little to its supporters.[1]

This paradoxical trend—the efforts of a westernized intellectual elite to defy the West (and its own "westernized" regime) in exchange for an imagined native Arcadia—is not exclusive to Russia. Ian Buruma and Avishai Margalit recently argued that it is not all that different from anti-Western feelings among westernized urban intellectuals in modern Asia and the Middle East.[2]

vii

Rather than zeroing in on these sociopolitical sentiments themselves, this study focuses on their transformation into a prominent gender metaphor around the turn of the twentieth century: namely, the representation of Russia as unattainable bride, which turned into a pivotal constituent of twentieth-century Russian intellectual thought. The bridal metaphor first attained supremacy in early twentieth-century literary, philosophical, and political debates—debates in which participants tended to envision their troubled self-views and worldviews in terms of a metaphoric amorous triangle. Within this triangle, the intelligentsia figured as Russia's symbolic suitor, Russia took on the role of female beloved, and the "westernized" tsarist regime appeared as the false husband from whom the intelligentsia needed to liberate the feminized Russia.

For obvious reasons, the intelligentsia's symbolic "liberation of the bride" was doomed to remain a utopian dream as long as the Russian Empire continued to exist. Little surprise, then, that those pre-revolutionary thinkers who used the metaphor invariably portrayed themselves or the intelligentsia as Russia's *ineffectual* suitors. After the fall of the tsarist government, however, one might have expected the concept of Russia as the intelligentsia's unattainable, oppressed beloved to have gradually vanished. Yet nothing of the sort occurred. On the contrary, the tendency to conceive of Russia as a bride-to-be, and of both state and intelligentsia as her male suitors, remained a key aspect of twentieth-century Russian intellectual thought. Far from disappearing after the Revolution of 1917, the concept continues even today as a vital cultural myth within Russian literature, philosophy, journalism, and, to a lesser extent, cinema, visual arts, tattoos, cartoons, and popular discourse. In 2009 it possesses the status of a cultural cliché that writers, thinkers, and artists travesty only too eagerly. This study affords the metaphor's development—from politically motivated image to object of postmodern parody—the meticulous exploration it merits.

As a prelude to this exploration, I would like to thank the Netherlands Scientific Organization (NWO) for funding my research on the project, and the University of Groningen for providing me with a welcoming and inspiring professional environment. For the final product, I am grateful to various people for various reasons. First of all, I am indebted to Joost van Baak for his part of our perfect collaboration, for motivating discussions, and for his unwavering support and acute editorial eye. Many thanks to Sander Brouwer for directing my thoughts to this topic and for more intellectual inspiration and support than any student could hope to receive. I would also like to express my gratitude to Viktor Erofeev, Aleksandr Iakut, Timur Kibirov, Andrei Nekrasov, and Vladimir Sorokin for sharing thoughts on their works; to Joe Andrew, Vsevolod Bagno, Wil van den Bercken, Otto

Acknowledgments

Boele, Gilles Dorleijn, Helena Goscilo, Rainer Grübel, Liesbeth Korthals Altes, Thomas Langerak, Vladimir Piskunov, Franziska Thun, Boris Uspenskii, Kees Verheul, Helen Wilcox, and Andrei Zorin for making time to shed light on (elements of) this study; to Miriam Finkelstein, Angela Livingstone, Sergei Nekliudov, and Clint Walker for generously providing unpublished research material; to Linda Edmondson, Karen Evans-Romaine, Antonia Napp, Riccardo Nicolosi, Brigitte Obermayr, Johanna Valenius, and Susanna Witt for taking the trouble to send recent publications; to Donna de Vries and the editors at Northwestern University Press for both a sharp eye and a convivial editing process; to Marina Konstantinova for sharing an amazing range of relevant Russian phone numbers; to Ann Perneel for extensive e-mail backing; to Frans and Victoire Rutten for their support; and to Wim and Geke van Dalen for a wonderful place in which to complete the writing. For an electrifying presence and for uplifting purrs, I thank those who make home a home: Thomas van Dalen and Pliushkin.

Unattainable Bride Russia

Introduction

IN 2000 IN MOSCOW, a new collection of poems by the poet Timur Kibirov opened with the following lines:

> You have only to utter the word "Russia,"
> and especially "Rus'," and into your mind
> immediately creep such platitudes,
> rubbish, nonsense so trivial.[1]

As examples of "Russia-platitudes," Kibirov mentions several nineteenth- and twentieth-century literary and philosophical national stereotypes. They include a reference to Russia's representation as female spouse in Aleksandr Blok's poetry.

> To Blok a wife.
> To Isakovskii a mother.
> To Dolmatovskii a mother.
> What do you want me to call you?
> A grandmother? No way![2]

Although the metaphor of Russia as wife or beloved has indeed become a cliché in contemporary Russia, it has received little attention in literary research to date.

This study is devoted to adaptations in twentieth-century Russian culture of the metaphor to which Kibirov refers. It focuses on gendered representations of the relationship among the Russian intelligentsia, Russia in the form of the Russian land or its people, and the Russian state.

In Russia, debate on these essentially sociopolitical relationships traditionally took place at the intersection of literature, philosophy, and political journalism: the Russian discussion on national identity was formulated to a large extent in literary circles.[3] Russia is not unique in this respect, as has sometimes been deemed: in most countries, as Joep Leerssen argues, it is in the literary field "that national stereotypes are first and most effectively formulated, perpetuated and disseminated."[4]

Thus an investigation of the political metaphor discussed here must walk the tightrope that connects literary analysis to sociopolitical and cultural-anthropological research. This inquiry attempts to do justice to this precondition by blending literary analysis with a study of nonliterary codes—philosophical treatises, political journalism, visual genres (paintings, films, cartoons, tattoos) and the like—and of social behavior, as reconstructed from letters, memoirs, interviews, and sociohistorical studies.

GENDERED LOVE TRIANGLE

This study explores a persistent sociocultural construct: the tendency to depict the relationship among the Russian intellectual elite, state, and people in gendered terms. This trend has ancient roots, but it is only in Russian twentieth-century intellectual thought that its ingredients meet to form a popular, elaborate metaphoric constellation with a set of more or less stable features. This metaphoric constellation renders the intelligentsia-state-Russia triangle as an amorous rivalry of two masculine forces competing for the same feminine entity. If Russia appears as the feminine component, then the Russian state is represented as its symbolic captor or husband, and the intelligentsia as its true bridegroom. The nature of their mutual relations is problematic: the symbolic "true bridegroom" is always an ineffectual bridegroom, for whom the desired "bride Russia" remains unattainable.

The concept described here occurs so often in twentieth-century Russian culture that by 2000 Kibirov can rightly treat it as an outworn cliché. Its outlines can be reconstructed in several twentieth-century literary works, philosophical and esoteric treatises, political essays, artworks, and films. Cartoons, tattoos, pop lyrics, and discussions on chat forums—some of which I briefly discuss—attest that it is solidly rooted in popular discourse as well. An exhaustive analysis would exceed the scope of this study, therefore, which focuses on the following selection of literary and philosophical texts.

> Aleksandr Blok's collection of poems *Native Land* (*Rodina*, 1907–16) and his play *Song of Fate* (*Pesnia sud'by*, 1908)
>
> A number of philosophical-journalistic texts by Nikolai Berdiaev from the 1910s
>
> Andrei Platonov's novel *Happy Moscow* (*Schastlivaia Moskva*, 1932–36, published 1991)
>
> Boris Pasternak's novel *Doctor Zhivago* (*Doktor Zhivago*, 1946–55, Russian publication 1988)
>
> Pasternak's play *Blind Beauty* (*Slepaia krasavitsa*, 1959–60, published 1969)

Daniil Andreev's esoteric treatise *Rose of the World* (*Roza mira*, 1950–58, Russian publication 1989)

Vasilii Grossman's historical novel *Forever Flowing* (*Vse techet . . .*, 1963, Russian publication 1989)

Venedikt Erofeev's novella *Moscow to the End of the Line* (*Moskva-Petushki*, 1969, Russian publication 1989)

Viktor Erofeev's and Vladimir Sorokin's novels *Russian Beauty* (*Russkaia krasavitsa*, 1982, Russian publication 1990) and *Marina's Thirtieth Love* (*Trídtsataia liubov' Maríny*, 1983, Russian publication 1995)

A number of stories and novels by Viktor Pelevin from the 1990s and 2000s

Mikhail Berg's short novel "Ros and I" ("Ros i ia," 1990)

A number of poems by Timur Kibirov from the 1990s and 2000s

This selection covers the twentieth century from beginning to end, and it represents the principal artistic phases (modernism, postmodernism) that Russia underwent during this time.

The attentive reader will notice that the selection includes no female authors. There is a simple reason for the lack of female voices: women writers and philosophers rarely take recourse to bridal images of Russia. On those occasions in which they do—and which I discuss in passing—as a rule, the bridal image is no more than a minor theme. Female authors' reluctance to address the topic continues to remain a riddle, although a possible explanation may be "bride Russia's" status as the mere object of male strivings—more on this later.

Those texts that I do discuss should not be interpreted as variations on an invariable theme. Each author adapts elements of the metaphor in question in a different way and within his or her unique poetics. To start with, some artists represent Russia allegorically rather than metaphorically. Pasternak's *Blind Beauty* is an allegorical play, which as a whole can be interpreted as a symbolic depiction of Russia as a young woman. It can be read on both literal and metaphoric levels. By contrast, Blok's poetic exclamation "My Russia! My wife!" is a metaphoric comparison, one which is made explicit within the text.[5] Since the latter approach dominates most of the texts discussed, this study applies "metaphor" rather than "allegory" as an umbrella term. In doing so, it benefits from Ivor Richards's theory of metaphor. According to Richards, every metaphor consists of a *tenor* (an "underlying idea"), a *vehicle* (a metaphoric term or "figure" through which the tenor is expressed), and a *ground* (a set of "common characteristics" of tenor and vehicle, or the reason for creating the metaphor).[6] Employing his terms, one can reduce the metaphor discussed here to the following:

Tenor: Sociopolitical triangle: Russia–intellectual elite–state

Vehicle: Amorous triangle: female beloved–(ineffectual) lover–husband

Ground: Problematic mutual relations, alienation, clash of interests

In other words, the subject or tenor to which the metaphor is applied—
"what is really being thought of"—is the problematic Russia-intelligentsia-
regime relationship. The image used to represent this subject—"what it is
compared to"—is that of a female beloved for whose love husband and lover
vie.[7] The shared ground of vehicle and tenor consists of those features that
the amorous intrigue and its social subject have in common: problematic
mutual relations. As a rule, these problematic relations are presented from
the lover's perspective: central is the question of whether his claim to the
"bride Russia" is legitimate, a concern accompanied by the anticipation of
his inability to free her from the symbolic husband, the state.

The different texts also vary in other than strictly metaphoric respects.
They rely on social categories that are defined uniquely by the individual authors. In the works involved, the term "Russia" refers to rather abstract eth-
nic concepts.[8] It is treated as a synonym of, alternately, the Russian people,
Kievan Rus', the Russian earth, and traditional rural Russia. It refers to an
invented, "imagined" national essence—to use Benedict Anderson's term.[9]

An ill-defined concept in and of itself, the imagined Russia is not represented consistently as a clear-cut metaphor throughout these works. In
certain texts—Blok's poems, for instance—the words "Russia" and "bride"
or "wife" are juxtaposed or openly equated. In others, a description of the
Russian landscape or people gradually coalesces with the depiction of a female beloved. Similar to this device, of which *Doctor Zhivago* is a prime
example, is the tendency to liken a concrete female character to Russia. In
novels and plays, as a rule, the latter two strategies prevail: the reader is confronted with a heroine who is likened to Russia in such a way that she can be
considered its metaphoric equivalent.

Heterogeneity also tinges the depiction of the intelligentsia, Russia's
symbolic suitor. The subject of "intelligentsia" as a problematic cultural
term has been discussed by a number of contemporary scholars.[10] This study
agrees with Victor Erlich that by the early twentieth century it is best cir-
cumscribed as the educated elite that had in common a "repudiation of tsarist autocracy, a strong disposition toward fundamental social change, and
a burning compassion for the dispossessed (the 'people'), accompanied by
a gnawing sense of moral obligation toward them."[11] Obviously, those who
shared such characteristics did not form a cohesive social group. Thus, both
the traditional aristocracy and the radical socialists who had worked their
way up from a disadvantaged social status were considered *intelligenty,* but
in reality they had little in common.

The protagonists in the works discussed are connected with "the intelligentsia" in various ways.[12] Blok and Berdiaev see the intelligentsia as a
matter-of-course social category with which they identify. The male characters in Platonov's novel *Happy Moscow* are typified as representatives of the
early Soviet intelligentsia, which formed a distinct professional group that—

6

in contrast with the pre-revolutionary intelligentsia—did not traditionally oppose the regime. Doctor Zhivago is linked with the intelligentsia primarily in a literary sense: a traditional cultural *intelligent* to the fingertips, he consciously poses as an heir of Pushkin and other giants of intellectual culture in nineteenth-century Russia. Finally, postmodern authors tend to use the term "intelligentsia" ironically. Instead of identifying with it, they distance themselves from its sociopolitical commitment. In particular, they are eager to mock Soviet dissidents, who often regarded themselves as spiritual heirs of the traditional intelligentsia.

No less multiform than the representation of the intelligentsia is that of the Russian state in the texts selected. If Helena Goscilo and Andrea Laroux rightly oppose "the sphere of the state" as "observable" and "visible" to "the mythological space of the nation," then it is hard to reduce the concept of the state, as found in the works discussed here, to one coherent definition.[13] All these authors are inclined to personify the state as an older, powerful antagonist who holds the feminized Russia in his power, and from whom she needs to be freed.[14] In some cases, however, the antagonist is associated explicitly with the Russian state, varying from tsarist authorities to Vladimir Putin, whereas in others he is simply characterized as a socially successful or dominant figure in opposition to the protagonist. In yet others, he is associated with the West or literally comes from the West. This association with the West is not fortuitous: from the nineteenth century on, Russian intellectuals traditionally saw the regime as a Western-oriented, foreign entity.

Thus, we are dealing here not with one metaphor but with a number of metaphoric representations that all revolve around one and the same theme. Depending on time and setting, such representations vary from the pre-revolutionary intelligentsia's problematic relationship with the tsarist regime to the clash between today's oligarchs and the Russian state. What they do have in common is the use of amorous metaphors to refer to the problematic sociopolitical tripod of official authority, intellectual opposition, and an imagined Russian native essence. In addition, they share a preference for translating essentially internal political tensions into matters of Russia's identity as distinct from that of the West—a classic device in Russian cultural history, in which Russia defines itself "in an entirely conscious opposition to the West, itself employing elements of Western culture for that goal."[15]

EXISTING RESEARCH

Its frequent occurrence notwithstanding, the gendered representation of Russia, intelligentsia, and state has sparked relatively little attention in literary research. Literary scholars and historians have explored relations among intelligentsia, state, and people extensively, but they have not traditionally

7

assigned a central place to the category of gender. From the 1980s on, the Slavic community did witness the appearance of a growing number of feminist and gender-oriented studies, including scholarly investigations of representations of masculinity and femininity in Russian culture.[16] The personification of Russia as a (maternal) female figure became a central trope in studies by Joanna Hubbs, Adele Marie Barker, and Oleg Riabov.[17]

As a rule, however, studies of gender representation in Russia either focus on cultural representation in general or tend to stress the image of Russia as a maternal force. As late as 2004, Christa Ebert is able to assert that in Russia, "wives . . . do not occupy a constitutive part in national symbolics."[18] This study offers a revision of the view of the Russian national myth cloaked primarily in a maternal mantle. It emphatically abandons the traditional mother myth in favor of the more recent, politically motivated concept of Russia as the intelligentsia's unattainable bride.

The overall neglect within literary theory of the gendering of Russia-intelligentsia-state into a love triangle does not mean the topic has gone completely unnoticed. As a rule, however, either it has been mentioned briefly without detailed analysis of its outlines in concrete works, or the discussion has been limited to the work of one author or period only.[19] Thus, in the past ten years Oleg Riabov has extensively discussed gendered representations of Russia-intelligentsia-state in the Silver Age as part of a larger investigation of womanhood in Russian literature and philosophy.[20] More recently, Sander Brouwer and Aleksei Makushinskii have published articles devoted to the same theme in nineteenth-century cultural history and literature.[21]

As yet, an integral discussion of the metaphor in question is lacking, however. This study attempts to change that situation, not only by providing substantial empirical and theoretical additions to existing research, but also by continuing where earlier research tended to stop. Revealing is Makushinskii's claim that Blok's gendered representation of Russia can be considered an "epilogue" to the nineteenth century.[22] Without disputing Makushinskii's view, my analysis does the opposite: it takes Blok as a *prologue* or starting point for a discussion of the metaphor in the twentieth century. It traces the gendered representation of Russia, intelligentsia, and state through the twentieth century and to the present, when it has been virtually abandoned by scholars. My objective is to offer the detailed discussion that this modern cultural myth deserves.

TEXT AND THE "REAL WORLD"

This analysis focuses primarily on texts—literary, philosophical, political. It does not treat them as strictly textual events, however, isolated from the historical or cultural issues of the day. Instead of interpreting literary texts as reflections of a recoverable absolute reality, these analyses regard them as representations of a reality that is always subjective and, as such, always the product of the experience of one concrete person or group. Accordingly, the question of a "true" course of events "behind," or leading to, the gendered representation of intelligentsia-state-Russia in the diverse texts does not interest me. What does fascinate me is how sociopolitical reality is represented in the texts in question, as well as how these textual representations eventually merge into a modern myth.

In answering these questions, I support my analyses with extraliterary expressions of self-view and worldview. Such a strategy is influenced by a number of scholarly approaches that focus on the interaction between different levels of culture: in this case, especially between literature and political or cultural history.

The focus on an interaction between literary and cultural or political codes formed a theoretical point of departure for both the Moscow-Tartu school of semiotics and—in a somewhat different context—the "New Historicism."[23] Without identifying totally with one or the other, this analysis profited from the way in which a number of studies that can be linked with Soviet semiotics or New Historicism approach the inextricably related fields of literary and cultural history.[24] The project also benefits from Hayden White's early explorations of history as a "verbal structure in the form of a narrative prose discourse" and from the study of cross-national perceptions known as imagology.[25] Although not set up as an "imagologist" project, my analyses do subscribe to most of imagology's main theses, such as the endeavor to explore national *stereotypes* rather than fixed identities and the "discourse of representation rather than a society."[26]

On a general note, this analysis allies with a trend in recent humanities research to question the possibility of objective data and to focus on interdisciplinarity. Both premises are crucial to deconstructionist thought, as well as to a number of other fields, including feminism, cultural studies, and postcolonialism.

It would be a mistake, however, to use terms like "deconstructionist," "semiotic," "New Historicist," or "feminist" to label this study. Its use of the aforementioned approaches to literature and culture is eclectic: to me, they are above all useful metalanguages, or tools that help refine one's thoughts about texts and their interaction with the "real world."

FROM CANON TO MARGIN TO CANON

Kibirov's ironic complaint about the triviality of the metaphor under discussion indicates the extent to which it has taken root in contemporary Russian culture. The bridal metaphor did not occupy an equally central place throughout the twentieth century, however. Within the total corpus of twentieth-century texts that turn to it, the stress clearly falls on the first and last decades of the century. If one were to present them on a timeline, there would be large gaps surrounding Platonov and his contemporaries. By contrast, the first and last decades of the century would be crowded with numerous titles of literary and philosophical texts, films, works of art, and cartoons, among other discursive genres.

This disproportion is illustrative of the prominence of the metaphor in the years between the early twentieth century and today. In both the pre-revolutionary and post-Soviet years, representations of the Russia-intelligentsia-state triangle as a problematic amorous intrigue can be found on every proverbial street corner. By contrast, in the Soviet era they rarely occur in either official or underground literature. Consequently, whereas chapters 2 and 4 touch upon the mere tip of the iceberg, the Soviet texts that appear here are practically the only works from their time in which the metaphor occurs.[27]

In the course of the twentieth century, the change in popularity of the Russia-bride metaphor is radical, but not inexplicable. Among other factors, its recurrence in the first decades can be explained by Symbolism's preference for metaphoric and allegorical representation, by a general vogue of gender and sexuality, and by an all-pervading sense of national crisis and favorable conditions for polemic debate.

In the Soviet Union conditions changed. Shortly after the revolution, as Victoria Bonnell argues, the artistic fashion for allegorical themes began to make way for more "concrete visualization[s] of social categories and concepts."[28] Moreover, from the late 1920s on, the way in which Russia was portrayed in literature was determined largely by official views. According to socialist realism, the Soviet system had led to a disappearance of social differences and to a successful union between intellectuals and ordinary people. Socialist realist literature was supposed to reflect that happy union, in obligatorily optimistic creations that left no room for "lost illusions, broken hopes, unfulfilled dreams" or, for that matter, amorous tragedies.[29] As a critic asserted in 1936, the heroine-centered love triangle of classic Russian literature had "lost its meaning" in the 1930s' Soviet novel.[30]

Within such a literary climate, the metaphoric portrayal of the Russian people as unattainable for the intellectual elite was taboo. By problematizing the relationship among intelligentsia, state, and people, this concept did anything but describe a blissful union of intellectuals and workers.

Harder to explain is the metaphor's marginal place in underground Soviet literature. This absence can be linked, in any case, to the impossibility of critical public debate. As a result, the tradition of polemical discussion that led to the birth of so many pre-revolutionary publications on Russia's national identity disappeared. In addition, the pre-revolutionary bride-Russia metaphor no longer worked after 1917, when the social labels "state," "intelligentsia," and "people" underwent substantial change.

After the relative silence of the Soviet years, the metaphor emerges as a prominent device again in late and post-Soviet culture. It is argued here that the renewed attention to representations of Russia as the intelligentsia's unattainable bride can be explained by a number of factors, including the postmodern focus on a play with national stereotypes, the resumed possibilities for open critical debate, and the easy accessibility and popularity of pre-revolutionary texts that make use of the concept. In this cultural setting, the metaphor returns to the forefront as a popular cultural stereotype in both artistic genres and public discourse. Undoubtedly, it was this popularity that caused Kibirov to include it in his list of "trivial" Russia clichés in 2000.

FROM MODERNISM TO POSTMODERNISM

Any study confronted with a time span of a century faces questions of continuity, and this project is no exception. Between 1900 and today, the metaphor of Russia as bride undergoes a substantial shift, which can be linked to the general transition from modernism to postmodernism that marks the twentieth century. Pivotal to its development in recent decades is the rejection of ideological commitment that marks the postmodern worldview.

Early twentieth-century Russian culture offers a sharp contrast to that view. In the pre-revolutionary years, a writer's ideological convictions functioned as a guiding principle for the creation of art. If Russian Symbolists propagated "art for art's sake," at the same time they used their work to express personal political and ideological views. As Aage Hansen-Löve argues, Symbolist artists paradoxically combine extraliterary and purely aesthetic considerations in works that exude an "ambivalent intentionality."[31]

Such an "ambivalent intentionality" marks several pre-revolutionary versions of the bride-Russia metaphor. Aleksandr Blok, for instance, is known as a strictly aesthetically oriented Symbolist, but he also considered the "gap" between the intelligentsia and the Russian people a "vital" and "real" theme.[32] When discussing this theme, he wanted people to listen only to the "*content* of the *issues*," rather than to "the *form* of my statement" or its "aesthetic style features."[33] In Ivor Richards's theory, Blok's bridal Russia images would belong, therefore, to those metaphors in which "the vehicle . . . become[s] almost a mere decoration or coloring of the tenor," and the metaphor's "underlying idea" is the center of attention.[34] Not surprisingly, the fictional characters through which Blok expresses his views on Russia are abstract beings, whose physical appearance receives little attention.

For the Soviet-era authors discussed here—with the possible exception of Platonov—literature and philosophy remain tools for the expression of sociopolitical views. Although they do not ascribe the same mythical-religious function to literature as their pre-revolutionary predecessors, the attitude of these authors toward issues of national identity links them unmistakably with the Russian tradition of regarding "literature as 'nation-builder.'"[35] Programmatic is Pasternak's assertion that, as a writer, he served as the voice of the Russian people.[36] As shown in this study, this conviction tangibly tinges his gendered rendition of Russia, intelligentsia, and state in *Doctor Zhivago*.

Toward the end of the twentieth century, under the influence of postmodernism, the focus on the sociopolitical function of literature and philosophy loses ground. Where Blok's gendered view of Russia and intelligentsia was motivated by deep political convictions, postmodern Russian writers deny any such political commitment. Instead, they stress the strictly literary-aesthetic intention of their works. Sorokin revealingly defines his texts as "just letters on a piece of paper."[37] Accordingly, postmodern writers claim to represent Russia as unattainable bride primarily out of interest in its status as a cultural cliché. To remain within Ivor Richards's terminology, they are interested not in the metaphor's "underlying theme" but rather in its "vehicle," or the characters which metaphorically represent that theme. Indeed, for postmodern writers, a feminized Russia is not an abstract female figure but a woman with a prominent bodily presence; in their hands, the concept of a union between the intelligentsia and Russia becomes an intensely physical, sexual affair.

This study examines the effect of the diverging approaches to the political marriage metaphor throughout the twentieth century. It argues that, on the one hand, in postmodern texts the concept largely loses its politico-ideological dimension. On the other hand, the myth's popularity in contemporary literature and its similar outlines in several recent texts contradict the idea that it serves as merely one of many random "letters on a piece of paper." These developments suggest that the writers who portray Russia as a metaphoric bride nevertheless share a distinct thematic preference for this particular myth and for a relatively standardized way of depicting it.

GENDER ISSUES

At first glance, this study may seem to focus on a female image: the personification of Russia as a bride or a wife. A closer look reveals that the female image invariably serves to underline the problematic identity of a *male* counterpart: the Russian intelligentsia. Although not explicitly adopting a feminist perspective, my study does owe this and other insights to feminist literary scholarship.

It was with the emergence of feminism in the 1960s that the division between "masculine" and "feminine" stereotypes came to be widely recognized as a sociocultural construct rather than as a biologically determined classification. Following Derrida's deconstruction strategy, French feminists in particular strove to show the socioculturally determined character of gender categories. Exemplary is Hélène Cixous' list of dualities in classic Western thought.

Activity/Passivity
Sun/Moon
Culture/Nature
Day/Night

Father/Mother
Head/Heart
Intelligible/Sensitive
Logos/Pathos[38]

Relating these opposites to another pair, man/woman, Cixous observes that in philosophy, "woman is always on the side of passivity."[39]

Rather than merely pointing to this and other gender mechanisms underlying Western thinking, feminism tried to overthrow the notion of a natural link between gender and non-biologically determined concepts. It did so in part in scholarly spheres—including the field of literary history, where feminists called for a revised look at literary representations of womanhood. Since women have been kept out of the literary field, and most of the texts that we read were written by men, they argued, the view that literature and philosophy represent a universal culture ought to be adjusted. They asserted that literature and philosophy express a patriarchal view of the world and of society. Feminist literary scholars also pointed out the status of the average female character (or of femininity in general) as "the Other," or as merely a male projection. In a feminist study of American literature, Judith Fetterly concluded that its female characters serve only "to indicate the involutions of the male psyche with which literature is primarily concerned . . . . They are projections, not people."[40]

Feminist and gender studies in the Slavonic field have shown that in Russian literary works the heroine likewise functions as no more than a "projection of male fantasy and desire."[41] They claim that, as a rule, in modern Russian literature these "male projections" refer specifically to the issue

13

of Russia's national identity: in Barbara Heldt's words, "the Russian heroine is generally taken as a marvelous given of nature, a being in whom not only her own and her family's virtue, but the future hope of Russia resides."[42] Rosalind Marsh similarly argues that Russian writers tend to depict their heroines as a "'non-cognating' symbol of the Russian soul."[43]

By implication, it is principally impossible to discuss feminized representations of Russia without taking into consideration the male perspective from which they originate. The feminized Russia is always feminized *in relation to* a masculine opponent—in this case, the (male) intelligentsia and the Russian state. Therefore, an analysis of metaphoric representations of Russia as an unattainable female beloved invariably involves a discussion of these male categories.

If in this and other premises this study employs a gender-sensitive outlook, then it is greatly indebted to feminist scholarly achievements for that sensitivity. At the same time, it differs from those feminist studies that underscore the problematic relationship between women and cultural representation. According to Helena Goscilo, for instance, the tendency to allegorize femininity may be artistically effective, but its effect on women's real lives can be very harmful, "eras[ing] them as human beings and ignor[ing] women's genuine daily plights." Goscilo considers this situation especially destructive in societies that, like Russia, "undergo . . . rapid, destabilizing change amidst economic chaos."[44]

I agree with Goscilo's view—what's more, I believe that Russia's masculine myths (such as that of the weak-effeminate *intelligent*) also negatively affect real men's lives—but I do not address the metaphor's problematic effect here. The extent to which our heroines function as female sounding boards is not explored in this study.

It could prove worthwhile, however, to examine the Russia-as-bride myth from a critical feminist perspective. Did, for instance, the classic Russian view of marriage as "an almost obligatory stage in the passage to adulthood" influence this political-marriage metaphor?[45] And how do ecstatic visions of Russia as an exalted female figure—who never so much as polishes her nails—correspond to the reality of pre-revolutionary Russia, where "the everyday duties of marriage, motherhood, and housekeeping continued to govern most women's lives"?[46] That these questions go beyond the scope of this monograph does not make them less relevant for the study of Russia's cultural history.

GENDER, NATION, REPRESENTATION

Feminists, as said, stressed the link between female characters and the issue of national identity in Russian literature. This link was not noted by feminism alone, however. Iurii Lotman also observed it when he stated that in modern Russian literature

> the hero, destined to transform the world, can be the executor of one of two roles: he can be an "undoer" or a "savior" . . . in this context "the world," Russia, is assigned the function of the feminine character "to be devastated" or "to be saved," and the active character transforms the male part.[47]

Such fusions between the national and the feminine spheres are not uncommon in modern Western culture. Since the late eighteenth century, an internationally rife narrative can be discerned in political as well as in literary circles, in which issues of national identity are formulated in terms of gender oppositions. This narrative was first placed on the academic agenda by feminists.[48] Among other things, feminist studies claimed that since the discussion of national identity was pursued in predominantly male circles, "nation becomes feminized . . . in service to male needs."[49] Subsequently, from the mid-1980s the intersection of national and gender concepts has proven to be a major source of general—not strictly feminist—academic interest.[50] An exploration of some of the outcomes of these existing studies of nation and gender helps us to understand the broader international context of the bride-Russia metaphor.

Despite controversies over the term "nation," scholars today seem to agree that it refers to a mental construct rather than to a historically, ethnically, or geographically motivated entity. Concepts of national identity began to arise in the eighteenth century—and in Russia, toward the nineteenth century—as a result of, among other factors, the growing possibilities of travel, war, and increasing trade contacts.

From the very start, debates on national identity dovetailed with thinking about gender differences. It is difficult to determine which factors contributed to this intersection, but most probably it sprang from a combination of historical developments: the fact that national debates were conducted by predominantly male groups, who identified with the role of (masculine) protector of the (feminized) nation;[51] the appearance of new theories on sexual difference at the end of the eighteenth century;[52] and, as George Mosse argues, the Romantic trend to envision abstract categories in concrete objects, whereby "a beautiful woman . . . exemplified the romantic utopia just as she represented the national ideal."[53] In Russia, as several scholars point out, grammatical categories also enhanced a gendered nationalist discourse: not only are Rus' and the Russian terms for Russia (*Rossiia*), country (*strana*), native land (*rodina*), and Moscow (*Moskva*) feminine nouns; but by lack of a pronoun referring to inanimate objects, the Russian language forces users to opt for the personal pronoun "she" in referring to these spatial categories.[54]

As a rule, in nationalist rhetoric state and nation tend to be gendered as male and female, respectively.[55] Masculine national allegories do exist, however. Like feminine representations of nationhood, they personify a set of characteristics that is traditionally associated with the gender stereotype in question: in the "male case," these characteristics include progress, change, and modern, urban society, or—in a negative variant—force and authority.[56] Female national symbols, on the other hand, generally represent morality, tradition, and virtue; they stand for sedateness, immutability, and pastoral ideals.[57] Katherine Verdery has presented nation-gender antinomies in a schematic overview that is not unlike Cixous' list of contrasts. In Verdery's view, Western thinking tends to equate the opposition woman/man with antitheses such as

    beloved/lover
    body/soul
    nature/culture
    land/people[58]

In the eighteenth and nineteenth centuries, these and the other gendered distinctions mentioned were employed in nationalist debate in different ways. The intersection between gender and nation sometimes consisted of the creation of a female national symbol or allegory with a proper name, which then occurred in political and literary texts as well as visual images—think of statues and paintings, but also of cartoons or portraits on coins. Examples include the French Marianne, Britain's Britannia, and the German Germania.[59] That they not only enjoyed popularity in distant history is indicated by the large-scale exhibition "Marianne and Germania: 1789–1889" held at the 1989 Berliner Festspiele.[60] The 1980s also saw Margaret Thatcher pictured as a smiling Britannia, dressed in armor and high heels, on the cover of the British tabloid *The Sun*.[61]

Although the Russian tradition lacks such an individualized national icon, it is linked with international nationalist tradition through its veneration of Mother Russia.[62] In nineteenth-century literature, political debates, and visual imagery, maternal national allegories occupy a prominent place in (especially European) nation-building.[63] If erotic connotations are never far away in their representations—illustrative are Mother Russia's all-too-prominent breasts and voluptuous hips in Volgograd's famous *The Motherland Calls Upon You* (*Rodina-mat' zovet*, 1967) statue—then, as a rule, the maternal figures are connected with nurture and tradition. By contrast, national allegories of the Britannia type act as repositories of virtue and moral strength.

Another nationalist rhetorical strategy involves the characterization of different nations or races as essentially feminine or masculine. Nineteenth-

and early twentieth-century political and historiographic thought tends to define the German people, or northwest European nations in general, as preeminently masculine races; whereas southern European nations, Jews, and Slavs are usually portrayed as feminine races.[64] The gender division of Germany and Russia as masculine and feminine, respectively, is pivotal to the work of Berdiaev and certain contemporaries, a subject addressed in chapter 2.

That gender metaphors are employed for political ends is illustrated best in times of war or when war threatens. In wartime discourse—in political and literary texts, cartoons, tattoos, visual art, and films—the tendency to phrase national concerns in gender terms heightens palpably.[65] Particularly popular is the strategic representation of one's country as a female figure who is (threatened with being) raped or captured by a masculinized enemy.[66] The prevalence of this rhetorical device, even in recent times, is demonstrated by the Iraqi novel *Zabiba and the King*, allegedly written by none other than Saddam Hussein. In the allegorical love story that *Zabiba* tells, Iraq appears as an attractive woman, for whose love a bad character (an allegorical amalgam of "the Jews" and the United States) and a positive hero (Saddam) strive. The U.S. invasion of Iraq appears here as Iraq-alias-Zabiba's symbolic rape.[67]

The concept of the rape of one's country is relevant to the bride-Russia metaphor, but in foreign imagery Russia has been appointed the opposite role, that of male oppressor or violator—of, for example, a feminized Poland or Finland.[68] In a more optimistic scenario, Adam Mickiewicz stages the same feminized Poland as the happy bride of a masculine Lithuania, in his *Book of the Polish Nation* (1832).[69]

Similar erotic-violent imagery is rampant in the depiction of colonizing versus colonized countries. Postcolonial studies show that in literature and in travel memoirs, these are often opposed as dominating masculine and dominated feminine entities, respectively.[70] In this context, Russia once again acquires the role of male counterpart: nineteenth-century Russian authors repeatedly conceived of its relationship to the Caucasus as that of a dominant male force subjugating a passive female victim.[71] The recurring gender paradigm in this scheme is one of erotic tension between colonizing force—the male "lover"—and colonized territory—the female "bride-to-be."[72]

Of particular interest to the current study is yet another way in which modern cultures have genderized issues of national identity. This is a situation, occurring in literary texts as well as in propaganda and political statements, in which a protagonist, poet, or autobiographical author is described as the lover of his native land and in which this land appears as his female beloved. Such a metaphor can be reconstructed in the nineteenth and twentieth centuries both inside and outside Europe. As said, it has been observed in Russian literature by Lotman and others, but its outlines are also found in Finnish poetry, prose, and nationalist memoirs;[73] in Romanian patriotic poetry;[74] in Iranian patriotic poetry and essays;[75] in German nineteenth-century poems;[76] and in the work of the Czech poet Jaroslav Seifert.[77] One of many examples of the same metaphor in a regional context—and a smart sample of city marketing—is a claim by the mayor of Groningen, the city where this study was conceived, that "Groningen is like a girl you fall in love with at first sight."[78]

Intimate amorous rhetoric is particularly widespread in the context of the (emigrant) artist's nostalgia for a distant homeland or long-lost childhood. Pamela Chester has reconstructed how, in the childhood reminiscences of a number of Russian and English writers and painters, "the landscape itself is feminized" and identified with "the feminine Other."[79] In late nineteenth-century letters written in Italy, Peter Tchaikovsky asserts that there exists no man "more in love with mother Russia . . . than I" and that he loves Russia "with a passionate kind of love."[80] Marina Tsvetaeva labels Konstantin Bal'mont's attitude to Russia during his exile the "being-in-love of a foreigner" and a "romance with Russia."[81] As an elaboration on this theme, one might consider Viktor Shklovskii's novel *Zoo, or Letters Not About Love* (*Zoo, ili pis'ma ne o liubvi*, 1922). Constructed as a correspondence between an autobiographical male character in Berlin and his beloved Alia in Petrograd, *Zoo* concludes with the confession that "Alia is a realized metaphor. I have made up a woman and a love affair for a book about . . . a foreign world. I want to return to Russia."[82] A few decades later, the Vitebsk-born U.S. emigrant Marc Chagall addresses his native town as an abandoned girl, who probably wonders "why I left you for so many years when I loved you. No, you thought: the lad's gone off somewhere . . . and yet there was not a single one of my pictures in which your joys and sorrows were not reflected."[83] Vladimir Nabokov, another Soviet emigrant to the United States, concludes the story of his first love in his autobiographical *Speak, Memory* (1967) by stating that "the loss of my country was equated for me with the loss of my love."[84]

The representation of the native land in the texts mentioned involves the intimate-emotive aspect of a feminized land and the male struggle for it, both of which mark the metaphor of Russia as bride. As a rule, they stress the physical aspects of heterosexual love that will become so crucial to this metaphor. Thus, in a 1900 essay Iran appears as a "heart-stealing beauty" whom one should "embrace . . . bite her lips, suck her neck, taste her sugar, fulfill one's desire."[85] Late nineteenth-century poems by the Finnish poet J. H. Erkko personify the Finnish landscape as a blonde, blue-eyed girl, who is awakened by spring's "warm kisses of love" and whose white shroud

18

"flowed down the maiden's breasts."[86] Nabokov calls his homesickness for Russia "a sensuous . . . matter."[87]

In other words, the trend to speak metaphorically of the nation as a beloved woman is far from unique to the works explored here. There is, however, one crucial difference between the examples mentioned and the selection of texts in this study. The former consist primarily of patriotic statements. As such, they are imbued with positive images: they stress the happiness felt by the poet or speaker in expressing love for his country. Those tragic images that do occur are mainly depictions of wartime or exile, where the feminized native land is temporarily unreachable or humiliated because of external reasons. Introspection or questions of guilt on the part of the speaker or writer are touched upon only marginally.

By contrast, this study deliberately targets introspection and guilt. It deals with representations that pinpoint Russia as the intelligentsia's *unattainable* bride, representations that underline the problematic attitude that Russia's westernized intellectual elite takes toward Russia. It examines a metaphor springing from the belief of this select group that it has become alienated from a native Russian "essence." Separating them from national allegories such as the ones discussed above, this sociopolitical problematization is what unites the texts to which we now turn.

Apocalyptic Riders, World Souls, Westernized Boys, and Russian Girls: Before 1900

RECALLING A TRIP to the countryside, in 1826 Aleksandr Griboedov describes in an autobiographical sketch being captured by the sound of

> melodious dancing songs, male and female voices, coming from the hill where we were earlier. Native songs! . . . We walked back: already the place was full of blonde curly-haired peasant girls, all dressed in ribbons and beads; there was a boys' choir as well; I found the plucky features and free movements of two of them especially pleasing. Leaning against a tree, I involuntarily turned my eyes from the sweet-voiced singers toward the listeners-observers, that damaged class of half-Europeans to which I too belong. Everything they heard and saw seemed alien to them: those sounds were inaudible to their hearts, those dresses strange to them. What sort of black magic has made us foreigners among our own people![1]

Iurii Lotman has claimed that in this fragment "the tragic gap between aristocratic intelligentsia and people is first formulated in Russian literature."[2] In the decades that followed, not only would the sense of such a gap be expressed more often; it would also become the leading theme in Russian intellectual discourse prior to the 1917 Revolution. Eventually, it would turn into the explicit gender metaphor of interest here.

The previous sections sketched the outlines of this gender metaphor. They tackled some of the theoretical questions that a study of its role in Russian culture needs to address. Before turning from these introductory remarks to the in-depth literary analyses, it is vital to answer one last preparatory question. As said earlier, the twentieth-century tendency to depict the land–intellectual elite–state relationship in terms of gender does not come out of the blue. Accordingly, this inquiry starts with an investigation into pre-twentieth-century developments that affected the meta-phor's formation.

FOLKLORIC MOTIFS: PENETRATING THE EARTH

The tendency to conceptualize space in gender terms may be as old as man-kind. It can be traced to folkloric motifs, such as the cult of feminizing the earth that existed in a number of primitive civilizations, including that of the Eastern Slavs.[3] Ordinarily, female representations of the earth have a maternal nature, but in certain situations the earth is imagined in alterna-tive terms, as a bride or a sexually attractive woman. Certain cultures, for example, regard a deceased man as the "bridegroom" of the earth, and in some agrarian civilizations, men literally penetrate and "impregnate" the earth in order to increase the harvest.[4]

The ancient Russian designation for the earth was *mat' syra zemlia* or "moist mother earth." Here, too, the maternal dimension prevails but occasionally makes way for bridal connotations. Thus, as two possible hy-postases of the Russian "mother earth" Sergei Domnikov discerns "the earth-maiden-beauty, dressed in grasses and decorated with flowers" and "the chaste maiden."[5] In one legend, the folkloric character Iarilo appears as the groom-to-be of feminized "mother earth," asking her to be his beloved.[6]

Associations of spatial with marital imagery also mark Russian marital folklore, in which marriage was compared to a battle[7] and "the fiancé was likened to an invading force, the future bride to the land or a garden or or-chard about to be despoiled."[8]

Another important folkloric motif for the unattainable-bride metaphor is that of the *izgoi*. A key social category in early Russian culture, the term *izgoi* usually referred to a stranger or social outcast. The collective's atti-tude toward this stranger was often ambivalent: he was either treated as a foreign enemy and, as such, a demonic "object of animosity" to be avoided; or he was regarded as a magical sorcerer or shaman, and thus an object of "fear and respect."[9] In characterizing the *izgoi*, Iurii Lotman and Boris Us-penskii point to his position "outside the home" and his "active opposition to society."[10] As will be seen, the traditional image of the *izgoi* can easily be recognized in nineteenth- and twentieth-century conceptualizations of the westernized Russian intelligentsia. It plays a key role in the depiction of the modern *intelligent* as Russia's symbolic bridegroom.

The same is true of the other folkloric concepts mentioned here. It is important to realize, however, that in themselves these motifs do not refer to a distinctly national-Russian context. The battle motif in wedding rituals bore no allusion to concrete political frictions. Nor did the "moist mother earth" concept have national implications, for the simple reason that in ancient Russia people did not think in terms of national identity or pride. In Old Russian literature, *mat' syra zemlia* gradually came to designate specifically the Russian earth or land, but it was only in the nineteenth century that the notions mentioned appeared within the context of a debate on Russian national identity.[11]

APOCALYPTIC RIDER MEETS SLEEPING BEAUTY

The metaphor as it appears in the twentieth century can also be traced to biblical concepts. A key pretext is the apocalyptic plot of the "woman clothed with the sun"—a personification of the people of God—and the dragon from which she is defended by the archangel Michael. The dragon passes his strength to a seven-headed beast that is ultimately defeated by a messianic rider on a white horse.[12]

In later Christian culture, the "woman-clothed-with-the-sun" motif blends with fairy-tale plots and medieval chivalric imagery. Relevant for our metaphor is its inextricable fusion with the Christian legend of Saint George, who defeats a dragon in defense of his faith. Indicative of the popularity of this legend in Old Russian culture is the status of Saint George as patron of the Muscovite tsars.[13] His legend by no means acquired a stable form in Russia, though: in time it coalesces with numerous other narratives, among which the dragon-slayer plot of Russian folktales is of prime importance. This plot can be summarized as the hero's attempt to liberate a captive princess from a snake, a dragon, or the evil folk character *kashchei*. His endeavors invariably end in triumph, which consists of both a marriage to the princess and the inheritance of her father's kingdom.[14]

In modern Russian culture, the dragon-slayer plot is interlaced with yet another ancient plot: the fairy tale of the sleeping beauty, a girl bewitched by evil forces and in need of liberation by a prince.[15] Under the influence of medieval imagery as reflected in the knighthood novels of Miguel Cervantes and Walter Scott, it has also merged with Western-oriented tales of knights fighting for the honor of their ladies.[16]

While in no way referring to concepts of national identity as we understand them today, such plots do imply social or political collision. In Russian folktales, according to Vladimir Propp, "the struggle for the throne between the hero and the old tsar" reflects "the transition of power from the father to the son-in-law through a woman." In his words, this plot deals with "the replacement of one social system with another and the disparities and contradictions resulting from it."[17] Its implication of political conflict is reinforced by the opposition of dragon and hero as *foreign* enemy and *native* prince, respectively. The sociopolitical implications were reinforced in later centuries: Savelii Senderovich has shown that both inside and outside Russia the political potential of the Saint George myth was exploited eagerly in military and political propaganda.[18]

In the political metaphor discussed here, traditional dragon-slayer and sleeping-beauty narratives have undergone substantial changes. First of all, their outcome is inverted from invariably positive into just as invariably negative: where the hero traditionally conquers the dragon and marries the princess, the hero in the unattainable-bride myth succeeds neither in triumphing in battle nor in becoming the princess's husband. The seeds of this pessimist revision were sown previously in Russian wonder tales and *bylinas,* which often pit a distinctly "passive," "infant" hero against an "active" and "morally and spiritually superior" heroine.[19] Secondly, in the traditional Saint George myth the dragon slayer represents the regime and its struggle against a foreign element, whereas in the works discussed here, the oppositional intelligentsia takes the role of the dragon slayer, and the state acts as the dragon.

Although the national-political appropriation of age-old plots becomes prominent only in the twentieth century, its roots lie in nineteenth-century Russian culture. Famous nineteenth-century adaptations of traditional *kashchei* and sleeping-beauty plots—by éminences grises like Pushkin, Gogol, and Dostoevsky—indicate the high degree of popularity they enjoyed in Russia at that time, albeit not yet in a sociopolitical context.[20] In addition, in the second half of the century a sociopolitical dimension did figure in musical variations on the story. A prime example is Aleksandr Borodin's version of the sleeping beauty in lyrics for "Sleeping Princess" ("Spiashchaia kniazhna"). Written in 1867, this song is generally considered to reflect Borodin's ideas on the abolition of serfdom in the 1860s.[21] Modest Mussorgsky explicitly interpreted its heroine as a symbol of Russia.[22] If Mussorgsky was right, then Borodin offers the first inversion of the plot's traditional happy ending: his lyrics stage a "mighty *bogatyr'*" who is supposed to rescue his dormant beloved but fails to arrive.[23] In the allegorical reading of the song, this failure was clearly understood as the intelligentsia's inability to free the Russian people.

Zara Mints has argued that the public saw similar political allegories in Peter Tchaikovsky's ballets, *Sleeping Beauty* (*Spiashchaia krasavitsa,* 1890) and *Iolanta* (1891)[24]—and a Soviet study of Tchaikovsky's *Sleeping Beauty* states matter-of-factly that "in Russian history, Desire is associated with Peter, Russia's reformer, who has concluded a treaty with the capital [Petersburg] as female beauty."[25] Chapter 2 tracks the increase of stories featuring captive princesses as political allegories in the first decade of the twentieth century, which culminates in the reception of Nikolai Rimsky-Korsakov's opera *Kashchei the Immortal* (*Kashchei Bessmertnyi*, 1905).

Thus, reconstruction of the political dimension of Borodin's, Tchaikovsky's, and Rimsky-Korsakov's works relies not on hints in the creations themselves but in public perception. By contrast, Semen Nadson's 1881–82 poem "Spring Tale" ("Vesenniaia skazka") overtly links sleeping-beauty motifs with sociopolitical concerns: its narrator states that it is in the "old legend" of the sleeping beauty that the hope of the present-day "dark times" resides.[26] In the 1880s, the tale of an abducted princess was superimposed yet more openly on political concerns by the philosopher Vladimir Solov'ev. In his essay "The Russian Idea" ("Russkaia idea," 1880), he depicts the Russian idea as a human—supposedly female—figure, captured by "nasty and jealous eunuchs," and the tsar as her potential liberator.[27]

Like Borodin's song, Solov'ev's and Nadson's adaptations of the classic narratives in question do not adopt their happy endings: in neither is the princess liberated. The tragic inversion of traditional plots in a political context does not take flight, however, until the early years of the twentieth century.

RELIGIOUS PROTOTYPES: WORLD SOULS

Apart from dragon-slayer motifs, Christian tradition provided the metaphor with another crucial element. This is the identification with Russia of female figures in Christian religion.

In Muscovy, the Mother of God acquired the ideologically motivated function of patroness of Russia and a number of its cities.[28] In the Muscovite period—well before debates on Russian identity took shape—"the Mother of God, the Church, and the Russian earth" fuse "into one image," writes Mariia Pliukhanova.[29] In architecture and iconography of this period, the cult of the so-called *pokrov*—the intercession or protection of the Mother of God—was transferred to the national sphere as well. One example is Red Square's crown jewel, the sixteenth-century Pokrovskii sobor (also known as Saint Basil's Cathedral), which was intended as an "ideal image of the Muscovite state" over which "the Mother of God spread out her *pokrov*" (literally, protective cloak).[30] Linked to this concept was the tendency to conceive of Russia as the "House of the Mother of God," a frequently used phrase.[31]

If the identification of the Mother of God with Russia appeared mostly in a context of maternal protection, then marital connotations dominated the Russian interpretation of another legendary female figure: Saint Sophia, or Divine Wisdom incarnate. First personified as a female figure in the Old Testament,[32] "Divine Sophia" was linked simultaneously with the sacred and

the "lower" human world in Gnostic thought.[33] According to Sergei Domnikov, Russian folk belief regarded her as the mother of Saint George—the
"founder of the Russian earth"—and the Russian people were considered
her "direct descendant."[34] She was prominent in Russian orthodoxy, and the
notion of patronage of Russia was no less vital to her myth than to that of the
Mother of God.[35] Muscovy saw the appearance of several Russian Sophia
icons, and some of Russia's most famous churches are devoted to her.[36]

Despite her ostensible "Russification," in this traditional-religious context Sophia should not be understood as a distinctly national image, even
though she begins to appear as such in the second half of the eighteenth
century. Influenced by a Sophia cult in German mysticism, at this time a
number of Russian Freemasons and Romantics glorified the concept of a
mystical marriage between man's soul and Sophia[37] and cloaked this union in
chivalric terms.[38]

Toward the end of the eighteenth century, the Sophia cult moved into
the national sphere. In 1789 Ivan Elagin suggests in his *Essay for a Narrative on Russia* (*Opyt povestvovaniia o Rossii*) that it was Sophia who asked
him to describe Russia's history.[39] Aleksandr Shakhovskoi's religious tragedy *Debora* (1809) is imbued with the Sophia-Russia idea,[40] and according
to Sander Brouwer, Sophia, "the marriageable girl around whose fate the
dramatic plot" of Denis Fonvizin's *The Minor* (*Nedorosl'*, 1782) "is built . . .
allegorically represent[s] Russia."[41]

The fusion of Sophia veneration with nationalist ideas was no random
development. It was enhanced by the nationalist revival that ensued from
the Napoleonic Wars. These wars are mentioned explicitly in an ode by
Nikolai Karamzin: envisioning Divine Wisdom as a female figure, the writer
has her address the Russian people in a speech that prophesies their future
triumph over Napoléon.[42]

If Karamzin's Sophia embodies the strength of the Russian state in
relation to other countries, then the same period also witnesses national
conceptualizations of Sophia that do the exact opposite. It is here that the
metaphoric constellation in which I am interested comes into view. Around
1820, the prevailing mood among the Russian intellectual elite begins to
shift from state-oriented to anti-state. This change of mood coincides with
representations of Sophia that, rather than associating her with the tsarist
regime, portray her as "the embodiment of a genuinely free Russia."[43] As
such, Sophia features in the poetry of the Decembrist and poet Prince Aleksandr Odoevskii. In his "Old Prophetess-Nun" ("Staritsa-prorochitsa," 1829),
the hero's inability to enter into a mystical marriage with "Saint Sophia" coincides with his failure to defend Novgorod.[44] For Odoevskii, Saint Sophia
unmistakably embodies this city, which the Decembrists glorified as the traditional ideal Russia as opposed to the contemporary Russian regime. In his

"Virgin of the Year 1610" ("Deva 1610," 1827–30), the contraposition of a nationally characterized Sophia figure and the poet is similarly rendered as a failing amorous relationship.[45] The poem shows Russia as a "heavenly virgin" who complains to the poet about the changes that her relationship to him— and to "the Slavs' sons" in general—has undergone. In intimate-amorous rhetoric, she accuses them of having "estranged yourselves from my beauty" and of failing to "hear my reproaches / . . . where are the swords for the holy motherland, / for Rus', for fame, for me? / Why are you waiting?"[46]

In Odoevskii's poem, several aspects of the Sophia concept (as it had taken form by that time) coincide, such as the association of the "heavenly virgin" with Rus' and the construction of her relationship to her devotees as that of a maiden to male suitors. New in his vision of the "virgin Rus'" is the tragic turn taken by the poet's relationship to her. Instead of defending their feminized homeland, the "alienated . . . Slavs' sons" represented by the lyrical ego wait and fail to act.

Written by a die-hard Decembrist, Odoevskii's poems no doubt refer to the failed uprising of 1825 against Nicholas I in which he had participated. Readers who are familiar with Russian history will remember that the Decembrists—a group of oppositional liberal intellectuals—had regarded their attempt at a revolt as an important step in improving the fate of Russia and its people. Thus Odoevskii's poems express, in gendered terms, what he saw as a problematic relationship between the intellectual elite, to which he belonged, and Russia or the Russian people.

The sense of distance between poet-intellectual and Russia that oozes from Odoevskii's poetry would only grow in the course of the nineteenth century. Russian intellectuals increasingly wrestled with the widening gap that separated them from both the Russian people and the tsarist regime. In literature, this expanse is articulated in a series of works in which a hero, representing the westernized intelligentsia, faces a quintessentially Russian heroine. A more detailed discussion of the subject follows, but what matters here is the manifest influence of traditional representations of Divine Wisdom on this "Russian" heroine. She appears as a feminine creature who incarnates precisely those abstract principles—moral wisdom, authenticity, harmony—that the hero who falls for her lacks and seeks. Explicitly linked to the divine sphere, she represents to the hero life itself, or an ideal state of harmony for which he strives.

An example of such an ideal feminine principle was supposed to appear at the end of the third part of Nikolai Gogol's *Dead Souls* (*Mertvye dushi*, 1842). The author allegedly wanted to conclude with the appearance of "a beautiful Russian maiden who is as yet not to be found anywhere in the world" and who would incarnate "generous aspiration and selflessness itself."[47] Mikhail Vaiskopf has asserted that, in general, Russia appeared in *Dead Souls* as a continuation of the Sophia concept of Masonic odes.[48]

While Gogol's novel merely alludes to the allegorical Divine Wisdom concept, other quintessentially Russian heroines are linked with it more openly. Sophia in Griboedov's *Woe from Wit* (*Gore ot uma*, 1824), for instance, not only shares a name with Saint Sophia but is also associated with ideal virtues like sincerity and truthfulness. In Sander Brouwer's view, the decision to name such a markedly Russian heroine Sophia might well be an "ironic commentary" on the "association Sophia/Premudrost'/Russia" of Fonvizin's Sophia.[49] Referring to the combination of this ideal status with her unfortunate choice of lovers, Vaiskopf links her to the inverted version of Sophia in Gnostic belief: "fallen" or "foolish Sophia."[50] Rather than copying the traditional myth, however, Griboedov places his symbolic Sophia in a distinctly Russian-Muscovite context and confronts her with the play's westernized hero, Chatskii.

Similar allegorically charged female figures occur in Dostoevsky's work—and even more in its reception. While Dostoevsky's heroines are never overtly associated with the concept of Sophia or its "fallen" inversion, this association has become a key ingredient in interpretations of his novels. In the mythopoetic tradition of the Silver Age, Dostoevsky's work was interpreted as highly Sophiological.[51] Thinkers and poets tended to read his heroines as hypostases of a Sophiological World Soul, and particularly of a feminized Russian earth, as will be seen in chapter 2. Today the view that the Sophia concept is pivotal to Dostoevsky's oeuvre has become generally acknowledged by scholars of his work,[52] who have pointed to a conceptual link connecting Sophia and Russia, the Russian people, or "the earth" in his texts.[53]

It is true that Dostoevsky repeatedly represents the earth as a divine female principle—one reminiscent of both the pagan "moist mother earth" and the concept of feminized Divine Wisdom. In *The Brothers Karamazov* (*Brat'ia Karamazovy*, 1880), Dmitrii Karamazov muses on entering "into an eternal union . . . with the ancient mother earth."[54] His specific allusion to the *Russian* earth in this passage imparts a maternal dimension to the recurring reference to Russia elsewhere in the novel.[55] The mother-Russia concept acquires distinctly sensual tones when Dmitrii's brother, Alesha, "suddenly threw himself on the earth like someone whose legs gave way" and "kissed her [the earth], crying, sobbing, overwhelming her with his tears, and furiously swore to love her, to love her forever."[56] This feminized Russian earth is symbolically linked to Dmitrii's beloved, the promiscuous Grushen'ka, whom he describes as "Russian, Russian to the backbone, she longs for mother native earth."[57]

The "longing for mother earth" recurs in *The Demons* (*Besy*, 1872), in which Mar'ia Lebiadkina proclaims that she kisses "moist mother earth" each time she prays: "I kiss it and I cry. . . . I fall to the earth, cry and cry."[58] And finally, the heroine in *Crime and Punishment* (*Prestuplenie i nakazanie*, 1866)—Sonia, alias Sofiia, a name that could hardly have been chosen unwittingly—not only reenacts the Gnostic Sophia's angel-cum-whore paradigm but also urges Raskol'nikov to kiss the Russian earth. The latter heeds her exhortation with near-erotic fervor, literally "kiss[ing] that dirty earth with passion and joy" while enduring public condemnation at Petersburg's Sennaia Square.[59]

Although Dostoevsky never openly linked Russia to a female Sophiological principle, such an association does occur in Vladimir Solov'ev's philosophy. Influenced by Gnosticism, as well as by Russian Orthodoxy and German mysticism, Solov'ev's Divine Sophia often appears as a mystical female world soul.[60] Paradoxically, for him this "world" soul possesses a distinctly national character. In a recent study, Manon de Courten examines four occasions upon which Solov'ev intervened in socially or politically problematic situations, concluding that his interventions were "guided" by "the link that he made between Sophia and the Russian mission in history."[61] The complex relationship between universal and national-political dimensions epitomizes Solov'ev's philosophy as a whole, which attributes a messianic role to Russia in a future unification of mankind.[62] In Sophiological terms, this paradox is articulated in the essay "The Idea of Humanity of August Comte" ("Idea chelovechestva u Avgusta Konta," 1898), in which Solov'ev represents Sophia as both an embodiment of all people and a being anticipated specifically by Russians.[63] He follows a similar logic when identifying the "woman clothed with the sun" as Russia in his *Three Speeches in Memory of Dostoevsky* (*Tri rechi v pamiat' Dostoevskogo*, 1881–83).[64] To Solov'ev,

> Dostoevsky applied to Russia John the Theologian's vision of the woman clothed with the sun . . . wanting to deliver the male child: the woman is Russia, and what is to be delivered by her is the new Word that Russia has to say to the world. . . . Dostoevsky correctly predicted the new Word of Russia. It is the word of reconciliation for East and West in a union of the eternal truth of God and man's freedom.[65]

In *Russia and the Universal Church* (*La Russie et l'église universelle*, 1889), Solov'ev again connects the "new Word of Russia" with Sophia. Here the idea of the Divine Sophia is called a "truly national and absolutely universal idea," associated with the "living Word . . . the new Russia has to say to the World"—a "living Word" that should be formed by complementing the Russian Sophia idea with a "rational expression."[66]

28

In the Dostoevsky speeches, Solov'ev interprets the "living Word" as a "word of reconciliation for East and West." His *Lectures on Godmanhood* (*Chteniia o bogochelovechestve*, 1878–81) show that in this context, he sees the East as the Sophiological, nonrational Russia and the West as its rational counterpart. He depicts the former as "the people who have accepted Byzantine culture headed by Russia"[67] and opposes this Eastern-Russian culture to "rationalism's supremacy" in "European politics and science."[68] In his view, the West moved away from Christianity through its focus on rationalism: it developed an "anti-Christian culture," which was diametrically opposed to the "Christian people" he believed Russians to be.[69]

To Solov'ev, the Eastern and Western worlds relate to each other as a divine and a human principle, respectively. In their union he envisions—in distinctly gendered formulations—the birth of the new "godmanhood."

> The spokeswoman of the immovable divine basis in humanity is the Eastern Church, and the spokesman of humanity is the Western world. . . . The human principle . . . can . . . enter into a free conjunction with the divine basis of Christianity . . . , and as a result . . . it can give birth to a spiritual humanity.[70]

The gendered terms in this fragment—spokes*woman* versus spokes*man*, and the notion of a new manhood *born* from their *free conjunction*—indicate that Solov'ev's union between East (Russia) and West should be understood, above all, as a (mystical) marriage.[71] Not coincidentally, in the same passage he represents the East-West union as "the impregnation of the divine mother . . . by the active human principle";[72] and not coincidentally does he envision the impregnation of an Eastern-Russian by a Western principle as the fertilization of a Divine Sophia by man's reason (ratio):

> Just as in pre-Christian history, the foundation or matter was nature . . . the active . . . element was the divine ratio . . . and the result (birth) the God-man—thus, in the Christian process the foundation or matter is nature or the divine element (the Word incarnate, or the body of Christ, Sophia), the active and form-endowing principle is human reason, and the result is the man-God.[73]

Solov'ev's idea of a mystical wedding between Russia/Sophia and the West/ratio has been discussed by Boris Groys, in whose view "the West should be understood as the Russian westernized intelligentsia, including Solov'ev himself, rather than as the real, geographical West."[74] In Groys' reading, Solov'ev's union between Russia and the West forms "in the soul of the Russian *intelligent* an inner mystical marriage between his Western culture and Russian subconsciousness, which lends him the intensely desired wholeness . . . or, in Solov'ev's terms, the 'all-unity.'"[75]

Indeed, Solov'ev's "West" refers less to concrete areas of the West than to the Western orientation of Russia's intellectual elite. A prominent member of this elite, Solov'ev saw himself as representative of the intelligentsia that felt alienated from its native country. Revealingly, in his poetry he conceives of the union with Sophia in highly personal terms, as an amorous relationship between her female hypostasis and himself or his lyrical ego.[76] In doing so, he attributes to himself the very same role of Sophia's groom-to-be that he ascribes to the West in the *Lectures*.[77]

Discernible in Solov'ev's Sophiology, therefore, is an interdependence that not only connects Russia to Sophia but also links the West, the Russian intellectual elite, and human reason. The philosopher conceives of the relationships involving these opposite spheres in marital terms, by contrasting Sophia/Russia as a feminine principle with the West—or the Russian westernized elite—as a rational masculine principle. While his view of their interaction initially seems binary, it implies a third element: the Russian state. His correspondence shows that he saw the conservative politicians of his day as oppressive rulers who needed to leave if Russia's fate were to improve. "What is now praised here as 'national politics,'" he writes in an 1886 letter, "is kept together only by the evil triumvirate of false clergyman P., false statesman T., and false prophet K., which . . . visibly weakens and approaches its end. And with the disappearance of those people . . . one can await a definitive change for the better."[78] Emerging from the combination of this personal political comment and Solov'ev's philosophical views is the concept of a mystical marriage between a feminized Russia, freed from its reactionary "false" rulers, and a westernized "intelligentsia." This concept would become a crucial source for later gendered representations of Russia.

POLITICAL ALLEGORIES: BRIDE-CUM-WHORE

The next weighty element in the history of our topic is a mythical plot based on political frictions, in which the conquest of a city or land is compared either to a marriage or to the rape of the territory in question. These equations, to borrow Sergei Averintsev's formulation, symbolically connect female "chastity . . . with the wholeness, the inaccessibility, and the orderliness of the city."[79]

The metaphor of the city as a virgin in danger of being unfaithful or impure is yet another concept with biblical roots. Throughout the Bible, the city appears as "a woman in all life phases and situations: as a virgin, a bride and mother; as childless, violated, abandoned, separated, and married anew."[80] Examples include elaborate depictions of Babylon as "the great whore" and, at the same time, the lofty bride of the lamb; and Jerusalem and Israel as either utopian bride or unfaithful harlot.[81] As a rule, the infidelity of which the personified loci are accused alludes to their occupation by non-native forces, an intrusion sometimes viewed in distinctly sexual terms. Jerusalem, for instance, is charged with lustfully "open[ing] thy feet" for "the Egyptians thy neighbours, great of flesh."[82] The author of Lamentations, on the other hand, represents the destruction of the city as the rape of an innocent, chaste woman.[83]

If the bridegroom to whom the biblical city/bride-cum-whore was supposed to remain faithful was Christ or God, then in medieval political rhetoric the worldly ruler gradually came to fulfill the role of husband to his city or country. Metaphors of a marriage between ruler and land can be encountered in both Russia and the West. In his study of medieval political metaphors, Ernst Kantorowicz quotes several writers and political figures—from antiquity to seventeenth-century England—who speak of the land and its ruler in terms of bride and bridegroom.[84] Medieval Arabic-Hispanic poets referred to occupiers of various regions as "husbands," and Andalusian poetry abounded in images of the city as its ruler's bride or wife.[85]

Nor is the idea of a marriage between land and ruler a rarity in Russian cultural history. Joanna Hubbs claims (though without adding sources or concrete examples) that the Russian peasant population traditionally conceived of its tsar as a "father" (*tsar'-batiushka*) married to "mother Russia" (*matushka-Rus'*).[86] Sergei Domnikov defines the Kievan "city-cum-church" as an "embodiment of a feminine principle, which awaited its heavenly spouse"—that is, the Russian ruler, who appeared as the "guardian of the Church's chastity and the defender of her body-City" against the end of time or the devil.[87] In a strictly textual sphere, scholars have traced a similar marital metaphor in the *Igor Tale* (*Slovo o polku Igoreve*, 1185–87), in which Prince Igor' appears both as son and bridegroom of "mother earth";[88] his wife, Iaroslavna, personifies this "earth in its role of bride" or "the Russian land that mourns for a ruler in captivity."[89] Somewhat later, in the Muscovite period, the metaphor of the land as a ruler's bride abounds in both literary works and political events.[90]

In modern Russian history, the metaphoric representation of ruler and land as husband and wife remains constant. Scholars have reconstructed it in Aleksandr Sumarokov's *Dmitrii the Impostor* (*Dmitrii Samozvanets*, 1771), Vasilii Narezhnyi's play of the same name (1800), and Fonvizin's *The Minor*.[91] In the same period, laudatory odes allude to the metaphor through their repeated opposition of a personified "Russia"—whose grammatical gender automatically renders it a feminine entity—to Peter the Great and several other rulers portrayed as strong male figures.[92] In 1834, Vasilii Zhukovskii conceives of Tsar Alexander II's tour through his land as an "all-national betrothal with Russia."[93] That the concept has remained of topical importance to this day is suggested by Boris Yeltsin's electoral campaign of 1996, which featured the slogan: "Yeltsin is a real man, and Russia a feminine creature."[94]

Besides the metaphoric marriage of ruler and land, Russian culture also takes recourse to the notion of the city as a virgin whose chastity must be defended. As such, the town of Vladimir is allegorized in the twelfth-century *Tale of Bygone Years* (*Povest' vremennykh let*) and in the *Igor Tale*.[95] In the song "Taking of the Kazan' Reign" ("Vziatie Kazanskogo tsarstva"), the occupation ascribed to Kazan' is defined as a "marriage" and the city a "princess."[96] As recently as 1999, in the widely read newspaper *Argumenty i fakty*, mayoral candidate Borodin compares Moscow to a bride and himself to a bridegroom who is inviting everyone to their wedding.[97]

In modern Russian literature, the city-as-virgin concept is not rare either. Iurii Mann reconstructs the "mythologeme of the entry into a city of a divine character, who turns out to be its savior and bridegroom" in Gogol's novel *Dead Souls* and his play *The Inspector General* (*Revizor*, 1836).[98] Sergei Nekliudov argues that whereas the later stages of life (motherhood, widowhood) are stressed in traditional representations of the city, its depiction in "premarital and marital situations (girl, bride, wife)" takes over toward the end of the nineteenth century.[99]

A special case in the context of this study is the city of Moscow. As Nekliudov shows, in the legend of Moscow's foundation "motifs of conquest of the city and of a marriage become intermingled in a single semantic complex."[100] In time, the concept of Moscow as a feminine entity develops into a forceful Russian myth. It forms part of a rhetorical tradition in which Moscow and Petersburg are opposed as feminine versus masculine and Russian versus foreign, respectively.[101] Colloquial expressions and literary metaphors accentuate the allegedly natural, organic, "feminine" growth of Moscow as opposed to Petersburg's unnatural, rational, "masculine" character. In the twentieth century, the prevailing view of the two cities was summarized by Georgii Fedotov, who opposes Petersburg as the receptacle of "all that is masculine, rational-conscious, all that is proud and aggressive in the Russian soul" to "Rus', Moscow, the village, the long-suffering earth, wife and mother."[102]

After Napoléon's occupation of Moscow in 1812, the gendered Moscow-Petersburg concept fuses with the traditional metaphor of a city entered by foreign forces as sexual profanation. Illustrative of this fusion is Mikhail Zagoskin's essay "Two Characters: Brother and Sister" ("Dva kharaktera: Brat i sestra," 1841), whose author knows many who prefer the careless ways and far-from-European behavior of the sister [Moscow] to the correct movements and aesthetic poses of the brother [Petersburg]. . . . She is a very frivolous girl and quite credulous; some little braggarts told her something, God knows what, about a certain monsieur, a renowned rowdy and bawler . . . ! My lady went crazy; she raved about him day and night.[103]

Given the story's subsequent events—"the monsieur" visits "the lady," who is so outraged at his unannounced visit that she "burns" him "out"—any contemporary reader will have understood that the French monsieur was, in fact, Napoléon and that his visit to the "lady" stood for the invasion of Moscow. Similarly, in Tolstoy's *War and Peace* (*Voina i mir*, 1863–70), Napoléon looks at the conquered Moscow as a "beauty lying before him," and compares "a city occupied by an enemy" to "a girl who has lost her virginity."[104]

Of particular importance to this study is the nineteenth-century association of Moscow and Petersburg with the Russian people or state and the Europeanized intelligentsia, respectively.[105] In his *Petersburg Notes for 1836* (*Peterburgskie zapiski 1836 goda*), Gogol famously asserts that

Moscow is an old homebody, who bakes pancakes . . . without rising from her armchair to find out what happens in the world; Petersburg is a sharp young man who never sits at home . . . Moscow is feminine, Petersburg masculine. In Moscow there are only brides, in Petersburg only bridegrooms.[106]

It is not hard to spot the link between Gogol's image of the "young man who never sits at home" and the nineteenth-century Russian intellectual who is abroad most of the time. The association of the pancake-baking "homebody" with the common people is equally obvious. Within twentieth-century intellectual Russian culture, this intermingling of the people-intelligentsia and female Moscow–male Petersburg antitheses becomes a recurring ingredient.

THE NINETEENTH CENTURY: WESTERN(IZED) BOYS, RUSSIAN GIRLS

The relationship of the unattainable-bride metaphor to emerging nationalist debates of the eighteenth and nineteenth centuries has been noted. While the tendency to conceive of nations in gendered terms was widespread throughout Europe at the time, the works examined here rely on the specific twist that nationalist discourse took in Russia. In Boris Groys' apt definition, this twist is summarized as the persistent Russian tendency to conceptualize the country's national identity "as the West's 'Other.'"[107]

The specificity of Russian nationalism is perhaps best reflected in Slavophile philosophy. Regarding the West as the rationalist counterpart of a truly Christian Russia, Slavophiles envisioned a messianic role for Russia and glorified the country's past as a harmonious coexistence of state and people. While their ideas were rooted in western European—and particularly German—Romantic concepts of national identity, Slavophiles at the same time refuted Western cultural influences in Russia.

Pivotal to Slavophile philosophy is the notion of a "dual image of Russia," in which "unofficial," "popular Russia" is opposed to and preferred to "official Russia."[108] Although broadly expressed only in the second half of the nineteenth century, the dual view originates in Slavophile thinking, which regards Russia's Western-oriented state as "official Russia" and the common people as its "unofficial," authentically Russian opposite.

Influenced by Schelling's view of the universe as a living organism, the Slavophiles are avid users of anthropomorphic terms. In the poetry of Aleksei Khomiakov, for example, Russia is repeatedly addressed in the second person; the setting—a male poet who expresses himself in emotional terms—and Russia's feminine grammatical gender suggest that the nation to whom the poet turns is an absolutely feminine Russia.[109] The poem "Foreign Girl" ("Inostranka," 1832) implies an amorous link between the poet and this feminized Russia when the former rejects a foreign girl for her inability to understand his love for Russia's "wild beauty."[110]

Even more than by Khomiakov's poetry, the Slavophiles' gendered view of Russia and the West is illustrated by Nikolai Danilevskii's philosophical treatises. In his *Russia and Europe* (*Rossiia i Evropa*, 1869), Danilevskii characterizes Russia in traditionally feminine terms—he sees Russia as "alien to violence," "soft," and "submissive."[111] Danilevskii defines the relationship between Peter the Great and Russia in even more distinct gender terms when he claims that "having met Europe, he [Peter], so to say, fell in love with her and wanted to turn Russia into Europe. . . . He both loved and hated her [Russia]."[112] Danilevskii's opposition of Peter the Great as a lover with Europe and Russia as two female rivals for his love anticipates the gendered view of Petrinian Russia of his early twentieth-century successors.

Akin to Slavophile thought is the messianic view of Russia in Gogol's later works. Especially significant for the works discussed here is the famous conclusive passage of *Dead Souls*, part 1, in which the narrator addresses Russia in personified terms that undeniably suggest romantic involvement.

Rus'! Rus'! I see you, I see you from my wonderful, beautiful distance: how wretched, scattered and uncomfortable is your life . . . what is this inscrutable, mysterious force that draws me to you? Why do my ears ring unceasingly with your plaintive song . . . ? What is in it, in that song? Why does it so beckon, and sob, and tug at the heart? What are those sounds that caress so painfully, steal into my soul and hover about my heart? Rus'! What is it that you want from me? What is the hidden, inscrutable tie that binds us? Why do you gaze like that, and why has everything in you turned to gaze at me with eyes full of expectation?[113]

Mikhail Vaiskopf rightly, I think, tracks the "beautiful distance" from which the narrator addresses Russia to the paradigm of the alienated Russian intellectual who spends large chunks of his life abroad.[114] Vaiskopf links the concept to Mikhail Zagoskin's novel *Homesickness* (*Toska po rodine*), published shortly before *Dead Souls* in 1839, whose protagonist states: "Rus'! . . . And I, one of your sons, a voluntary exile, live abroad and can look at you, my dear one, only from a distance."[115]

Important here is the fact that Gogol's "alienated" narrator formulates his attitude to "distant" Russia as that of a lover toward his beloved. Together with this amorous pathos, another detail in the Rus' fragment that several twentieth-century texts would inherit is the motif of the meeting glances between the lyric male ego and a feminized Russia. I argue that one can trace this motif to eighteenth-century odes that repeatedly depict a feminized Russia as "looking around" or looking at its ruler.[116]

From Gogol and Slavophilism, it is a small step to the classic nineteenth-century novel and the sense of alienation from people and state that its haunted protagonists express. This feeling, which lies at the heart of the gender metaphor, has its roots in the eighteenth century. Drastic reforms, particularly under the century's two "Great" tsars, Peter and Catherine, result in a fundamental change in social position for the aristocratic elite. This change can be summarized as a shift away from the status of state representatives ensconced in the countryside and toward that of an urbanized, westernized elite deprived of direct participation in state affairs.

If not immediately, then surely toward the end of the century, this altered social status results in a feeling of moral crisis within aristocratic circles. Increasing numbers of nobles experience the loss of their positions as statesmen as problematic; in addition, they retrospectively criticize Russia's inclination toward Western models since Peter the Great.[117] In Robert Tucker's words, "the autocratic state power" was regarded more and more "as an alien power in the Russian land."[118]

At the same time, the nobles' assault on the "turn toward the West" should be read as a self-critique: not only is the aristocratic elite at this time infatuated with western European (particularly French) literature and philosophy, but it also has a weakness for European fashion. Nobles increasingly travel and live abroad. Particularly after the Napoleonic Wars, this passion for anything Western paradoxically coincides with what James Billington has called a "hyper-sensitive national self-consciousness."[119] The aristocracy's ambivalent self-view leads to the feelings later cultivated by Griboedov and like-minded others of a "damaged half-European" Russian aristocracy that is out of touch with its native culture. Resulting in a defiance of the regime that culminates in the failed Decembrist uprising of 1825, the relationship between the intellectual elite and the state only deteriorates in the course of the nineteenth century.[120]

Important to our topic is the coincidence of the sociopolitical developments mentioned with a cult of veneration aimed at the common people. Following German Romanticism, with its heightened interest in individual national cultures, Russian aristocratic intellectuals eagerly pick up the trend to glorify the common people as bearers of a national essence. In the course of the nineteenth century, the "cult of the people" merges with French socialist thought, yet another foreign doctrine that Russian intellectuals project onto an imagined Russian "nation"—and one that leads to a rapid spread of populist ideals in Russian society in the second half of the century.

By this time, a preoccupation with the common people and their fate has entered the agenda of not only aristocratic intellectuals, but also that diffuse slice of society eventually designated as "the intelligentsia." The problematic nature of this term has been mentioned: it refers in no way to a stable social class or to an absolute majority of the thinking sector of Russian society. With respect to the second half of the nineteenth century, however, it can be defined as a mixture of representatives of the aristocratic elite and *raznochintsy*.[121] This socially heterogeneous group is unified by the longing—to quote Geoffrey Hosking—to "reunite elite and people and thereby to create a new society which was both more humane and more authentically Russian."[122] While initially motivated by optimistic conceptions of an idealized "authentic Russian people," in the course of the century the intelligentsia increasingly feel that they are divided from those people by an unbridgeable mental gap.

In another derivation of western European thought, the idealization of the common Russian people merges with the Romantic tendency to regard woman as the repository of a divine, harmonic, feminine principle. More than a one-sided masculine affair, this trend is enhanced by women themselves: they follow behavioral models that prescribe a pastoral appearance intended to evoke images of peasant culture and common people. The pseudo-pastoral fashion heightens during the Napoleonic Wars, when simplicity is a buzzword and women stop wearing wigs and corsets.[123]

By the mid-nineteenth century, this veneration of the common people has led to an intellectual culture in which, in Jane McDermid's words, "it is as if the peasants were the female side of the Russian nation, and the westernized aristocracy the male side."[124] In such a context, according to another scholar, it is hardly surprising that "an acute sensitizing of attitudes about the social condition of women coincided with the liberation of the serfs in 1861."[125] In some cases, this abstract coupling of social to gender categories has concrete consequences: during the second half of the century, in particular, progressive intellectuals treat real-life love relationships as platforms for the enactment of social ideals, such as "fictive marriages" initiated by the husband solely to emancipate his wife—unions that require no physical proximity between the spouses. The 1860s see several fictive marriages between prominent intellectuals and "liberated women," who openly display extramarital affairs. Irina Paperno has considered a number of these ménages à trois involving radical intellectuals who "link . . . the liberation of a woman to the liberation of humanity": Aleksandr Herzen, his wife, and the German poet Herwegh, for instance; or Nikolai Chernyshevskii, who urges his wife to have amorous affairs.[126]

For Herzen, the fusion of "the people" and feminine categories resonates both in his biography and in his writings. In 1863 he states that

> only he who is called to action and understands the way of the people . . . ; who harmonizes his actions with its strivings and, on this basis, works for the national common cause; this man only shall be the bridegroom who cometh. . . . Who then will that longed-for lover be?[127]

That it is the Russian people who should serve as the female bride of Herzen's "longed-for lover" is not only suggested by his literal reference to "the people"; the idea is also implicit in his conceptualization, elsewhere, of "the masses" as a feminine entity when he labels them "children, women, capricious, wild, inconstant."[128]

Thus, in the course of the nineteenth century the glorification of an idealized Russian people coalesces with a cult of veneration of the feminine. In itself, this fusion is hardly unique to Russian culture, but what typifies the Russian context is its reference to the problematic social status of the westernized intellectual elite.

Not unexpectedly, given the function of nineteenth-century Russian literature as a vehicle for social debate, this typically Russian dimension is best seen in the classic Russian novel. In literary Russian fiction, the sociopolitical issues mentioned are expressed in a plot with a recurring pattern. This plot opposes a distinctly Russian heroine to a westernized protagonist and, in many cases, to an antagonist who is associated with the state or political authority. With some variations, it can be discerned in a good number of canonic nineteenth-century Russian texts: Pushkin's *Eugene Onegin*

(*Evgenii Onegin*, 1833), Herzen's *Who Is to Blame?* (*Kto vinovat?* 1847), Goncharov's *The Precipice* (*Obryv*, 1869), Tolstoy's *War and Peace,* and several texts by Turgenev, such as the novella *Asia* (1858) and the novel *Nest of the Gentry* (*Dvorianskoe gnezdo*, 1859), to name but a few.

It is in the recurring plot constellation of these prose texts that the unattainable-bride metaphor can first be anticipated with some degree of clarity. Referring to several of the works mentioned, Aleksei Makushinskii has compiled a list of features attributable to hero and heroine, respectively:

masculine	feminine
city	country (earth)
Petersburg	Russia
intellect	soul
reflection	intuition
reason	faith
dichotomy	wholeness
European	autochthonous
culture	nature
educated class	people
groundlessness	rootedness[129]

Evocative of the oppositions that Mosse and Verdery discern in European national allegories (and that I enlist in my introduction), these antithetical features apply to a surprisingly large number of nineteenth-century Russian hero-heroine pairs. Their consistent occurrence in a great many publications shows a more marked inclination toward the allegorical sphere than one would expect in realist fiction.

As a rule, the plot in question opposes a quintessentially Russian heroine to a westernized hero. A talented man, the latter serves as the prototype of the nineteenth-century "alienated *intelligent.*" The hero emerges from outside—from either the "big city" or abroad—in the distinctively Russian estate or village where the heroine lives. A social outcast, estranged from his country and appearing as either her potential "savior" or "undoer," he can be considered a modern version of the folkloric *izgoi.*[130] Ultimately, the hero is unable either to establish a romantic relationship with the heroine or to make himself useful in Russian society.[131]

The socially unsuccessful hero is not without a rival: he is often compared with an antagonist who acts as his diametric opposite, both socially and amorously. Succeeding where his rival fails, the antagonist does enter into a romantic relationship with the heroine and does function well within Russian society. He is often associated with the regime and with state authority.

As opposed to the hero's characterization as a poetically inclined person, a thinker, the antagonist is a practical doer. In certain cases, he is referred to not by name but merely by title, which emphasizes his function as a socially successful figure.[132]

In itself, the parallel between the hero's social and amorous failures does not link the two spheres metaphorically. What does weld a metaphoric link is the consistent identification of the heroine with the Russian people and Russian society. A familiar figure in Russian literature is Pushkin's Tat'iana, with her famous "Russian soul" and love for the Russian winter.[133] Tat'iana's pronounced "Russianness" is echoed in the portrayal of a number of contemporary heroines. Liuba in *Who Is to Blame?* has inherited her "mother's peasant blood" and claims to "talk with the peasants, as with anyone else . . . and they love me."[134] Vera in *The Precipice* "grew up in the servants' room, among the common people"; Goncharov labels her and her sister "sprouts" of "old Russian life."[135] In *War and Peace*, Natasha not only performs her renowned Russian dance—making her uncle wonder "how . . . this little countess, raised as a French emigrant, had imbibed that spirit from the Russian air she breathed" and had obtained "those inimitable, artless, Russian devices"—but is also defined as a "patriot" who is "able to understand everything that went on . . . in every Russian person."[136] In Turgenev's *Nest of the Gentry*, Liza appears as a Russian "patriot," "delighted with Russian mentality" and "sympathiz[ing] with the Russian people."[137] Another Turgenevian heroine, Asia, is called "an entirely Russian girl."[138] Dostoevsky's "Russian-to-the-backbone" Grushen'ka and his other earth-loving heroines—discussed earlier in this chapter—led one critic to conclude that "in Dostoevsky's consciousness, all Sophiological female images have a deeply national character," unlike the "typical *intelligenty*" whom their male lovers represent.[139]

Together with several other nineteenth-century Russian heroines, these female characters grow up in the countryside and are raised by a *niania* who endows them with a deep love for popular Russian culture. As a united image, they become one nineteenth-century "meta-heroine" who, more than being characteristically Russian, features as the very embodiment of Russia and the Russian people.

The heroine's Russianness is reinforced by the status of the hero: he is a typical man harboring the inclinations of his time—dandyism, Romanticism, rationalism—which entered Russia from the West. Directly opposed to her rootedness in Russian culture is his status as a westernized intellectual who feels out of touch with his country and people. Onegin in *Eugene Onegin*, Bel'tov in *Who Is to Blame?*, Rudin (in Turgenev's novel of the same name, 1856), and Lavretskii in *Nest of the Gentry*: after spending time in western Europe, these men and their peers have turned away from the

Russian society of their youth. Revealing is Herzen's Bel'tov: for this "foreigner both at home and abroad," Russia is "a country that he absolutely did not know, foreign to such an extent that he could not assimilate into it."[140] Then, too, Rudin's tragedy is explained by the fact that he does "not know Russia." Similarly, in *Fathers and Sons* Bazarov is reproached for not understanding the Russian people and for having a "false impression" of them.[141]

The heroes in question are prime examples of the "superfluous man," a Russian literary type characterized by a "radical alienation from society and an inability to take personally meaningful or socially useful action."[142] The weakness of these talented but powerless personalities is expressed mainly through metaphors of femininity or childishness. Turgenev's heroes are repeatedly pictured as children or irresponsible little boys.[143] Eugene Onegin, Goncharov's *Oblomov*, P. B. in Turgenev's *Faust,* and Pierre Bezukhov in *War and Peace* are all equated symbolically with either a vain or a weak woman.[144] This representation of the *intelligent* as childish, feminine, or weak culminates in the 1880s in a cult of illness among Russian intellectuals and goes on to become a leading rhetorical device in the pre-revolutionary debates on Russia explored in this study.[145]

In the aforementioned texts, the identification of the heroine with Russia and the hero with a socially alienated intelligentsia is hard to miss. In fact, this symbolic layer is recognized from the outset: in the politically charged atmosphere of the 1850s and 1860s, leading critics eagerly discuss the many indecisive heroes and manifestly Russian heroines of their contemporaries in sociopolitical terms. Reviewing Turgenev's *On the Eve* (*Nakanune,* 1860), Nikolai Dobroliubov draws an overt parallel between the heroine and "Russian society."[146] In an illustrious speech in honor of Pushkin, Dostoevsky reads Onegin as a product of "our intellectual circles, which have become alienated from the people," and Tat'iana as the embodiment of "contact with the native soil" and people.[147] In 1858 an indignant Chernyshevskii writes about Turgenev's *Asia:* "The scene, inflicted upon Asia by our Romeo . . . is a mere symptom of a disease that ruins all our affairs."[148] By "our affairs," as he explains in the same passage, he refers to "administrative and legislative improvements, financial reforms, the liberation of the serfs"; in short, to sociopolitical developments.[149] Guilty of the hero's weakness is, in his eyes, Russian society, which treats the Russian citizen and intellectual as a child who can "never" develop "into a man."[150] With respect to Turgenev's heroes, Dmitrii Pisarev similarly asserts that from the day "our men . . . stop being children," they "become old men," whose senile "softness . . . corresponds to childish naiveté and immaturity."[151] As Rufus Mathewson shows, this tendency "to view a novel's intimate personal settings . . . as testing grounds for behavior in more dangerous, frequently unmentionable, arenas of action" continues to epitomize Russian literature deep into the twentieth century.[152]

The above suggests that nineteenth-century prose anticipates, in several respects, the tradition that serves as the subject of this analysis. Indeed, the link between nineteenth-century prose and later metaphoric representations of Russia as the intelligentsia's unattainable female beloved has not been left unnoted by scholars. Iurii Lotman points to a tendency in nineteenth-century Russian literature to assign to "'the world,' Russia . . . the function of the feminine character 'to be undone' or 'to be saved'" by a "hero, destined to transform the world."[153] David Bethea speaks of a recurring plot in nineteenth- and early twentieth-century Russian literature involving the liberation "of a heroine, who represents the country's vast potential, by a Christ-like paladin";[154] Sander Brouwer highlights the nineteenth-century motif "of depicting the heroine as a representative of the Russian national spirit from which the intelligentsia had estranged itself";[155] and Aleksei Makushinskii labels the amorous tragedy between a westernized intellectual and a heroine who "embodies" a "Russian dimension" the "basic plot of nineteenth-century literature."[156] Makushinskii and Brouwer both emphasize the plot's invariably tragic outcome when naming its hero a "rejected bridegroom" and—in an erotic twist—a "bridegroom who did not come," respectively.[157]

While the analyses in question all stress the persistent existence of this plot in twentieth-century literature, in practice they focus on a discussion of nineteenth-century texts. This study extends the discussion to include twentieth-century Russian culture, in which the gendered representation of the Russia-intelligentsia-state triangle emerges as a prominent political metaphor.

Wooing "My Rus'! My Wife!":

(Pre-)Revolutionary Russia

IN THE SUMMER OF 1918, the Russian philosopher Nikolai Berdiaev expresses the following view of Russia in his *Philosophy of Inequality (Filosofiia neravenstva)*:

> In the soul of the Russian people, the inner marriage never took place. . . . The Russian earth remained feminine, always posing as a bride, always expecting its bridegroom to arrive from outside. It yielded to several husbands that entered from without, but this never resulted in true marriage. . . . You, Russian boys, you *intelligenty* . . . with your feminine nature, constantly searched for spiritual marriage elsewhere. You never managed to reveal an innate masculine spirit . . . you borrowed it from the West, from Western male doctrines. (4:269–70 and 273–74)[1]

Berdiaev's words are programmatic for a vehement debate that is conducted by leading Russian intellectuals between approximately the 1890s and the late 1920s. "The thoughts of its participants," in the words of one scholar of early twentieth-century intellectual culture, "kept circling around one theme: the position of the intelligentsia in relation to the state and society."[2] At the time, this issue figures prominently in literary and philosophical texts, as well as in political essays, cartoons, memoirs, personal correspondence, and even (the reception of) music and painting. Central to the discussion is the element of self-critique: as a rule, those involved consider themselves representatives of the intelligentsia, which they criticize for its weakness and lack of initiative in the sociopolitical sphere.

As previously shown, such a concern is not new within Russian cultural history. What distinguishes these discussions from earlier ones, however, is the tendency to render the subject explicitly in gender terms, as an amorous intrigue between a feminized Russia and a masculine intelligentsia and state. The implicit coalescence of the heroine with Russia in the nineteenth-century novel is now replaced by a direct equivalence, by an equal sign, as it were, between Russia and femininity.

The sudden popularity of this political gender allegory can be explained by the interaction of several factors. First, it should be regarded in the context of a general transition from "latent tropes" in realism to the "realized metaphors" that Renata Döring and Igor' Smirnov have discerned in Russian Symbolism.[3] In their view, the literature of this period can be classified as a "secondary artistic system," in which "a situation from life . . . becomes a realized metaphor" and a work of literature tends to arise from "wordplay."[4] In such a system, social or political reality is depicted not primarily through realistic description, but rather through a play with earlier literary sources and metaphoric images. This turn away from realistic spheres is reflected in the "conversion" of a growing number of Russian intellectuals "to idealism, aestheticism, even religious mysticism"—all three being tendencies that are permeated by a symbolic view of the everyday world.[5] The sociopolitical triangle of intelligentsia, state, and Russian people is discussed accordingly, in highly symbolic terms. Hence the concept of a future marriage between Russia and intelligentsia—influenced as it is by Gnostic and mystical notions of androgyny—cannot be understood in terms of traditional amorous affairs. Instead, it is envisioned as a mystical androgynous entity in which the masculine and the feminine halves merge to become substantially transformed.

Another factor contributing to gendered readings of Russia is the interest in femininity that marks turn-of-the-century Russian philosophy.[6] An important source for the authors discussed here is Sophiological philosophy—or, more specifically, the interaction between the feminine and the masculine within this philosophy. In the words of Olga Matich: "One of the central metaphysical concerns of the Silver Age was the transcendental mystery of sex."[7] The preoccupation with sexual relationships arises against the background of a general European focus on sex and irrationalism. In the fin de siècle era, both inside and outside Russia, readers devour theoretical-philosophical studies of sexuality, such as Otto Weininger's 1903 *Sex and Character* (*Geschlecht und Charakter*). As Evgenii Bershtein recently argued, in Russia the latter's ideas did not merely affect thinking about sexuality per se, but served "as a source of ideas and categories for importing gender and sexuality into the literary analysis of . . . the revolution."[8]

A factor that enhances the popularity of metaphors of Russia specifically as *unattainable* bride is the sense of sociopolitical crisis that pervades early twentieth-century Russian culture. As stated, in the course of the eighteenth and nineteenth centuries the intellectual elite increasingly views its social status in problematic terms. After Russia's defeat in the war against Japan and the failure of the 1905 Revolution, this pessimistic self-view reaches its zenith. In philosophy, political journalism, and poetry, close attention to the issue of Russia's fate and future can be discerned from this period on. It continues during the First World War, which further intensifies national awareness, and remains throughout the 1917 Revolution and the ensuing civil war.[9]

The fact that part of the intellectual elite views itself as Russia's ineffectual suitor is not surprising in a period marked by a coalescence of the social with the personal or amorous spheres. Many artists perceive the sociopolitical crisis as a personal failure, and their attempts to overcome social wrongs merge with a striving for personal—particularly amorous—happiness. Emblematic is Andrei Belyi's conviction that the amorous crisis he experiences in the first decade of the twentieth century reflects "an attack on the whole of Russia."[10]

A final, more practical, stimulus in the development of the metaphor into a commonly used concept is the abrogation of censorship in 1905. In the years that follow, freedom of the press allows for its occurrence in a vivid, critical analysis of Russia's future in a dazzling number of journals and newspapers that are widely read and discussed in intellectual circles.

These factors—the turn toward metaphoric thinking, a preoccupation with sexuality, a sense of social crisis, the merging of the personal with the social, and the abolition of censorship—are crucial to the birth of a conception of "intelligentsia," "state," and "Russia" as a gendered tripod. The use of quotation marks indicates that any analysis of that conception is hampered by the rather imprecisely defined social categories from which it stems. The term "intelligentsia," long saddled with a problematic status, is no less indistinct around 1900. While virtually all participants in the debate in question regard themselves as part of the intelligentsia, no two apply precisely the same label to this enlightened class of society. Its speakers vary from individual artists to representatives of the Social Democratic, neo-populist, and liberal branches that project from the tree of Russian intellect during this period.[11]

Equally nebulous is the (pre-)revolutionary use of the term "state." The concept of the Russian state as a foreign force that has intruded upon an authentic Russia is a vital rhetorical device by this time. Charges against it encompass criticism of the late imperial regime and of topical political issues, along with a retrospective condemnation of the state—from the reign of Peter the Great on—for its dictatorial inclinations and strong orientation toward the West. In this context, the Russian state is equated with foreign forces that have oppressed or mentally influenced Russia in the past, including the Norsemen, German bureaucracy, and philosophical models from western Europe. Added to the list after the revolution, the "foreign" Bolshevik regime comes to be referred to as more or less interchangeable with the earlier "invaders." At the same time, the westernized intelligentsia criticizes

44

itself for an excessive susceptibility to Western thought—a paradox that often leads to contradictory arguments concerning the latter's opposition to the state and to Western influences.

Finally, in the period in question the term "Russia" becomes a common denominator for a miscellany of abstract concepts: it can mean traditional Russia, the Russian land, the Russian earth, "the people"—and sometimes it specifies Russia's peasant population. It may be possible to summarize these varying notions as the Russia of the ordinary people, as opposed to that of the ruling classes, but reducing them to a rational, lucid definition is out of the question.

Thus, the categories involved in this discussion are unclear, to say the least. A similar fogginess tinges the role played by a feminized Russia: her bridal hypostasis overlaps that of the more classic role of nurturing mother. Blok, whose attitude to Russia is "always erotic,"[12] is perhaps an exception, but a mixture of bridal and maternal imagery marks most representations of a feminine Russia from this period. It is a guiding principle behind Esenin's personifications of the nation; and it is salient in Belyi's essay "The Green Meadow" ("Lug zelenyi," 1905), in which the image of Russia as an attractive beauty coincides with the narrator's conception of it as "my mother," to name but two examples.[13]

In a 1930 essay, Dmitrii Merezhkovskii defends the simultaneous attribution of bridal and maternal roles to the earth, which he links to Dostoevsky's mother-bride earth and to similar concepts in ancient cultures.[14] Oleg Popov recently proclaimed this duality exemplary for Russia: "for a Russian," he asserts, "the basic symbolic embodiment of the Mother will always be an image of the Motherland, the Russian Land. . . . His longing for *Matushka-Rossiya* resembles the longing a man feels for the woman he loves when he is separated from her."[15] Although I do not adopt this psychoanalytic perspective, I do wish to underscore the deliberate coalescence of two female roles in the works to be discussed. Their incestuous implications become a favorite intellectual toy for Russian postmodernists, as discussed in a later chapter.

1890s–1920s: OUTLINES OF A DEBATE

The prominent status of the allegory of a feminized Russia between the 1890s and the 1920s obviously precludes a complete overview of the literary, philosophical, and political (con)texts in which it occurs. Instead, this chapter focuses on two authors, Aleksandr Blok and Nikolai Berdiaev, who act as figureheads in debates in the literary and politico-philosophical spheres, respectively. Particular attention is paid to Blok's 1908 play *Song of Fate* and to a number of poems from his collection *Native Land* (1907–16), and to

certain philosophically and sociopolitically oriented texts by Nikolai Berdiaev, mainly from the 1910s. The works of both authors are regarded in the
context of their inclusion in more general sociopolitical debates.

A division of the analysis of this period into two spheres, each centered on a key author, does have its disadvantages, owing to the inextricably
interwoven nature of literary, philosophical, and political forms of expression in Russian culture. These are particularly hard to separate in the period
discussed here. Blok, for example, is renowned not only for his poetry but
also for his politico-philosophical articles. Viacheslav Ivanov was both a philosopher and a prominent poet. And Berdiaev combined his work as a
philosopher with political journalism.

There are several reasons, however, for presenting separate views of
the predominantly literary and politico-philosophical spheres of this era.
Most importantly, in poetry the image of Russia as an unattainable beloved
is particularly popular in the first decade of the twentieth century. While
several contemporary poets use the image as late as the 1920s, the metaphor
on which this study focuses appears most prominently in a poetic context
between approximately 1905 and 1910. By contrast, politico-philosophical
representations of the intelligentsia and Russia as an impossible marriage
take flight only after 1910. Most philosophical texts discussed here date from
the period of the First World War.

Thus both discourses depart from the same metaphoric character
constellation, but the political reality to which they refer differs. For Berdiaev, the struggle against German military power is a major stimulus for his
writings about Russia's "wrong husbands," whereas Blok's works are written
too early to be concerned with a concrete German threat. Then, too, Blok
and several contemporary poets are known generally as Symbolists or post-
Symbolists. Berdiaev and the other politico-philosophical thinkers who pass
in review should be placed in the context of the so-called Russian Religious
Renaissance. Consequently, their works establish different preferences and
take place within a different cultural setting.

Nonetheless, one cannot speak of two completely unrelated debates.
In practice, these poets, philosophers, and journalists parry with one another
continually. The following chronological overview of the works involved offers a basic impression of the extent to which their various statements form
part of an ongoing discussion.

1890s–1905: Sophia Returns

Roughly speaking, the turn toward gendered thinking began in the 1890s.
In an 1898 book review, Vasilii Rozanov epitomizes Russian civil culture as

excessively masculine and out of touch with the feminine Russian earth.[16] Personal correspondence suggests that by that time the concept of the intelligentsia as Russia's ineffectual lover has gained a foothold among the intellectual elite. In an 1893 letter, the painter Mikhail Nesterov summarizes a conversation about Russia that he has had with a group of Russian archeologists: "We all love Russia, but alas! We are unable to love her with genuine love; in our love for this extraordinary, peerless woman we are horrible despots."[17] That Nesterov conceived of this feminized Russia as a beloved woman rather than as a mother can be inferred from memoirs covering the same period in which he compares the relationship between Russia and Venice to the dilemma of two women competing for the love of one man.[18] As I have argued elsewhere, these and other memoirs and letters indicate that Nesterov's 1896 painting of a young woman, *On the Hills* (*V gorakh*), should really be read as a symbolic rendition of Russia as female beloved.[19] What is more, it appears during a period in which Russian canvases are populated by a remarkable number of beautiful young women with markedly Russian characteristics: Surikov's *Siberian Beauty* (*Sibirskaia krasavitsa*, 1891) and *Cossack Woman* (*Kazachka*, 1882), as well as Wassily Kandinsky's *Woman in the Russian Land/Bride* (Russian title unknown, 1903) are but a few examples.[20]

Crucial to the popularity of the metaphor around 1900 are, first and foremost, Solov'ev's philosophical ideas. The influence of Sophiology—and, by implication, mystical and Gnostic thought—on the concept of femininity in the work of Blok and his contemporaries is by now commonly acknowledged.[21] What matters here is their perspective on the national dimension of the Solov'evian World Soul.

That this dimension is relevant to Blok from the beginning of his writing career can be inferred from his 1904 *Verses on the Beautiful Lady* (*Stikhi o prekrasnoi dame*), as well as from his correspondence and personal notes dating from around 1900. Blok's early association of Sophia with Russia occurs in the context of the "Solov'ev circle," an intellectual-mystical group that meets in 1900–1901 at the home of Vladimir Solov'ev's relatives to discuss his ideas.[22] Apart from Belyi and Blok, prominent members include Zinaida Gippius, Dmitrii Merezhkovskii, and the philosopher's nephew, Sergei Solov'ev. They see the World Soul in distinctly Russian or earthly terms. In Merezhkovskii's 1901 novel *The Resurrection of the Gods* (*Voskresshie bogi*), for example, a sixteenth-century icon painter envisions Sophia as Christ's bride in a rural setting, which he recognizes as "the Russian earth."[23] The earth stars as a Sophiological "bride" in Gippius's 1905 poem "To the Earth" ("Zemle"), which is published in the prominent avant-garde journal *Vesy* in 1906.[24] Belyi defines Russia as bride and "Woman, clothed with the Sun" in his 1905 essay "The Green Meadow," published in the same journal.[25]

In 1905 Merezhkovskii associates Russia with the figure of a female be-loved—in this case, the object of Peter the Great's affections—in his novel *Antichrist: Petr and Aleksei* (*Antikhrist: Petr i Aleksei*).

Coming from a very different literary tradition, around this time Anton Chekhov represents the Russia of the 1860s as an attractive young girl who is "call[ed] on . . . to awake" in "The Fiancée" ("Nevesta," 1903)—that is, if we are to believe Joe Andrew's convincing analysis of the story.[26] In the same year, the poet Sofiia Parnok also takes recourse to the sleeping-beauty metaphor in her poem cycle "Russia" ("Rossiia"). In the words of her biogra-pher Diana Burgin, Parnok "compared Russia to a sleeping beauty awaiting her savior prince . . . who was far away and oblivious to the moans of the beauty's 'embattled Truth'"; according to Burgin, Parnok's poems "expressed the 'sleeping' poet's underlying desire to have her course directed and to be saved from her dormant state."[27] Here the masculine outlook, in which masculine strivings are projected onto a feminized Russia, is replaced by the feminine view of a poetess who personally identifies with that feminized country. Around this time Parnok's brother, Valia, also stresses Russia's femi-nine character, although in somewhat less complimentary terms: his Russia is "a very broad *baba*-monster with an inordinately small vagina!"[28]

1905–1914: Echoes of the '05 Revolution

"The power and the people"—thus sounds a major slogan of early twentieth-century Russian politics. From the way in which it is used in Nicholas II's Russia, Sergei Domnikov deduces that it consciously revives "the . . . arche-typal image of a sacred marriage between . . . power and people."[29] If one subscribes to the thoughts of Blok and like-minded authors, however, this marriage was becoming a notoriously unhappy one. Pessimistic tones domi-nate artistic representations of Russia, particularly after the uprisings and failed revolution of 1905. "All the 'great literature' of 1907–1917," writes Zara Mints, can be summarized as "an analysis of the experience of a failed revolution."[30] This is also the period in which a metaphoric representation of Russia as the intelligentsia's female beloved reigns supreme in literary, political, and public discourse. Rather than assuming the shape of a future mystical wife, the "nation" now increasingly poses as a principally unattain-able bride. It has acquired a dual status, often appearing as both an exalted, saintly figure and a vulgar, fallen woman.

Russia repeatedly appears as a captive princess in the overwhelming number of satirical journals that come into being after the revolution and the abolition of censorship in 1905. The failed revolution also reverberates in Blok's and Belyi's work at this time. It triggers the latter to write "The Green

Meadow," as well as "Adam," a short story written in 1906 and published in *Vesy* in 1908. The hero in "Adam" imagines himself as heir to the Slavophiles and as bridegroom-to-be of the riotous Russia of 1905;[31] in "The Green Meadow," Russia is compared to a sleeping beauty faced with the choice of staying with her husband or marrying a *kashchei* from abroad.[32] In 1906 Blok, too, envisions Russia as a sleeping beauty in the poem "Rus'" (2:106–7).[33] And in 1905 Rimsky-Korsakov's opera *Kashchei*—which features the liberation of a princess from a sorcerer—causes a scandal when it is received as an allegorical call to revolution. Its alleged anti-governmental stance led to such fervent reactions among the public that Korsakov was dismissed from his post as conservatory professor.[34] If, as Lynn Sargeant has pointed out, the sorcerer was associated with the influential conservative statesman Konstantin Pobedonostsev, then, by implication, the audience must have understood the princess as the object of the latter's political "sorcery": to them, she represented contemporary Russia. As I argue later, such an interpretation was in line with a trend in public discourse at the time to represent Pobedonostsev as a sorcerer and Russia as a princess whom he has bewitched.

To return to Belyi. He asserts that "The Green Meadow" is the result of conversations he has had with Blok.[35] At that moment Blok is working on an article similarly titled "The Green Meadows" ("Zelenye luga"; 8:135), which is published in *Zolotoe runo* in 1906 as "Dark Days" ("Bezvremen'e"). By this time Blok's increasing interest in politics has resulted in a number of poems that depict the revolution as a female beloved (2:50–57, 324).[36] "Dark Days" is set quite plainly amidst the revolutionary turmoil of 1905. To its narrator, "reality is passing in a red color," and the "days become ever louder with screams, with flying red flags" (5:71). Depicted in gender terms clearly referencing those used by Belyi, the Russia in "Dark Days" symbolically merges with a sensuous gypsy bride who encounters several male suitors.[37] A year earlier, Blok had addressed Russia in similar terms in the poem "Autumn Freedom" ("Osenniaia volia," 1905), whose poet listens "to the voice of drunken Rus'" without whom he can neither "live nor cry" (2:76).

As 1907 approaches, gendered representations of Russia, intelligentsia, and state begin to figure even more prominently in Russian intellectual culture. On the first of January, the newspaper *Novoe vremia* features an article by Vasilii Rozanov, who refers to the war against Japan and Russia's internal political tumult in undeniably marital metaphors. He depicts Russia in its need for a new leader as a bride awaiting a bridegroom in vain.[38] A year later, in the same newspaper he refers to the 1905 Revolution as a "*baba*-revolution" rebelling against the "*muzhik*-state."[39]

The same year marks Blok's growing infatuation (influenced by letters from the poet Nikolai Kliuev) with the struggle to eliminate the alienation between the intelligentsia, with whom he personally identifies, and the people. His initial interest in this theme, in early 1907, coincides with the first drafts for the play *Song of Fate* and for the *Native Land* collection.[40] In both works, the poet (or hero) and Russia are symbolically equated with a lover and an unattainable female beloved, respectively. In both, the hero is a rival for her love with an antagonist who incarnates the Russian regime as well as foreign influences. In the essay "The People and the Intelligentsia" ("Narod i intelligentsiia"), which Blok writes the following year, Russia and the intelligentsia are explicitly gendered (5:321). Blok would later remark that *Song of Fate* and *Native Land* dealt with the same theme as this essay,[41] which focuses on "the question of how the intelligentsia can find a connection with the people" (8:264).

In 1908, Blok finishes *Song of Fate.* In the summer and autumn of that year he writes the cycle *On Kulikovo Field* (*Na pole kulikovom*) and the poem "Russia" ("Rossiia"), both crucial to the theme discussed here.[42] A Gogolian notebook entry in October defines Russia as a mystical beauty in a troika who needs to be freed from a "demonic coachman."[43] On the first day of 1909, he finishes "Autumn Day" ("Osennii den'"), yet another poem in which the poet addresses Russia as a wife.[44]

Blok's "bride-Russia works" are discussed eagerly in the literary-cum-mystical-cum-political network formed by the intellectual elite of those days. For the definitive versions of *Song of Fate* and *Native Land,* he consults contemporaries such as Konstantin Stanislavskii and Georgii Chulkov.[45] He is acquainted with several other authors who represent Russia as a female beloved. Apart from Andrei Belyi and Nikolai Kliuev, Blok personally knows Vasilii Rozanov as well. The two follow one another's writings scrupulously and repeatedly react to each other publicly.[46] On the very day that Blok claims to be writing his 1908 article on the people and the intelligentsia, he has an extensive talk with Rozanov and calls him a "close (if incomprehensible) person" (8:259).

More important than the degree to which existing examples inspire Blok's version of the metaphor, however, is the degree to which *he* influences his contemporaries. Without a doubt, it is the representation of Russia as unattainable bride in Blok's 1908 works that first give this metaphor the status of a national stereotype. The resonance in the press and among contemporaries who have reviewed, in particular, *Native Land* and "The People and the Intelligentsia" is enormous.

Blok repeatedly reads the works in question for a broad audience and in the presence of several renowned intellectuals. He reads a draft version of *Song of Fate*—along with some of his gendered-Russia poems—in an intimate setting before fellow artists such as Georgii Chulkov, Maksimilian Voloshin, and Fedor Sologub (4:579); and at one of Viacheslav Ivanov's "Wednesdays," where the intellectual elite of the first decade of the twentieth century gathered.[47] It is here that Blok meets with a number of writers and thinkers who will elaborate on the same metaphor; apart from Chulkov, Voloshin, and Sologub, these include Ivanov himself, Rozanov, Sergei Bulgakov, and Berdiaev,[48] who allegedly counts Blok and Belyi among his literary favorites.[49] On November 13, 1908, Blok reads "The People and the Intelligentsia" at a crowded meeting of the so-called Religious-Philosophical Society (Religiozno-filosofskoe obshchestvo). More readings follow: on November 25, for a smaller group of prominent poets and thinkers, including Merezhkovskii, Rozanov, and Ivanov; and on December 12, at a meeting of the Literary Society (Literaturnoe obshchestvo) for representatives of populist, Marxist, and social democratic groups, and eminent intellectuals such as Chulkov and—again—Merezhkovskii.[50] On these occasions, the essay sparks vivid debate. At the first meeting, the police are called in to quell vehement reactions to the lecture, a fact that attracts a great deal of attention in the press (5:742).

The publication of the works in question causes considerable commotion as well. Contemporaries avidly discuss and debate them in widely read media.[51] In the course of the 1910s and 1920s, Blok's gendered view of Russia is singled out—for both praise and criticism—in numerous reviews and essays by prominent contemporaries such as Viacheslav Ivanov, Nikolai Gumilev, and Kornei Chukovskii.[52] Here, and in memoirs on Blok, his gendered view of Russia is extended and incorporated as a vital image into the worldview of the author in question.[53] Sergei Gorodetskii, for example, claims in a 1909 review in the newspaper *Rech'* that, upon viewing the juxtaposition of land and wife in Blok's poem "Autumn Day," "we are surprised to see that this is . . . indeed a new revelation of the symbol of the Eternal Feminine."[54] Together with Ivanov's review of Belyi's and Blok's 1908–9 works, Gorodetskii's piece is generally seen as the starting point of neo-populist discussions of the years 1909–10.[55]

Blok's gendered representations of Russia, state, and intelligentsia are not only reproduced and expanded in memoirs and reviews: many leading writers, thinkers, and journalists of the time respond to them in their own writings. In 1909, similar metaphoric imagery marks Belyi's novel *The Silver Dove (Serebrianyi golub')*. Published in *Vesy,* this work of fiction had been conceived from 1905 on, in reaction to the first revolutionary period.[56] In an obvious dialogue with Blok, Belyi presents an amorous triangle involving the hero-*intelligent,* his fiancée, and a promiscuous peasant woman. The two women incarnate, respectively, an exalted and a fallen feminine representation of Russia or the Russian people. *The Silver Dove* also echoes "The Green Meadow"[57]—and Belyi again returns to the feminized view of Russia in that essay in an article on Gogol, which appears in *Vesy* together with part of *The Silver Dove.*[58] Like Blok's writings on Russia, Belyi's novel leads to fervent and emotional reactions,[59] and contemporary reviewers regarded it from the start "as a novel about the relationship between the people and the intelligentsia."[60]

Apart from *The Silver Dove,* the year 1909 also witnesses Ivanov's elaboration of a Sophiologically inspired view of man as the "heavenly Bridegroom" and the "earth as Wife" in his essay "Terror Antiquus" ("Antichnyi uzhas"), published in the journal *Zolotoe runo.*[61] Ivanov does not yet refer specifically to Russia here, as he will in a similar context in later essays.

Finally, 1909 sees the appearance of a collection of essays titled *Milestones (Vekhi).* Written by high-ranking liberal intellectuals such as Berdiaev, Bulgakov, and Petr Struve, the *Milestones* essays proffer ethical-religious solutions to the alienation of "the intelligentsia" from the Russian people. Intended more as self-criticism than as a concrete program for social change, *Milestones* has a huge influence on ongoing intellectual debates: within a year, it is discussed in more than 220 articles, reviews, and other written reactions.[62] In itself, the collection is of little interest to the theme discussed here, with the exception of Sergei Bulgakov's contribution, which concludes with a gendered view of Russia and the intelligentsia. It does, however, serve as a major frame of reference for the Russia-as-bride metaphor in the years to follow. Contemporary critics of *Milestones* believe the collection to be closely linked to Belyi's *Silver Dove,* often calling this novel its "literary companion."[63] Belyi and the contributors to *Milestones* reinforce this impression by commenting on one another's work in terms of personal recognition and sympathy.[64] Emblematic is Berdiaev's reaction to *The Silver Dove* in the journal *Russkaia mysl'* in 1910, in the form of a philosophical essay, "The Russian Temptation" ("Russkii soblazn"). Berdiaev looks at the relationship between Belyi's hero and his temptress as a failing amorous union between the Russian intelligentsia and the Russian people or earth, respectively (3:414–15). Whether or not in direct reaction, Rozanov's essay "Near the Russian Idea" ("Vozle 'russkoi idei,'" 1914), written in 1911, echoes a number of the concepts from this article, although it focuses on the relationship between the "feminine" Russia and the "masculine" West rather than on the issue of intelligentsia and people.[65]

Berdiaev's review marks the beginning of his personal conception of the relationship between Russia and intelligentsia as a problematic gender opposition. Again, interaction with contemporaries plays a crucial role in this formation of gendered Russia views. Referring to the period around 1910 in his autobiography, Berdiaev speaks of Belyi as a "friend of the family" who "constantly visited our house, ate, drank, and even slept at our place" (1:224). From 1905 until after the October Revolution, Berdiaev repeatedly sees Belyi and Rozanov.[66] As members of literary and philosophical circles, they meet in the company of several other authors in whose work the metaphor of Russia as unattainable beloved will figure prominently; this group includes Sergei Bulgakov, Viacheslav Ivanov, Vladimir Ern, Evgenii Trubetskoi, Pavel Florenskii, Chulkov, and the poets Voloshin and Sologub.[67]

During the same years, Kliuev publishes poems that refer to Blok's feminized Russia. In his 1910 cycle "To Aleksandr Blok" ("Aleksandru Bloku")—a direct response to Blok's "Russia"[68]—the poet asks a feminine figure: "O, who are You: A Woman? Russia?"[69] A year later, Kliuev's lyrical ego addresses Russia as a "mighty-eyed wife" in "In the Frozen Darkness . . ." ("V moroznoi mgle . . .").[70] Both poems inherited from Blok the notion of a tragic separation between the poet and Russia. Later, Kliuev just as openly enters into a dialogue with Belyi's depiction of Russia by having the lyrical ego in "Don Psalm" ("Poddonnyi psalom," 1916) claim: "O my native land . . . / I do not see you as the woman clothed with the sun, / . . . / But as a *baba*, a housewife."[71]

Blok has distanced himself from the literary community at this time,[72] but Kliuev and Blok do meet in 1911, and the latter's contact with Belyi remains strong. In letters to Blok dated 1911, Belyi portrays the two as lovers who flirt with and duel over Russia.[73] During these years, Blok himself is no less preoccupied by the idea of Russia as an object of amorous admiration. A draft from March 1911 for the epic poem *Retribution* (*Vozmezdie*, 1910–21) represents Russia as a sleeping beauty who has been enchanted and captured by a "sorcerer": a role Blok attributes to the same Pobedonostsev who is allegorized in Rimsky-Korsakov's opera *Kashchei* (3:328). Pobedonostsev later functions as sorcerer-captor of a feminized Russia in Georgii Chulkov's historical treatise *The Emperors: Psychological Portraits* (*Imperatory: Psikhologicheskie portrety*, 1927).[74] Whether or not in response to Blok, Igor' Severianin also embroiders on the concept when, in his 1925 poem "Sleeping Beauty" ("Spiashchaia krasavitsa"), he compares Russia to a "princess who fell asleep" and needs to be "courted" but ultimately dies.[75]

In 1913, Blok again reverts to the concept of the poet as Russia's male suitor in "New America" ("Novaia Amerika"), first published in the newspaper *Russkoe slovo* on December 25. Belyi will later interpret this poem as a continuation of his female-Russia hypostasis in "The Green Meadow."[76] The same issue of *Russkoe slovo* contains a poem by Bal'mont, "The Silent Country . . ." ("Strana, kotoraia molchit . . ."), which refers to a snow-covered Russia as a "bride, dressed in a veil."[77] If Blok's influence is less than crystal clear in this passage, there can be no question about the stimulus he provides for Bal'mont's "I" ("Ia"), written in 1927 after Bal'mont has emigrated. This poem undeniably draws inspiration from the "My Rus'! My Wife!" of Blok's Kulikovo cycle when the poet asserts that "for one only am I prepared to take it all: / My sister and mother! My wife! Russia!"[78]

1914–1917: War

Toward the mid-1910s, more poems appear in which the poet poses as Russia's ineffectual lover. By this time, the First World War and the Russian fight against Germany begin to play a vital role in literary—as well as in political and philosophical—representations of Russia.

Gendered takes on political relations have now become commonplace. Many a Russian has been confronted with feminized Russias and markedly masculine states and intelligentsias in newspaper articles, in satirical journals, in cartoons, and on political posters, which offer a state-endorsed version of the metaphor. Russia is transformed into a militant fairy-tale princess, for instance, in the 1914 poster "Russia for the Truth" ("Rossiia—za pravdu").[79] In the satirical journal *Novyi satirikon,* the nation appears as a sleeping beauty waking to the roar of German artillery.[80] A 1915 popular print personifies the war between Russia and its central European enemies as a men's fight between a brave knight and a dragon, respectively.[81]

At this time Blok—who spends the war partly in isolation on the family estate and partly as a soldier at the front—retreats into the background. Russia is now glorified as the poet's beloved in the work of a number of his colleagues. One example is the lyrical ego in Sologub's poem "Russia" ("Rossiia"), published in the newspaper *Otechestvo* in 1915, who addresses Russia as "still a bride" awaiting a "lofty destiny."[82] Voloshin's poem of the same name, also written in 1915, appears in *Vlast' naroda* in 1917. In Voloshin's "Russia," the poet stresses his love for Russia's "profaned" appearance. Although the maternal aspect dominates, the poem suggests an amorous relationship between Russia and the poet when the latter claims to love "you [Russia] . . . / Mystically enlightened / With all the beauty of the world."[83] That the war has provided the background for his gendered view of Russia can be inferred from both the poem's inclusion in the "War" cycle and its original subtitle, "During the Galician Retreat."[84]

Finally, in the mid-1910s the poet poses as Russia's lover in Nikolai Kliuev's and Sergei Esenin's "peasant poetry." In the reading of Natal'ia Solntseva, Kliuev's 1915 poem "February" ("Fevral'") interprets the revolution as a fertilization of the Russian earth or as a "marriage dance."[85] Just how literally one should take this fertilization is indicated by the violently erotic wish of the lyrical ego of another Kliuev poem—"To Enter Your Wounds . . ." ("Voiti v tvoi rany . . . ," 1916–18)—"to spurt my seed into the womb of the Earth."[86] In Esenin's work of the same years, numerous poems focus on the poet's relationship to a personified rural Russia, with the war as a vital background motif.[87] In his personifications, maternal imagery merges with distinctly bridal metaphors. In "Again Decoratively Stretched Out . . ." ("Opiat' raskinulsia uzorno . . . ," 1916), for instance, the poet opposes himself as a "tender novice" to Russia as a "loose wife."[88] That this concept also tinged the myth surrounding the author himself is implied by a friend's observation that "Esenin's . . . sometimes blind love of Russia seemed to bar him from falling in love [with any other place]."[89]

In the war years, philosophical and political thought also takes repeated recourse to gendered oppositions of Russia and intelligentsia. Such an opposition plays a vital role in a polemic revolving around a performance of Dostoevsky's *Demons* at the Moscow Art Theater (MKhAT) in 1914. Contributions to the discussion in *Russkaia mysl'* (nos. 4 and 5) by Berdiaev, Ivanov, and Bulgakov view Russia or "the Russian people" and "the intelligentsia" as a mystical bride and a lover incapable of conquering that bride, respectively.

By this time, the First World War has led to a revival of messianic Slavophile sentiments and renewed interest in the Sophia concept, which is projected onto Russia's present-day political situation.[90] How Sophiological concepts have come to function in a neo-Slavophile, nationalist context is perhaps best illustrated by Evgenii Trubetskoi's religious-philosophical essay "The National Question, Constantinople and Saint Sophia" ("Natsional'nyi vopros, Konstantinopol' i Sviataia Sofia"). Written and read as a public lecture in 1915, it associates Sophia with the Russian people and the "national soul."[91] Trubetskoi's conception of the relationship between Sophia as "national utopia" and her (male) devotees in mystical-marital terms highlights his claim elsewhere that a suitor wanting to reach Sophia feels "like a man who doesn't have the right clothes in which to enter the marriage palace."[92] Sophiological concepts acquired a similarly political role in the 1910s in the work of the philosopher Pavel Florenskii, who branded Sophia the "essence of infantile Rus'" and the mystical bride of Saint Constantine-Cyril in his essay "The Holy Trinity–St. Sergius Monastery and Russia" ("Troitse-Sergieva Lavra i Rossiia," 1918).[93]

Equally infatuated with national gender metaphors at this time is Viacheslav Ivanov. In his 1915 essay "Living Legend" ("Zhivoe predanie"), he defends the Slavophile view of Russia as a fairy-tale hero's perspective of a bride captured by evil forces.[94] Slavophile echoes resonate with particular force, however, in Berdiaev's politico-philosophical texts of the war years, beginning with his treatise *The Soul of Russia* (*Dusha Rossii*), published in 1915. Written in reaction to the war, *The Soul of Russia* marks Berdiaev's shift of attention from the Russia-intelligentsia relationship to the Russia–intelligentsia–foreign forces triangle. He now criticizes Russia's attitude to Germany as that of a passive bride who married the "wrong" bridegroom.[95]

Berdiaev again elaborates on the relationship of a feminized Russian people with the state and with foreign authorities in his "On the Eternally Womanish in the Russian Soul" ("O vechno-bab'em v russkoi dushe"), published in *Birzhevye vedomosti* in January 1915. He writes the essay in reaction to Rozanov's self-proclaimed "feminine" veneration of the "masculinity" of military displays of power in *The War of 1914 and the Russian Renaissance* (*Voina 1914 goda i russkoe vozrozhdenie*, 1915)[96]—a monograph in which Rozanov clearly poses as representative of the intelligentsia in opposition to the state.[97] The philosopher Vladimir Ern, in turn, criticizes Berdiaev's article in the same *Birzhevye vedomosti*, but he preserves the metaphoric concept of the Russian people or earth as mystical bride. Sticking to Christian tradition, Ern opposes that bride to Christ as bridegroom-to-come.[98]

In 1916 Berdiaev expounds his previous views on Russia or the intelligentsia as a feminine entity in the politico-philosophical articles "On the Personal and Historical Look on Life" ("O chastnom i istoricheskom vzgliade na zhizn'"), published in *Birzhevye vedomosti*, and "Nationalism and Messianism" ("Natsionalizm i messianizm"), published independently.[99] He and Trubetskoi participate in a 1916–17 polemic in *Russkaia mysl'* on the need for either an ethical or an erotic attitude toward the native land, even if not in a manifestly Russian-national context.[100]

The Revolution and After

As described, Russian intellectual culture brews with revolutionary sentiments from 1907 to 1917, the year in which the Russian Revolution causes years of political unrest to culminate in an actual shift of power. The intellectual and artistic elite is divided in its attitude toward this transition: some consider it a long-awaited blessing; others vehemently oppose its undemocratic and violent aspects.[101]

In Russian poetry, the events of 1917 do not annihilate the image of Russia as a feminine figure. Now, however, it is revolutionary Russia to whom the poet relates as to an (unattainable) bride. Her potentially demonic or promiscuous dimension comes to the fore more than in the past. In addition, female Russia tends to merge with either the bride of Christ or Christ himself, who figures as the revolution incarnate in certain works by Blok, Belyi, and Esenin.

Blok finds himself in an awkward position at this time, being one of only a few former Symbolists who sympathize with the Bolsheviks' seizure of power. Scholars have repeatedly discussed his positive, primarily aesthetic-mystical, view of the revolution and the social isolation this caused him.[102] Written and published in 1918 in two Bolshevik newspapers, the poem "The Twelve" ("Dvenadtsat'") is generally considered to be the ultimate expression of this view. It depicts Christ and his disciples as a group of revolutionaries who march through snowy Petersburg and whose wish to shoot "fat-assed" "Holy Rus'" coincides with the shooting of the poem's heroine, Kat'ka (3:350 and 353).

Apart from this symbolic association of Kat'ka with Russia, "The Twelve" is of importance to the metaphor discussed here for its connection to earlier works by Blok and Belyi. Chukovskii calls it "the logical conclusion" of the *Native Land* collection. Belyi interprets it as an extension of "The Green Meadow."[103] Sergei Hackel argues that the depiction of its heroine might also have been inspired by Georgii Chulkov's prose sketch "The Snowstorm" ("Metel'"), which appeared in the newspaper *Narodopravstvo* in January 1918.[104] In this essay, Chulkov criticizes Russia's political situation and the "semi-intelligentsia," as he calls it, in terms of a mystical vision of Russia as an attractive girl, who looks at the author through a snowstorm and then disappears.[105]

That same Chulkov detests "The Twelve," as do many of Blok's friends and admirers, such as Gippius, Sologub, and Ivanov. Yet the poem is even more of a commercial success than his 1908 works on Russia.[106] Generally speaking, Blok's gendered view of Russia is disseminated actively at this time through the 1918 publication of the second chapter of *Retribution*—with its equation of Russia with a captive sleeping beauty—and through his reading of this poem at numerous well-attended performances.[107] In the words of one critic, the years after 1917 saw a "revival of a second general infatuation with Blok," and with *Retribution* in particular.[108]

Within the literary scene, Blok was now close to the group of authors known as the "Scythians" or Skify. Sharing a view of Russia as half-European, half-Asian in character, the Scythians sympathized with the revolution as the mystical manifestation of Russia's Asian element. The close interaction in 1917 and 1918 of poets who identified with this idea—specifically Blok, Belyi, Esenin, and Kliuev—is reflected in several similarities in their poetic depictions of Russia. A month after the publication of "The Twelve," Belyi reacts to Blok's text with his epic poem "Christ Has Risen" ("Khristos voskrese").[109] Belyi's poem is published in May in the same Bolshevik newspaper, *Znamia truda*, in which "The Twelve" had appeared earlier that year. It superimposes the story of Christ's crucifixion on contemporary Russia, which appears as a "Bride" and a "Wife, Clothed with the Sun"; the revolution is envisioned as the arrival of her heavenly bridegroom, Christ.[110] In 1923 the philosopher Gustav Shpet quotes this passage in his *Aesthetic Fragments* (*Esteticheskie fragmenty*), claiming that in its relationship to European culture Russia ought to behave as a susceptible bride.[111]

The crucifixion of Christ also plays a role in Sergei Esenin's personifications of the Russia of 1917 and post-revolutionary years. In poems that at times openly refer to the revolution, he envisions Russia varyingly as the

Virgin Mary, a crucified Christ, and a drunken, promiscuous woman.[112] Although Russia's maternal dimension remains prominent for him, the designation of Rus' as "Virgin" and the poet's stance as her "only herald" and "guard" add a courtly amorous dimension to their relationship.[113] Significantly, Kliuev labels Esenin a "bridegroom of the Riazan' earth" in his 1922 epic poem "Lion Bread" ("L'vinyi khleb").[114] At this time Kliuev, too, identifies with the role of Russia's lover in "The Fourth Rome" ("Chetvertyi Rim," 1922); and—again in an erotic context—in "A *Zurna* on a *Zyriane* Wedding . . ." ("Zurna na zyrianskoi svad'be . . . ," 1918–19): this poem's lyrical ego expresses the wish to "lie down like a seed in the furrows / Of the eager earth-bride!"[115]

Another poet who eagerly eroticizes national imagery in this period is Maksimilian Voloshin. In "Holy Rus'" ("Sviataia Rus'," 1917)—a highly popular poem during the post-revolutionary civil war—the lyrical ego addresses Russia as a bride who turns from princess to prostitute. Rather than to one of the princes to whom she is promised, she gives herself to "a robber and a thief."[116] Voloshin repeats the image of Russia as a fallen woman who consorts with the enemy in other poems of the post-revolutionary years; invariably, each of his lyrical egos personally addresses Russia and poses as its potential savior.[117] His opponent embodies, alternately, Germany and the Bolsheviks.[118]

Voloshin's poems coincide with nonliterary representations of the Bolsheviks in Russia: in 1917, for example, the journal *Novyi satirikon* publishes "Romance of Lenin and Russia" ("Roman Lenina i Rossii"), a cartoon narrative in which Lenin courts, embraces, and kisses a feminized Russia, who ultimately bears his unwanted child.[119] By now the concept of Russia as a captive bride has become such a commonplace that the public spots metaphoric connotations even in works that have none; in another publication I show how this happened, for instance, to Viktor Vasnetsov's fairy-tale paintings from the mid-1910s on.[120]

Voloshin is likely to have been affected by this politically charged atmosphere; more particularly, we know that Blok was a source of inspiration for his political poems.[121] Voloshin clings to a feminized view of Russia as late as 1929, when he equates the face of the "virginal" "Sophia Holy Wisdom" with that of "Russia itself" in "The Vladimir Mother of God" ("Vladimirskaia Bogomater'").[122]

Voloshin's and Blok's mystical visions of Russia unite in the poetry of the last poet to be mentioned here. Mariia Shkapskaia meets Voloshin and Blok face to face in 1916 and 1920, respectively.[123] The strong influence that Blok makes on Shkapskaia in the year before his death is clearly present in her poem "Russia" ("Rossiia") and in a cycle of the same name, both written in 1921–22 and both representing Russia, addressed by the poet, as the bride of Christ.[124] In addition, the cycle portrays Peter the Great and Russia as husband and wife.[125] In the manner of Parnok, however, this female poet identifies not with the male perspective but with a feminized Russia: "You are a woman and you are my sister."[126]

From a philosophical point of view, it is most notably Berdiaev who sticks to a metaphoric representation of Russia as female beloved in and after 1917. The revolution prompts him to adapt his views on Russia and the intelligentsia—as a disturbed amorous relationship—to the contemporary situation. He does this in a number of articles, some of which are published in popular journals and newspapers of the time and some of which are compiled in two collections: *The Spiritual Bases of the Russian Revolution* (*Dukhovnye osnovy russkoi revoliutsii*, 1917–18) and *The Fate of Russia* (*Sud'ba Rossii*, 1918).[127] In 1918 he extends his version of the metaphor substantially in *The Philosophy of Inequality*, written as a direct reaction to revolutionary events. Although Berdiaev retains his ideas on the status of Russia as a metaphoric bride, he now conceives of the nation as the slain victim of the new rulers, whom he sees as the intelligentsia's "feminine" radical wing (4:273 and 276). At a later date, in exile, he renounces this view (1:265).

Berdiaev takes our journey into the 1920s, when the conception of Russia as an unattainable bride begins to wane. In the 1930s, offshoots of the debate emerge only occasionally. These include Kliuev's 1934 epic poem "Devastation" ("Razrukha"), whose lyrical ego identifies with the role of potential liberator of a "native land-cum-bride" defiled in 1918.[128] Emigrants like Sergei Bulgakov and Georgii Fedotov continue to use the metaphor. In Bulgakov's essay "My Native Land" ("Moia rodina"), written in 1938 in exile, the concept of Russia as bride is formulated in Sophiological terms: the narrator calls his life a constant search for the Divine Sophia, with whom he has "fallen in love" and whom he associates with Russia.[129] Throughout the 1920s, 1930s, and 1940s, Fedotov writes a number of essays in exile in which an erotic relationship with Russia prevails.[130] These are, however, isolated exceptions in a period in which the vivid debate witnessed earlier had practically fallen silent.

ALEKSANDR BLOK: COURTING "MY POOR WIFE" RUSSIA

Aleksandr Blok, as noted, is not the first to represent the Russia-intelligentsia-state tripod in gendered terms. What he does do, though, is to turn this gendered view into an elaborate metaphor that recurs in several of his works and that colors his personal behavior as well. Blok explores the bride-Russia theme most extensively in *Native Land* and *Song of Fate*. *Native Land*, a collection of verse about Russia, contains several poems in which the poet addresses Russia or the Russian landscape as beloved, bride, or wife. In the play *Song of Fate,* Russia is equated symbolically with the heroine, Faina, a promiscuous young singer-performer. In mystical terms, the play recounts her relationship with the hero, German. A stereotypical *intelligent,* he falls for Faina but is unable to establish an amorous relationship with her and to snatch her away from an older suitor—Faina's so-called Companion—who incarnates the tsarist regime.

As mentioned, *Song of Fate* and *Native Land* inspired a number of contemporary writers, thinkers, and journalists. What is more, Blok's vision of Russia, intelligentsia, and state as an amorous intrigue remains of topical importance beyond the early twentieth century. In one way or another, it finds its way into a large number of twentieth-century Russian (literary and nonliterary) texts. From Platonov's *Happy Moscow* to Kibirov's poems on Russia: when Russia appears as unattainable female beloved, Blok is never far away, either in implicit allusions or in explicit quotations.

Accordingly, whereas Makushinskii is probably right in arguing that Blok serves as an "epilogue" to nineteenth-century symbolic equations of Russia and intelligentsia with bride and bridegroom, at the same time Blok forms a point of departure or *prologue* to twentieth-century gender-biased views of Russia.[131]

Given this immense influence, it is not surprising that today Blok's rendition of Russia, intelligentsia, and state as a tragic amorous plot is a widely recognized theme in Russian literary history. Scholars repeatedly discuss his preference for this topos, and literary handbooks frequently mention his view of Russia as a beloved woman.[132] Considering the undisputed status of Blok's leitmotif, this study does not seek to prove once more the existence of such imagery in his work. Here the aim is to place his "bride Russia" in a broader sociopolitical context. Having viewed Blok's metaphor against the background of similar concepts in the work of his contemporaries, I continue my exploration with a look at what Richards would call the *ground* of the metaphor. My interest lies in the shared characteristics of three matching sets: Russia and the woman to whom Blok compares her, "the intelligentsia" and his poet-hero, and the state and Blok's antagonist. It is these common qualities that best reveal the core of the political issues to which the metaphor refers. The discussion opens with a review of Blok's general attitude to the theme of Russia.

Blok and Russia: Life or Death

In the words of Aleksandr Etkind, Blok can be characterized as a "poet-visionary" in whose life "the literary stance merges with real-life behavior" and "literary work blends with political struggle and mystical service to an unknown God."[133] This rather dramatic fusion is in keeping with what Vladislav Khodasevich famously defined as the "life-building method" of the Symbolists, who "did not wish to separate . . . the literary biography from the personal."[134] On the one hand, Symbolists experience life as part of their art and put their experiences into a literary-aesthetic context. On the other, "life building" is epitomized by a wish to transcend the aesthetic sphere and make contact with real life. This desire prevails in the years following the 1905 Revolution, when many Symbolists express an increasing sociopolitical awareness.[135] For Blok, the post-1905 years are marked by a "growing interest in . . . topicality, history, social and political problems" and by an orientation toward "outer-literariness."[136] This shift in orientation can be seen quite clearly in his attitude to the theme of Russia and the intelligentsia. Regarding his essay on this theme, Blok asks

> that note be taken, above all, of the *content* of the *issues* that I discuss—particularly relations between the intelligentsia and the people, the intelligentsia and Russia—and *not* of the *form* of my statement, not of the aesthetic style features that I cannot do without, although sometimes I would like to do so. (5:688; italics in original)

In a letter Blok expresses his "panicky terror of literariness, specifically regarding *this* issue" (8:264; italics in original). Illustrative of this fear is his correspondence with the theatrical director Konstantin Stanislavskii, in which he defends the alleged neglect of formal aspects in *Song of Fate*. While claiming that he would "by no means overlook 'form' in favor of 'content,'" Blok also stresses that the play's sociopolitical themes are more important than its "words" (8:264–66). In a famous passage, he confesses that "to the *theme of Russia* (and, particularly, to the matter of the intelligentsia and the people) . . . I . . . irrevocably *dedicate my life*. I realize more and more that this is a primary issue . . . here lies life or death, happiness or ruin" (8:265–66; italics in original). The feeling of near-physical emphasis that imbues this statement is confirmed by Kornei Chukovskii's assertion that "when Blok spoke about Russia, it sometimes seemed as if he also felt it with his whole body, as if it were pain."[137] A similarly personal, emotive stance to Russia pervades the work of several of his contemporaries.[138]

In the case of Blok, the intense wish to convey his ideological message eventually results in a simplification of style. Zara Mints speaks of the shift from the "multi-layeredness of the symbol" in his early work to an "allegorical two-layeredness" and synecdoches in the years 1907–9.[139] In *Native Land*, the link between Russia and a female beloved occasionally takes the form of such "two-layered" symbols—think of explicit equations such as

"My Russia! My wife!" "my poverty-stricken country . . . my poor wife," and "Bride, Russia" (3:249, 257 and 269).[140]

But Blok's "allegorical two-layeredness" becomes especially obvious in *Song of Fate*. Faina and German unequivocally function, respectively, as an "allegorical" and a "synecdochic" representation of Russia and the intelligentsia.[141] Significantly, in his draft of the play, Blok openly refers to Faina as "you, Russia" and "native Rus'" (4:445 and 447), explicit comparisons that he removes in the published text in an attempt to hide what has been called the play's "allegorical-constructivist schematic basis."[142] He does not succeed in shaking off the "curse of abstractness" that haunted him while writing *Song of Fate*, though (4:578). Among scholars, the play's transparent symbolism has been singled out repeatedly; consequently, it is generally considered to be an inferior work within Blok's oeuvre.[143] That Blok himself endorsed such a view is suggested by the typification of Faina within the play as a "bad allegory," as well as his ultimate rejection of the work as "foolish," "vulgar," and "silly"; and its hero as "dull" (4:135 and 581).

Thus the outlines of Blok's "bride Russia" metaphor are affected strongly by his wish to convey a sociopolitical rather than a literary message. As shown in the following chapters, similar outer-literary motivations continue to tinge the metaphor in the years leading to postmodernism.

It would be wrong, however, to dismiss Blok's texts as primarily sociopolitically motivated statements. Despite his assumption that the Russian theme "exceeds the boundaries of literature" (8:264), his view of Russia as a beloved is influenced to a great degree by existing literary models. Of particular importance to its outlines are the literary achievements of his nineteenth-century predecessors: as Zara Mints argues, in his texts from the years 1907 to 1909 one can speak of an "*integral* juxtaposition of Blok's poetic worldview and the system of ideas of nineteenth-century democratic journalism and literature."[144] Indeed, the influence of nineteenth-century thought on the Blok of that period can hardly be underestimated; he wrote extensively about the discussion between Slavophiles and Westernizers, about populist writings, and about several literary classics that share a preoccupation with national issues.[145] As pointed out in the following analysis, neither *Native Land* nor *Song of Fate* can be understood without this persistent focus on nineteenth-century literature.

Blok's "Bride Russia"

It is hard to narrow down Blok's feminized Russia to a single depiction. His "bride Russia" encompasses the Sophia-like presence in his Kulikovo cycle, but also the waving girl dressed in a shawl in "Russia," the invisible young bride in "New America," and the sensually promiscuous Faina in *Song of Fate*. These different hypostases share a number of recurring qualities, however. The "national-populist" aspect of the feminized nation provides us with a good place to start exploring those qualities.

Populist Motifs: National Tsarina

From the very beginning of his writing career, Blok attributes a national dimension to his muse. As early as 1901, he heralds the exalted feminine principle of his *Verses on the Beautiful Lady* as a "Russian Venus" (1:91). In a 1903 letter to Belyi he states that the beautiful lady is "*potentially* embodied in *the people* and in *society*."[146] In another letter the year before, he had addressed her prototype, his wife Liubov', as a "national Tsarina."[147]

In *Native Land* and *Song of Fate*, Blok intensifies the tendency to nationalize his muse. She now appears as a young woman carrying a crimson ribbon and dressed in a *sarafan,* decorated sleeves, and a patterned shawl: the traditional costume of Russian village women.[148]

In *Song of Fate*, the identification of the heroine with the common people of Russia is at its most palpable. As Petr Gromov argues, if the play's "basic conflict situation" is the supposedly problematic relationship between intelligentsia and people, then Faina clearly "represents the people."[149] Not fortuitously does she appear as a peasant girl, dressed in shawl and *sarafan* (4:115–16, 142, 149). Initiating the hero's confrontation with her is his need to "go to the people," a phrase that, in the context of the play, unmistakably evokes the "going to the people" movement of populist radicals in 1874 (4:110). The connection between Faina and the people is made explicit when an admirer claims that Faina "brought us part of the soul of the people" with her song (4:135)—a song that Schamma Schahadat has linked to Nietzsche's notion of the *Volkslied* as the ultimate expression of national essence.[150]

Blok's association of his muse with "the people" is reinforced by gypsy motifs.[151] The two themes are first linked in "Dark Days," in which the feminine figure with whom Russia symbolically merges has the "glance of a gypsy girl" (5:72). In *Song of Fate*, the hero German describes Faina/Russia as another "gypsy girl" (4:129). By connecting the common people with gypsy culture, Blok joins a tendency in Russian literature—which began with Pushkin's *Prisoner of the Caucasus* (*Kavkazskii plennik,* 1820–21)—in which the "key to the national character is sought in the 'gypsy' or 'Moldavian' theme," according to Zara Mints.[152] In Blok's appropriation, this theme blends with the revolutionary or "Scythian" sentiments that he feels are distinctive to the Russian people.[153]

But Blok does not focus on gypsy culture alone. In his work minorities of religious dissent serve as the supreme embodiment of the common people. In 1907 and 1908, his preoccupation with the theme of Russia and the intelligentsia coincides and merges with a repeatedly uttered wish to study dissident religious movements.[154] In 1909 he identifies these with a native essence when writing of his longing to go "to the sectarians—to Russia."[155] One need not be surprised, then, that Blok repeatedly associates his metaphoric Russia-beloved with religious sects. In a draft of the *Native Land* poem "The Densely Forested Slopes . . ." ("Zadebrennye lesom kruchi . . ."), the poet addresses a girl "under the glow of the old faith" in terms that recur almost literally in his other evocations of a feminine Russia; he does this in a setting that recalls the Old Believers' self-burning protests.[156] In *Song of Fate* Faina is introduced in similar surroundings, as a young girl looking "like a nun" from an Old Believer community (4:115–17).[157]

Through this identification of the common people with sectarianism, Blok once again adheres to nineteenth-century cultural traditions. In the second half of the nineteenth century, movements of religious dissent, particularly those of Old Believers, had gone through "booms of popularity" as allegedly quintessential representations of a pre-Petrine, native Russian people.[158] The same role was assigned to them in the early twentieth century. As Aleksandr Etkind asserts, "In Symbolist and post-Symbolist literature, various people explained their life and art in terms of truths or fantasies about sectarians . . . at the same time, they all talked about something else: religion, nationality, revolution, poetry, sexuality."[159]

A note shows that Blok's conception of Faina as an Old Believer was inspired by a nineteenth-century source: she was grafted onto a heroine with the same name in Pavel Mel'nikov-Pecherskii's novels involving Old Believer communities.[160] By implication, Blok's conception might have drawn inspiration from Mikhail Nesterov's painting *On the Hills:* Nesterov's canvas depicts Pecherskii's Faina in a riverside setting that Blok mirrors in several details on a textual level in his portrayal of Faina.[161]

Thus the association of Blok's heroine with the Russian people is established not only by explicit comparison, but also by her identification with social minorities, such as the gypsy and Old Believer communities. Blok associates this feminized Russian people with the outdoor world (vast expanses, open streets, windstorms), as opposed to the indoor world (big city, academic society) in which he places the (male) intelligentsia.[162] Such a geographical antithesis—which embroiders on the classic opposition of feminine-masculine to form rural-urban—reverberates strongly in both *Native Land* and *Song of Fate.* In both, a feminized Russia is associated with rural spheres: it is linked with a river and riverbanks, the steppe, forests, fields, meadows, villages and dilapidated village houses, mist, smoke, and open fire, the wind, vast distances, and open spaces.[163] The same elements occur in "Dark Days," "Rus'," and "Autumn Freedom" in connection with a personified Russia. In fact, the muse in *Verses on the Beautiful Lady* is already linked to a specifically Russian rural area when the poet associates her with his "native shores" and "native steppe" (1:117, 141).

Blok is not alone in his view of Russia as a feminine and rural entity: his contemporaries feminize the nation in similar terms. Several poets and writers of the time identify Russia with a rural *baba*-bride—one who appears in a rural setting and blends with sectarian motifs.[164] In Sologub's "Russia," the country as symbolic bride is connected with spring fields and a "clouded distance";[165] Shkapskaia's feminine Russia appears against a background of steppes, forests, and fields;[166] in Merezhkovskii's *Resurrection of the Gods*, Sophia is associated with Russia's "fields, blue bushes . . . and endless distance";[167] Belyi's "sleeping beauty" in "The Green Meadow" is equated with the meadow of its title and linked with "the free space" and Cossack population of the Russian countryside;[168] and, in *The Silver Dove*, specifically represented as mystical "bride" are the "huts, farmers, straw" of rural Russia.[169] For the hero of Belyi's novel, Rus' is embodied primarily in his mistress, Matrena, a peasant woman who draws him into a religious sect and who is most often depicted near rivers, fields, forests, and in her wooden hut.[170]

Sectarian motifs also echo in the "burning villages" and the "roaming people" among which Voloshin's personified Russia appears in "Streetwalker Rus'" ("Rus' guliashchaia").[171] In other Voloshin poems, the setting for his Russia-bride is replete with forests, rivers, and steppes; she is found, among other places, in "the silence of the fields."[172] In Kliuev's poetry, a feminized Russia emerges from a similar wilderness of fields, forest, huts, snowstorm, wind, mists, and smoke.[173] The personified Russia in his "Lion Bread" is connected with Avvakum and the Old Believers.[174] Finally, a direct link with Blok strikes the reader of Esenin's personifications of Russia in a poem whose poet addresses Russia as a "loose wife"; endowed with a "chestnut braid," his feminized Russia appears in meadows, beneath "misty smoke," and in the "wind."[175]

In their symbolic link with the Russian rural landscape and its people, the "brides Russia" of this era hark back to nineteenth-century literary and social models. It was nineteenth-century literature—and particularly the poetry of Nekrasov and Tiutchev—that set the trend for poetic declarations of love for Russia's deteriorating rural landscape. And it was nineteenth-century populism that created "important connections between the idealization of the *narod* and that of the countryside" for Russian artists, to borrow Christopher Ely's words.[176]

But more than of populist tradition, the female figures in the works mentioned are heiresses of the quintessentially Russian heroine of nineteenth-century prose. This literary type resonates tangibly in *The Silver Dove*'s Katia, whom the reader first encounters at her grandmother's estate as a naive girl with "innocent and pure" eyes, "leaning over the grand piano, a volume of Racine in her hands; she had been brought up on the French classics. . . . In a blue dress, a trifle short and closely clasping her waist . . . a little girl she looked, quite a little girl!"[177] With her hyper-innocent looks and manners, Katia can be understood as little other than a parody of her nineteenth-century predecessors.

Folklore Elements: Sleeping Princess

The national dimension of Blok's Faina, as scholars have argued, is accentuated partly through her folkloric use of language and intonations.[178] That Blok's play on tradition is a conscious device can be inferred from his interest in folkloric rituals, which he describes in detail in the essay "The Poetry of Spells and Incantations" ("Poeziia zagovorov i zaklinanii," 1906).

Blok's symbolic equation of Russia with a bride is reinforced by folkloric motifs as well. Heroine and hero in both *Native Land* and *Song of Fate* are opposed to one another as princess or swan and prince or foreign guest, the respective designations for bride and bridegroom in traditional Russian wedding lore and *bylinas*.[179] Faina is not only dressed as a Russian village woman; she also drops a crimson ribbon, an act traditionally performed by the bride or her female friends in Russian and Czech wedding songs.[180] Using a folkloric metaphor, she claims to be clothed "all in mists, like a bride in a bridal veil." She waves to German with her "patterned sleeve" (4:144 and 163); as Blok explains in his 1908 essay on folklore, "a girl sends her love when she waves her hand, according to a Ukrainian song" (5:38). He had applied this folkloric image to Russia earlier in "Autumn Freedom," in which a female figure who merges with "drunken Rus'" "happily wave[s]" at the poet with her "colored sleeve" (2:75). Esenin's bridal Russia similarly waves at the poet with "a decorated sleeve" in "Again Decoratively Stretched Out. . . ."[181]

Faina's character can also be traced to folklore-inspired heroines of the nineteenth century, such as Zhukovskii's Svetlana and Pushkin's Tat'iana.[182] Her predecessors loom large as her *niania* relates a fairy tale in which Faina is compared, in folkloric terms, to a swan bride awaiting her bridegroom (4:137–39). The story is followed by Faina's ritual attempt to predict her future bridegroom with a mirror (4:139–40). Here Blok echoes *Svetlana* and *Eugene Onegin* not only through the choice of folkloric designations of bride and bridegroom, but also through the heroine's ritualist prognostication, aided by the mirror.[183]

Apart from these folkloric elements, Blok's depiction of Russia as symbolic bride is tinged with what Zara Mints calls "one of the most widespread Symbolist myths: the symbolized folkloric plot of 'dis-enchantment' and liberation of the Sleeping Princess, captured by evil forces."[184] Symbolist adaptations of the sleeping-beauty plot fully exploit the social implications of the original folktale: the sleeping beauty now comes to represent, in Mints's words, the "Beauty (life, 'the soul of the world,' Russia)" over whose liberation the artist fights with the state.

Blok perhaps best illustrates this claim. "Sleeping Beauty" was among his favorite childhood stories, and the first ballet he attended was Tchaikovsky's adaptation of the tale.[185] In Blok's literary works, dragonslayer and sleeping-beauty motifs occur and merge from the outset. In the politically motivated texts of the years following 1905, they appear in an increasingly politicized context. In 1906, the sleeping-beauty theme first occurs in his representation of Russia in "Rus'" and "Dark Days" (2:106–7; 5:74–79 and 82).

Vital to its appearance in these and Blok's later works is the influence of Belyi's "The Green Meadow," in which Russia is equated explicitly with a "sleeping beauty, who some day will be awakened from her sleep."[186] The essay reverts to Gogol's "Terrible Vengeance" ("Strashnaia mest'," 1832), whose heroine Katerina was enchanted and taken away from her husband by a sorcerer: to Belyi, "in the colossal images of Katerina and the sorcerer, Gogol immortally expressed the languish of the sleeping native land—the Beauty."[187] Lending the image macabre features, Belyi suggests that Russia rested under a "veil of black death" or a "shroud of mechanical culture," which needed to be lifted in order for the land to awaken.[188]

Belyi's later work reveals palpable traces of "The Green Meadow." Research relates Katia in *The Silver Dove* to the essay's "sleeping beauty Russia,"[189] and Belyi himself recycles the same metaphor in his 1909 essay on Gogol.[190] But "The Green Meadow" also leaves profound marks on Blok's *Native Land* poems. In "Russia," for instance, the feminized nation is said to "give" her beauty to a "sorcerer"; the "bride, Russia" in "New America" "rest[s] not in a rich coffin"; and in "The Kite" ("Korshun"), Russia is depicted as a "sleepy meadow" beneath a circling kite (3:254, 268–69, and 281).[191] The sleeping-beauty story is reenacted, too, in the poem "Dreams" ("Sny"), albeit without an explicit national-metaphoric dimension. *Song of Fate* transfers the concept to the national sphere when Faina, alias the feminized Russia, delivers a folklore-tinted monologue in which she blames her old "Companion" for capturing her and begs to be liberated by a mystical bridegroom.

I sleep on swansdown—I forget everything in the world! . . . You guard me from all misfortunes, you let no one touch me, you tell me fairy tales, and you

make my swan's bed, and you guard my virgin's dreams. I wait for you, bright
one . . . I have slept my whole life away! . . . Out there, behind bars . . . the
white swan sleeps. (4:143–45)

Later, in *Retribution,* Blok explicates the association of Russia with
a sleeping beauty: in this poem, Russia is represented as a "beauty" who
"slept away hopes, thoughts, passions" in an enchantment brought about by
Konstantin Pobedonostsev (3:328). As several scholars argue, *Retribution's*
sleeping-beauty metaphor responds to "The Green Meadow." [192] In addition,
it is likely to have been inspired by Solov'ev. Just one year before writing
this fragment, in 1910, Blok had summarized Solov'ev's philosophy as "the
issue of freeing the captive Princess, the Soul of the World, who passionately
grieves in the embrace of Chaos" (5:451).

Blok's interest in folkloric concepts emerges against the background of a
general preoccupation with folklore and popular art in early twentieth-
century Russia. [193] The same preoccupation tinges his contemporaries' feminine representations of Russia. In the early twentieth century, as we saw
the sleeping-beauty tale is turned into a sociopolitical metaphor in poems
by Parnok and Severianin; in Chulkov's historiography; and in the reception
of Rimsky-Korsakov's *Kashchei.* In more than one of these works, Pobedonostsev fills the role of Russia's enchanter. The metaphor is extended in
contemporary criticism of Blok's work, such as Sergei Gorodetskii's 1909
review in *Zolotoe runo.* [194] It also plays a role in Kliuev's "In the Frozen
Darkness . . . ," in which Russia appears as a woman whose features are
"clouded" by the mists of "the sorcerer January" and who is held in "som-
ber captivity"; [195] in Esenin's poetry, in which the poet addresses Russia as
a "sleepy princess" and wants to "guard the Rus' that has fallen asleep"; [196]
and in Voloshin's portrayal, in "On the Station" ("Na vokzale"), of a feminized Russia "unable to awaken from her sleep." [197]

The sleeping-beauty legend as revised by Blok and his colleagues is
linked to more than old folktales. Even more directly, it echoes the political
revisions of such tales in nineteenth-century Russia, as shown in the previous chapter, and the repeated application of the sleeping-beauty myth
to Russian politics in neo-populist journalism in the years around 1905—a
phenomenon whose analysis will follow shortly.

Immutability: Primordial Beauty

In keeping with traditional feminine stereotyping, the association of a
feminized Russia with rural regions coincides with a focus on eternity or

immutability. The idealized Russia addressed by early twentieth-century authors is envisioned as an archetypal (feminized) force as opposed to a modern urbanized (masculine) intelligentsia. As we have seen, this opposition is inherited partly from the nineteenth-century Russian novel, in which heroine and hero represent the static-rural and dynamic-urban spheres, respectively.

Blok first connects the figure of a "Tsarevna" and "Bride" specifically to the Russia of the past or to "the spirit of Rus'" in 1902.[198] He reverts to this association in 1906 by emphasizing the "primary purity" of the personified Russia in "Rus'."[199] *Native Land* and *Song of Fate,* as well as "The People and the Intelligentsia," reinforce the link between a feminized Russia and a static primordial idyll. They do so primarily by transferring contemporary sociopolitical events to historical Russia and, more particularly, to the 1380 Battle of Kulikovo. Blok regarded this battle—traditionally considered a decisive victory in Russia's struggle for liberation from the Mongols—in cyclical terms as one of the "symbolic events in Russian history," which were "destined to return."[200] Significant is his repeated evocation of a feminized Russia in the works in question as Rus'; as Robin Milner-Gulland points out, since the eighteenth century Russians had regarded this term as representative of "the essential Russia . . . irrespective of the great moments of change that have punctuated its historical destiny."[201]

In *Native Land,* the feminized Russia is not only repeatedly associated with a historical Rus', but the motif of immutability is intensified by the poet's repeated evocation of the gendered country as "still the same" and as possessing a "primordial" beauty.[202] In a similar vein, the heroine in *Song of Fate* is equated with a "Russia, invariable in its very essence" and called "eternal, like a star" (4:134, 141). Here, again, the setting is defined by a historical Russia. The hero associates Faina with the Nepriadva River at the Battle of Kulikovo, and her thoughts of a future bridegroom have been traced to Iaroslavna's lamentations in the *Igor Tale.*[203]

In associating the symbolic "bride Russia" with historical immutability or with eternity, Blok is again far from unique. In a letter penned in 1893, Nesterov muses on the "pensive, quiet physiognomy contemplating the depths of bygone and future ages" of a feminized Russia.[204] Esenin stresses Russia's invariability in "I Am Tired of Living . . . " ("Ustal ia zhit' . . ."), where the lyrical ego claims that a future "Russia will be just the same, / Living, dancing, and crying at the fence";[205] and the feminized Russia of Kliuev's "In the Frozen Darkness . . ." is "eternally invulnerable."[206] Several years later—in the 1933 essay "On National Penitence" ("O natsional'nom pokaianii")—Georgii Fedotov reverts to the same paradigm when wondering if all that "will be left on Russia" will be "the earth . . . the only invariable, always beloved one."[207]

Religious Backgrounds: Bright Wife

The concept of a feminized Russia as an immutable static force is rooted partly in religious and specifically in Sophiological notions. The previous chapter demonstrated that Solov'ev tied the mystical bride Sophia directly to Old Russia and its religious iconography. Blok's "bride Russia"—in its capacity as repository of tradition and eternity—is similarly identified with the religious sphere.

In most cases, for the Symbolists and post-Symbolists discussed here, religion and art are kindred areas. In Hansen-Löve's definition, Symbolism is characterized by a "striving . . . to constantly shift, redefine, and transcend the 'borders' between . . . art and religion, philosophy and science, theory and practice, work and life."[208] Not fortuitously, Blok and several of his contemporaries actively interact with representatives of the Orthodox clergy. Many of them conceive of themselves as religious thinkers rather than as writers. At one point Blok himself becomes infatuated with dissident movements, and his feminine representations of Russia are openly associated with Old Believer faith. In fact, his feminine muse is surrounded principally by a religious aura. In the words of Kornei Chukovskii, "For Blok the saintliness of his beloved was indisputable dogma. . . . Her image often appeared to him amidst the holy objects of a church and was associated with such things as: bells, choirs of angels, icons, lecterns, monasteries, and cathedrals."[209]

Blok's saintly muse would have looked different without the poet's juvenile infatuation with Solov'ev's Sophiological philosophy. According to Belyi, Blok already conceives of this muse as a nationalized Sophia around 1900, when he supposedly claims that Sophia's revelations "could be announced to different nations . . . to a Russian . . . she is the essence of all Russia."[210] Mother of God and Sophia metaphors color the conceptualization of a feminized Russia in *Native Land*—think the "bright wife" and the undefined feminine "You" of the Kulikovo cycle, who descends from heaven "clothed in the streaming light."[211] On the one hand, the universal-exalted dimension of Blok's Beautiful Lady largely vanishes in the depiction of the female figures in this collection;[212] on the other, Blok himself affirms that both they and the heroine in *Song of Fate* are an extension of the Sophiological "She" of his early poems.[213] Contemporaries certainly conceive of them as such.[214]

The same contemporaries themselves eagerly transfer a Sophiological feminine World Soul to the national sphere. We have seen that Merezhkovskii, Gippius, and Belyi transplant the Sophia concept to a national-Russian context in the years preceding the 1905 Revolution. A similar shift can be observed in the politico-philosophical writings of the so-called Sophiologists, as well as of Berdiaev, Rozanov, and Ivanov—a subject of further discussion in this chapter, in relation to Berdiaev's work. Research also interprets Katia in Belyi's *Silver Dove* as both a "version of Vladimir Solov'ev's Divine Sophia" and "Russia in potentiality."[215] Sophiological notions echo in Kliuev's depiction of the feminine Russia as "flicker[ing], breath[ing] and liv[ing] / Everywhere, imperceptible"; and as tangible in "the forest's murmur, / The flickering of stars and the whistling of storms";[216] and they tinge Voloshin's view of feminized Russia as "enlightened mystically / With all the beauty of the world."[217] Finally, Esenin's personifications of Russia in the mid-1910s as a female figure are set among icons, churches, and monasteries.[218]

After the revolutions of 1917, Sophiological representations of Russia become particularly popular. As mentioned, Blok's "The Twelve," Belyi's "Christ Has Risen," and Esenin's and Shkapskaia's poetry all allude to a mystical marriage between Russia—in the guise of a Sophiological feminine figure—and the revolution, embodied in Christ as her celestial bridegroom. Even later, in the 1920s, the figure of Sophia continues to influence female representations of Russia: Voloshin equates Russia's "Face" with that of Sophia in his 1929 "Vladimir Mother of God";[219] and in his 1928 poem "To Return from the Reindeer Trade . . ." ("Vernut'sia s olen'iego izvoza . . ."), Kliuev equates "Sophia," who "flutters her wings," with "the eternal spinster, Russia."[220]

Corruptions of the Ideal: Fallen Stars

On the night of June 26, 1902, Blok describes in his diary the feminine "Earth" as a "universal prostitute"—one with a "made-up face" (7:51). While his poetry of this period rather glorifies an exalted feminine principle, Blok's muse is principally a dual figure, who simultaneously embodies the ideal and the corruption of that ideal.

Blok's dual vision of his female muse is no exception within Symbolist artistic culture, which is crowded with angelic-demonic female figures. The demonic pole of this opposition becomes dominant for him with time, and specifically in the aftermath of the 1905 Revolution. She who was once a Beautiful Lady is now increasingly associated with drunkenness, sexual promiscuity, love of destruction, and gypsy culture. This new hypostasis is closely linked with the motif of metaphysical captivity. Summarizing Blok's poetry from the post-1905 years, Zara Mints states that "again [the central female figure's] genuine essence as 'soul of the world' . . . is elucidated, although it is stressed that this is a 'soul of the world' held captive by earthly chaos."[221]

Crucial to Blok's depiction of the Beautiful Lady's bewitched, profane pendant are national-revolutionary sentiments. Russia is associated with a morally depraved woman in "Autumn Freedom" in 1905, in which the poet listens to the "voice of drunken Rus'" (2:75). In "Dark Days," Russia's "poor people" are represented as "the thousand-eyed Russia, who has nothing to lose; she has given all her flesh to the world and now, freely hurling her hands in the wind, has begun to dance across her pointless, uninvented expanses" (5:74).

A year earlier in "The Green Meadow," Belyi imagined Russia in similar terms as a female beauty who "dances on a green meadow" and "spins around pointlessly."[222] In Belyi's case, the dancing metaphor is inspired by a performance he attended, together with the Bloks, of the dancer Isadora Duncan. In "The Green Meadow," Belyi describes Duncan's dancing as "the image of our future life";[223] and in his memoirs he writes of the (American-born!) dancer as the female embodiment of revolutionary Russia.[224]

Belyi's view of Duncan is in line with reviews in the Russian press, which similarly conceive of the ballerina as Russia or as the Russian people incarnate, an interpretation prompted particularly by her performance of Tchaikovsky's *Marche slave.*[225] In her interpretation of the march, Duncan consciously sought to embody the Russian people. I have elaborated elsewhere on Gordon McVay's observation that an "interesting inversion of nationalities" would later mark the public view of Duncan and her one-time husband, Sergei Esenin.[226] During one foreign tour, for instance, Esenin dresses as a western European gentleman and applies for an American passport, while Duncan asks her audience to sing the "Internationale"; she eventually dies a Russian citizen, with a Soviet passport in her bag.[227] In the American press, the native Californian is announced as a "sensational Russian dancer," and one *New York Tribune* reviewer goes so far as to label her an "epic figure . . . the figure of Russia."[228]

Belyi's metaphoric reading of Duncan is unlikely to have been inspired by this reception of her art, which reigned supreme only in the 1910s and 1920s. It may possibly rely on Natasha's Russian dance in *War and Peace,* though. Belyi alludes to this scene elsewhere—in *The Silver Dove*—when he has Matrena burst into a typically Russian dance in a setting that unmistakably evokes Tolstoy's dancing scene.[229]

Representations of Russia as a dancing woman stress her sensuality, but they contain no demonic elements. Such elements do appear in female personifications of Russia in *Native Land* and *Song of Fate.* In the former, the feminized Russia differs radically from the exalted muse in Blok's early works: the poet mentions her "tear-stained" or "rogue beauty," "deceptive" character, "sly eyes," and "ruinous traits," which show a "drunken freedom"; and she is designated as a "fatal land" (3:254, 268, 281, and 590). In *Song of Fate,* Faina-Russia's angelic-demonic character is highlighted when the hero speaks of her transformation from "elevated dream" into "gypsy," and when she brands herself a "fallen star" (4:129, 141). When singing the song that lends the play its title, Faina poses as a promiscuous "snake" with "black . . . snake eyes," who lashes the hero's face with a whip (4:127–30).

According to Schamma Schahadat, in this scene, among others, Faina can be traced to the saint-cum-whore Nastasia Filippovna in Dostoevsky's *Idiot*.[230] By and large, for the dichotomy of his female figures Blok is indebted to Dostoevsky's saint-sinner heroines.[231] In Blok's case, though, the two dimensions are not always embodied within one character: *Song of Fate's* antithetical pair, Faina and Elena (the hero's wife), forms a two-headed example of the same angel-demon opposition. Faina and Elena function simultaneously as each other's mystical doubles and opposites. Apart from their parallel positions as the hero's beloveds, they are linked by a number of manifestly antithetical qualities: Faina is associated with the color black, open spaces, and the bustle of the big city; by contrast, Elena is consistently connected to the color white and to an archetypal sheltering home.[232] A similar antithetical pair is seen in Belyi's Katia and Matrena, who are opposed in *The Silver Dove* as the naive daughter of an aristocrat and a sensual, demonic peasant woman, respectively.

The conception of a feminized Russia in such pairs cannot be explained by Symbolist dichotomous thinking alone. Another source may be found in the (older) tendency to oppose a "conformist," "domestic" heroine with a "non-conformist," "illegitimate" heroine in the classic epic novel.[233] More importantly, the feminized Russia relies on the dualistic Gnostic concept of Sophia that imbues Solov'ev's philosophical writings. Blok alludes to such a background when he describes Elena in a draft—as opposed to the "fallen star" Faina (4:141)—as "saintly, pure and beautiful" (4:444).

A demonic or fallen woman: not only Blok and Belyi represented Russia as such. The same motif tints Kliuev's "Psalm of the Don," which appears to draw a direct parallel to Belyi's double-sided vision of Russia. Where Belyi first conceives of Russia as the "Woman clothed with the sun" and later identifies it with the "dirty, silly" *baba* Matrena, Kliuev's poet views his native land "not as the woman clothed with the sun" but as a village "*baba* with hips like a shock of oats."[234] Esenin, meanwhile, calls Russia his "loose wife" and repeatedly refers to it in terms of drunkenness and ecstatic dancing.[235] The recurrent motif of a "dance on a green meadow" in this context suggests a direct link with Belyi's dancing Russia.[236]

But the motif of Russia as a fallen and sexually depraved woman appears most prominently in Voloshin's poems of the second half of the 1910s, which were inspired in part by the First World War and the October Revolution. In his 1915 "Russia," the poet addresses Russia as a "defeated, profaned," "slavish" woman who is whipped in the face by her "master."[237] In

1917 and 1918, Voloshin includes the same motif in poems on the German threat and the Bolshevik regime: in a profusion of adjectival constructions, he portrays a feminized Russia as "homeless," "drunk," "foolish," "stinking," "disgraced," and "ruined." He calls her a "streetwalker," a figure tied to "sinners and whores," and has her "screamed at, betrayed, nibbled on, ruined through drinking, spat on, defiled on dirty squares, sold out on the streets"; lying "covered with blood, naked, wounded, exhausted"; singing "shameless songs"; creating "obscenities"; and, to top it all off, exhibiting "private parts."[238]

Masks and Facial Metaphors: Veiled Brides

In all these examples, the fallen metaphoric bride Russia appears as the reverse side of a saintly hypostasis. Rather than an irreversible transformation, we are dealing with a dualistic appearance of the same figure or—to use a metaphor to which the authors themselves repeatedly revert—of "two faces" of the same entity.

In the dualistically oriented language of late Symbolism, in particular, images of double faces and masks play a central role. As Irene Masing-Delic notes, for Blok and his contemporaries "the mask . . . represented the apparent (the flat perspective), but through the slits of the mask . . . one could see, or perhaps only suspect, the 'real' (the deep perspective)."[239] It might prove fruitful to trace the influence on this worldview of the legend of the Egyptian goddess Isis, the unveiling of whose statue symbolized the disclosure of truth—and whose story was a beloved topic of several German Romantic poets ardently read by the Symbolists.[240]

Mask motifs figure prominently in representations of Russia in the given period, which witnesses a strong tendency to speak of Russia's "face" (*lik*, *litso*) or two faces.[241] Masks are salient in the feminine representations of Russia discussed here: from the works examined, a common myth can be reconstructed in which Russia appears as a veiled woman and the poet as her male suitor, who wishes to look beyond the veil at the symbolic woman's true face. The precise form of this veil differs from one text to another—it may be a plain shawl, a veil, a funeral pall, a shroud, or even an altar cloth.[242] Pivotal to the trope is the motif of eye contact or the momentary glance that the poet hopes to catch from the veiled, invisible Russia.

The function of the various coverings shifts according to their traditional religious or folkloric meaning. One function is an attempt to conceal the truth: saintly Russia in the guise of a misleading sinner. This notion of Russia's veiled inner glory is far from unprecedented. It was prominent in Slavophile thought, especially in Khomiakov's personifications of Russia, as mentioned in the previous chapter. It was also central to the Kitezh legend, which enjoyed tremendous popularity in early twentieth-century Russian intellectual culture.[243] Voloshin's 1919 poem "Kitezh"—to mention but one example—speaks of "holy Rus', covered with sinful Rus'"; in his poem "War" ("Voina"), the poet declares to a feminized Russia that he specifically loves her sinful outer appearance.[244]

Blok's poetry displays a particularly strong preoccupation with the idea of Russia's veiled inner beauty. In *Native Land* and *Retribution*, Russia's beauty is "clouded" (3:254 and 328). The hero in *Song of Fate* blames Faina-Russia for having veiled her true face or "soul" under the "mask" of her black dress (4:149 and 129).

The metaphor is extended to the relationship between this veiled feminized Russia and the hero or poet: their alienation is represented as the latter's inability to look into Russia's eyes or to see her face from behind her cover.[245] In *Song of Fate*, Blok opposes the hero-*intelligent* to a group of "people with a new soul" who do "look Faina straight in the face" (4:134–35). Fedotov, in whose essays the metaphor of Russia's face figures repeatedly, elaborates on this image when he writes in a 1929 essay: "We need to study Russia, to amorously peer into its traits."[246] Georgii Chulkov embroiders on the same metaphor in the "Snowstorm" essay, which portrays Russia as a girl under whose "white scarf enormous eyes shone, austere as on icons."[247]

Related to the facial metaphor is the passing glance that Blok's poet or hero—and the protagonists of several of his contemporaries—wishes either to give to or receive from the feminized Russia.[248] As precedent for this image, one can point to the monologue addressed to Russia in *Dead Souls*, part of which serves as the motto for *Song of Fate* (4:103). That Blok inherited Gogol's motif of brief glances between the narrator-hero and Russia can be inferred from a note written by Blok during his work on *Native Land* and *Song of Fate*. Virtually mirroring the "eyes filled with expectations" that Gogol's Russia turns to the narrator, the note envisages Russia as flying past in a troika with "starry eyes, addressed to us with the entreaty 'Love me, love my beauty!'"[249] Blok explicitly turns to Gogol's vision in a 1909 essay on the author, in which he portrays Russia as veiled beneath a deceptive outer grayness and speaks of the "curtain of age-old ordinary life" in *Dead Souls* that opens to reveal the "future Russia" (5:378).

Apart from hiding the feminized Russia's inner beauty, in Blok's poetics the veil also fulfills the opposite function: of a mask that hides a true face, sinful or promiscuous, under a misleadingly pious outward appearance. This concept can be traced to Solov'ev's evocation of the earth, in his 1886 "Earth Mistress!" ("Zemlia-vladychitsa!"), as a female figure through whose "fragrant *pokrov*" the "fire of a dear heart" could be felt.[250] Along parallel lines, Blok's feminized Russia repeatedly appears as a nun, but hiding under her outward austerity—often beneath a shawl—are "glowing cheeks" and "beckoning," "sly," "laughing," or "shining" "black" eyes that "burn" the poet.[251] Similarly, in the 1920s, Mariia Shkapskaia's Russia has both the "unutterable face of an icon" and a "wild-eyed glance."[252]

Memoirs and essays on Blok further amplify the concept of the pious veil that masks an underlying promiscuity. Belyi speaks of Blok's "unmasking" of the "Slavophile face of the Muse," adding that this face reveals "not Sophia, not Russia, but ancient, dark Rus'."[253] In an allusion to the early poem "I Anticipate You . . ." ("Predchuvstvuiu tebia . . ."), Fedotov states that to Blok's Russia, "the same thing happens . . . as to the Beautiful Lady: as the poet closely observes her face, he discovers other, frightening traits."[254]

Apart from a typical Symbolist mask, the veil can also serve as a more traditional cover: as the bridal veil of Russian wedding ceremonies, which must be lifted to see the bride.[255] Blok's texts repeatedly allude to this function of Russia's shawl or "covered face" (3:268 and 4:164). It is emphasized in the folklore-inspired depiction of morning mist as a *fata* or bridal veil:[256] in *Native Land* and *Song of Fate*, the Nepriadva River and Faina are alternately said to be dressed in mist, like a bride or a princess (3:251; 4:144, 149). Also identifiable as a bridal veil are the clouds that hide Russia's "beautiful traits" in "Russia" (3:254), an image that is virtually duplicated in the "clouding" of the "beauty" Russia in *Retribution* (3:328) and in the snow-clouding of Russia's "traits" in Kliuev's "To Aleksandr Blok."[257] In a similar vein, Esenin describes Riazan' prior to the Tatar invasion as a bride under the "veil of Varangian sleep" in his 1918 *Song on Evpatii Kolovrat* (*Pesn' o Evpatii Kolovrate*).[258] Finally, in Bal'mont's "Silent Country" snow functions as the "bride Russia's" cloak.[259]

In addition, the gendered view of Russia of Blok and his contemporaries reconsiders the Christian *pokrov* (cloak) legend, the story of the cloak that descends on earth as a symbol of Mary's protection. First, the clothing of the feminized Russia can serve to offer the poet a shelter. In Blok's "Rus'," for instance, the lyrical ego claims to hide "the nakedness of my soul / In the shreds of [Russia's] rags" (2:106). Second, the covering can function as a protective cloak for Russia itself, as in Belyi's "Adam," in which the hero covers the Russian earth with what he calls a *pokrov:* his chasuble.[260] While the mask motif does not play a palpable role here, it does so in Esenin's description of the devastation of revolutionary Russia as the tearing off of her *pokrov.*[261] In kindred terms, Fedotov phrases Blok's turn to the theme of a feminized Russia as his "throwing off" of her *pokrovy* and his confrontation with "a Rus', far from saintliness."[262] Shkapskaia speaks of Russia's "widow *pokrovy*" and imagines Peter the Great "commandingly taking off the *pokrovy* of his wife [Russia] with a male hand."[263]

Death motifs, finally, lurk in Belyi's "The Green Meadow," where the corpse of a feminized Russia is covered with a shroud. In his essay, the "sleeping beauty Russia" is covered with a "shroud of black death," the "shroud" of mechanical culture; to the author, its "fetching down" will mark her awakening from death or sleep.[264]

It will be clear from the above that feminized Russia represents a wide range of concepts in both Blok's work and that of various contemporaries. Whether appearing as gypsy culture, rural settings, demonic forces, or covering masks, all such associations spring from a male perspective. Thus the burning question is: which male force is opposed to the "sleeping princesses" and "veiled brides" that represent Russia of this era?

The Poet: The Bride's Suitor

In a speech on the occasion of his friend's death, Andrei Belyi asserted that "all the aspirations of Aleksandr Aleksandrovich Blok added up to" his striving to write "for the intelligentsia."[265] The same holds true for Blok's gendered view of Russia. His image of Russia as unattainable bride invariably serves as a foil for the sociopolitical strivings and frustrations of the male hero or poet. This poet-hero is an unmistakable exponent of "the intelligentsia." Vital to an examination of the metaphor in question is a closer look at this character and, specifically, at its sociopolitical dimensions.

Representing the Intelligentsia

Born and raised in an aristocratic family, Blok strongly identified with the role of repentant aristocrat who needs to bridge the gap between aristocracy and the common people. As early as 1901, this theme dominates his correspondence with the composer Semen Panchenko, who urges him to "worship the Ordinary man . . . cry, fall on your knees, and bang your head against the earth in tears and in moans at the feet of the Peasant. So that he will forgive you."[266]

In time, Blok's preoccupation with the alleged gap between intelligentsia and people increases. In the period before and immediately after the 1905 Revolution, like several contemporaries he experiences a phase of intense political commitment, going so far as to carry a red flag at a workers' demonstration.[267] Mints writes that 1906 and 1907 are marked by Blok's shift "from a 'mystical' panegyric to the 'fire' of the revolution . . . and a striving to understand the socio-historical anticipations of 'Russian rebellion.'"[268] Not only does Blok turn to nineteenth-century realist and political-democratic traditions toward the end of this decade, as discussed earlier, but the poetry of the contemporary "anti-intelligentsia poet" Pimen Karpov also exerts an influence on him at this time.[269] From 1907 onward, his social views are affected by a series of personal letters from Kliuev, who makes him reconsider his position as a member of the aristocratic intelligentsia. In a strategic move rather than in a truthful account of his position, Kliuev introduces himself to Blok in the first letter as "a farmer" and a "poorly educated" man—someone who has turned to Blok as a representative of "you, gentlemen."[270] Here and in later correspondence, he urges Blok to annihilate "the spiritual alienation between 'you' and 'us.'"[271] Blok is deeply moved by Kliuev's concerns about a growing civic unrest and his antipathy toward the aristocratic intelligentsia among the people in his region.[272]

As important as the theme may have been to him, Blok's own understanding of the term "intelligentsia" is difficult to determine. His critique of it in the 1908 essay covers "every member of cultural society, regardless of parties, literary directions, or classes" (5:319). In a 1911 letter, however, he specifically attacks the Social Democrats for their "unwillingness to know the village" (8:346). His views on his own status are no less equivocal. In 1905 he refers to himself in a letter, albeit sarcastically, as a "SOCIAL DEMO-CRAT" (8:141; capitalization in original). Two years later, he describes himself to Belyi as "representative of . . . the hundreds of 'repentant noblemen'" as opposed to the "forty simple millions" of ordinary Russians (8:198). In letters and essays of 1908 and 1909, he poses as a representative of "the intelligentsia" as a whole (5:319, 327; and 8:258, 274).

Equally inconsistent is the sometimes positive, sometimes negative stance toward the intelligentsia that Blok has inherited from his nineteenth-century predecessors. While emphasizing his own status as an *intelligent,* at the same time he claims in a letter to his mother that "the closer a man is to the people . . . the more fiercely he hates the intelligentsia" (8:258–59). On the one hand, as Victor Erlich rightly asserts, "the feverish intensity with which abstruse metaphysical and aesthetic questions were debated at the sessions of the influential Religious-Philosophical Society smacked to Blok of an ideational 'feast during the plague'"; on the other hand, he eagerly engages in the same debates.[273]

Blok's sociopolitical position remains ambiguous when the Bolsheviks gain power in 1917. He does participate in public institutions established by the new regime, but his political views, still mystically oriented, are not directed toward concrete activity.[274] In diary entries from January 1918, he repudiates "the intelligentsia"—citing its negative view of the revolution and its instinctive "hatred of parliaments, institutional gatherings, and so on"—and bitingly remarks that "the chief gentlemen *intelligenty* do not want to go to work" (7:314–15). In the same entry he personally identifies with that very intelligentsia, however, calling it "dear" and "native" scum (7:315).

A similar sort of ambiguity colors Blok's relationship to the West. In his own words, he has received "the *éducation sentimentale* of a Russian gentleman" for whom foreign influences have formed an organic part of life from the very start.[275] In a letter, he calls Europe his "other native land" (8:284). That he shares with the classic repentant aristocrat the wish to deny such influences is suggested by a comment on a public reading of *Retribution* in 1921. A viewer describes how Blok deliberately posed as a simple man and somewhat artificially maintained a Russian pronunciation of French words during his performance.[276]

Thus Blok both identified with and bore a troubled attitude toward the intelligentsia. To a large extent, this attitude defined his vision of Russia as an unattainable beloved. In the "People and the Intelligentsia" essay, he compares the intelligentsia and the people to the "two camps" at the Battle of Kulikovo: opposing forces separated by an "unbridgeable gap" that has to be crossed (5:323–24). He claims that the removal of that gap requires the intelligentsia to love Russia as "a mother, sister, and wife," and places himself in the role of that wife's lover by repeatedly stressing his status as an *intelligent* (5:321, 319, 327).

Native Land and *Song of Fate* are linked directly to this metaphor. As said earlier, Blok observed that these two works and his essay all deal with the same theme. This indication is confirmed in the texts, in which the hero-poet—identifying with a warrior at the Battle of Kulikovo—addresses Russia as his wife or appears as her "promised husband" (3:251–54; 4:148–49, 144). In the opinion of Zara Mints, this protagonist's opposition to and tragic relationship with Russia or the Russian people irrevocably leads the reader to interpret him as a "synecdoche" for the intelligentsia.[277]

The metaphoric dimension is particularly obvious in the depiction of German, the hero in *Song of Fate*. Populist aspects of his wish to "go to the people" have been discussed.[278] In this respect, German has been compared to Dostoevsky's Raskol'nikov and the latter's "fusion with the principles of the life of the common people."[279] German's own milieu is typified as that of the cultural intelligentsia when, on first meeting Faina, he is set amidst a public of "only writers, painters, artists," who "live an intelligentsia's life" (4:110, 133–34). He has been considered a lyrical double of Blok, the self-declared representative of the intelligentsia.[280] Research has perceived another possible twin to Blok in the "man in glasses," a character in *Song of Fate* who openly identifies with the intellectual elite and the Symbolists in a monologue that equates Faina with Russia.[281]

If the hero's role as an *intelligent* is made explicit in *Song of Fate,* the same can be said of his association with non-Russian culture. In general, as Mints has argued, Blok's opposition of "people" to "intelligentsia" equals that of "Russia" to "the West."[282] German's association with the West can be inferred, first of all, from his foreign name: the very word "German" is linked etymologically to Germany. Given its rare status in Russian, German's name can hardly be read as anything other than an allusion to the thoroughly foreign Germann in Pushkin's "Queen of Spades" ("Pikovaia dama," 1833).[283] But his connection with non-Russian elements is not limited to his name: in a reiteration of folkloric characteristics, he is equated with a "brave fellow . . . from a far-off refuge" in an "outlandish cap" in the *niania*'s fairy tale (4:138). The worldview that this semi-foreign hero expresses echoes that of a stereotypical nineteenth-century *intelligent:* German passionately cares for Russia—embodied in Faina—and he identifies strongly with the Russian warriors who fought for their country at the Battle of Kulikovo (4:148–49).

Among Blok's contemporaries, a similar link binding Russia's symbolic suitor to the intelligentsia prevails. Take the classic westernized, populist *intelligenty* who populate Belyi's work: the hero of "Adam" is the characteristic repentant nobleman, who identifies with the Slavophiles and returns from "the big world" to implement reforms on his father's estate and "help the common people"; and *The Silver Dove*'s Dar'ial'skii is—in a near-parodic recapitulation of the nineteenth-century hero-*intelligent*—"part of the intelligentsia," "anti-governmental," "a newcomer," "a gentleman," "a writer," and a populist who sees himself as "the future of the people" from whom he simultaneously feels alienated.[284] A completely westernized intellectual, Dar'ial'skii is typified as one of many who are shaped by Western ideas and who "run from you, Russia, to forget your spaciousness in a foreign land; and when they return . . . they use foreign words, they have foreign eyes; they twirl their mustache differently, the Western way."[285] In "Christ Has Risen," Belyi extends the implicit satirical dimension of these earlier heroes: here the identification of Russia with a bride is followed by the appearance of "the spine of a weakened *intelligent* in glasses" who "mumbles indignant words on the meaning of Constantinople."[286] Given his striking similarity to the man in glasses in *Song of Fate* and the long-haired writer in "The Twelve," this character is likely to be a deliberate response to Blok's texts.

The other authors examined here do not always stage their heroes or lyrical egos as explicit exponents of the intelligentsia. The status of many of these male figures as *intelligenty* is probable, though, at the very least: most of their creators considered themselves to be part of the intelligentsia, a social segment they tended to experience as problematic. Two examples that openly incorporate this self-view in bride-Russia works are the 1918 essay "Snowstorm," in which Chulkov represents "us," the "wretched semi-intelligentsia," as Russia's ineffectual savior,"[287] and Voloshin's "On the Bottom of the Inferno" ("Na dne preispodnei," 1922), whose poet poses before a feminized Russia as a tragic "Russian poet"—an heir of "Pushkin" and "Dostoevsky."[288]

Nineteenth-Century Resonances: Weak and Childish

As said earlier, Blok's bride-Russia works can be regarded as an ongoing dialogue with nineteenth-century realist and democratic traditions. They tangibly rely on the paradigm of the *intelligent* or hero that prevails in the texts Blok is rereading at this time, such as Pushkin's *Onegin,* Turgenev's novels, and Pisarev's and Dobroliubov's critical essays. As we have seen, these authors tended to attribute a set of fixed characteristics to "the intelligentsia" in its relationship to Russia—think weakness, passivity, childishness, lack of masculinity—the very qualities that apply to the poet-hero in Blok's writings.

In *Native Land,* it is primarily the intelligentsia's alleged "weakness" that reverberates. This feature is salient in the Kulikovo poems, where the poet confesses to his female companion, "I don't know what to do with myself, / Or how to follow your flight!" (3:252); in "Russia," when he claims not to "be able" to pity Russia and meekly implores it to give its beauty to a "sorcerer" (3:254); and in "New America," whose poet—"unable" to see Russia's "face"—experiences its spaciousness as "frightening" and "incomprehensible" (3:268).

Blok expands the link with nineteenth-century predecessors in *Song of Fate.* This play's "man in glasses" defines the "soul of the intelligentsia" as "deserted" and "flabby" (4:134)—a definition that certainly holds true for German. The latter describes himself as an "insignificant, alien, weak" person who is "incapable of anything," does not know "how to apply my strength," and who realizes "how much there is to do" but does not "know where to begin . . . !" (4:146). He whines, "I don't dare to fight; I don't know what to do; I ought not; my hour has not yet arrived!" (4:149), a complaint repeatedly echoed by Faina's accusation that he is incapable of putting "beautiful words" into practice.[289]

Blok's play recycles the lack of masculinity in the attitude that the nineteenth-century hero-*intelligent* takes to Russia. German's relationship with Faina, or Russia incarnate, is marked by stereotypically feminine characteristics like passivity, fear, and childishness.[290] Like his nineteenth-century prototypes, German is depicted as a figure saddled with the negative aspects of childhood, such as irresponsibility and immaturity: he is accused, for instance, of "reasoning like a child" (4:436).

German emerges from the given context as a typical *izgoi* or social outcast—one more feature he shares with nineteenth-century models. Several aspects that Iurii Lotman and Boris Uspenskii discuss as being typical of the ancient Russian category of *izgoinichestvo*—such as the position "outside the home," the "traveling along roads," and the status of foreigner or demon—are easy to recognize in Blok's German.[291] Not only is this hero linked openly with a foreigner; the connection with Pushkin's hero, who has the "soul of Mephistopheles," also gives German's character a demonic cast.[292] *Song of Fate* narrates his departure from home and his subsequent route from the city to a wasteland and, eventually, to a deserted road. His position as an *izgoi* does not result in his portrayal of the traditional role of sorcerer, however. That role, yet to be analyzed here, is ascribed to the antagonist.

Blok is an heir to nineteenth-century tradition in yet another respect. His play reenacts the same combination—the hero's ineffectuality and a messianic consciousness—that marked many a nineteenth-century protagonist. Feeling "chosen" by an unknown force, German is equated symbolically to Christ and to an apocalyptic messiah (4:146 and 139). He appears before Faina on "the sun's face" as a "triumphant figure . . . with a glowing face" that burns "with a godly fire" (4:150). That he serves as an embodiment of the revolution in this passage is suggested in a 1909 letter in which Blok defines the revolution incarnate in highly similar terms, as "youth with a halo around its face . . . often unwise as an adolescent, perhaps, but it will grow up tomorrow" (8:277). The association of German with Christ foreshadows Blok's explicit personification of the October Revolution as Christ ten years later, in "The Twelve" (3:359).

In his 1908 essay, Blok attributes several of the same characteristics to the intelligentsia even more openly. He denounces the "abstractness," "fear," and "incomprehension" of this elite with regard to the Russian people; he notes its tendency to "turn in a vicious circle"; and he mentions its "weaknesses" (5:322, 325–26). Once again, nineteenth-century echoes reverberate, but in Blok's texts the slumbering association of the intelligentsia with a failing bridegroom is out in the open: here the hero-poet appears overtly as Russia's ineffectual lover.

Again, Blok's work forms the mere tip of an iceberg packed with similar heroes and lyrical egos. In Belyi's "The Green Meadow," Russia's symbolic husband is a Cossack, a classic social outcast.[293] Belyi's Adam conceives of himself in messianic terms but is, in fact, an unhealthy, "pale, pale, pale" young man who fails abominably in his attempts to save Russia or humanity.[294] His Dar'ial'skii is a talented but "weak," passive character who "hung about" while "nobody could ascertain his goal"; in his relationship to Matrena—

alias the feminized Russia—this hero is defined as a *baba* and a child.[295] The *intelligent* in the same author's "Christ Has Risen" is marked as "weakened" and as faintly "mumbling" his Slavophile views.[296] Chulkov blames the "unstrung, blind and wretched semi-intelligentsia" for not being able to "save" the feminized Russia and for moving "backward instead of ahead."[297] Voloshin's lyrical ego and "Russian poet" in "On the Bottom of the Inferno" poses as a dropout who does not know how to "call, or scream, or help" and who "will decay at the bottom of [Russia's] cellars" or "slip in a bloody pool."[298] In Severianin's "Sleeping Beauty"—to conclude a mere selection of pessimistic examples—the lyrical ego who wants to liberate Russia is literally a (powerless) child.

Folkloric-Chivalric Roots: Riders Astray

Labeled a prince and a foreign guest, the "weak" suitor of Blok's feminized Russia is depicted as a bridegroom in folkloric terms. In general, elements from folklore characterize his heroes no less than his heroines. In his oeuvre, metaphors of the poet as horseman, knight, or warrior abound. In part, these are historically motivated: in both *Native Land* and *Song of Fate*, the poet or hero identifies with Russian cavalrymen at the Battle of Kulikovo.[299] In the Kulikovo cycle, the poet refers to himself as a classic warrior.

> I am neither the first combatant nor the last,
> The native land will long be ill.
> Thus remember at the early Mass
> The poor friend, the bright wife! (3:250)

The link with a warrior-knight who defends his lady is intensified when the poet's "chain mail" is "touched up" by that same bright wife, whose face "is bright forever in my shield" (3:251). In *Song of Fate,* German defines himself as a "warrior in an ambush" at the same battle (4:149).

Folkloric images, fused with the medieval concept of the knight errant, also underlie *Native Land's* representation of the hero as a horseman in search of his lady. The poet in the Kulikovo cycle "roam[s] on a white horse" (3:252), and in a draft for "Autumn Day" the poet claims his "horse is tired" (3:592). Earlier, in "Dark Days," Blok's "powerless" "horseman on a tired horse, astray at night in the swamp" is confronted by a female figure whose image blends with that of Russia (5:74–75, 82).[300] In this essay, as well as in *Native Land* and *Song of Fate*, the poet acts as a knightly personage who fails to liberate a feminized Russia from a figure reminiscent of the dragon in folkloric tales.

Zara Mints has argued that, in the years when the works in question were written, in most cases Blok's hero becomes an (ineffectual) "fighter for the 'holy cause,' a knight-savior."[301] Surely this transition motivated his contemporaries' mythical perception of Blok himself as Russia's mystical lover-knight: descriptions varied from Bal'mont's interpretation of "Blok, who reads his wonderful poems about Russia" as "a knight who loves an Un-achievable Lady"; and Gippius's description of Blok's "knightly adoration" of Russia, which "is to him . . . the Beautiful Lady"; to Belyi's view of Blok as "warrior of the bright Wife, to Whom two eagles' wings were given . . . to let her fly from the Dragon" and as the man to whom "the reflection of the Bright Wife is Russia."[302]

The contemporary reading of Blok's poetry and person was inspired by the importance that chivalric and dragon-slayer imagery played in his work from the start. A 1907 essay shows that his notion of knighthood was inspired in part by Western medieval models and their refraction in Pushkin's "Poor Knight" and other nineteenth-century Russian texts.[303] By implication, the projection of Pushkin's character on Prince Myshkin—the hero in Dosto-evsky's *Idiot* and a nineteenth-century pendant of Don Quixote—is likely to have affected Blok's view of the "poor knight" figure as well.[304]

Another plausible pretext for the protagonist's status as knight or dragon slayer is the biblical background that Belyi's "Bright Wife" metaphor brings to the fore. The poet's white horse in the Kulikovo cycle links him with the apocalyptic image of the Messiah, as well as with Saint George, who appears on a white horse in iconographic tradition.[305] The association is not fortuitous: as Savelii Senderovich has shown, the Saint George legend is piv-otal to Blok's poetry.[306] The depiction of the protagonists in *Song of Fate* and *Native Land* also prompts a reading of their characters as tragic alter egos of Saint George: they define themselves as warriors and strive (but fail) to liberate a feminized Russia from a male rival.[307] That they were understood in terms of this legend at the time of publication is suggested by Belyi's com-ment that Blok's poetry was the "concrete and real express[ion]" of Saint George's "meeting with the Dragon."[308]

Blok's chivalric heroes may have alluded to ancient legends, but at the same time they embodied topical political concerns. As mentioned in chapter 1, sociopolitical implications were inherent to the Saint George legend from the start. Blok's work continues that tradition: in the words of Zara Mints, it revolves around the relationship between a chivalric "'I' as a contemporary *intelligent*—the carrier of a tragic guilt . . . and 'you' as the daughter of the common people, the Native Land—as a victim in need of an act of liberation."[309]

This concept—of the hero-poet as a knight, a horseman, or a dragon slayer who fights for the liberation of a feminine force—enjoys general popularity in early twentieth-century Russian culture.[310] In the context of the metaphor discussed here it reverberates in Parnok's poetry, as we have seen. Russia's symbolic husband in "The Green Meadow" is also marked as someone who "struggles" with a rival for his beloved and "defends the native meadows from a vile attack"; his status as the Russian horseman par excellence—the Cossack—links him symbolically to knightly figures.[311] In Voloshin's poetry, demonic or other evil forces are opposed to "princes" or to a "chosen" hero in their struggle for power over the "bride Russia"; her "chosen" bridegroom is represented symbolically as a warrior with a "sword of prayers."[312] The poet in Severianin's "Sleeping Beauty" wants to "court" Russia in order to awaken her from sleep and rescue her from evil forces.[313] And in Kliuev's "Devastation," a depiction of Russia as bride is preceded by the poet's identification with Saint George, who rides his horse and is threatened by wolves.[314]

The Rival: Sorcerer-Seducer

Zara Mints saw the story of the sleeping beauty and her capture by evil forces as a key myth of Russian Symbolism. Within this myth, Russia and the intelligentsia tend to fulfill the role of sleeping beauty and the prince who is to set her free, respectively. Inevitably, these two actors in the narrative are opposed to an evil captor. Writers of the time represent the latter in varying terms: in one instance his character may be traceable to the dragon of the Saint George legend, in another to the antagonistic sorcerer of folkloric tales, in yet another to the seven-headed beast of the Apocalypse, and in a final example to forces that separate knights from their ladies in medieval chivalric imagery.

From a political perspective, Russia's symbolic captor tends to incarnate either the tsarist regime or foreign forces. These forces and the intelligentsia relate to each other as two rivals vying for Russia's love—but, unlike the situation in traditional plots, here the hero or poet assumes a tragic role. If Propp writes that in the wonder tale "the struggle ends, of course, with the hero's triumph," then its early twentieth-century revisions just as invariably conclude with the hero's defeat and the victory of the symbolic dragon.[315] This victory should be understood primarily as a preservation of the status quo, since a struggle in the strict sense of the word seldom takes place. In this respect, the texts in question are closely linked to the nineteenth-century Russian novel, whose hero so often passively yielded a "Russian" heroine to a stronger authoritative antagonist.

In its purest form, Blok applied the classic dragon-slayer plot in a 1910 essay on Vladimir Solov'ev, in which he proclaimed the latter a knight trying to liberate "the captive Princess, the World Soul, grieving passionately in the embraces of Chaos" or of a "dragon" (5:451). The essay concludes with the author's appeal to "us, Russians," to liberate the symbolic princess from the dragon (5:454).

If the Solov'ev essay shows that Blok did think in terms of a dragon-slayer plot, in his portrayals of Russia it is not a dragon but a sorcerer who fulfills the role of evil captor. In his work, this figure has its roots in folklore. It appears prominently for the first time in his 1906 study on folkloric rituals, in which he appoints a crucial role to sorcerers in the life of the common people when he claims that "all the rays of the joys, sorrows, consolations, and songs of the people invisibly cross, interlace so to say, in the one face of the sorcerer" (5:43). In the same year, sorcerer motifs appear next to a feminized Russia in "Rus'," although without being openly linked (2:106).

A link between Russia and a mystical evil force does occur in "Dark Days." In this essay, the female figure that symbolically merges with Russia is opposed, on the one hand, to a prince-like male horseman and, on the other, to a demon. As so often with Blok, the nineteenth century is not far away: the narrator envisions Lermontov, Gogol, and Dostoevsky as the three "demons" or "sorcerers" of nineteenth-century Russian literature (5:76–79). They function for him as mystical doubles of their own literary characters—Lermontov of his lyrical ego, Gogol of the sorcerer in "Terrible Vengeance," and Dostoevsky of Rogozhin in *The Idiot*.[316] The "demons," according to Blok, have lulled contemporary literature and reality into a dreamlike state, in which it "wanders" idly, like a modern-day errant knight (5:82). Blok would rather that the literary world hear "the Russian revolution, the hungry and repressed screams," which he links to the symbolic captive bride (ibid.). This line of thinking illustrates what Victor Erlich terms the author's "growing impatience with the esoteric fiddling of some of his fellow Symbolists as Rome was about to burn"—a feeling that coincides with Blok's focus on the theme of the people and the intelligentsia in the same period.[317]

Modeling the sorcerer in "Dark Days" on the *kashchei* in "Terrible Vengeance," Blok takes recourse to the same prototype that had appeared in "The Green Meadow" a year earlier, when Belyi envisioned the feminized Russia held captive by a sorcerer in a "foreign castle."[318] The latter's representation of this figure—which is in keeping with the folkloric association of the sorcerer with a demonic stranger—can be considered programmatic for a number of later literary-philosophical metaphoric representations of the state or the West.[319] Belyi associates his sorcerer with the "smoke of factories" and with the "mechanical deadliness" and "dead cities" of industrialization.[320] This industrial world is opposed to the "primitive rudeness" of traditional Russian culture, with which Russia's true husband is connected.[321] In the essay, this opposition blends with the opposition foreign-native: in keeping with traditional tales, the sorcerer and the true husband represent foreign and native space respectively. The authority of the sorcerer over the hero is formulated in terms of age: the former is depicted a number of times as an "old man" "whom they call your father."[322] In the essay's politicized context, the father role unmistakably evokes the traditional image of the tsar as a father, an association that reappears in Blok's later works. For Belyi, the sorcerer is also overtly linked to the classic evildoer of folkloric tales: he is compared to *Zmei Gorynych* and to a "werewolf," both traditional wonder-tale hypostases of the dragon.[323]

It is no big step from Belyi's to Blok's evil antagonist. Both in *Native Land* and *Song of Fate*, the protagonist is opposed to a rival who is linked organically to Belyi's sorcerer. Within *Native Land*, the connection is most obvious in "Russia," where the poet yields his beloved Russia to a "sorcerer" (3:254). The kite—the bird of prey in the poem of the same name—"circles above a sleepy meadow," which serves as the symbolic equivalent of the "beauty" Russia (3:281).[324] A similar force occurs in what appears to be a nonpolitical context in the poem "The Wild Wind" ("Dikii veter"), in which the wind is a "brutal guest" who tries to steal the poet's bride (3:279–80). A traditional hypostasis of the dragon in wonder tales, here the wind can be seen as an extension of the sorcerer-rival in "Russia" and "The Kite."[325]

As discussed later in this chapter, in the years before Blok wrote these poems the Russian press commonly associated the ultraconservative statesman Pobedonostsev with a *kashchei* or vampire. Blok himself would represent Pobedonostsev as such in 1911 in *Retribution*, and scholars have pointed to a possible link between the sorcerer figures in Blok's poems and the statesman.[326] The poems themselves, however, do not openly mark these figures as embodiments of a concrete sociopolitical force.

The situation is different in "New America" and in drafts of "Russia," which show that Blok originally sought to represent the sorcerer as a bridegroom who loved, bewitched, and ultimately imprisoned Russia (3:591). In these drafts, Blok equates his sorcerer with the "haughty fabric frame" of industrial Russia, which the poet sees as its "executioner" (ibid.). In "New America," the poet opposes the allegedly authentic Russia of the Battle of Kulikovo to "plant chimneys," "factory sirens," "a multilayered factory building," and "cities of workers' shacks" (3:269); in what seems a continuation of the "Russia" drafts, this antithesis is envisioned as the gendered opposition of the "bride, Russia" to "black coal" as her "tsar and bridegroom" (ibid.). Thus for Blok, industrial civilization—in its role as "new America"—functions as a foreign rival to whom the poet yields the feminized Russia (3:270). If this view resulted from his growing preoccupation with Russia's industrial development,[327] then—given the striking similarities—Belyi understandably credits "The Green Meadow" as its poetic inspiration.[328]

As elsewhere, what is simply implicit in *Native Land* is plain to the eye in *Song of Fate*. Here, the hero-*intelligent*, German, is opposed in his love for the heroine to a rival—"Faina's Companion"—who holds her in his power and repels German's attempts to liberate her. In the figure of this antagonist, a miscellany of political and literary predecessors meet. They include Konstantin Pobedonostsev; the former minister of finance (1892–1903) and prime minister (1903–5) Sergei Witte; the sorcerer in Gogol's "Terrible Vengeance," whom Blok and Belyi had revived in earlier works; and the antagonist of Dostoevsky's "Landlady" ("Khoziaika," 1847)—like the Companion and Gogol's *kashchei,* an old "undoer" and "sorcerer" whose powers over the heroine prevent the young hero from uniting with her.[329]

To Blok's attitude to Pobedonostsev, to whom he openly attributes a similar role in *Retribution,* I come back shortly. Of additional importance to *Song of Fate* is Witte, on whom, according to Liubov' Blok, the Companion's image was first grafted.[330] To judge from photographs of Witte, the "corpulent," "tall" Companion could easily be his twin, with his long beard, walking stick, and "movements, costume, and stance reminiscent of an emperor or a notable foreigner who wishes to visit a foreign, befriended country incognito" (4:127, 143).[331] Within the political allegory that *Song of Fate* is, the last comparison likely alludes to the view of the imperial regime as an alien force within Russia—a pet subject for Blok's beloved Slavophiles, as we saw earlier. The Witte that Blok knew can also be recognized in the Companion's sympathetic, tragic character. Although generally denouncing the imperial regime, Blok speaks highly of this politician in his diary, calling him "if not a mountain, then a height; from his time on . . . nothing has been 'elevated'; everything is 'flat'" (7:262). Such a positive view is in keeping with the general trend among liberal intellectuals, who sympathize with Witte for his moderate liberal policy and his successful attempts to modernize Russia industrially.

In Blok's portrayal of the Companion, this political prototype blends with Belyi's *kashchei* and his predecessors. The relationship of the Companion to the heroine is saturated with metaphors of sleep and involuntary imprisonment; Faina repeatedly speaks of being abducted and lulled to sleep by him, and of wanting to be freed by the hero (4:145, 149, 150). Scholars rightly identify this dimension of his character, via Belyi's and Gogol's sorcerers, with the traditional folkloric sorcerer that Blok introduced in his 1906 essay.[332]

With the Companion, Blok reenacts the traditional opposition of the old, socially powerful sorcerer to a young, ineffectual protagonist—an antithesis that also marked nineteenth-century variations on the bride-Russia theme. Faina's Companion is not only compared to an emperor and a foreign notable, but also repeatedly called "the authoritative one" (4:115, 164, 166). His sheer size, probably dictated by Witte's physical appearance, emphasizes his powerful status: German refers to himself as insignificant, whereas the Companion is "massive" and "enormous" (4:127, 143). German's child-ishness is contrasted with the Companion's "old" age, an epithet attributed to him seven times throughout the play (4:145, 150, 164, 166). Having first been pictured as a man "in the prime of his life," the Companion soon slips into the chronic state of physical exhaustion of old age (4:127, 129, 145). His authoritative aura and advanced age unite in Faina's song, which implicitly addresses the Companion with the words: "He who is old and gray and in the prime of life, / He who gives the most clinking coins, / Come to my ring-ing voice!" (4:129).

The association of this old, powerful man with the "old" world of the imperial state is prompted not only by his connection to Witte, the ancien régime incarnate at the time of the first revolution. Blok exemplifies the link by depicting the Companion as an exponent of faded glory. His face is "swol-len, with traces of bygone beauty," and his melancholic sadness is stressed throughout the play (4:127, 143–45, 151, 166). Significantly, in a letter to Rozanov, Blok later personifies the Russian state, in terms evocative of the Companion, as "foul, slobbery, stinking old age, a seventy-year-old syphilitic, who infects a healthy young hand with his handshake" (8:277).

If affiliated with the regime, however, the Companion is also linked with the industrial culture that figured as Russia's seducer in Belyi's essay and in *Native Land*. His two appearances in the play are set against the background of an international industrial exhibition and a wasteland littered with building materials and far-off factories; as was the case in *Native Land*, this world—the official Russia of modern civilization—contrasts drastically with the world of the poet-hero, who identifies with the historical Russia of the Kulikovo battle.

Song of Fate thus forms an unequivocally allegorical representation of the relationship among intelligentsia, Russia, and the Russian state (or modern industrial Russia) as a tragic amorous triangle—one in which the antagonist enacts the role of the Russian state, which prevents the lovers from uniting.

The antagonistic role of the state within this constellation concurs with Blok's reference to the Russian state in a 1909 letter as "our only com-mon enemy" (8:281). While this enemy still has human traits in the play, Blok allegorizes it far more negatively somewhat later, in *Retribution*. Here the same Pobedonostsev who served as one of the prototypes for the Com-panion openly enacts the role of "winged sorcerer" who enchants a femi-nized Russia. That Pobedonostsev represents what Blok sees as state au-thority at its ugliest suggests this character's frightening "iron hand," which "pressed" Russia's powers "into a useless knot" (3:328). In a 1908 essay Blok had already called Pobedonostsev, with reference to his reactionary atti-tude to political opposition, an "old vampire" ruling over "sleeping, tired . . .

Russia" (5:301). As mentioned, Chulkov would apply the very same meta-phor to Russia and Pobedonostsev in a gendered context in *The Emperors* in the 1920s. Belyi does the same in *Petersburg* (*Peterburg*, 1916–35), the novel in which he grafts the character of the conservative senator Apollon Ableukhov onto that of Pobedonostsev.[333] Not only is Ableukhov compared to a *Retribution*-like bat "with a stony glance," but—in a fragment over which Gogol's troika passage looms large—the narrator also warns a per-sonified Rus' to beware of the man.[334] Under the guise of Count Dubl'e, Ableukhov's sworn enemy, is the clearly recognizable alter ego of that other well-known political character of the day, Sergei Witte.[335]

An obvious link connects characters in *Petersburg* and *Retribution* to the sorcerer in Belyi's and Blok's earlier work.[336] In both books, however, an additional source is provided by the depiction of Pobedonostsev in po-litical journalism. Leonid Dolgopolov has argued that after the latter's death in 1907, "not a single newspaper in Russia failed to publish an article (and often more than one) on Pobedonostsev."[337] It was in these articles that "Pobedonostsev was first called . . . a 'sorcerer,' a 'night owl'" in a context that reoccurs almost literally in *Retribution;* thus, one local newspaper de-fines him as "he, whose name repressed the Russian earth for so many de-cades . . . who strangled everything alive . . . with his cold bony hand."[338] The image of the sorcerer never stood on its own: according to Zara Mints, for readers of those days, representations of Pobedonostsev as a sorcerer inevi-tably "called to mind the Russia that was 'enchanted' by him, and the fight-ers for its freedom."[339]

If rampant from 1907 on, this view—of Pobedonostsev as a winged sorcerer who dominated the allegorical sleeping beauty, Russia—is strongly entrenched in public thought well before his death. It can be traced at least as far back as 1905. It is in this politically turbulent year that the public spots a reference to Pobedonostsev in Rimsky-Korsakov's *Kashchei;* following its performance, mocking satirical verses in the *Peterbugskii listok* newspaper symbolize the regime as "here and there, the Sorcerers are everywhere."[340] The scandal might have been anticipated at a time when numerous satirical journals are reacting to the failed revolution of January 1905. In Petersburg alone, 178 publications with ominous titles such as "Post from Hell" and "Poleax" are called into being for the sole purpose of vehemently deriding and attacking tsarist authorities.[341] In 1905 and 1906, cartoons in these pub-lications repeatedly depict Pobedonostsev as a bat or vampire, and in a 1905 edition of the journal *Strely,* the bat looms over a feminized sleeping Rus-sia.[342] Even postcards of Pobedonostsev as a bat are said to have circulated at the time.[343] *Retribution* expounds on precisely this myth.

In addition, Blok's sorcerer may have drawn inspiration from other po-litical cartoons or posters: as Victoria Bonnell has argued, in the early twentieth century this is a genre in which women rarely appear as anything other than allegorical figures.[344] I have discussed a few examples in passing, such as the wartime posters of Russia as an attractive young woman. In 1905 and 1906, cartoons in "Post from Hell" and its like similarly represent Russia as a beautiful woman or princess. Here the evil-captor plot prevails: feminized Russia is chained by a spider (bureaucracy), for instance, or has her blood sucked by a vampire (the state and its representatives).[345]

Whether or not he is incited by such examples, Blok presents his readers with a broad range of allegorical "Russia-captors." Last in line is Van'ka in "The Twelve." Sergei Hackel has compared this poem to "The Green Meadow," claiming that like Belyi's feminized Russia/Katerina, Kat'ka in Blok's verses "has abandoned her true love (Pet'ka)—the agent and guardian of Rus''s rediscovered integrity—in favor of a renegade who has betrayed the national cause."[346] In Hackel's reading of the poem, Van'ka—a soldier of Kerensky's provisional government and of the bourgeois—becomes a direct heir of Belyi's foreign sorcerer.[347]

As said earlier, the tendency to depict the contemporary state as an evil force that enchants Russia is a common constituent of public discourse at this time. Not surprisingly, then, it recurs as a popular device in the poetry of Blok's contemporaries. A not necessarily political reaction to the sorcerer in Blok's "Russia" appears in Kliuev's poem "In the Frozen Darkness . . . ," in which he allegorizes a snowstorm as a sorcerer who has enchanted a feminized Russia.[348] In his "Devastation," howling wolves and demons threaten the poet, who refers to Russia as the "native land—bride."[349] Wolves also function as captors and killers of a feminized Russia in Severianin's "Sleeping Beauty."[350] As early as 1903, Parnok speaks of the "embattled Truth" of the sleeping beauty Russia, albeit without designating an imprisoning force.[351] In Belyi's *Silver Dove*, the joiner Kudeiarov serves as the hero's demonic opponent and as the captor of Matrena, alias Russia incarnate. In Voloshin's poetry of the late 1910s, the poet envisions a feminized Russia as the captive of an evil "master," "enemies," "robbers," and "demons."[352] In a lecture, he identifies these demons as symbolic stand-ins for the young Bolshevik regime.[353]

From Blok to Esenin, from Belyi to Voloshin: as shown, several early twentieth-century authors share a tendency to conceive of Russia as a female figure captivated by evil forces. The influence exerted by Blok is hard to underestimate in this context. Perhaps even more than the mark his metaphor made within the poetic sphere is the impact it had on politico-philosophical writings. Berdiaev, our next focal point, is a key advocate of the view of Russia as unattainable bride that dominates philosophical and sociopolitical discourse in the 1910s. An analysis of his texts shows that in many respects his thoughts on this theme are indebted to Blok's "wife Russia."

NIKOLAI BERDIAEV: THE FEMININE
SOUL OF RUSSIA

This chapter opened with a quotation from Nikolai Berdiaev's *Philosophy of Inequality*, which proclaimed Russia a bride and the intelligentsia her ineffectual bridegroom. This text and others by Berdiaev can be considered explications of Blok's gendered views of Russia. Berdiaev was well acquainted with both Blok and his work, and in a 1937 essay on Russian literature, he calls Blok the "greatest poet of the beginning of the century."[354] Blok's "astounding" poem "Russia" he sees as "prophetic."[355]

It is not Blok, however, but Belyi who first triggers Berdiaev's interest in gendered conceptualizations of Russia and the intelligentsia. In the period when Berdiaev's contact with Belyi is at its peak, *The Silver Dove* appears. The novel makes a deep impression on Berdiaev, who reviews it in 1910 in *Russkaia mysl'*. The review—in which he calls the intelligentsia-people opposition an "age-old Russian theme" that Belyi has transposed to a deeper level (3:413)—shows that Berdiaev has a specific interest in the novel's gender-related dimension. "Matrena is the Russian earth," he states, and "the unity between Dar'ial'skii and Matrena is at the same time the unity between the intelligentsia and the common people" (3:414–15). Whereas he himself has devoted articles to the "mental demoralization" of the intelligentsia ever since the 1905 Revolution, it is at this point that his rendition of the theme acquires an explicit gendered dimension.

Between the publication of the Belyi review in 1910 and the end of the civil war, Berdiaev repeatedly uses amorous metaphors to depict the triangle consisting of Russia, intelligentsia, and state. He does so in popular journals and newspapers of the time—such as *Russkaia mysl'*, *Birzhevye vedomosti*, and *Narodopravstvo*, which were read by a broad intellectual public—in articles that can be categorized as political journalism rather than philosophy. At times, their explicit, didactic tone nudges them to the verge of political propaganda. In other words, we are dealing here with Berdiaev the "born publicist," as one contemporary typifies him, and not with a systematic philosopher.[356]

In his rendition of the metaphor, Berdiaev both relies on and differs from Blok and his like. Differences between Berdiaev's and Blok's "bride Russia" are not hard to pinpoint. Central to Berdiaev's version is the androgynous ideal that is so popular in Russian culture at the time. In his autobiography, he explicitly opposes this ideal to Blok's Beautiful Lady and Solov'ev's Eternal Feminine principle—two concepts that, in Berdiaev's view, lack androgynous-erotic implications (1:89–90). In truth, Solov'ev and Blok both did identify with androgynous thought; but by the time Blok writes *Native Land* and *Song of Fate*, this dimension is no longer central to his poetics.[357] Berdiaev's consistent point of departure, on the other hand, is an androgynous philosophy that is focused on "conquering" gender and erotic love (1:89–91). His political gender metaphors presuppose a "disunity of the masculine and feminine elements" in Russia that needs to be overcome.[358] Thus, in *The Philosophy of Inequality* Berdiaev claims that whereas Western nations have found a successful balance between their masculine and feminine dimensions,

> the secret of the Russian soul . . . lies in an undue, false correlation between the masculine and feminine principles. In . . . the soul of the Russian people, no inner marriage has taken place, no marital union of a masculine and a feminine principle; no androgynous form has been realized. The masculine spirit did not organically unite with Russia's feminine soul. (4:269–70)

Considering the intelligentsia and the people as the ultimate exponents of Russia's dissociated masculine and feminine principles, respectively, Berdiaev sees their desired marriage primarily as a metaphysical concept.

One more distinction between the two authors is found in the role that the First World War plays in Berdiaev's work. He, as well as Rozanov, takes recourse to a gendered view of Russia in distinctly political journalistic articles, many of which are devoted to the German threat in the years 1914 through 1917. It is an aspect that does not appear in Blok's work for the simple reason that most of the latter's "bride Russia" texts were written long before the war started.

The two authors differ in another respect. Although relying on presuppositions similar to those of the poet, the philosopher offers a less personal version of the metaphor. Contrary to Blok, whose poetic representations of a feminized Russia often need to be deciphered from implicit metaphors, Berdiaev offers explicit comparisons. He overtly states that "the Russian people always pose as a bride" and that "the male German spirit . . . imposed itself upon the Russian earth as husband" (3:414, 4:274). This directness asks for a different approach than that required for Blok's texts, whose metaphors often need to be reconstructed from correspondence, memoirs, or biographical facts. An analysis of Berdiaev's philosophical texts is in less need of such complementary sources.

Having said this, I must note that Berdiaev, as well as other contemporary philosophers, was quite emotionally involved in his musings on the intelligentsia, which emerged in the context of active *zhiznetvorchestvo,* or life-building tendencies. On the one hand, he poses as a neutral, analytic observer of the purported conflict between "intelligentsia" and "people." He refers to the former as radical revolutionaries or (later) Bolsheviks, with whom he sympathizes but from whom he generally dissociates himself; he emphatically distances himself from populism (1:76, 132). He writes about achieving an agreeable level of contact with the common people rather than the mystical coalescence that interested Blok and Belyi (1:132–33). On the other hand, a mystical union between the intelligentsia and the common people is precisely what Berdiaev is after in his writings. He may not experience the alleged dissociation between the two as a personal tragedy, but in his autobiography he does pose distinctly as an exponent of the intelligentsia in general, and its aristocratic segment in particular.[359] His writings on the gap between the intelligentsia and the people result partly from post-1905 talks with sectarians, followers of Leo Tolstoy and Aleksandr Dobroliubov, and peasants from the village where he spent his summers.[360] He experiences these conversations as occasions upon which "any opposition" disappears "between the ordinary man and the gentleman."[361] As the "basic fact" of his personal biography, he names "my departure from the aristocratic into the revolutionary world" (1:43). Thus personal commitment to the theme does affect Berdiaev's take on the intelligentsia-versus-people opposition, even though his involvement is less radical than Blok's.

What Blok and Berdiaev also share is an infatuation with nineteenth-century literature. The nineteenth century is, generally speaking, a crucial prism through which early twentieth-century philosophy must be viewed. With reference to the metaphor examined here, the need to do so is perhaps best indicated by the fact that Berdiaev, Bulgakov, and Ivanov all projected their gendered view of the intelligentsia and Russia onto the heroes of Dostoevsky's *Demons*. Nineteenth-century sources reverberate throughout Berdiaev's writings. He claims to identify personally with nineteenth-century heroes like Stavrogin, Tolstoy's Prince Andrei, Griboedov's Chatskii, and Pushkin's Onegin (1:43). In an effort to define his philosophical roots, he singles out the Slavophile-westernizer debate and Solov'ev's philosophy (1:10, 43, 91, 160, 186). With respect to his ambiguous feelings about his aristocratic origins, he writes that he has always felt "linked to . . . Chaadaev, some of the Slavophiles, Herzen . . . Vladimir Solov'ev" (1:43). Together with Bulgakov, Trubetskoi, Ern, and Ivanov, among others, he is an active member of the religious-philosophical circle "In Honor of Vl. Solov'ev" in the years between 1905 and 1910 (1:181). In addition, a direct connection has been reconstructed between implications of gender in Chaadaev's philosophical letters, the semi-explicit gendered view of Russia in Slavophile thought, and, ultimately, Berdiaev's openly gendered perspective on Russia.[362] "One might say," writes Robin Aizlewood with regard to visions of the artist-*intelligent* and Russia as a tragic amorous couple, "that what is 'potential' in Chaadaev is realised in a maximalist way in Berdiaev."[363] The same can be said of the relationship between Solov'ev's Sophiology and Berdiaev's philosophy: whereas a national dimension merely glimmers through in the former, in Berdiaev's work this dimension is maximally realized.

Berdiaev is not alone in this respect. A similarly "maximalist" nation-gender philosophy emerges from the writings of a number of contemporary philosophers, among whom Rozanov and Ivanov appear most prominently. The following sections provide a closer look at the gendered conception of Russia by Berdiaev and some of his contemporaries.

Russia: Posing as a Bride

A reader of Berdiaev's work of the 1910s can hardly fail to notice the writer's view of Russia as a metaphysical bride or female beloved. "Matrena embodies the Russian earth." "The Russian people . . . always pose as a bride." "The image of the native earth is . . . that of a bride and wife." "The Russian earth has always . . . posed as a bride." Berdiaev's variations on this gendered theme are found throughout his articles and treatises of the period.[364] To him, as shown in his 1910 review of *The Silver Dove*, a feminized Russia embodies the same rural concepts that Blok used in describing the gendered nation: Berdiaev equates it with the Russian earth, the Russian people, "Russian nature, . . . the Russian *baba*," and "Russian fields, ravines, and taverns" (3:415, 422–23).

The bridal metaphor is a topical concept for many a philosopher and journalist at this time. In 1907 Rozanov had already spoken of Russia as a "poor bride" in his article "To the New Year" ("Na novyi god").[365] In 1911 his essay "Near the Russian Idea" brands Russia as a "bride and wife" and a "woman, eternally searching for a bridegroom, leader, and husband."[366] In a mixture of Christian and mystical rhetoric, Ivanov speaks in 1909 of the earth as a bride and as Christ's "wife clothed with the sun" in "Terror Antiquus."[367] He transposes this concept to a national-Russian context in 1914 in "The Basic Myth in the Novel *The Demons*" ("Osnovnoi mif v romane *Besy*"). This essay identifies Dostoevsky's Khromonozhka as a "Russian Earth-Soul," "languish[ing] in expectation of her intended bridegroom, the hero of Christ."[368] In Berdiaev's and Bulgakov's reviews of the novel, the same heroine is similarly equated in her role of languishing bride with the Russian earth and "the Russian soul."[369] Ivanov's review is, moreover, reminiscent of Blok's and Belyi's writings when it compares Russia to a "Sleeping Beauty . . . in captivity."[370] In his 1915 article "Living Legend," Ivanov repeats this metaphor.[371]

From a strictly Sophiological point of view, Russia is represented as female beloved in Florenskii's "Holy Trinity–St. Sergius Lavra and Russia." In this essay, Florenskii treats the Divine Sophia as the "bride" of Saint Cyril and a symbol of "the feminine receptivity to life" of Kievan Rus'.[372] Sophiological views also permeate Evgenii Trubetskoi's essay "The National Question, Constantinople, and Saint Sophia," in which he links the Divine Sophia with Russia's "national soul," to whom he ascribes a future messianic role; as another article shows, the bridal role of Sophia is of topical importance to him in this respect.[373] While an emigrant in the 1930s, Bulgakov likewise equates Russia with the Divine Sophia, with whom he claims to have fallen in love and to have longed to meet all his life.[374]

The Bride: Chaos, Passivity, Submissiveness

Thus, the metaphor on which Berdiaev relies in the 1910s is far from uncommon in intellectual debates of the time. Like most of his contemporaries, Berdiaev uses it to express what is essentially a sociopolitical critique of the intelligentsia. He formulates this critique at a time of turmoil for Russia, when recent events—the war against Japan and internal political unrest—are still fresh in everyone's minds. Berdiaev does not want such agitation to be read in concrete political terms, however: in his work, it points to a disturbed balance between Russia's "feminine" and "masculine" elements.

Here I want to take a closer look at the features that epitomize the first ingredient of this opposition. In a large number of works of the 1910s, Berdiaev repeatedly circumscribes Russia and the Russian people with the help of terms like "spontaneity,"[375] "chaos," "weakness," "servitude," "passivity," "submissiveness," and the desire to "dissolve" in the collective.[376] In keeping with traditional Western thought, which has branded these concepts stereotypically feminine, Berdiaev summarizes them in what he alternately calls the "femininity of the soul of the Russian people" and the "feminine Russian earth." "On the Eternally Womanish in the Russian Soul" not only forms the title of one of his 1914 essays: dominating his characterization of Russia's alleged weakness, passivity, and submissiveness as childish or immature[377] is his representation of such traits as feminine.[378]

Berdiaev applies the characteristics in question in varying, and at times paradoxical, contexts. In one passage he specifically calls the Russian "people" passive, and in another he blames the Russian "element" for its passivity. Here he speaks of the alleged passivity of the Russian people toward the Russian earth, in particular, and there he mentions the people's submissive attitude toward the Russian state.[379] What does unite his depictions of Russia's femininity is their reliance on Slavophile thought. Inverting them into blameworthy features, Berdiaev echoes those qualities that the Slavophiles traditionally praised in their nation: think of Danilevskii's attribution of softness and servitude to Russia, discussed in chapter 1.

By defining the features mentioned as essential to Russia's "feminine" nature, Berdiaev is again far from unique. Distinguishing him from many of his contemporaries, however, is his negative bias. Oleg Riabov groups contributions to the dialogue on Russia's femininity into three perspectives. Berdiaev, who views Russia as excessively feminine, shares his perspective with thinkers like A. Nemov (pseudonym of the philosopher Aleksei Toporkov), who implores the Russian nation to turn from a feminine toward a more masculine self-consciousness in his 1915 treatise *The Idea of a Slavic Renaissance* (*Idea slavianskogo vozrozhdeniia*).[380]

A more optimistic perspective is offered by philosophers such as Viacheslav Ivanov, Vladimir Ern, and, later, Nikolai Losskii, who proclaim that in any nation, including Russia, a feminine and a masculine principle coexist.[381] At the same time, Ivanov paradoxically calls modern Russia a predominantly feminine entity, whose future he imagines in terms of a mystical union with a Christlike, masculine spouse.[382] His view of that feminine dimension is determined by the same terms—passivity, spontaneity—as Berdiaev's.

Rozanov, finally, regards what he labels the femininity of the Slavs as an exclusively positive notion.[383] As early as 1898, he asserts that European civilization has lost touch with the "motherly womb" of the earth; and that contact with European culture has made Russian civilization just as "one-sidedly masculine, in other words, out of balance."[384] Later, in "Near the Russian Idea," he defines the Russians themselves—along with Russian literature, Russian ideals, and Russian socialism—as predominantly feminine.[385] Rozanov ascribes to this feminine Russia characteristics similar to those mentioned by Berdiaev, but extends the list with positive features. For him, the Russians are "weak, tender, soft, compliant"—but he commends that last feature, as well as their ability to "submit themselves."[386]

Strikingly, in 1945 Berdiaev himself labels the view of the Russian nation as feminine a German invention: the Russian people are, he claims, in fact, "capable of displaying great masculinity."[387] Drastic as it is, this turnabout is possibly the result of Russia's defeat of the Germans in the Second World War.[388] Berdiaev sticks to the androgynous nation as ideal, however: even after radically altering his position, he preserves the gendered philosophy that typifies his earlier work.

The Nineteenth-Century Prism:
Sophias and Mystical Brides

As noted earlier, the nineteenth century functions as a major prism through which to view Berdiaev's personifications of Russia. He and several of his contemporaries tend to ascribe the role of the nation's female embodiment to nineteenth-century literary heroines.

For example, Berdiaev not only points to the status of Belyi's Matrena as an "artistically brilliant symbol of the Russian national element";

in retrospect, he also identifies Liza and Khromonozhka in *The Demons* as "the Russian earth . . . awaiting its bridegroom" (3:419). Ivanov likewise reads Dostoevsky's heroines as models of a feminine Russia: he interprets Khromonozhka as "symbol of the Earth-Mother," "Russian Soul," "the Eternal Feminine in its aspect of the Russian soul," and the "Russian Earth-Soul" awaiting its "intended bridegroom";[389] and conceives of Sonia in *Crime and Punishment* and Aglaia in *The Idiot* as equivalents of the Russian people and earth, respectively.[390] Rozanov projects his views of Russian socialism and the revolution as feminine entities onto Dostoevsky's Sonia as well, in addition to other nineteenth-century literary characters such as Turgenev's heroines, Ekaterina Maslova in Tolstoy's *Resurrection* (*Voskresenie*, 1899), and Ulen'ka in Gogol's *Dead Souls*.[391]

The politico-philosophical orientation of the thinkers in question accounts for a high degree of abstractness: unlike Blok and other poets, they devote little attention to clothing or other outward manifestations of the female characters they mark as personifications of Russia. What they do share with Blok is a dual concept of the feminized Russia. In his review of *The Demons*, Berdiaev associates Russia with an exalted "eternal feminine principle" (3:108), and in *The Meaning of Creation* (*Smysl tvorchestva*, 1916) he reverts to the concept of the "Earth-Bride" as Christ's lofty spouse, referring explicitly to Boehme's and Solov'ev's Sophiology (2:220). Yet Berdiaev follows these same thinkers—and, through them, Gnostic tradition—by stressing the inherently darker side of the figure.

The existence of a direct link between this dual concept and Gnosticism is explicated by Ivanov in his interpretation of *The Idiot:* he sees Nastasia Filippovna as the alter ego of the alleged "Russian Earth-Soul" Khromonozhka and labels her "the Eternal Feminine," "having descended to save the world . . . but subsequently, like the Gnostics' Agamot . . . being held in captivity and profaned by substance."[392]

A similar view influences Berdiaev's depictions of a sacred-cum-profane feminized Russia. He stresses Russia's sexual promiscuity in "On the Eternally Womanish in the Russian Soul." In this essay he accuses Rozanov, whom he sees as representative of the "feminine" Russian people, of "female-womanish feelings that have an almost sexual character" in relation to the state (3:358). As said earlier, in the debate on Russia's gender, Rozanov himself identifies with the feminine perspective. In *The War of 1914*—to which Berdiaev's article responds—Rozanov describes his "feminine" reaction to a display of state power in sexually ambiguous terms.[393] In "Near the Russian Idea," a sexual bias again emerges when Rozanov claims, with reference to his "bride Russia," that "to the eternal cry of the he-man . . . 'I want,' the Russian tribe . . . answers: 'Take me!'"[394]

It is not only with reference to Rozanov that Berdiaev speaks of the darker or sexually promiscuous side of feminine Russia. In the *Silver Dove* review, he defines Matrena in her role as Russia incarnate as "dark-spontaneous and demonic, terrifying" and equates her with "the Russian mystical element, with its terrifying and dark chaos" (3:415, 423). Berdiaev links Matrena-Russia's darker side with religious dissidence when he emphasizes her involvement in a religious sect; later, he associates Rozanov with "pre-Christianity" and "paganism" (1:167, 3:351). On a more general note, he defines a preference for paganism and sectarianism as typical of the feminine "Russian national element"—which he opposes in this respect to Orthodox religion as "chaotic," "Dionysian," "primordial," and "anticultural."[305] The same Rozanov that Berdiaev criticizes so vehemently had defined the revolution in 1908, in similar terms, as being a "hysterical," "sectarian" *baba*.[396]

Berdiaev himself comments on this duality when he proclaims Russia "a sacred country in its sinfulness."[397] Man must love his native "earth-bride," he proclaims, "with all her contradictions, sins, and defects."[398] If this angelic-demonic representation of Russia is reminiscent of Symbolist poems, then the analogy is even more obvious in Berdiaev's adaptation of bifacial metaphors. In *The Soul of Russia*, the philosopher ascribes to his personified Russia "two faces," which he compares to Dostoevsky's "divided" face: "fathomless depth and unbounded height are combined with a kind of baseness."[399] Facial metaphors and the veil motif that figures so prominently in Blok's poetry appear in Berdiaev's texts specifically when he refers to the First World War. Here, the *pokrov* functions as both a symbol of divine protection and a "feminine" mask that prevents the true Russia from revealing itself by keeping its "masculine" dimension out of sight. "The world war," Berdiaev argues, "will show the world Russia's face, forge a masculine spirit."[400] So far, the "Russian spirit" has been "wrapped in the *pokrov* of the national mother"; now the war is poised to "reveal Russia's face . . . unmask the falsehood of life, throw off *pokrovy*."[401] The mask motif is reinforced when Russia is accused of not "exposing" or "revealing" its "masculine principle."[402] In a later essay, Berdiaev reverts to the *pokrov* motif in a more traditional manner and speaks of the "eternal wish [of the Russian people] to hide in the folds of the garments of the Mother of God."[403]

In 1909 Ivanov also takes recourse to the *pokrov* motif in "Terror Antiquus," albeit in a universal-mystical rather than a national context. Referring to the Vedantic goddess Maya, he proclaims the earth a bride and speaks of her "virginity behind . . . the deceptive charm of her eyes, under the splendidly woven veil of the mysteriously and dualistically smiling Maya."[404] In his Dostoevsky review, Ivanov compares Russia in its hypostasis of bride to the Mother of God, whose "most invisible *pokrovy*" are out of the reach of the "demons" who threaten her.[405]

Clearly, both Berdiaev and his contemporaries personify Russia as a mystical bride. These personifications merge with those of Blok and other poets in a number of respects, including the emphasis put on a rural Russia and a "Russia of the people," rather than on the official Russia. They also share Blok's preoccupation with nineteenth-century prototypes. More than his poetic antipodes, however, Berdiaev focuses on the place of feminized Russia within an androgynous philosophy. Central to his thought, therefore, is her interaction with a masculine counterforce.

The Intelligentsia: Bridegroom, Husband, Leader

In an early text, Berdiaev notes that the feminine question is to an equal extent a masculine issue.[406] This is certainly true of his view of Russia as a feminine entity, whose correlation with a masculine force is at the very heart of the works discussed in this study. Over and over, Berdiaev stresses the need for a feminized Russia to unite in a mystical marriage with a masculine force. Crucial to his view of their union are motifs of anticipation: the personified Russia needs to shift "from expectation to creation"; and the Russian people always "wait for a bridegroom, a husband, a leader" and "for chosen ones of such high quality that they can authoritatively lead [the feminized people] toward a more humane life."[407]

Berdiaev's concept of a feminine-masculine union recycles elements of the pagan cult of the earth as a feminine force, including the tale of the earth's fertilization. In *The Soul of Russia*, for instance, he claims that man "fertilized [the earth] with his logos."[408] In "Terror Antiquus," Ivanov similarly speaks of the feminine earth's "fertilization" by "masculine energy" and masculine "Logos."[409] At the same time, as these quotations suggest, the marriage of the two principles is envisioned as a mystical communion in the manner of Gnostic and mystical-alchemic tradition. For Berdiaev, elements of both are refracted, as light through a prism, at frequent meetings in 1909 with groups of religious sectarians in the Iama café in Moscow and, later, at his house.[410] A general admirer of Gnostic and German mystical thought, Berdiaev regards his religious acquaintances as "Gnostics of the common people" (1:228). In his autobiography, he observes that during his talks with sectarians, "I often recognized thoughts that I knew from reading J. Boehme and other Christian mystics-theosophists" (1:229). In *The Meaning of Creation*, Berdiaev elaborates on the influence of Boehme and Gnostic thought on his own philosophy (2:220). His vision of the symbolic marriage of a feminized Russia and her metaphysical spouse is in keeping with their view of gender: he envisions it as a mystical union in which the masculine and feminine counterparts not only meet, but also coalesce. Hence, the works discussed here contain, besides marital metaphors, numerous calls to Russia to *become* masculine. In *The Soul of Russia*, for instance, Berdiaev speaks of an "immanent awakening of a masculine, light-bearing conscience" as a basic need for Russia.[411]

Thus, Berdiaev opposes a feminized Russia to a force that is depicted either as her mystical bridegroom or as an immanent masculine element. As in the case of the feminine category, he attributes a set of recurring stereotypically masculine characteristics to this counterforce. It is "strong," "active," "creative," "form-endowing," "light-bearing"—and associated with "logos," "consciousness," or "the spirit," as opposed to the "chaos," "spontaneity," and "soul" of its feminine counterpart.[412] In addition, if Berdiaev associates the mystical bride Russia with nature and calls her anticultural, then he connects her masculine counterforce with culture or alienation from nature (3:417). He stresses the importance of Orthodox Christianity or "the Church" as the masculine counterforce for Russia's femininity par excellence (3:418, 422, 427).

As implied by this comparative analysis, the characteristics of Berdiaev's masculine counterforce form antithetical pairs with Russia's "feminine" features. Schematically represented, his conception of the feminized Russia and her masculine consort would look like this:

Mystical bride	Mystical bridegroom
Feminine principle	Masculine principle
Weakness	Strength
Passivity	Activity
Chaos / Formlessness	Logos / Form-endowment
Spontaneity (*stikhiinost'*)	Consciousness
Soul	Spirit
Darkness	Light
Paganism	Christianity
Nature	Culture

Similar antithetical pairs can be reconstructed from Ivanov's and Bulgakov's views on Russia and the intelligentsia. Ivanov opposes a feminine earth to a masculine principle that he associates with the sun, energy, fertilization, Christianity, and logos in "Terror Antiquus."[413] In his interpretations of Dostoevsky, Myshkin and Stavrogin appear—in a specifically Russian context—as precisely such masculine principles.[414] "Russian Tragedy" ("Russkaia tragediia"), Sergei Bulgakov's review of *The Demons*, projects a similar view of a feminine Russian earth and her alleged need for a male "Logos."[415] Florenskii echoes most of the features mentioned when speaking of a "feminine" Russia's need for "male self-awareness and spiritual self-determination, the creation of 'stateliness,' a stable way of life, a display of all its creative activity in art and science, and a development of the economy."[416]

As Oleg Riabov has argued, in their attribution of antithetical features to the masculine and feminine spheres, the authors in question were inspired by Aristotelian thought and the Apollonian-Dionysian opposition in Nietzsche's then-popular philosophy.[417] They also followed traditional feminine-masculine oppositions. As mentioned earlier, the feminist theoretician Cixous marked the same passivity-activity, nature-culture, and dark-light antitheses as recurring feminine-masculine oppositions in Western thought. In addition, the chaos-logos antithesis links Berdiaev's philosophy with Solov'ev's philosophy, in which the opposition of Sophia/chaos to ratio/logos figured prominently. Solov'ev also formulated this opposition in terms of feminine/passive/formless as opposed to masculine/active/form-endowing features.

Berdiaev is linked to Solov'ev by more than his view of gender, however. Their works correspond in a sociopolitical sense, too. As we saw, to Solov'ev the opposition of a feminine Sophia to a masculine logos mirrors the antithesis between Russia and a westernized intelligentsia. A relatively marginal concept for Solov'ev, this sociopolitical gender metaphor becomes pivotal to Berdiaev's writings of the 1910s. Although at times he appeals to "Russian man" in general to counterbalance what he sees as Russia's excessive femininity, to him no social category can better fulfill the male role than "the intelligentsia."[418]

Berdiaev's definition of this category is even vaguer than Blok's. In his 1910 review, the philosopher speaks of the "union between the intelligentsia and the people" as a marriage between, quite specifically, the "cultural intelligentsia" and the common people (3:416). As representatives of this group—which he describes as a broad social stratum, containing "the old-style Russian revolutionary and populist, and the new-style Russian decadent and mystic"—Berdiaev appoints Belyi's hero Dar'ial'skii and Belyi himself (3:417). In "On the Eternally Womanish in the Russian Soul," he tags Rozanov as the intelligentsia's representative. Berdiaev links him in this respect to Dostoevsky and the Slavophiles and, in a contemporary context, to the neo-Slavophile sentiments of Bulgakov, Ivanov, and Ern (3:351, 353). In his article "Stavrogin" (1914), Berdiaev projects the metaphor of the intelligentsia as Russia's bridegroom onto Dostoevsky's hero, whose aristocratic origins are stressed and who is proclaimed a "symbol of metaphysical squiredom" (3:108).

In the examples mentioned, "the intelligentsia" is embodied in a concrete—literary or historical—exponent of the cultural intelligentsia. In his work from the period of the October Revolution and the civil war, Berdiaev abandons this personifying tendency. At this time he ascribes the role of Russia's predestined bridegroom-*intelligent* specifically to contemporary revolutionary segments of the society. In *The Philosophy of Inequality*, written in direct response to the October Revolution, he addresses "people of the revolution of today," "populists," "Social Democrats," *and* "radicals" as that part of the intelligentsia responsible for a feminized Russia's welfare (4:267ff., 276–77, 282–83). Elsewhere in this treatise, he appeals to a broader circle, which he calls the "Russian intelligentsia boys": "you, Russian revolutionaries, socialists, anarchists, nihilists," and—indicating the liberal aristocratic intelligentsia with which he identified—"some of us" (4:273). Further in the text the circle widens even more: as Russia's intended masculine counterpart, the philosopher now addresses "you, more moderate Russian socialists and Russian radicals of all nuances, Russian enlighteners, you, descending from Belinskii, from the Russian critics, from the Russian populists" (4:279). Berdiaev regards the Bolsheviks as a radical variant of these categories, which ultimately destroys all others (ibid.). While earlier associating "the intelligentsia" with the aristocracy, he now opposes the Bolsheviks' *"intelligentskaia* moral" to an "aristocratic" creation (4:281).

Berdiaev's "intelligentsia" thus encompasses a number of varying social categories. It is this diffuse group, in his view, that should fulfill the role of Russia's bridegroom or its "form-endowing" masculine counterpart.

Contemporaries likewise tend to see the—seldom clearly defined—intelligentsia as Russia's supreme masculine consort. To Bulgakov, Stavrogin, in his role as Khromonozhka's lover, represents "the intelligentsia" that needs to provide Russia with the "masculine principle of the Logos."[419] Ivanov, if never explicitly reverting to the term "intelligentsia," does point in that direction by appointing Stavrogin as the Christlike "intended bridegroom" of the Russian earth.[420] Florenskii's depiction of Russia's sorely needed male stimulus suggests that he specifically saw the religious and intellectual elite as obliged to fulfill this role.[421]

As shown, the thinkers in question undoubtedly envisioned the intelligentsia as Russia's primary mystical bridegroom. The works discussed here were written, however, mostly as a critique of that very intelligentsia. They all circle around the notion that the intelligentsia is not capable of the task for which it is predestined—in other words, that it is an *ineffectual* bridegroom.

Berdiaev, to start with, subscribes to the traditional view that the intelligentsia's relationship with Russia is troubled. He claims that Russia's *intelligenty* have "lost touch with the people" (3:417, 423), but, in a paradoxical twist, he also blames its problems on the fact that—being Russian—the Russian intelligentsia inevitably forms part of that people and of Russia itself. Hence, he asserts, the intelligentsia suffers from the same weakness—and, consequently, femininity—that afflicts the Russian people as a whole. Programmatic is his assertion in the Belyi review that "the Russian intelligentsia [was in fact always feminine]: (it was) capable of heroic deeds, of offers, of giving its life, but it was [never] capable of masculine activity . . . it gave it-self to the elements; it did not appear as a bearer of the Logos" (3:416–17).

In his article on Rozanov, Berdiaev extends the view of a feminine in-telligentsia. He declares Rozanov to be a representative of "the intelligent-sia" as well as "the people," with whom he shares a "feminine passivity," "lack of masculinity," and "pre-Christian" "paganism" (3:351–52, 356, 361). Throughout the writings discussed here, Berdiaev continues to attribute this list of characteristics to the intelligentsia.[422] In a virulent pun, he summarizes the attitude of both the Russian people and the intelligentsia (embodied in Rozanov) toward the state as *bab'e i rab'e*, or "womanish and slavish" (3:356, 361). Whether or not intentionally, this designation immediately evokes Rus-sia's nineteenth-century authors and their "womanish" heroes-*intelligenty*.

As he did in his critique of the Russian people, Berdiaev links the features in question not only with femininity but also with childishness. He repeatedly equates the intelligentsia's alleged lack of masculinity to "ado-lescent immaturity" and the *intelligenty* themselves to "boys" who need to "become men."[423] Rozanov similarly speaks of a tradition of "boyishness" within Russia's intelligentsia: "all—professors, academicians—are boys."[424] In a more positive vein, Ivanov refers in "Living Legend" to himself and his colleagues as "Dostoevsky's former 'Russian boys.'"[425] If Ivanov explicitly refers only to Dostoevsky, then Turgenev and the radical critics are likely to have served as an additional source of inspiration for the childhood meta-phor of him and his colleagues. As shown in chapter 1, nineteenth-century metaphoric representations of the intelligentsia as children accentuated the same weakness, submissiveness, and passivity that become crucial in Berdi-aev's philosophy. That radical critics might have influenced his views directly is suggested by a number of observations about Chernyshevskii and Pisarev in Berdiaev's autobiography.[426]

Riabov has argued that Berdiaev's view of the intelligentsia makes him part of a general historiosophical-political discourse in which the intel-ligentsia is envisioned, simultaneously, as a near-saint and ultimate *Kultur-träger* and as weak, submissive, and excessively effeminate.[427] This opposi-tion is formulated repeatedly in terms of the savior-undoer paradigm that Iurii Lotman discerns as a central concept in nineteenth-century literature. The thinkers discussed here particularly saw Stavrogin, in his alleged role of representative of the intelligentsia, in such terms. Given their rootedness in the Russian religious renaissance, it is not surprising that they use religious terms in references to the intelligentsia's double-edged position. Berdiaev ascribes Stavrogin's failure to unite with Khromonozhka or "the Russian earth" to a combination of "the divine" and "the demonic" in his character (3:104, 108). Ivanov equates Stavrogin's betrayal of Khromonozhka with a betrayal of Russia, branding him a "divine envoy" and, at the same time, a "carrier of Satanic force."[428] Bulgakov literally applies the "savior-undoer" opposition to Stavrogin's inner struggle—and, by extension, to that of the Russian intelligentsia—involving the Antichrist and "Christ, loved and desired by the Russian soul."[429] Five years earlier, in "Heroism and Asceticism," he had labeled "religious recovery" the only solution to "the intelligentsia's ugly maximalism."[430]

A question to which Berdiaev pays little attention is that of the origins of the alleged femininity of both Russia and its intelligentsia. Riabov has asserted that Berdiaev ascribes it to three key factors: the purported femininity of the Slavs in general, the pagan or sectarian elements in Russian religion, and the "want of a chivalrous principle in Russian history."[431] To Berdiaev, however, the first two notions are aspects rather than causes of Russia's femininity.[432] He does offer two possible explanations for the intelligentsia's or Russia's "feminine-weak" character: the "boundlessness" of Russian space and the lack of a chivalrous tradition in Russia comparable to that in medieval Europe.[433] Here Berdiaev strikes a tender chord—or so one is led to believe from the work of his colleagues, who repeatedly describe the intelligentsia in knightly terms. In his 1907 critique of the First Duma, Rozanov discusses the need for a political-intellectual alternative in the form of a "noble knight" who needs to liberate the "bride" Russia;[434] Ivanov represents the Slavophiles in their quest for an authentic Russia as "a fairy-tale hero" in search of his bride in "Living Legend";[435] and, in his essay on the Holy Trinity–St. Sergius Lavra, Florenskii opposes a feminine Kievan Rus' to Saint Cyril, portraying the latter as a bridegroom who preserved "his chivalry to the Heavenly Virgin."[436] Contemporaries even perceived of Berdiaev himself—as had been done in the case of Blok—as a knight.[437]

Thus, although Berdiaev and other early twentieth-century thinkers do regard the intelligentsia as Russia's mystical savior-bridegroom, they see it as incapable of fulfilling its task. They insist that the intellectual elite, as part of Russia, suffers from the same "feminine" deficiencies endured by the Russian people: passivity, weakness, and servitude, or a "womanish and slavish," *bab'e-i-rab'e*, mentality. What is the object of this supposed *bab'e-i-rab'e* attitude of the intelligentsia? This question brings us to the metaphor's third component: the state.

The State and the West: False Bridegrooms

As I pointed out at the beginning of this chapter, Berdiaev claims that Russia has submitted herself to "several husbands that entered from without." Similar formulations abound throughout his oeuvre. In *The Soul of Russia*, Russia "awaits a bridegroom . . . but instead of the one promised her, a

German bureaucrat ... takes possession of her";[438] in "On the Eternally Womanish in the Russian Soul," "the great problem of the Russian soul ... lies in its tendency to marry a foreign and alien husband" (3:361); and in "The Religious Foundation of Bolshevism," "the Russian soul ... is always awaiting a bridegroom and always mistaking the false one for her promised one" (4:35).

Politics is never far away in Berdiaev's amorous images, and the same is true here. He sees the intelligentsia as Russia's true but ineffectual mystical bridegroom. As such, he opposes it to a "false" or "unpredestined" foreign bridegroom, who successfully serves as its amorous rival. In his works, this rival is a metaphoric representation of either the Russian state or the West.

What Berdiaev understands precisely by "the state" or "the West" in this context is difficult to pinpoint. The Belyi review marks the start of his use of gendered terms to inveigh against the huge impact that Western philosophical ideas are having on Russian intellectuals. He criticizes Western thought as "masculine doctrines" to which a "feminine" Russian intelligentsia has submitted itself (4:274). In language that can be traced to Solov'ev and the Slavophiles, he repeatedly blames the Russian intelligentsia for a superficial or "unmanly attitude" toward "Western consciousness."[439] Berdiaev specifically denounces German thought as "the masculine German spirit" from which the intelligentsia seeks its "fertilization."[440] Thus, he defies Belyi's passion for gnoseology and the philosopher Heinrich Rickert, and he repeatedly criticizes Russian intellectuals' infatuation with the unexpected threesome of Karl Marx, Immanuel Kant, and Rudolf Steiner.[441] In his revolutionary-era writings, Berdiaev refutes Social Democratic thought as "German attire" for the revolutionary *intelligenty* to parade in.[442]

The critique of the intelligentsia's preoccupation with Western thought coincides with Berdiaev's repeated attack on Western influences in Russian state policies. Relying on the dual image that developed in the nineteenth century, he asserts that in Russia the state "often seemed a foreign authority"—one saturated with German influences and particularly German bureaucracy.[443] Although he ascribes the mental dependency on the West specifically to the intelligentsia, he blames the Russian people as a whole for the "exclusive power of Germanism in ... the life of our state."[444]

If Berdiaev relies on old traditions here, he does the same in his depiction of Peter the Great as the cardinal representative of Western or bureaucratic influences within the Russian state. In his view,

> Peter was a masculine appearance in the Russian state. But Peter was a violator rather than a husband. He violated the feminine soul of the Russian people. ... Part of the people saw Peter as the Antichrist. Later, however, the

people submissively obeyed the German bureaucratic principle that entered through Peter. (4:270)

This gendered concept of the relationship between Peter the Great and Russia virtually echoes the portrayal of Peter as Europe's lover in Danilevskii's *Russia and Europe* (see chapter 1). Berdiaev proves to be equally cognizant of Danilevskii when asserting in *The Soul of Russia* that, for Russia, western Europe—particularly Germany—is "the object of passionate feelings and dreams of love and, alternately, of enormous hate and fear."[445]

Rozanov ponders the relationship between Russia and "the West" in similar terms, but his conclusion differs radically from Berdiaev's. He opposes Russia to an authoritative foreign principle as well, the latter of which he embodies in three guises: the Norsemen, the Germans, and the European mentality.[446] He also views this relationship in gendered terms, but his opinion of Russia's role is more optimistic.

> If we turn to . . . the eighteenth and nineteenth centuries, when vivid contact between the Russians and the "masculine" European principle is renewed . . . it is as if from outside . . . one sees the "subordination of the Russians," but now, in fact, a more *inner possession* of these very subordinators is taking place. . . . Alas! The husband does not "possess the wife" . . . actually, the wife "possesses the husband."[447]

Here Rozanov distinguishes Russia's outer appearance—subordinate to foreign influences—from its alleged inner superiority. He interprets the relationship between the Norsemen and Russia in similar terms.[448] To him, "the more devoted" and "unselfish" the submission of the "bride" Russia to "foreign influences" is, "the stronger . . . her effect on the one to whom she 'submit[s]'" will be.[449]

While both Rozanov's and Berdiaev's views on Russia and the state clearly rely on Slavophile thought, their adaptations of it are embedded in their philosophy of androgyny. Berdiaev's view of Peter the Great, for example, centers on the interaction between a "masculine" and a "feminine" element. In "On the Eternally Womanish in the Russian Soul," the Russian people "pose as a bride . . . in relation to the colossus of the state" (3:352). *The Soul of Russia* relays this thought: "State authority has always been an external instead of an internal principle for the stateless Russian people; it . . . came, as it were, from outside, as a bridegroom comes to his bride."[450]

Stressing the state's "masculinity" and "authority," Berdiaev diametrically opposes this metaphoric bridegroom to the "feminized" intelligentsia.[451] Pivotal to this opposition is, again, the focus on a disturbed gender balance. If Berdiaev claims that Russia and the intelligentsia suffer from excessive femininity, he accuses the West or the state of overdeveloped masculinity. He calls the "German spirit"—the West's representative par excellence—"limitedly masculine" and too "abstract, alienated from femininity."[452] In 1908, in the same vein, Rozanov opposes the Russian state, as a "cruel" and "practical" muzhik, to the revolution, as *"baba"*—comparing the former to both Chichikov and "little daddy the general" in *Dead Souls.* [453] In *The War of 1914,* Rozanov later stresses the "hyperbolical masculinity" of military state power as opposed to his—the Russian *intelligent*'s—femininity.[454] During the war years, he opposes a feminine Russia in "Near the Russian Idea" to "the Germans—a masculine tribe," the Norsemen, and a "masculine 'European principle.'" He associates these three male opponents with, respectively, "violence, rule, and authority"; a "warlike, iron" character; and "pride, seizure, and rule."[455]

The view of the German mentality as masculine also marks the writings of Berdiaev's and Rozanov's contemporaries. Bulgakov speaks of "typical German unfemininity" (*bezzhennost'*) in his treatise *Unfading Light* (*Svet nevechernii,* 1916).[456] In a 1915 collection of essays, *The Sword and the Cross* (*Mech i krest*), Ern observes an "anomaly of abstract masculinity and a denial of a positive feminine essence" in the German people.[457] In approximately the same period, the journalist-satirist O. M. Men'shikov attributes a "beastly masculinity" to the Germans as opposed to what he considers the Slavs' meek femininity.[458]

Obviously, the tendency to represent a foreign force as excessively or aggressively masculine is universal in wartime rhetoric. The same cannot be said of the interpretation of Peter the Great as Russia's violator, which is motivated by internal political friction. In Berdiaev's adaptation, the concept is embedded fully in his gendered view of state and intelligentsia. Contemporaries—both in the philosophical and literary sphere—also stage Peter I as the violator of a feminized Russia, albeit never as directly related to the intelligentsia as in Berdiaev's work. Christa Ebert reconstructs a view of Peter's reforms as the "rape of Russia's soul" in Aleksei Remizov's fairy tales.[459] In 1905 Merezhkovskii symbolizes Peter's infatuation with the West in *Antichrist* through the ruler's erotic interest in a statue of Venus shipped to Russia from Europe. If Peter's sense of revulsion at Russia's purported backwardness is expressed through his physical disgust toward a Mother of God icon, then the imported statue is equated to the "new Russia" and Peter, who "grabbed her with both hands, as if in embrace," to its sculptor.[460] A critical indication of the problematic relationship between Peter and his "new Russia" resonates when he is imagined hacking at the statue—which is about to fall apart—"in the air."[461]

Where Merezhkovskii's novel can be considered a pretext for Berdiaev's view of Peter the Great and Russia, Mariia Shkapskaia's poem cycle

"Russia" is likely to have been a reaction to that view. Written in the early 1920s, the cycle offers a view of Russia as a meek wife who forgives Peter the Great his amorous escapade with "another," the West:

> Russia awaits Peter to come to her.
>
> . . .
>
> And he walks with confident step,
> Leaving his council behind,
>
> . . .
>
> Authoritatively, he tears off his wife's
> Veils with a masculine hand,
> And for a long time their amorous whisper
> Disturbs the rest of the fortress.
>
> . . .
>
> Torn to blood were her hands,
>
> . . .
>
> You [Russia] stood like a stone *baba*,
> When the Master appealed to you.
>
> . . .
>
> And, in answer to his
> European mistake, Russia, You,
>
> . . .
>
> Softened your Scythian traits.[462]

The link between this poem and Berdiaev's philosophy is not hard to recognize. Shkapskaia echoes not only his representation of Peter I and Russia as an amorous couple, but also the characterization of Peter as a feminized Russia's authoritative masculine violator. The association with Berdiaev is reinforced by Shkapskaia's use of the term *baba*, a crucial concept in Berdiaev's critique of Russia.

Aside from the concepts mentioned, the fairy-tale motif of evil forces that capture a princess colors Berdiaev's gendered representations of the state and the West, although less prominently than it does in Blok's work. The captor motif can be felt in his assertion, in *The Soul of Russia*, that "bride Russia" is in "eternal danger of being held captive, of being submissive to that which is outside it."[463] Berdiaev envisions the "disclosing of its inner masculinity" as Russia's mystical "liberation from any captivity."[464]

Before Berdiaev appeared on the scene, Rozanov had already used the metaphor of a captive beauty in his 1907 "New Year" article, which represented Russia as a bride in need of a knight to free her from the humiliation imposed by the First Duma.[465] In 1909 Bulgakov, referring to Dostoevsky's *Demons*, described Russia and the intelligentsia as "possessed" by a "legion of demons" from which they needed to be "freed."[466] He equated the "possessed" intelligentsia with the biblical Shulamit and her eternal search for a bridegroom.[467] In what seems to be a response to Bulgakov's essay, Rozanov recalls the figure of Shulamit in the same context in the 1910s, in *The War of 1914,* in which he identifies himself—as self-proclaimed "feminine" exponent of the intelligentsia—with Shulamit's vain search for a male lover.[468]

Most elaborately, however, the plot of a feminine Russia held captive by evil forces appears in the writings of Viacheslav Ivanov. In "Living Legend" he appeals to the Slavophiles to liberate Russia, whom he envisages as a bride held captive by evil forces.[469] He summarizes the plot of a number of Dostoevsky's novels with these words: "A divine envoy . . . needs to free the World soul who lies in the chains of evil spells; and to dissolve the chains of Andromeda, to . . . awaken the Sleeping Beauty."[470] By superimposing this mythical plot on the relationship between Stavrogin and Khromonozhka, Ivanov links it with his symbolic view of the intelligentsia and Russia as a mystical marriage.[471] In an interpretation that is evocative of Bulgakov's thoughts on the subject, Ivanov reads *The Demons* as a symbolic intrigue involving the "feminine" Russian earth, a "masculine" mystical bridegroom, and demonic forces.[472] From Ivanov's perspective, Dostoevsky envisions "how a demonic 'Legion' excludes the masculine principle of inner life from the sphere of influence affecting the soul of the people . . . and how its feminine principle, the Russian Earth-Soul . . . languishes in expectation of its groom, the Christian hero."[473] In the novel, the "mystical bridegroom" Stavrogin is, in fact, a demonic force, a Pretender—a politically fraught plot development that Ivanov, however, does not take into consideration.

If the religious-mystical perspective dominates Ivanov's work, in Ern's *The Sword and the Cross* this point of view acquires an overtly political dimension. To Ern, the German army represents a "German Dragon"; both Russia and "the soul of the German people themselves" are its "female prisoners."[474]

There can be no doubt that Berdiaev and contemporary thinkers viewed the tripod Russia, intelligentsia, and state (or alternatively, the West) as a gendered triangle. In their works, the concept of Russia as unattainable beloved—a notion poetically shaped by Blok—gains an explicitly politico-philosophical basis. Whether their response to Blok's gendered metaphor was always a conscious one is not the issue here. What does make Berdiaev a crucial figure in the history of the metaphor is the reappearance in his work of concepts that Blok formulated in the poetic sphere and which

Berdiaev underpins with a more explicit and more elaborate intellectual argumentation. One could say that Berdiaev brings the metaphor even more into the open. Not surprisingly, intellectuals of later generations will develop a view of Russia that is firmly rooted in both Blok's poetically gendered metaphors and Berdiaev's androgynous philosophy. This group includes the canonical writers and thinkers of the Soviet period whose texts we turn to next.

Virgin Russia Meets Lenin and Stalin:

The Soviet Years

TECHNICALLY SPEAKING, a discussion of bridal Russia representations in Soviet culture would encompass the years 1917 through 1990. This chapter focuses solely on the period between the late 1920s and the late 1960s, however. There are reasons for this perhaps unconventional categorization. In the previous chapter we saw that 1920s (and even some 1930s) renditions of the metaphor tend to be mere repetitions of moves by authors who had used the same concept earlier. Most of them were written in emigration and were utterly inaccessible to Russian readers at the time of writing. In addition, the end of the 1920s marks the onset of what Billington calls a "new monolithic culture"—a cultural era that coincides with Stalin's consolidation of power and replaces the experimental, cosmopolitan atmosphere that had prevailed until well into the 1920s.[1] This uniform culture is unable to ban dissident voices completely, however, and in the 1960s it begins to dissipate gradually. From the late 1960s on, artistic developments take place that should be linked to international postmodernism rather than to a strictly Soviet setting. These developments are discussed in more detail in the next chapter. The focus here is on the presence of the metaphor in the intervening years.

At first glance, the gendered metaphor seems to disappear during this time. The very specific metaphor of Russia as *unattainable* bride is indeed missing from official Soviet culture. Elements of pre-revolutionary philosophical discourse do leave their mark on socialist realist art, though. In fact, socialist realism preserves several symbols and dichotomies that had typified intellectual debate during the early decades of the century. As Katerina Clark asserts in 1981, Soviet literature uses "signs" which "encapsulate the polemics and dilemmas of the Russian intelligentsia that have been constant from at least the mid-nineteenth century to the present day."[2] One of these signs is the spontaneous-conscious antithesis to which the late-imperial intellectual elite reverted in discussions on the people-and-intelligentsia issue.

In Leninist and socialist realist discourse, this dichotomy is preserved and "transcoded" to the Soviet context.[3] Lenin's rhetoric, for example, "is full of imagery about bringing 'light' to the 'darkness' of the Russian people"—an act that he views as a triumph of the consciousness of intellectuals over the spontaneity of the people.[4]

It is difficult not to see the similarities between this rhetoric and, in particular, Berdiaev's opposition of people to intelligentsia in terms of dark versus light or spontaneity versus consciousness. In Lenin's rendition, however, the terminology does not appear within the problematic gendered context so typical of the early twentieth century: he focuses on an oncoming union between workers and intellectuals rather than on the lack of such a union, and he does not allegorize their contact in gendered terms.

This is not to say that female representations of Russia were uncommon in formal Soviet culture. According to Hans Günther, "in the 1930s we constantly encounter a parallel modeling of a woman and the Native land, a woman and the earth and so on."[5] The tendency to personify Russia as a female figure also flourished during the Second World War. As Lynne Attwood points out, a number of Soviet films feature "war heroines [who] symbolize both the Soviet Union and its moral fortitude."[6] Pat Simpson discerns a trend in the early 1940s to lay "particular emphasis on the mother as incarnation of the Motherland" in paintings and posters.[7] These personifications should be regarded within the context of the Stalinist myth of the "great family." In Clark's words, in the "great family" myth "the society's leaders became 'fathers' . . . ; the national heroes, model 'sons'; the state, a 'family' or 'tribe.'"[8] Günther's studies have shown that, within this myth, Russia or the Russian earth fulfills the role of archetypal nurturing mother.[9]

Accordingly, research did pick up on allegorical representations of Soviet Russia as a mother. It has paid less attention to the bridal or erotic connotations that this figure can acquire. Yet such connotations are far from uncommon in Soviet literature and art. Lebedev-Kumach's lyrics to "March of the Native Land" ("Marsh o rodine"), for example—sung in the popular Soviet musical *Circus* (*Tsirk*, 1936)—conclude with "Like a bride we love our native land, / we cherish it, like a tender mother."[10] In Mikhail Sholokhov's *Virgin Soil Upturned* (*Podniataia tselina*, 1932–60), one of the canonical novels of socialist realism,[11] the Russian earth is characterized as "a mare; when she's in heat you must hurry to put the stallion to her, for she won't look at him when her time is past. That is how the earth relates to man."[12] The Russian earth is sexualized even more explicitly—and in terms that evoke pre-revolutionary discourse—in Maxim Gorky's praise of his colleague, Mikhail Prishvin, whose works focused on rural life in the Soviet Union. "In your books, this sense of the earth . . . sounds to me remarkably comprehensible, as you are husband and son of the Great Mother. Does this sound like incest? But after all, that's just what it is: man, born of the earth, makes her fruitful with his labor."[13] Together with the other examples mentioned, Gorky's words may suggest that the pre-Soviet tendency to discuss Russia in bridal terms continued unbroken in Soviet culture. Crucial to all of them, however, is the exclusively *un*problematic relationship of the poet or "the Russian man" toward the feminized Russia. Only Sholokhov's tone is not unequivocally positive, but man attains a (sexual) union with the earth in his novel, too.

By contrast, gender allegories of Russia with a more negative or tragic bias are harder to find in official Soviet culture. This is due largely to the rigid cultural atmosphere of the age, in which any notion of political or social discord is considered taboo. As a result, the fierce political debate that marks the first decades of the century becomes virtually paralyzed. What commences are "decades of constrained formulaic commentaries about politics, nationality, ethnicity, human rights, and the economy," which "precluded reflection and discussion"—in the words of Jeffrey Brooks.[14] Within this obligatorily optimistic public culture, conflict of either a social or an amorous nature is basically nonexistent. Within the literary realm, this is particularly true of the years after socialist realism is proclaimed the leading dogma. In Vera Dunham's words, in socialist realism "happy endings abounded: boys got girls; tractors got repaired; job and family conflicts were resolved."[15] Hence, if parallel modeling of the amorous and social spheres stands firm in Soviet literature, it does so in a distinctly positive context. Quite obviously, the boy-does-*not*-get-girl plot and the social critique of the "unattainable bride" metaphor are a poor fit for official literary formulas.

Nor can the concept of an adversarial intelligentsia as Russia's symbolic suitor be accepted in an official culture pervaded by "the precept that one's true spouse and parent is the Party and the nation-state."[16] In general, "the intelligentsia" is a problematic social category within the socialist utopia. Before coming to power, the revolutionary movement formulated the same desire to bridge the gulf between the intellectual elite and the ordinary people as did the writers discussed in chapter 2. Once the revolution has taken place and Soviet power is consolidated, however, the gulf has supposedly dissolved. The tendency to conceive of the intelligentsia-people relationship as problematic contradicts this official view. Not fortuitously, the term "intelligentsia" is given a new meaning in official Soviet usage: it is now applied, in one scholar's definition, to "urban professionals and service personnel of a recognizable modernizing twentieth-century sort."[17]

To this group as a whole, the authorities are not unsympathetic. Less congenial is the official attitude toward those who identify with the traditional aristocratic and artistic intelligentsia. The strivings and self-image of these intellectuals are, by definition, contrary to the new political regime.

They—and other profoundly critical thinkers—are viewed by the Soviet state as "little short of an internal enemy."[18] As a result, any literary expression of the cultural intelligentsia's traditional preoccupations, including the "bride Russia" metaphor, is doomed to be denied official publication, at the least.

Thus, the debate on Russia and the intelligentsia as a problematic amorous relationship practically vanishes from official Soviet culture by the 1930s. One might have expected that the metaphor would survive outside official circles. At first glance, however, even within alternative Soviet culture it seems to have become a marginal phenomenon. In critical texts that appear during this time, the allegory occurs far less often than it did in pre-Soviet years. Although dissident authors do revert to gender stereotypes when depicting Russia, they mostly turn to the same concept of the Russian land or earth as "mother" that dominates official Soviet literature.

This is particularly true of the Village Prose or Country Prose of the post-Thaw period, whose shared themes—as defined by Kathleen Parthé—include "the rural/urban split, criticism of government policy in the countryside, the revival of Russian national and religious sentiment, a search for national values, a concern for the environment, and a nostalgia generated by the loss of a traditional rural life."[19] Village Prose writers tend to personify Russia as a female force within a framework of dichotomies that are crucial to the pre-revolutionary debate: Russian versus non-Russian, male versus female, rural versus urban. They do not copy the pre-revolutionary conceptualization of Russia as a bridal figure, however. In David Gillespie's words, in Village Prose "little attention is paid to sexual relationships. . . . The dominant relationship . . . is . . . between parents—often grandparents—and children, in particular."[20]

From a sociopolitical perspective, it seems appropriate that the young bride of the early twentieth century is replaced in Village Prose—with its focus on the decay of Soviet Russia—by the ultimate monument of bygone days, an elderly (grand)mother. That erotic dimensions are nevertheless not inimical to Village Prose's babushka is demonstrated by the heroine in Aleksandr Solzhenitsyn's story "Matrena's House" ("Matrenin dvor," 1963). An elderly village woman, Matrena symbolically merges, in the eyes of the narrator, with traditional Russia. Throughout the narrative, this feminized Russia appears to him as an elderly, weakened woman, but in one passage he sees

> a pink-shaded twilight, from which Matrena appeared. Her cheeks seemed to me . . . to have a pink glow . . . I imagined . . . her blushing. . . . And [I imagined] . . . a song, a song under the sky, which the village had stopped singing long since. . . . Matrena's round face . . . tied with an old [*starcheskim*] faded shawl [*platochkom*] looked at me . . . afraid, girlish.[21]

115

Who else could this Matrena be but an older version of the Russia that Blok portrayed as a bride with "not an old [*starcheskim*] face" under its "colored shawl" (*platochkom*) and "glowing cheeks," whose "windblown songs" the poet connected with the "first tears of love"?[22] Solzhenitsyn's heroine is an exception, however: in general, the association of Russia with maternal, aged female figures dominates Village Prose.

There are several reasons for the small number of Soviet-era works in which Russia is personified as an unattainable beloved, the first and most obvious being the repression of nonconformist culture under Stalin. In contrast to the sphere of vivid intellectual debate that marked the early twentieth century, the Soviet era suffers from a total lack of possibilities for critical intellectual discourse and for the expression and publication of critical ideas. Those unofficial writings that do appear are often done in secrecy. Many are destroyed by the authorities and others published abroad or not until after the collapse of the Soviet regime.

Second, the marginalization of the metaphor during this period can be explained, from a thematic perspective, as a result of the change of regime. The new status quo entails a new balance of power and a shift in previous sociopolitical categories. The term "intelligentsia" undergoes a particularly substantial change. Not only is part of the traditional intelligentsia repressed and not only does the term refer officially to a professional social stratum, but several radical left-wing intellectuals have come to represent the very state they formerly opposed. As a result, as Clark tells us, "in the Soviet Union there is not something extrahistorical called 'the government' or 'the Party'. . . . The Party itself is in a sense only one group of that larger class called the intelligentsia."[23] Neither "the people" nor the notion of a struggle for the people preserves its previous meaning in this new social setting, where the state turns the task of improving the lot of the common man into a political propaganda instrument. Depriving it of its main discursive issue, the authorities thus leave the traditional intelligentsia empty-handed.

Hence, while intellectual opposition to the regime does not vanish as such in the Soviet period, the categories "intelligentsia," "state," and "people"—from which the early twentieth-century debate emanated—become diffuse, and opposition to them loses its topicality.[24] Consequently, the tendency to conceive of these categories as a problematic romantic intrigue plays a less prominent role in Russian culture of the Soviet period than it played earlier.

A closer examination, however, shows that the metaphor in question does retain a foothold in nonofficial Soviet culture. As mentioned in chapter 2, offshoots of the gender debate on state, intelligentsia, and Russia continued to surface occasionally after the 1920s, although mostly in work by emigrant authors recycling earlier ideas. The original debate and its by-products resonate in texts that are more Soviet-bound as well. Take Iurii Olesha's novella *Envy* (*Zavist'*, 1927), with its variation on the plot that features an outsider-*intelligent* (Kavalerov) and a representative of the state (Babichev) vying for the love of an attractive woman (Valia). If Olesha's Valia does not explicitly represent Russia, then the novel's male characters do describe her nostalgically as an exalted female hypostasis of "the glory of a past century" and of "our era"—in other words, of the tsarist Russia that has been replaced by the here and now of Soviet life.[25]

Envy is illustrative of a small but prominent body of nonofficial texts from the Soviet period in which the metaphor does occupy a central place. Focusing on these works, which run the gamut from drama and prose through political and esoteric writings to tattoos, I pay particular attention to two novels now considered canonical within Russian literature of the Soviet period: Andrei Platonov's *Happy Moscow* (written 1932–36) and Boris Pasternak's *Doctor Zhivago* (written 1930s–1955). A number of thematic similarities between *Doctor Zhivago* and Pasternak's *Blind Beauty* (a play written 1958–60) are also discussed. In addition, I briefly consider the occult treatise *Rose of the World,* written between 1950 and 1958 by the poet-cum-religious thinker Daniil Andreev; a politico-historically oriented passage from Vasilii Grossman's novel *Forever Flowing* (1963); and adaptations of the image in prison tattoos.

Although not discussed extensively in this analysis, another relevant Soviet-era work is the pseudo-academic "diary" of the philosopher and literary critic Georgii Gachev. In *National Images of the World: Kosmo-Psycho-Logos* (*Natsional'nye obrazy mira: Kosmo-psikho-logos,* published 1995), Gachev defines Russian culture in terms that rely palpably on existing gender metaphors. Marrying a rather eccentric literary criticism to philosophy and mysticism, he writes in 1967:

> In literary plots . . . it was organic for the woman (= Russia) to have at least two masculine hypostases: the State and the People (the legal, respectable husband and the intoxicating lover). In its purest form this [woman] is Tat'iana, . . . Goncharov's women . . . , Turgenev's women. . . . For the Russian man, however, it is natural to have . . . a heavenly . . . and earthly woman or, in Dostoevsky's case, an infernal and a rational one. . . . But it was between the People and the State . . . for their mutual contact, for these rivaling men . . . it was for them that the Word arose: literature, the intelligentsia, like a "stratum." Characteristic of the Russian intelligentsia are . . . feminine traits: softness, offer, and self-sacrifice. . . . The Russian man-*intelligent* is . . . effeminate . . . a monk who has devoted himself to Russia (loving in his heart only her, like a poor knight).[26]

The state as Russia's "respectable husband," a "feminine" intelligentsia: it is virtually impossible to read Gachev's gendered social categories as anything but a conscious echo of the early twentieth-century debate on Russia and the intelligentsia.

Obviously, Gachev's text could not have been influenced by an ongoing public debate involving Russia and the intelligentsia; at the time of writing, such a debate would have been out of the question. The same applies to the other works discussed in this chapter: their outlines are never motivated by a broad public discussion on the fate of Russia. Although most of the authors cited were acquainted with one another, they could not exchange ideas as actively and openly as their predecessors had done some decades earlier. Their works were mainly written in seclusion and, apart from *Blind Beauty*, were not published in Russia until the perestroika years.[27] Although *Doctor Zhivago*, *Rose of the World*, and *Forever Flowing* circulated in *tamizdat* and/or samizdat, they did so only from the 1970s on[28] and thus were unable to influence one another.[29] Nevertheless, in highly individual ways all the works discussed here expound on the debate from the foregoing decades— that in which Russia, state, and intelligentsia are represented as an amorous intrigue. At this point, however, the metaphoric intrigue is transposed to the particulars of the Soviet period, and emerging to play a decisive role in the romantic entanglement are developments leading to and following the October Revolution.

ANDREI PLATONOV: NEW MAN
SEEKS SOVIET SOPHIA

In some editions of *The Foundation Pit* (*Kotlovan,* 1929), the last lines are followed by a note in which Platonov explains the sociopolitical idea underlying this novel. Referring to the tragic fate of a central character—the little girl, Nastia—Platonov writes:

> Will the USSR-ess [*esesersha*] perish like Nastia, or will she grow up to be a whole person, a new historical society? This disquieting feeling shaped the theme of the work in question at the time the author wrote it. If the author made a mistake in depicting the downfall of the socialist generation in the form of a little girl's death, then this mistake originated only in his excessive anxiety over something dear, the loss of which would equal the destruction of not only the past but also the future.[30]

The decision to personify Soviet Russia as a female figure is no random choice for Platonov: he expands on the same metaphor in the unfinished novel *Happy Moscow*, which he begins a few years later. *Happy Moscow* relates the life and fate of Moskva (Russian for "Moscow") Ivanovna Chestnova, a girl growing up in early Soviet Russia. As research has shown, Moskva

118

functions as an allegory for both the city of Moscow and the whole of Stalinist Russia, particularly in its capacity as a future socialist heaven.[31]

In his typification of Moscow as Russia incarnate, Platonov echoes—in a distinctly Stalinist setting—feminine representations of Russia used by Blok, Berdiaev, and the like. Platonov deviates from early twentieth-century discourse, however, when he refuses to adopt the pro-Russian pathos of his predecessors.

Blok and Berdiaev used gendered metaphors to express social or political views on the problematic relationship involving the Russian state, the intelligentsia, and the people. Both identified with the issue personally. Platonov's explanatory note in *The Foundation Pit* might suggest that he is equally committed to the fate of the Russia personified in his writings. As Pia Berger-Bügel asserts, Platonov sincerely believes in "a new mankind . . . a better world."[32] However, as research has often noted, in his works Platonov "seems not to want to persuade anyone of anything, or to ask his reader to feel any particular feelings."[33] The "unsettling" effect of his language can also be observed in *Happy Moscow*, a text that differs from Blok's and Berdiaev's work in that it does not reflect unequivocal sociopolitical views.[34] Contrary to Blok's and Berdiaev's "brides Russia," Platonov's female personification of Russia can hardly be read as the expression of a specific author's personal view on political reality. In this sense, *Happy Moscow* forms a departure from the texts discussed earlier, as well as a prelude to the postmodern treatment of the metaphor, which largely dismisses authorial commitment.[35] The next chapter devotes more attention to the implications of this gradual shift from political to strictly literary spheres.

Moscow: Soviet Sophia Versus Soviet Lolita

Unlike *The Foundation Pit*'s allegorical Nastia, who enacts the role of a needy child, the heroine of *Happy Moscow* is depicted as a marriageable young woman.[36] A supreme beauty, Moscow is surrounded by male admirers who court her, propose marriage, or fantasize—mostly in vain—about her as their wife. To her suitors, Moscow embodies much more than seductive love: as illustrated in the sections that follow, a complex web of allegorical links ties Moscow to her spatial surroundings.

Moscow: Sophia

Platonov gives Moscow's body cosmic proportions. She is said to sense "the origin of all kinds of things" and to fill "the whole world with her attention" (19).[37] She appears as something akin to a divine creator of life when one lover asserts that "had it been possible to connect the whole world" to Moscow's heart, the result "could have regulated the course of events" (15).

Together with a number of other passages, those mentioned suggest a symbolic equivalence between the heroine and Solov'ev's concept of a feminine World Soul or Sophia—a connection repeatedly noted in research on the novel.[38] Platonov scholars have observed that the Sophia concept—particularly its erotic implication—is, in fact, pivotal to several of the author's works.[39] This is not surprising for a man who, at the start of his career, had written an essay entitled "The Soul of the World" ("Dusha mira," published in 1920). The extent to which the World-Soul concept in this early essay relies on pre-revolutionary models of femininity is indicated by Eliot Borenstein's claim that it is "more derivative than groundbreaking."[40]

Research also draws analogies between Platonov's heroine and that other feminine hypostasis of the otherworldly: Blok's Beautiful Lady.[41] Moscow Chestnova is particularly evocative of Blok's and Solov'ev's feminine principle in her fundamental duality: serving as both an ideal and the corruption of that ideal, this exalted female figure is linked inextricably with degeneration and sexual promiscuity.[42] A metaphoric allusion to corruption is the literal mutilation she suffers in losing a leg,[43] but hers is also a "vulgar, lying mind" in a "shameful state"; she says "foolish things" (38); and her walk is designated as "so self-important, so mocking" (67).

Within Platonov's poetics, the heroine's transformation comes to revolve around a "preoccupation with the life of the body, particularly in its unsavory or grotesque aspects."[44] A genuine "Soviet Lolita" (Natal'ia Kornienko's apt label), Moscow simultaneously embodies an ethereal feminine principle and a manifestly physical presence.[45] The novel highlights such markedly sexual elements of her body as nipples (66) and pubic hair (75), and opposes her to men who love even the most repelling aspects of her physique. Programmatic is the claim that "neither Moscow . . . herself, nor anything about her, however dirty, could have made Sartorius [an admirer] feel in the least squeamish, and he could have looked at the waste products of her body with the greatest of interest" (44; see also 75, 76).

In combination with her cosmic proportions, this dark-physical side allies Moscow with the Gnostic (fallen) Sophia idea which was so pivotal to early twentieth-century feminine representations of Russia.[46] As scholars have observed, her depiction echoes not only Solov'ev's version of this concept,[47] but also—and very explicitly so—the metamorphosis of Blok's Beautiful Lady into the promiscuous, demonic figure of "The Stranger" ("Neznakomka," 1906).[48]

Moscow: Nature

In the depiction of Moscow, the connotation of a world-regulating femi-nine force is linked closely to her allegorical relationship with nature and the pastoral idyll. Whereas scholars rightly emphasize her function as an embodiment of either an exalted feminine principle or the city of Mos-cow, it would be wrong to overlook the rural dimension of her character.[49] As a young girl, Moscow felt that "everything in [the world] was right for her," particularly while wandering "through the fields, over simple, poor land" (11). Upon seeing a collective farm, she muses: "There'll be a smell of bread, and little children snuffling away in the barns. And cows are lying in the pasture, and a dawn mist is forming above them. How I love seeing all this and being alive!" (45). Illustrative of her organic ties to the bucolic life are descriptions of her face, which is "peaceful and kind, like bread" (90); her body, which is made of the "same glittering nature" (*prirody*) as her dress (47) and oozes a "smell of nature and kindness" (54); and the smell of her sweat, which is reminiscent of "bread and of wide expanses of grass" (75).

Underlining her amorous affairs is Moscow's oneness with nature or the countryside. To her lover Sartorius, "all of nature" is encompassed in her body (45). During their first rendezvous, in rye fields on the outskirts of the city, Moscow takes off her shoes and walks barefoot on "the softness of the earth" (44). Upon leaving Sartorius, natural elements "touch" her: "The sun was shining on the silk of her dress, and the last drops of morning moisture, gathered from the tall grass, were drying on her hair" (47).

Moscow's metaphoric coalescence with nature and an idealized coun-tryside links her both to the classic nineteenth-century Russian heroines discussed in chapter 1 and to Blok's feminine-Russia hypostases.[50] This co-alescence is not the only thing that connects her to these heroines: she also shares with them an affinity with ordinary people—and, more specifically, with the Russian people.

Moscow: Moscow

If *Happy Moscow*'s male heroes are loners who spend much time by them-selves in apartments and offices, Moscow is constantly surrounded by people. She wants to flee from the scene of her private love affair with Sartorius "into the darkness of people and crowds" (50). Upon leaving him, Moscow explains: "What good is my life to me without people, without the whole of the USSR?" (48). This dimension of Moscow—as a "sexual hypostasis of the communal ideal," to quote Eric Naiman—brings us to a more tangible spatial concept to which Moscow is linked allegorically: the city of Moscow, or Soviet Russia as a whole.[51]

This allegorical-political dimension is not unique to *Happy Moscow.* As Thomas Seifrid has argued, Platonov's work from the late 1920s and early 1930s shows an "elaborate attention to social and political themes, particularly that of the state."[52] In turning to these themes, Platonov relies on national gender metaphors on more than one occasion. Sonia in *Chevengur* (1927–29), for instance, is—in Eliot Borenstein's words—"little more than an abstraction to the novel's central character, while the man who does actually sleep with her views her as the embodiment of Russia."[53] In a feminist study of Platonov, Philip Bullock interprets Nadezhda Bostaloeva in the story "Juvenile Sea" ("Iuvenil'noe more," 1931–32) as a Soviet counterpart of Marianne or Britannia; he reads the heroine of "Girl of the Rose" ("Devushka roza," 1945), who is raped by a German soldier, as an allegory for the Russian landscape.[54]

It is in *Happy Moscow,* however, that Platonov exploits the allegory of a feminine Russia—or Moscow—to the full. Moscow's status as a universal feminine principle is tightly interwoven with her symbolic link to the more concrete geopolitical spaces of Moscow, Soviet Russia, and socialism. Crucial is a vision of her by Sartorius, in which amorous and political concepts coalesce.

> Unknown to anyone, two feelings had met and combined together inside him—love for Moscow Chestnova and anticipation of socialism. His vague imagination held out a picture of summer: tall rye, the voices of millions of people who, for the first time, were organizing themselves on earth without being dragged down by poverty and sadness, and Moscow Chestnova, coming towards him from far away to be his wife. She had gone the rounds of life; together with countless others she had lived life through and had left the years of emotions and suffering behind her, in the darkness of her past youth; she was returning the same as she always had been, only barefoot, in a poor dress, with hands that had grown bigger from work, and yet she was clearer and merrier than before; she had found contentment for her wandering heart. (52–53)

Several of Moscow's characteristics converge here: in a setting reminiscent of Blok's poems on Russia (rural poverty; the role of mystical wife; and the phrase "the same as she always had been," which occurs repeatedly in Blok's evocations of a feminized Russia), she blends symbolically with both the countryside (walking "barefoot" through the rye) and the people (her position among "the voices of millions of people" and her life "together with countless others"). The hero explicitly links his amorous feelings for the mystical bride Moscow to his expectations for Russia's socialist future.[55]

Moscow Chestnova is coupled allegorically not only with Russia but also with the city of Moscow. A symbolic equivalence is implied quite openly in Sartorius's reply when Moscow asks whether he loves her: "No, I'm admiring another Moscow—the city" (42). Natasha Drubek-Maier rightly asserts that what may appear to be an antithesis actually suggests that the hero's love for the girl and the city of Moscow forms one single manifestation.[56] As if to remove any doubt about Moscow's allegorical status, Platonov explicitly personifies the city of Moscow as a young "beloved" when he has Sartorius describe it as "the city he loved . . . excited by work, renouncing itself, it was struggling forward with a face that was young and unrecognizable" (91).

Merging within the novel are two allegorical links: one between Platonov's heroine and the city of Moscow, and another between her and socialism or Soviet Russia. Seen in this light, the novel embroiders on the Stalinist myth in which the city of Moscow comes to represent the whole of Soviet Russia.[57] The notion of Moscow as the heart of a socialist paradise was particularly popular in the 1930s, when Soviet newspapers and journals boasted a hierarchical worldview—one in which "the sacred center is the Kremlin, surrounded by the mundane quarters of Moscow; Moscow in turn is the center of the 'great Russian Native Land,' beyond the borders of which the hostile empire of capitalism begins."[58] In a draft of the novel, Platonov hints at the link between Moscow and Soviet Russia when the heroine asks her father for the origin of her name and is told: "A wonderful city! . . . [Moscow is the central hearth, the hearth of our native land]."[59]

There are no primary sources that explain what prompted Platonov's decision to equate the city of Moscow with a heroine. Sergei Nekliudov does convincingly link the allegory to earlier historical concepts, many of which are outlined in chapter 1: biblical female personifications of Jerusalem and Babylon as bride or whore; the representation of the conquest of a city as rape or marriage; the moist-mother-earth cult;[60] and the conception of the Moscow-Petersburg dichotomy as Russian-Western or feminine-masculine.[61] In a more direct vein, Platonov's feminized vision of Moscow might have been triggered by Velimir Khlebnikov's 1921 poem "Moscow, Who Are You?" ("Moskva, ty kto?"), which was published while Platonov was writing his novel in 1933.[62] Referring to Leninist Russia as envisioned by Gorky,[63] Khlebnikov's poem personifies Moscow as a female figure who oscillates between the roles of "enchanted" victim and victimizing femme fatale.[64] Significantly, in the same year Evgenii Zamiatin departed from Gogol's gendered Moscow-Petersburg vision in an essay that represents Moscow as a girl who craves anything new and revolutionary.[65] Zamiatin's essay was written in emigration and published only in 1963, however, so it could not have influenced Platonov's novel directly.

The works and concepts outlined here are elemental to an understanding of the cultural climate in which *Happy Moscow* arose. Yet, given the distinctly Stalinist setting of the novel and the period in which it was written, it was shaped above all by the allegorization of Moscow as a female figure in 1930s Soviet culture. Political journalism under Stalin tended to represent Moscow and its leader as mother and father, respectively.[66] Stalinist literature, paintings, films, and popular songs abound with feminine representations of Moscow as the "heart of Russia," as researchers have repeatedly observed.[67] Lidiia Fomenko points out that in Soviet musicals and comedies, as well as in a number of Soviet paintings, Moscow and the heroine are symbolically linked in a "chronotope" in which "the capital turned out to be the metaphoric embodiment of a new feminine fate."[68]

Although research has focused on a preference for the maternal archetype in this recurring chronotope, bridal connotations are far from absent in the myth.[69] Moscow is allegorized as a bride rather than as a mother, for instance, in what Günther considers the "concentrate of Soviet mythology": the mass songs of the Stalin era.[70] Thus, the lyrics of V. Semernin's "Springtime Moscow" ("Moskva vesenniaia") personify Moscow as a laughing, dancing girl who "waits for new dates" and "great happiness."[71] During the Second World War, certain female personifications of Russia on propaganda posters also harked back to amorous rather than maternal archetypes. In "Red Army Warrior!" ("Krasnoarmeets!" 1942)—a poster calling on soldiers to liberate the nation—the Russian people are represented by a young woman, with unmistakable physical charms, whose dress appears to have been ripped open by the enemy.[72] Her pose evokes not only violent but also sexual connotations. That the role of a physically attractive woman often merges with that of a mother is illustrated by a feminine image created at a later date: Vera Mukhina's statue *We Demand Peace* (*Trebuem mira,* 1950). If, as scholars assert, the women in this sculpture do indeed "embody the standard maternal allegory of nation," then Mukhina's mothers are no homely drudges.[73] Portrayed as beautiful young women, they have accentuated breasts and thighs made even more pronounced by a helpful, imaginary gust of wind.

Happy Moscow was written when some of these songs, films, posters, and statues had yet to appear, while others had already become an indissoluble element of mass culture. The outlines of Platonov's heroine are no doubt affected by them or by what Eric Naiman has summarized as the "yearning encouraged by Stalinist ideology—Moscow as the ideal centre which the entire nation strives to penetrate."[74]

Not coincidentally does Naiman hint at the Soviet "Moscow myth" and at Platonov's rendition of it as a concept with erotic implications. As said earlier, Moscow Chestnova's physical appearance and sexual promiscuity are emphasized throughout the text. This aspect of her character can be read as an indicator of Platonov's ambiguous stance toward Soviet Russia and the Stalinist conceptualization of Moscow. Such a reading is proposed by Pia Berger-Bügel, who claims that "with Moscow, who in the course of the narrative degenerates into a strumpet," Platonov symbolizes "his disenchantment with the abuse of ideals held by the Soviet regime, which transformed in the 1930s under Stalin's despotic leadership into unparalleled terror."[75]

And yet, as Heli Kostov rightly argues, Platonov's heroine should not be read in terms of an unequivocal critique of Soviet Russia. According to Kostov, in her depiction "a problematic field remains prominent until the end, in which the unmasking of the utopia coexists with the wish not to part with it."[76] What does occur as her story unravels is an inversion of the optimistic Stalinist Moscow myth into its tragic opposite. If, in official narratives staging Moscow as the heart of Soviet Russia, the personal and national levels coincide in happy endings, then here personal and general social strivings merge within a more pessimistic plot.[77] In other words, *Happy Moscow* problematizes the unproblematic identity of the Moscow of official Soviet culture—which acts as the direct "attainable" opposite of Platonov's degenerating and principally *un*attainable allegorical heroine.

Like Blok's and Berdiaev's "brides Russia," this feminized unattainable Moscow is primarily the product of a male perspective: Moscow specifically merges with "all of nature," with Russia's socialist future, or with the city of Moscow as seen through the eyes of her male lovers. As Berger-Bügel asserts, her role is that of a "mirror of wishes and hopes that the representatives of the new man—Bozhko, Sartorius, and Sambikin—read into her."[78] Hence, an exploration of Platonov's Soviet allegory would be incomplete without a closer look at the men who lend Moscow her allegorical dimension.

Moscow's Lovers

In 1933 a literary project launched in Moscow—"Moscow awaits its artist" ("Moskva zhdet svoego khudozhnika")—appealed to members of the Writers Union to depict the "New Moscow" in its role as the center of the Soviet Union and, by extension, the entire world.[79] "Moscow awaits its artist": in Russian the title suggests an amorous connection between the city of Moscow (whose grammatical gender is feminine) and the artist (for whom the male singular form is used). Platonov's novel may have been a direct response to the appeal;[80] in any case, it departs from a similar amorous suggestion: *Happy Moscow* describes the affairs of the allegorical heroine Moscow with Soviet intellectuals and artists. Her male admirers share both their love for the heroine and an intense commitment to the future of Soviet society. Eventually, in their minds the two passions merge.

True Soviet Men

Platonov's heroine is surrounded constantly by men with responsible and intellectually challenging professions. Not only does she come to live in a building which is a "home to pilots, aircraft designers, engineers of all kinds, philosophers, theoretical economists and members of other professions" (19); but the gathering at which she meets two of her lovers is described as an evening of "shared genius of vital sincerity and of happy rivalry in intellectual friendship" (37), which is attended by "young scientists, engineers, pilots, doctors, teachers, performing artists, musicians and workers from the new factories. No one was over the age of 27, yet each of them was already known throughout the new world of their motherland" (33).

The central male characters in *Happy Moscow*—Bozhko, Sambikin, and Sartorius—are, respectively, a geometrician-cum-town planner, a surgeon, and a mechanical engineer. Each feels intensely responsible for the development of socialism and for the future of Soviet Russia. Heli Kostov defines the trio as "a group embodiment of one hero," broken down into three "different realizations" of the Soviet myth of the "new man"—the human representative of an ideal Soviet society.[81] Most obviously, this myth is hinted at in the character Bozhko, whom Moscow calls a "true Soviet man" (44). Bozhko writes letters to convince people around the world of the benefits of socialism, and he has an extensive record of service within quintessentially Soviet social organizations, such as the local *stengazeta* (13–14). Bozhko, Sambikin, and Sartorius all perceive the creation of a picture-perfect socialist Soviet society as their personal responsibility. Their attitude toward (Soviet) Russia's future is characterized by emotionally charged notions— think the "heartbeat of happiness" (13), "passion" of the heart (69), the "terror of responsibility," and insomnia (26).

The members of this passionate trio combine their commitment to Soviet society with an intense but vain love for Moscow Chestnova. As we have seen, Sartorius's political commitment merges with the love he feels for the girl. His political and amorous endeavors unite, too, when, in an attempt to relieve the suffering of his futile love for Moscow, he manages to calm "his heart" only by working on technical plans of benefit to "the State and to the collective farm workers" (68). A similar coalescence marks the depiction of

Bozhko, who writes letters propagating socialism specifically after Moscow's visits (14) and who longs to connect "the whole world" with the help of Moscow's heart (15).

For the three heroes, Moscow's status as political allegory is reinforced by the conclusion of the unfinished novel. Eventually, their amorous failure vis-à-vis the heroine parallels their increasingly troubled stance toward the socialist utopia. None of the three has been able to establish a lasting relationship with Moscow, an amorous defeat that can be compared to their growing ambivalence toward socialism and Soviet Russia: as the novel ends, it is unclear whether or not they still support the Soviet utopia.[82]

Echoes of the Silver Age

In many respects, the relationships between the heroine and Bozhko, Sambikin, and Sartorius duplicate the gendered view of Russia and the intelligentsia that was rampant in preceding decades. That the link with Blok is particularly pertinent becomes crystal clear when the novel is juxtaposed with Blok's play *Song of Fate*.

As mentioned, Platonov's heroine is redolent of Blok's female figures—particularly of his feminine hypostases of Russia—in more than one sense. Not fortuitously did one scholar suggest that Moscow is a "reflex to Blok's image of Russia as a woman."[83] In *Happy Moscow*, the Soviet *intelligenty* who court Moscow mirror the "writers, artists, poets" who admire Faina in *Song of Fate*.[84] Then, too, the unattainability of Faina to the hero corresponds to the basic impossibility of any true amorous attachment between Platonov's Moscow and her male lovers. As Sambikin rightly surmises, Moscow "would never be able to exchange all the noise of life for the whisper of a single human being" (38). Like Faina, she is seen in this respect as a destructive force. Sambikin tells Moscow: "There are things that destroy everything—and you're one of them. When I saw you, I . . . thought I would die" (76). German similarly says to Faina: "You poisoned my heart . . . , / You trampled on the gentlest flower, / . . . / You wiped out my soul with the train of your black dress!"[85]

What is more, Platonov's heroes reiterate the weakness that Blok and his contemporaries attributed to the intelligentsia in its relationship with Russia.[86] What attracts Sambikin is the "power" of Moscow's appearance (35). When Bozhko notes her liveliness during a festive evening, he trembles "from fear" (38–39) and observes the vivid atmosphere of the party "submissively" (40). Sartorius repeatedly appears in her company either crying or on the verge of tears (43, 44, 47); during their first rendezvous, Moscow leads the way and he merely follows, "lagging behind," "helpless and worthless"

(44, 46). Moscow draws a contrast between the "virgin" Sartorius and the sexually experienced woman she sees in herself (60).

Finally, in both Blok's and Platonov's texts the hero, in his powerless attitude toward the heroine, is equated with a warrior: German identifies with a "warrior in an ambush,"[87] and Moscow leaves Sartorius standing "alone in the dawn . . . like a surviving warrior on a silent battle-ground" (46).

The coincidences between play and novel do not necessarily suggest that Platonov is consciously embroidering on Blok's play. They do show, however, that in terms evocative of those used by his predecessors, Platonov recycles and expands the early twentieth-century tendency to allegorize a heroine as a foil for male national-political aims and frustrations. Obviously, in the novel's Soviet context, this allegory undergoes substantial changes. In no respect can Moscow Chestnova's suitors, for example, be seen as equivalents of the representatives of the pre-revolutionary intelligentsia. They do enact the role of dyed-in-the-wool Soviet *intelligenty*, however. Not only does their status as urban professionals turn them into representatives of the "intelligentsia" as defined by Soviet rule; they are also driven by the same sense of moral obligation toward society and toward the Russian people that traditionally characterizes the intelligentsia. A link between Sartorius and the more conventional hero-*intelligent* is suggested when he is introduced to the reader as a man who is "carried away by intellectual imagination" (39) and who calls himself a rationalist (42). Sambikin is a troubled intellectual for whom Moscow represents "such an intellectual riddle that he began to devote the whole of himself to its solution" (79–80). That the tragedy of the intelligentsia is, in general, a topical theme for Platonov can be inferred from his essays on Pushkin: focusing, in one scholar's words, on the "historical fate of the Russian intelligentsia," these enter into a "dialogue, and sometimes even a direct polemic with . . . Blok's concept in the article 'The Intelligentsia and the Revolution.'"[88]

Clint Walker rightly compares the Soviet intellectuals who "woo the young utopian bride, Moskva Chestnova" to the traditional *intelligenty* in Griboedov's *Woe from Wit*, whose love for the heroine coalesces with their strivings to attain a useful position in Russian society.[89] But there is a crucial difference between Platonov's *intelligenty* and the intelligentsia of pre-revolutionary Russian literature. This discrepancy lies in the former's identification with the state, which contrasts sharply with the opposition to the regime that molded the classic (self-)definition of the intelligentsia. By implication, the metaphoric amorous triangle that was so popular in the preceding decades is absent in *Happy Moscow*: in their courtship of Moscow, Platonov's Soviet *intelligenty* are not opposed to any representative of the state. These characters support or embody the state themselves, albeit in a highly ambiguous way.[90] Thus, the idea of a fight between intelligentsia and state over the fate of Russia is no longer relevant to this novel.

In addition, whereas the association of a feminized Moscow with nature conjures up stock images of the Silver Age, Platonov's heroine is linked with the urban and the official spheres to a much greater extent than her predecessors were. More than a rural idyll, Moscow Chestnova represents urban Russia and the Soviet state. In Natasha Drubek-Maier's words, she offers an "expansion of the metaphor 'Russia-woman' through the personification with the state / the people / ideology."[91] Significantly, in a note Platonov calls his heroine a "living poster."[92]

In other words, if the early twentieth-century opposition of a feminine Russia and a masculine intelligentsia did leave its mark on *Happy Moscow*, within Platonov's poetics this opposition is transformed substantially. Opposing a feminized Stalinist Moscow to Soviet Russia's "new men," Platonov embroiders on the work of Blok and contemporaries, while re-creating their "brides Russia" in a Stalinist setting. Within this setting, the traditional boundaries separating intelligentsia, state, and people become blurred, and the original metaphor undergoes significant revision.

BORIS PASTERNAK: RUSSIA'S LOST VIRGINITY

As said earlier, in the Soviet period metaphoric representations of Russia as an unattainable bride featured only as a marginal phenomenon. Between the mid-1930s, when Platonov wrote his novel, and the late 1950s, the metaphor is practically absent from Russian intellectual thought. It finally resurfaces in Boris Pasternak's *Doctor Zhivago*, a novel published abroad in 1957.

While writing *Doctor Zhivago*, Pasternak defined the goal of his nascent novel as an attempt "to give a historical image of Russia over the last forty-five years."[93] This focus on the historical fate of Russia is embodied in his heroine, Lara, whom Evgenii and Elena Pasternak have defined as the "symbolic essence" of

> the fate of Russia, as a deceived and enslaved woman, the "stubborn, extravagant, crazy, irresponsible, adored Russia, with her eternally splendid, disastrous, and unpredictable gestures," from which he [Pasternak] suffered and which he adored in Ol'ga Ivinskaia [his lover at the time of writing].[94]

Scholars have repeatedly halted at this symbolic link between Pasternak's heroine and Russia.[95] In some readings, the novel has been placed specifically in the context of the political metaphor of interest here. Neil Cornwell, for example, argues that the plot suggests a reading of Zhivago's inability to commit to Lara as "the failure of the Russian intelligentsia to back adequately the ideals of . . . February 1917."[96]

This study provides a more detailed look at the sociopolitical implications found in *Zhivago*. Focusing on the central constellation of characters—Zhivago (hero), Lara (heroine), and Komarovskii (antagonist)—I explore the extent to which the triangle is informed by gendered debates on Russia and the intelligentsia from the beginning of the century.

Zhivago and Blok

In Pasternak's own words, the art which appealed to him most in the early days of his career was "the youthful art of Scriabin, Blok, Komissarževskaya and Bely . . . [which] was so striking that . . . one wished to repeat it again from the very foundations, yet even more speedily, fervently and wholly."[97] Among the artists mentioned, Aleksandr Blok is to remain a crucial figure in Pasternak's life and writing career.[98] The elder poet's role in the genesis of *Doctor Zhivago* is so fundamental that one commentator claimed the novel to be "unintelligible without Blok."[99] No less inextricable is the link tying the novel to the general culture of Blok's times. In the words of James Billington, its choice of "long-silent themes at variance with official Soviet culture" turns *Doctor Zhivago* into a direct "throwback to pre-revolutionary Russia."[100] One such theme revived in the novel is the symbolic identification of the heroine-beloved with Russia.

Pasternak's affinity with the "bride Russia" metaphor is not surprising in the light of his affinity with Russian Symbolism. Despite gaining notoriety as a futurist poet, in his early days he is "surrounded mainly by practitioners and adherents of Symbolist culture."[101] At the time, his work is closely affiliated with that of Symbolist artists.[102] If far from professing a strictly Symbolist philosophy, in 1958 he does call art "symbolical" in essence.[103] A key issue in the reception of *Doctor Zhivago* has been the question of whether or not it should be considered a Symbolist text.[104]

Pasternak's connection with the early twentieth century is more than strictly stylistic, however. What unites him with Blok, in particular, is a similar attitude toward the relation between the formal and thematic aspects of their art. Pasternak's definition of art as essentially symbolic does not prevent him from leaving the Symbolist Musaget group around 1910, claiming that "verbal music . . . consists not of the euphony of vowels and consonants on their own, but of the relationship of the sound of speech to its meaning."[105] A friend, Aleksandr Gavronskii, accuses Pasternak of overemphasizing content at the expense of form, thus echoing the charge previously leveled at Blok by Stanislavskii.[106] For both authors, the emphasis on content rather than form coincides with an increasing focus on sociopolitical issues at later stages in their careers. "As the decades passed," according to Christopher Barnes, "Pasternak's life and creativity . . . were becoming increasingly and inescapably bound up with human affairs and history."[107] The exact same is true for Blok.

Pasternak is particularly outspoken regarding his move toward the thematic sphere when issues of Russia's identity are concerned, as can be concluded from his 1945 meetings with Isaiah Berlin. Berlin characterizes Pasternak as a "Russian patriot," with a "passionate, almost obsessive, desire to be thought a Russian writer with roots deep in Russian soil."[108] In Berlin's words, Pasternak believed he was "in communion with the inner life of the Russian people"; that he served as "its voice as Tyutchev, Tolstoy, Dostoevsky, Chekhov and Blok had"; and that "he had something to say to the rulers of Russia, something of immense importance which only he could say."[109] Pasternak seeks to express that "something" in *Doctor Zhivago*. He refers to the novel in the same year as an endeavor to "do something dear to me and my very own," for which he needs "to break through to the public."[110] In order to realize this breakthrough, Pasternak allows his thematic—politico-historical—interests to prevail over aesthetic ones, as his comment on the novel shows.

> This second book [the second half of *Doctor Zhivago*] is probably poorer and less trimmed, stylistically . . . but from the perspective of plot, it is fuller, sadder, more tragic. . . . I have written this prose unprofessionally, without a consciously upheld creative goal, in the bad sense of the term "without ceremony," with some dullness and naiveté, which I allowed myself and for which I have forgiven myself.[111]

The language Pasternak uses to describe the clash between his thematic interests and his aesthetic aims is reminiscent, to say the least, of Blok's aforementioned comment on the theme of Russia and the intelligentsia. Equally eager to reach an audience, Blok, too, focused on the content of his message rather than on its aesthetic modeling.

A more tangible connection exists between *Doctor Zhivago* and Blok, who occupies a central role in the plot. An unfinished essay on Blok that Pasternak is writing in 1944 provides material for several outlines of *Doctor Zhivago*.[112] Pasternak started his novel while he "marked out several passages and made notes on Blok's verse" for this essay.[113] The two projects have become intermingled by 1946, when Pasternak writes in a letter to Nadezhda Mandel'shtam that he wants "to write some prose about the whole of our life from Blok up till the recent war"—referring to Blok as a chronological marker.[114] In the novel, he attributes a similar weighty status to Blok when "young people in both capitals" in the 1910s are said to be collectively "mad" about the poet (81);[115] when Blok is labeled a determining factor in the development of juvenile revolutionary pathos in 1905 (159–60); and when the revolutionary era is characterized by a quotation from Blok (510). In all these fragments, the younger generation is incarnate in Zhivago. That he acts as a fictive hybrid of Blok and Pasternak is suggested in the latter's claim that his hero "forms some resultant force between Blok and me."[116]

Putting aside the fact that Pasternak can be considered Blok's outright heir, it is relevant that he unites with Blok—and with most of the authors thus far discussed—in terms of his attitude to the metaphor in question. For Pasternak, as for these authors, the issue of Russia's future fate is a matter of personal commitment and social engagement. As is true of his predecessors, Pasternak's gendered view of Russia springs from this social, and intensely personal, motivation.

The Heroine: Marriageable Girl Russia

The story of *Doctor Zhivago* revolves around the fate of the doctor and writer Iurii Zhivago; it focuses particularly on his vicissitudes during the October Revolution and the civil war. Crucial to his story are a tragic extramarital affair with the heroine, Larissa Guichard, and his relationship with the lawyer Viktor Komarovskii, a rival for her love. Larissa—or Lara—is seduced by Komarovskii at an early age, after which she marries the future revolutionary Pavel Antipov. Some years later, Lara and Pavel begin leading separate lives. At this point, her relationship with Zhivago begins.

Lara enters the scene as an undisguised successor of the classic nineteenth-century Russian heroine whose wholeness, purity, and rootedness in the countryside diametrically oppose the cold rationalism of an urban-rooted, "split" hero. An attractive sixteen-year-old with a "clear mind and an easy nature" (27), Lara is said to be the "purest being in the world" (27), to move "with a silent grace" (28), and to read "as if it is the simplest possible thing, a thing which even animals could do" (289). In a draft version, Zhivago summarizes her "principal characteristics" as originality, wholeness, and spontaneity (607).

As suggested here, in relation to Zhivago, Lara functions as an embodiment of abstract phenomena rather than as a tangible human figure—a matter that has been singled out in feminist discussions of the novel.[117] Jane Harris argues that throughout Pasternak's work feminine images are "associated . . . with the personification of abstract forces: Nature (*priroda*), the Life Force or Life (*zhizn'*)."[118] Lara's status as such an abstract personification is beyond all doubt, if only because her physical characteristics remain nonspecific throughout the novel. To her lover, Komarovskii, Lara represents "the incorporeal" (48), and a draft of the novel states that "it seemed as if she did not have any body or weight" (632).

Edith Clowes is probably right in asserting that, generally speaking, Pasternak "deemphasizes or 'effaces' . . . physical and social being . . . in order to put into the foreground other, spiritual aspects of being."[119] In Lara's case, however, the supremacy of a spiritual over a physical dimension cannot be separated from her gender. This supremacy is singled out specifically in her relationship with the male hero. Not fortuitously, his friends reproach Zhivago for regarding the women in his life as "disembodied ideas for you to juggle with in your head" rather than as real human beings (476). While this quotation does not refer explicitly to Lara, the novel leaves little doubt that she is to him the supreme incarnation of such "disembodied" spatial and philosophical concepts as nature, life, the earth, and Russia.

Lara-Nature-Sophia

Above all else, Lara is associated with nature and rural landscapes. Walking through a country estate, she experiences the air of the "huge countryside" in personified, sensual terms as "dearer to her than her kin, better than a lover" (77).[120] Her link with the pastoral is brought out in the thoughts of her male suitors. As a juvenile, her husband—the future revolutionary leader, Antipov—is said to experience a joy upon seeing her as if "she had been some holiday landscape of birch trees, grass and clouds" (52). For Zhivago, too, the image of Lara merges with nature. Upon seeing a rowan that "held out two white branches welcomingly," he "remembered Lara's strong white arm, seized the branches and pulled them to him" (370); addressing the tree as a mistress, he says: "I'll find you, my beauty, my love, my rowan tree, my own flesh and blood" (ibid.). This passage reverberates when Zhivago later feels that "the whole breadth of heaven leaned low over his bed holding out two strong, white, woman's arms to him," and when he speaks of the "merciful, wonderful, beauty-lavishing hands" of nature (389). A draft stresses the amorous character of this mystical confrontation by referring to the hands as those of a "loving woman" (627).

The symbolic equivalence of Zhivago's spatial surroundings and Lara extends beyond the strictly natural world. Fundamental to their romance is her adaptation of a cosmic dimension. She and Zhivago are said to love each other because "everything around them willed it, the trees and the clouds and the sky over their heads and the earth under their feet. . . . Never, never . . . had they lost the . . . joy in the whole universe, its form, its beauty, the feeling of their own belonging to it" (494). Although theirs is a shared experience, it is through Lara that Zhivago first realizes the "feeling of belonging" to the universe. Not surprisingly, analyses of the novel have repeatedly traced her character to Solov'ev and his notion of Sophia or the Divine Feminine.[121] The novel alludes almost literally to such an "eternally feminine" principle when Lara is said to be "charged . . . with all the femininity in the world" (420) and when Zhivago experiences a moment of spiritual revelation in which Lara and his surroundings blend together as a metaphysical entity.

> [It was] as if the gift of the living spirit were streaming into his breast, piercing his being and coming out by emerging from his shoulders like a pair of wings. The archetype, which is formed in every child for life and seems for ever after to be the inward image of his personality, arose in him in its full primordial strength and compelled nature, the forest, the afterglow and everything else visible to be transfigured into a similarly primordial and all-embracing likeness of a girl. "Lara," he whispered and thought, closing his eyes, addressing the whole of life, all God's earth, all the sunlit space spread out before him. (339)

In several respects, Lara's symbolic equivalence with nature, life, and the earth recalls Solov'ev's notion of Sophia as a feminine World Soul, as well as the (related) figure of the Beautiful Lady whom Blok's poet so eagerly anticipates. A reading of Lara's character in this light is motivated by Blok's central role in the novel and by the remark that Zhivago and his youthful friends "had soaked themselves" in Solov'ev's *Meaning of Love* (42). Written in the 1890s, this treatise was crucial to the Russian development of a mystical cult of femininity around 1900.[122]

Lara-Russia

Apart from the cosmic aspect, the passage cited highlights another, more tangible, spatial dimension that Lara attains in the eyes of Zhivago: to him, she represents the earth and the space surrounding him. A closer look shows that "God's earth," with which Lara is symbolically equated, can be understood in both universal and specifically Russian contexts.

Just how central the earth motif is to the novel as a whole is demonstrated by another Pasternak creation: a 1943 poem in memory of Tsvetaeva, in which Pasternak refers to what must be *Doctor Zhivago* as a future "book about the earth and its beauty [*ee krasote*]."[123] The suggestion of personification in this definition is made explicit in the novel, in the hero's poem "The Earth" ("Zemlia"). Despite its universal title, "The Earth" evokes a quintessentially Russian setting of "Moscow houses" with "wooden stories," a river, and pussy-willow twigs. The Russian setting is personified when the poet wonders why "the horizon weeps in mist" and when he claims that "it is my calling / To see that the distances should not lose heart, / And that beyond the limits of the town / The earth should not feel lonely" (534–35). To a Russian reader, the feminine endings of the nouns "horizon" (*dal'*) and "earth" (*zemlia*), and of the corresponding adjective "lonely" (*odnoi*), suggest a bond uniting the (male) lyrical ego of the poem and a female earth.

If the gendered interpretation of "The Earth" relies on grammar alone, the symbolic coalescence of Lara with the earth is more overt. Lara is literally one with the soil in a dream in which, "buried under the ground," she sees a "tuft of grass sprout[ing] from her left nipple" (51). In a palpable allusion to Turgenev's Liza and similar characters, Lara is "attracted to the earth and to simple people" (107).

The link between Lara and the soil is particularly marked from the perspective of Zhivago, for whom she merges with the people and the earth of the provincial town of Iuriatino in the Ural Mountains. Zhivago first sees Lara there in the local library, where he witnesses how well she "was known and liked in the town" (288). When he visits her house, he is overcome by so much love and tenderness for the "little houses on the streets which led to her" that he "could have picked them off the earth and kissed them!" (302); upon returning to her after a long parting, he has to "force himself not to fall down on the earth and kiss the stones of this town . . . the sight of it filled him with happiness like the sight of a living being" (372).

Serving as such a blatant symbolic representation of the earth and of Iuriatino, Lara's image has been traced by scholars to the concept of moist mother earth and to Korè, the Greek goddess of spring, love, and fertility.[124] While it is not unlikely that Pasternak was inspired by such notions, another passage shows that Zhivago associates Lara far more specifically with the Russian earth and with Russia in general than with any thoughts of a universal earth-mother. Musing on his love for her, he asks himself:

> And what did she mean to him? Oh . . . he knew that perfectly well. A spring evening . . . the air is punctuated with scattered sounds. The voices of children playing in the streets come from varying distances as if to show that the whole expanse is alive. The expanse is Russia, his incomparable mother; famed far and wide, martyred, stubborn, extravagant, crazy, irresponsible, adored, Russia with her eternally splendid, disastrous and unpredictable gestures. . . . This was exactly what Lara was. You could not communicate with life, but she was its representative, its expression, the gift of speech and hearing granted to inarticulate being. (385–86)

Lara's allegorical function is underlined even more in a draft of this passage, which labels her the "humanization and embodiment . . . the voice of the distance and the future, the possibility of contact with the whole universe and discussion with heaven, the earth and fate" (606).

Above all else, in her role as the female embodiment of Russia, Pasternak's heroine represents a traditional, immutable Russia—akin to traditional female national allegories—as opposed to the official state. Not fortuitously, in the passage in question her character is identified with a provincial setting and with Russia's "eternally" splendid appearance. Upon leaving Lara, again Zhivago defines her and the joy she brings him as "eternal" (445). A connection between eternity and an alleged native essence glimmers through, too, in Pasternak's remark that his wife "aided the development of Lara in that she was an '*eternal* authentically Russian . . . enduring element.'"[125]

Set in a context of pastoral innocence, Lara's fate becomes inextricably intertwined with Russia's political development. A revealing comment about this fusion is offered by a minor character in the novel—a woman who compares Russia and the imperial and Soviet regimes to a young girl and her male admirers, respectively.

> And Russia too had been a marriageable girl in those days, courted by real men, men who would stand up for her, not to be compared to this rabble nowadays. Now everything had lost its gloss, nothing but civilians left, lawyers and Yids clacking their tongues day and night. Poor old Vlas [the speaker's husband] and his friends thought they could bring back those golden days with toasts and speeches and good wishes! But was this the way to win back a lost love? For that you had to move mountains! (307)

A symbolic link connects this feminized Russia with Lara: extending her gendered vision of Russia, the speaker muses on her favorite color and dress as "mauve-lilac" and concludes that "Russia . . . in her virginity before the revolution seemed . . . to have been the color of bright-lilac" (308); corresponding to this passage is Lara's first acknowledgment of her loss of virginal innocence while dressed "in her pale bright-lilac, almost white, lace-trimmed dress" (47). The lilac motif reappears toward the end of the novel: the last images that Zhivago sees before his death are glimpses of an old acquaintance—with the significantly "colored" name "Mademoiselle Fleury"—whom he does not recognize, but who is referred to four times as a stranger in a "mauve-lilac dress" (483–85).

The parallel between Lara and the personified Russia in the "marriageable girl" passage is expressed at the plot level as well: Lara appears as a marriageable young girl whose loss of virginity through an affair with a civilian lawyer coincides with the 1905 Revolution. More explicitly, a link between Lara and Russia in the revolutionary era is suggested by Lara's characterization as someone whose "expression" and "carriage" reflected "everything that made that time [the period of the first revolution] what it was—the tears and the insults and the hopes, the whole accumulation of revenge and pride" (455). Not surprisingly, scholars have repeatedly defended a reading of Lara as a symbol of Russia's historical fate, particularly during the revolutionary years. James Billington, for example, views her marriage to the revolutionary Strel'nikov-Antipov as "Old Russia" having "wed itself to the Revolution."[126]

This symbolic connection—of Lara with Russia's political fate has its roots in discussions on Russia and the intelligentsia from the early twentieth century. If we are to believe Evgenii Pasternak, the female characteristics that Zhivago ascribes to Russia "link her image with Blok's Russia, his female beloved, bride and wife" and with the transition of Blok's "Beautiful Lady into indecent and loose Rus'."[127] Academic comments on *Doctor Zhivago* link the passage on feminized Russia's "lilac" color with Blok's reference to the revolution as a "lilac phantom."[128]

Pasternak's biography and certain passages in the novel endorse a reading of Lara against such a Blokian setting. When Pasternak first lays eyes on Blok's poems as a young boy—a moment he considers crucial to his artistic development[129]—the *Verses on the Beautiful Lady* have just been published. Pasternak devotes a passage of his unfinished essay on Blok to the Beautiful Lady and claims that "without her, the reality of those years and places would have remained expressionless."[130] He is enthralled not only by the muse's exalted hypostasis but also by her demonic inversion. Among a list of poems noted as making "perhaps the biggest impression" on him in his youth, he mentions several that feature a "fallen" version of Blok's *Dama*.[131] As Guy De Mallac observes, Pasternak prefers those poems in which Blok's "duality is expressed" most distinctly.[132]

Lara's kinship with Blok's female muse can be inferred directly from the text as well, especially when her sexually depraved state comes in view. In June 1935, Pasternak discusses his future novel in terms that recall Blok's "Stranger" poem and his play of the same name ("Neznakomka," both 1906): *Zhivago* is meant to elaborate on the traumatic youth of Pasternak's real-life wife, Zinaida, a "veiled beauty in the private rooms of night restaurants . . . so young, so unspeakably attractive."[133] In the novel, "The Stranger" resonates when Komarovskii takes Lara "veiled to dinner in the private rooms of that ghastly restaurant where the waiters and the clients undressed her with their eyes as she came in" (51). Like Blok's stranger, Lara appears at night—as a beautiful female stranger in a veil—in a restaurant where footmen loiter.[134] Corresponding to the "harlot-woman" in Blok's poems is also Lara's notion of herself as a "fallen" and "bad" woman.[135] Finally, the opposition of Lara to Zhivago's legal wife, Tonia, reenacts the tradition of the illegitimate-nonconformist versus domestic-conformist heroine that was so vital to Blok's *Song of Fate.*

Naturally, Blok's female figures are not the sole inspiration for Lara's character. The combination of her angelic-demonic traits and cosmic dimensions also makes her a worthy successor of Gnosticism's "fallen Sophia"; and scholars have traced her character to the biblical depiction of Babylon as harlot and Jerusalem as bride,[136] as well as to the sinner-saint pair of Mary Magdalene and the Virgin Mary.[137] But the analogy between Lara and these historical concepts (which were so relevant to early twentieth-century "brides Russia") only intensifies her status as the Soviet-era scion of female representations of Russia by Blok and his contemporaries.

The Hero: Doctor, Poet, Outcast

It speaks for itself that the symbolic dimension of Pasternak's heroine cannot be regarded in isolation—that is, without taking into account her interaction with other characters in the novel. In early twentieth-century debate, it was "the intelligentsia" that turned to the image of an unattainable female beloved in order to express sociopolitical frustrations. In Platonov's novel, it was to a group of quintessentially Soviet *intelligenty* that the heroine appeared as a utopian allegory. In turn, Pasternak's heroine functions as an embodiment of Russia specifically for the novel's troubled hero-poet, Iurii Zhivago.

Superfluous Man in Soviet Setting

The novel's title hero is introduced to the reader as a gifted young intellectual, artist, and doctor. Ultimately, his life ends in personal and social failure, however. Iurii Zhivago spends his last years in "long periods of indifference to himself and to everything in the world" (459). As scholars have noted, his character conjures up a nineteenth-century literary type—the superfluous man—whose parallel personal and social alienation was a recurrent feature.[138] Zhivago becomes isolated both socially and personally in much the same way as his nineteenth-century predecessors did; toward the end of the novel, he has abandoned both Lara and his social position as a doctor. Not coincidentally is he a fan of Eugene Onegin, whose story he and his wife "go on endlessly re-reading" (278, 279).[139]

Within the narrative, the failure of Zhivago's social and amorous strivings is ascribed not to external circumstances but to character flaws that he shares with nineteenth-century prototypes. The key shortcomings attributed to the traditional "superfluous man" can be summarized as social maladjustment, lack of initiative, a meek submission to fate, and an inability to turn lofty thoughts into practical deeds. Each of these definitions applies to Pasternak's hero. His social status is that of an isolated outcast. His desire to "be writing a work of art or science" or to "be of use as a doctor or a farmer" (282) is expressed in a diary—written while residing at the isolated Varykino estate—rather than acted out in real life. Ultimately, Zhivago's friends blame him for letting his life pass by in vain (476). Passive resignation and want of initiative also characterize his attitude to Lara. Having promised to kill her former seducer if the man bothers her again (413), Zhivago eventually allows the same Komarovskii to take Lara away against her will, admitting that "all I can do now is to agree blindly and obey you as if I had no will of my own" (443).

In other words, Zhivago's parallel amorous and social failings reiterate the Russian hero's traditional inability to turn thoughts into deeds. By contrasting him with the revolutionary Strel'nikov, to quote Ian Kelly, "Pasternak was working within the literary tradition of 'Hamlet and Don Quixote,' or man of action versus man of reflection."[140] Indeed, Zhivago's portrayal can be connected with that of Hamlet—or rather, with the perception of Shakespeare's hero in nineteenth-century Russia, where Hamlet's reflective nature was seen as an obstacle to finding a useful social occupation and to establishing an amorous relationship. Pasternak establishes a similar parallel when Zhivago's friends reproach him not only for his social failure, but also for his conception of the women in his life as merely abstract ideas. This is certainly true in the case of Lara, whose function as an inspiring muse eclipses her status as a woman of flesh and blood for Zhivago. Revealingly, upon sensing that they will soon part, he is tormented less by the fear of losing Lara than by "his longing so to express his anguish that others should weep" (434).[141]

A final similarity between Pasternak's protagonist and the classic nineteenth-century hero is an adversarial stance toward official authorities. If Zhivago is not an active opponent of the regime, he unmistakably disapproves of it. As Henry Gifford asserts, the main opposition in the novel is that "between Yury himself and those who have capitulated to the ethos of the new system."[142] Throughout the narrative, Zhivago figures as a politically isolated figure, set apart from and hunted down by men of the new order. His status of social outcast makes itself felt even in his use of language, which is set against the "pompous" rhetoric of the authorities in a highly individual, poetic style.[143] Zhivago's condemnation of official Soviet language—with its pursuit of "all this 'dawn of the future,' 'building a new world,' 'torch-bearers of mankind'"—adamantly illustrates his disapproval of the regime as a whole (282).

Child of Russia's Terrible Years

If Zhivago's portrayal relies heavily on the depiction of the hero in the nineteenth-century Russian novel, it is shaped no less tangibly by early twentieth-century intellectual culture. *Doctor Zhivago* deals with developments dating to late imperial and early Soviet culture, and recaptures—as Edith Clowes asserts—"the religious and political thinking of the first decades of the twentieth century."[144] Zhivago's life spans a period from the late nineteenth century until 1929, and he is a perfect exponent of the generation that grew up with Blok and Solov'ev. With his intellectual talents and adversarial attitude to the regime, Zhivago acts as a representative specifically of the pre-revolutionary artistic intelligentsia. The last pages of the novel allude to his status as such when a friend refers to Zhivago's youth.

> The Russian Revolution came out of the Russian enlightenment. Take that line of Blok's, "We, the children of Russia's terrible years" . . . when he said it, he meant it figuratively, metaphorically. The children were not children, but the sons, the heirs of the intelligentsia, and the terrors were not terrible but apocalyptic. (509–10)

Serving as spokesman of the generation that was "collectively mad" about Blok's poetry, Zhivago is an unmistakable "child" or heir of the imperial intellectual elite to which his friend refers. Scholars have often discussed him as an exponent of the pre-revolutionary intelligentsia. Thus, on the basis of a number of plot developments, Cornwell defines Pasternak's hero as a supreme "representative of that westernized, pre-revolutionary Russian culture which had either to die or be violently transformed by 1929."[145]

Of pivotal importance to this study is the relation between this westernized *intelligent*'s love for Lara and revolutionary-era debates on the intelligentsia as Russia's lover. As James Billington claims, central to Pasternak's novel is "the idea that increasingly obsessed the literary imagination of the late imperial period: the belief that a woman, some strange and mysterious feminine force, could alone show the anguished intellectuals the way to salvation."[146] As we have seen, Zhivago—reverting to early twentieth-century categories—conceives of Lara as precisely such a salutary feminine force. The characterization of Zhivago himself is tinged by a popular concept of the same period: the intelligentsia as Russia's bridegroom. The depiction of his inability to keep Lara at his side echoes the metaphors that Berdiaev and his contemporaries used for the intelligentsia. Like Berdiaev's *bab'e-i-rab'e* intellectuals, Zhivago appears as a talented intellectual who lacks initiative and a will of his own. A detailed reading shows that Pasternak relies on early twentieth-century predecessors when attributing these features to his hero.

Examples begin with Berdiaev's urging of the Russian "boys" to "become men" (see chapter 2), an admonition that corresponds to the contrasting attitudes of Zhivago and Komarovskii toward Lara as, respectively, a "childlike" "boy" and a "fatherlike" "man with grey hair" who is "no boy" and who "could be her father" (447, 49, 47, 585). Linked to the boy motif was a claim by Berdiaev and his contemporaries that the intelligentsia was (excessively) feminine. As Clowes has argued, Zhivago is an equally effeminate hero: he has "'feminine' traits," and his "whole creative process is strongly feminine."[147] Pasternak recycles early twentieth-century debates about the failing intelligentsia in yet another respect: he opposes a weak, submissive Zhivago (443, 445) to an older rival who is physically imposing and determined not to "give in" to fears about Lara (40). The former's features echo the weakness, obedience, and tendency to submissively "give itself" of which Berdiaev accused the intelligentsia.

Given Zhivago's status as an early twentieth-century Russian poet-intellectual and the symbolic, "national" nature of his love for Lara, the congruities with Berdiaev and his contemporaries might be viewed as conscious philosophical echoes. Such an interpretation is plausible in the light of Pasternak's preoccupation and personal acquaintance with those writers who feature most prominently in the debates discussed. As Guy De Mallac asserts, the coincidence of Pasternak's school and student years with Russian Symbolism and the "intellectual effervescence rooted in those times was bound to engage and excite a precocious adolescent like Pasternak."[148]

Indeed, in the 1910s and 1920s, the author repeatedly meets poets and philosophers who have taken part or are still participating in the debate on Russia's femininity. In addition to Blok, these include Sergei Esenin, Viacheslav Ivanov, Konstantin Bal'mont, Viktor Shklovskii, and Andrei Belyi.[149] Together Pasternak, Shklovskii, and Belyi attend meetings and discussions held by the Russian Religious-Philosophical Academy, founded in 1921–22 in Berlin, where they give lectures, along with Nikolai Berdiaev and Fedor Stepun.[150] With a group that includes Belyi and Ivanov, Pasternak spends many hours in Berlin informally "debating both the literary activities of the day and the eternal metaphysical issues dear to Russia."[151] It is virtually unimaginable that the gendered concept of Russia and the intelligentsia—to which the poets and philosophers in question turned so eagerly in their writings—played no part in these conversations. In addition, scholars have repeatedly observed thematic links between Pasternak and Berdiaev, whom the former characterized as a "writer of our time," "in the same line of thought" as himself.[152]

Echoes of the Silver Age emerge with particular force in the identification of Pasternak's hero with a knightly figure, and specifically with the mythical Saint George so cherished by his pre-revolutionary predecessors.

That this myth was of topical political importance to Pasternak can first be inferred from his poem "Enlivened Fresco" ("Ozhivshaia freska," 1944), in which the battle at Stalingrad is represented in terms of a struggle between Saint George (the Red Army) and the dragon (the Nazis).[153] As research has demonstrated, the Saint George myth also forms a crucial subtext to *Doctor Zhivago*. A symbolic link between Iurii Zhivago and the figure of Saint George has been reconstructed both from their related names (Georgii-Iurii) and from a number of individual scenes.[154]

The Saint George legend might also explain the hero's highly personal relationship with Moscow, which is traditionally seen as the "city of Iurii," with George as its patron saint.[155] In the story, Moscow serves as "Iurii's city" not only in a literal sense, as the place where Iurii Zhivago grows up, spends most of his life, and dies. It is also, to borrow Zina Gimpelevich-Schwartzmann's typification, shown "again and again . . . to be the poet's true love, his muse and his main character."[156] Zhivago describes the city in explicitly amorous terms when returning after a lengthy absence as "breathing and blossoming with the color of her streets and clouds . . . whirling all round me, turning my head and willing me to turn the heads of others by writing in her praise" (482). The novel concludes with two friends who leaf through Zhivago's notebooks and claim that "Moscow . . . now appeared to them, not as the place where all these things had happened, but as the heroine of a long tale of which that evening, book in hand, they were reaching the end" (510).

Fundamental to the Zhivago–Saint George connection is the passage in which Zhivago fears losing Lara to "a prehistoric beast or dragon . . . who thirsted for Iurii's blood and lusted after Lara" (434). Overcome with fear, he pens a poetic version of the legend of Saint George and the dragon (435). His writings—as the narration suggests—result in the poem "Fairy Tale" ("Skazka"), in which a horseman tries to free a princess from a dragon-snake (522–24). In contrast to the traditional dragon-slayer plot, in the poem it is unclear whether the rider succeeds in his task. While he does manage to kill the dragon, in the end he and the girl try "to wake up" but fall into a deep sleep that might last for ages (524).

The allusion to a tragic end is mirrored in Zhivago's own failure: he does indeed lose Lara to his rival, Komarovskii. Hence the dragon-slayer motif, as Savelii Senderovich argues, emerges here "against the background of a presentiment of misfortune instead of triumph."[157] By doing so, it echoes the tragic inversions of the traditional Saint George myth which occurred so often in politicized terms in the early twentieth century.

For Pasternak, the myth functions no less in a political context: his captured princess (Lara) and hero (Iurii) serve as symbolic representatives of revolutionary Russia and the artistic intelligentsia, respectively. The two are divided by a "dragonlike" third character, on whom we zero in next: Viktor Komarovskii.

The Rival: Aged Parasite

A "cold-blooded businessman who knew the Russian business world like the back of his hand" (24), Komarovskii is the hero's antithesis in every respect. He appears as Zhivago's superior in all except the moral point of view: Komarovskii is older and more socially successful, and he outpaces Zhivago in the rivalry over Lara. Whereas Iurii fails in his social career, Komarovskii is a lawyer with connections to the top echelons of both tsarist and Soviet Russia, a man who is "applauded at meetings and mentioned in the newspapers" (49). As opposed to the lethargically inclined Zhivago, Komarovskii is literally labeled a "doer" (24).

The Komarovskii-Zhivago dichotomy follows the actor-thinker paradigm that was central to many a nineteenth-century Russian protagonist-antagonist pair. It is especially reminiscent of this type of coupling through the association of Komarovskii and Zhivago, in relation to Lara, with an old man or father and a child, respectively. The nineteenth century witnessed several similar Russian father-son sets—sometimes symbolic, sometimes genuinely familial—vying for the heroine's love.[158]

If Komarovskii thus recalls classic nineteenth-century antagonists, the triangle Komarovskii-Zhivago-Lara is particularly reminiscent of the plot, which Mints distinguishes somewhat later, in Symbolism, of the sleeping-beauty Russia who needs to be liberated from evil forces by the artist (see chapter 2). As was the case in the early twentieth century, here the Saint George legend is superimposed on a narrative in which the poet-*intelligent* appears as the dragon-slayer and the authorities as the dragon: if Zhivago identifies with Saint George, Komarovskii plays the part of the dragon. From the start, the man is associated with nonhuman spheres. His very name refers to mosquitoes,[159] an allusion that is reinforced when Lara calls him an "aged parasite" (393). In his longing for Lara, Komarovskii is compared to an aggressive "beast," who "gripped" the railing of his staircase "until it hurt his hand" and kicks his bulldog to let off some steam (48–49). His bestial nature is underlined by the "growling noise" (47) of his speech and by his dog's fear that Lara might "infect its master with something human" (49).

Not only Komarovskii the man is reminiscent of an evil, beastly creature. His relationship with Lara is likewise described in terms of evil sorcery: she is "his prisoner," whom he "enslaves" within a "bewitched circle"

(49–50). As stated, Zhivago anticipates the moment when Komarovskii takes Lara away from him as her abduction by a dragon (434, 523–24). In addition, in a draft of the novel, Pasternak represents Zhivago, Lara, and Komarovskii as Perseus, Andromeda, and the sea monster, respectively.[160] As we have seen, only decades prior to this time, Ivanov had taken recourse to the Andromeda-Perseus plot in his symbolic representation of Russia and the intelligentsia as an amorous tragedy.

Komarovskii's role as mythical evildoer is reinforced by the depiction of Lara, which is dominated by metaphors of sleep to such an extent that the sleeping-beauty myth makes itself strongly felt. Komarovskii has a vision of "her head resting on his arm; her eyes were closed, she was asleep, unconscious that he watched her sleeplessly for hours on end. Her hair was scattered on the pillow and its beauty stung his eyes like smoke and ate into his heart" (48). The analogy with a sleeping beauty who is literally in Komarovskii's hands is intensified by Lara's constant wish to sleep during their affair (50); she characterizes the romance as a "nightmare of sensuality which terrified her whenever she awoke from it" (73).[161]

The princess in the "Fairy Tale" poem mirrors Lara's role: the soul of this "beautiful prisoner and prey" is in the "power" of "a dead sleep" (523–24). Just as Lara is symbolically linked with Russia, the princess-to-be-saved is called a "daughter of the earth," and the poem is set in a specifically Russian steppe landscape (524, 522). If one bears in mind the Lara-Russia association, Zhivago's role as the artist, and Komarovskii's as representative of "the old order,"[162] then the parallel with the political allegory that Zara Mints discerns in the Silver Age is notable, at the very least. Striking is the analogy between the passages mentioned and the image of Russia— as a sleeping beauty waiting to be freed from an evil sorcerer—in Blok's *Retribution* and Belyi's "The Green Meadow." As the next section shows, it is not unlikely that Pasternak borrowed this story line directly from Belyi and Blok.

We now have an indication of how fundamentally *Doctor Zhivago* relies on the language and metaphors of early twentieth-century debates on Russia. Pasternak does deviate from the pre-revolutionary paradigm in one crucial respect, however: the historical setting of his story. In *Doctor Zhivago*, the myth of a bridal Russia is transposed largely to the political and historical reality of post-revolutionary Russia. Its political context is defined partly by the intelligentsia-and-people issue in imperial Russia, but decisive for Zhivago's story is the hostile attitude of the *Soviet* system toward artists belonging to the traditional intelligentsia. According to Pasternak's son, the same political theme—the ill-disposed attitude of Soviet authorities toward the cultural intelligentsia—informed his father's play *Blind Beauty*, which deserves some attention here, too.

Chapter Three

Sleeping Versus Blind Beauty

Although set in historic Russia, *Blind Beauty* allegedly articulated Pasternak's personal sense of being "in the grip of the feudal slavery of a system
that strived for the total suppression of creative talents and for spiritual en-
slavement."[163] The play was conceived in the late 1950s, as a dramatic trilogy
featuring nineteenth-century Russia and the developments involved in the
abolition of serfdom.[164] The title refers to a serf woman, Lusha, who is ac-
cidentally blinded by the master of her estate. At the end of the play, which
Pasternak did not complete, she was to regain her sight through the help of
a famous European doctor.[165]

The story echoes *Doctor Zhivago* in more than one respect. Pasternak
evokes Zhivago when qualifying the hero—Lusha's son, Petr—as a "deep,
slow, original, dreamy (à la Blok)" type.[166] The draft of one scene expands
upon the Hamlet and reflection-versus-action themes that are also explored
in *Zhivago*.[167]

More importantly, however, in *Blind Beauty* the feminine-Russia
metaphor that had marked Lara's character morphs into full-fledged allegory. Pasternak's comments on the play show how vital the idea of a feminized Russia has become for him. In conversation, he discloses that Lusha
is "of course symbolic of Russia, oblivious for so long of its own beauty, of
its own destinies."[168] In his eyes, the symbolic heroine specifically represents
traditional Russia or the Russian people. Lusha is equated implicitly with
the Russian peasantry when the sight of her master makes her fall down
in awe, and her colleagues beg her to "rise," commenting that "this is how
much peasant Rus' fears its masters."[169] When the tsar visits the estate where
she lives, he similarly urges its inhabitants to "rise with the words: 'Soon,
soon you will straighten your tortured spine, soon you will rise in full glory,
our poor, original, talented people.'"[170]

Evgenii and Elena Pasternak have commented that Pasternak brought
the allegorical dimension into the play in autumn 1959, when he began
to ponder the "possibility of showing the . . . growth of the creative powers of society: the awakening of the sleeping-beauty Russia."[171] That the
sleeping-beauty concept was pivotal to *Blind Beauty* is already indicated by
its title, which plays on that of the classic fairy tale: in Russian, "Blind Beauty"
and "Sleeping Beauty" share not only the same noun, but also an adverb with
the same first letter; each title consists of an adverb-noun combination with
the same feminine (*-aia* and *-a*) endings (*slepaia krasavitsa, spiashchaia krasavitsa*). The allusion to the sleeping-beauty tale deepens when the estate on
which Lusha is enserfed is branded a "bewitched kingdom."[172]

According to Evgenii and Elena Pasternak, the author claimed that
his view of Russia as a sleeping beauty "was based on Andrei Belyi's

145

symbolic reading of the 'image of the sleeping *pani,* Katerina, whose soul was stolen by a terrible sorcerer'"—a source to which the Pasternaks add Blok's extension of the metaphor in *Retribution.*[173] If this is true, then the foreign doctor who miraculously cures Lusha might serve as the alter ego of the sorcerer, who also comes from abroad and enchants the heroine with his magical talents.

Thus, Pasternak's texts are on a par with *Happy Moscow* in their thematic reliance on gendered representations of Russia, intelligentsia, and state in early twentieth-century Russian culture. However, the adaptation of the metaphor by Pasternak—an "internal émigré from late imperial culture," in Billington's words—relies more openly on the heritage of his predecessors than does that of Platonov.[174] It is true that both Pasternak's novel and the play were written and largely set in Soviet Russia, and that their visions of Russia as a metaphoric bride allude to the transformation of the Russian Empire into Soviet Russia. Nevertheless both flirt—elaborately and, sometimes, explicitly—with the concept as it was formulated in the first decades of the century.

DANIIL ANDREEV: THE RULER'S SWEET CARESS

While Pasternak was working on his novel and play, in a Stalinist jail Daniil Andreev created what he was to consider his magnum opus: *The Rose of the World.*[175] This mystical treatise recycles several of the concepts under discussion within an esoteric conceptual framework. It expresses a utopian vision of history and of the future—one allegedly dictated to Andreev by voices of the "highest spirits" in Russian and universal history.[176]

Andreev's adaptation of the metaphor examined here goes on to play a crucial role in contemporary Russian culture. Having circulated in samizdat from the 1970s on, *The Rose of the World* had achieved cult status by the time the Soviet Union collapsed. "Today," Mikhail Epstein asserted in 1994, "*The Rose of the World* is a source of inspiration and intuition for . . . liberal Westernizers, adherents of religious pluralism . . . and neo-linguists looking for the Aryan primal native land of the national spirit."[177] Fourteen years later, a Google search for *Andreev "Roza mira"* yields 31,200 hits (as opposed to, say, 101,000 for *Tolstoy "Anna Karenina"*; both entered in Cyrillic). Postmodern literature reflects this popularity in its use of the treatise as a prism for refracting the gendered Russia view of Blok and his contemporaries.

With *Rose of the World,* Andreev sought to create a survey of history as "part of a cosmic mystery, originating in several physical worlds at the same time."[178] Russia occupies a central place in this hierarchy of worlds. In keeping with Russian mystical tradition,[179] Andreev is oriented universally, but he assigns a messianic position within the future fate of humanity specifically to Russia.[180] A central role in his view on the fate of the country is assumed by Navna: the feminine "Ecumenical Soul of Russia" ("Sobornaia Dusha Rossii").[181] In esoteric and often contradictory terms,[182] Andreev contrasts this feminine principle with two masculine forces: a cosmic prince or "demiurge" and demonic creatures who capture Navna and who personify the tyrannical aspects of the Russian state. He foresees a future "Heavenly Russia" in Navna's liberation from the demons and her marriage to the demiurge.[100]

Andreev conceives of these events in terms of concrete political forces. He proclaims Peter the Great a puppet in the hands of Russia's demons and princes, alternately, and associates Stalin with the evil forces that capture Russia's Ecumenical Soul.[184] A similar politicization of esoteric concepts marks his poems, in which Ivan the Terrible appears as a mystical lover "whose caress is to Rus' like honey!"[185]

The source of Andreev's gendered mysticism is revealed in the text, which discusses the historical development of Russia's Ecumenical Soul and her relationships with masculine counterforces. His view on these phases— as rephrased by Epstein—forms an occult pendant to the history of the metaphor discussed here:

> In Russia the first embodiment of this ideal femininity [Navna] was Tatiana Larina in Pushkin's *Evgenii Onegin*. Then came Turgenev's women. . . . The highest manifestations of the Eternal Feminine are found in the works of Vladimir Soloviev . . . his sophiological insights . . . became reality in the works and fate of Aleksandr Blok . . . [Blok] fell into the abyss of the demonic feminine, following the steps of the fallen Sophia, who appeared to him as . . . a seductive combination of virgin and whore. . . . This error was not his alone but the entire country's, reflecting the tragic fall of her feminine soul. From the heights of Sophia, to whom many Russian churches were dedicated, the people were stepping into the chasm of revolutionary materialism.[186]

For the occult thinker that Andreev is, the female figures mentioned arose as the result of a conflict between the prince-demiurge and one of Russia's demons.[187] Rather than this gendered mysticism in itself, what is of interest here is the role it eventually comes to play in contemporary Russian culture.[188] More on this in the next chapter.

VASILII GROSSMAN: BRIDEGROOM LENIN

In the late 1980s, after a long ban, the Russian publication of Vasilii Grossman's novel *Forever Flowing* is acclaimed a "major literary landmark."[189]

147

The novel gives rise to fierce controversy, which focuses on Grossman's critical discussion of Lenin's role in the transformation of Russia into the Soviet Union.[190] Presented as notes by the hero, the passage in question is generally seen as a direct expression of the author's political stance.[191] Without rejecting such a view, I approach Grossman's text in the first instance from other—gender- and literary-oriented—perspectives, which have been largely neglected in its discussion to date.

According to the author, Lenin begins as a member of the adversarial intelligentsia and goes on to become the very state whose tyranny he once opposed. The critique is formulated in terms that allude to a number of texts cited here. It is argued that, in order to understand Lenin, one needs to relate his character to the "myth of the national character."[192] That "national character"—which Lenin allegedly shares with political and literary giants of Russian history like Peter the Great and Pushkin—consists of "an attachment to Russian nature . . . akin to the peasant feeling," "susceptibility to the world of Western thought," "universal responsiveness," "anti-stateliness," and, ultimately, slavish subordination to the West.[193]

If the narrator traces this description to nineteenth-century sources, then his gender categories and the context in which they appear particularly echo the gendered representation of Russia, intelligentsia, and state of late-imperial rhetoric. The "dozens of revolutionary theories, beliefs, party leaders," and westernized ideas of the nineteenth-century Russian intelligentsia are opposed to "the young Russia, which has shed the chains of tsarism," as a succession of suitors to a bride.[194] Eventually, the "searching, doubting, estimating glance" of this bride elects Lenin as its "chosen one."[195] As in *Doctor Zhivago*, Russia is thus personified as a virgin whose girlhood is brought to an end by the revolution.

Forever Flowing also shares with *Doctor Zhivago*—and its precursors—the tendency to use the sleeping-beauty myth as an expression of political views. Lenin is claimed to have "unchained" Russia's dream "as in the ancient fairy tale."[196] In Grossman's text, the prince and the captor of the traditional fairy tale merge in this political leader, who mutates from adversarial *intelligent* to become an incarnation of state power. In relation to feminized Russia, he is designated initially as her "chosen" savior, but he gradually reveals himself as a tyrant. This metamorphosis is again formulated in gendered terms, as that of a man physically oppressing a woman: Russia experiences "tighter and tighter . . . the iron hand that led her," whereas Lenin's "intellectual and revolutionary violence" grows more authoritative as his "tread became sterner, his hand heavier."[197]

The similarities between this criticism and that in other texts discussed here are salient. Grossman reproduces in detail Berdiaev's perspective on Russia as a bride, who subordinates herself to the West and marries a "wrong," authoritative "husband." Like Berdiaev's, his bridal metaphor refers to the relationship involving nation, intelligentsia, and regime. In this later text, however, the focus of attention is—understandably—revolutionary and post-revolutionary Russia. Accordingly, the political context to which the metaphor refers shifts: rather than the imperial state or Germany, here Russia's "wrong husband" is Lenin or the Soviet state.

Despite this shift, Grossman's text often corresponds literally to debates on Russia from the early decades of the century. Word for word, it repeats the qualities that Berdiaev and his contemporaries applied to Russia and the intelligentsia in relation to the state or the West: Grossman's feminized Russia is a "slave" characterized by "submissiveness" and "complaisance," and the intelligentsia's attitude to the West is described as "anti-stately," "susceptible," and "responsive"; Berdiaev, Rozanov, and Ivanov had applied precisely the same terms in a similar context.[198] Grossman's text also preserves images of Russia from Silver Age poetry, such as the "iron hand" with which the state leads a feminized Russia in Blok's *Retribution*[199] and the werewolf motif used for Russia's suitor in Belyi's "The Green Meadow." Like Belyi's sorcerer, Lenin appears as an apparent savior who awakens Russia from dreams but turns out to be an evil force. The association with "The Green Meadow" is reinforced when Grossman claims that the Russian "national character" is marked by an affinity for Russian nature "in its form as forest and meadow."[200]

A lack of information concerning Grossman's intellectual biography makes it hard to establish the extent to which he consciously relied on the authors and concepts mentioned. The novel does point in that direction: in one scene, reading Blok's works symbolizes the supposedly humane existence of pre-Stalinist times.[201] Critics have discussed *Forever Flowing*'s reliance on the political views of Berdiaev, Bulgakov, Voloshin, and Merezhkovskii.[202] The appearance of some of these authors' ideas in *Doctor Zhivago* might have revived them for Grossman, who read—and disapproved of—Pasternak's novel while working on *Forever Flowing* in 1958.[203]

Once again, however, the question is not whether the authors, publications, and views mentioned here served as concrete inspiration for this particular work. Significant is the simple fact that the concepts they expressed resurfaced decades later, in a critique of the Soviet regime.

PRISON TATTOOS: RAPING THE NATION

If the "bride Russia" idea appears sporadically in Soviet Russia's nonofficial literature, then the motif of Russia as unequivocal sex object is rampant in less highbrow Soviet images: tattoos worn by Russian prisoners. These tattoos are, at times, less distant from the gender metaphors of Platonov and other writers than one might expect.

Thus, an anti-Soviet tattoo represents the first head of the Cheka, Felix Dzerzhinskii, as an enormous figure with a hairy claw, in which he is about to clench a naked girl.[204] If commentators are right in claiming that in the tattoo, Dzerzhinskii "represents the Russian authorities in all their forms," then surely the girl whom he threatens must be Russia or the Russian people.[205]

The naked-woman motif, is, in general, popular in nationalist tattoo imagery. Anti-Semitic tattoos from the 1960s visualize, alternatively, Russia-cum-Estonia, Estonia, and Belarus as a voluptuous naked woman who is raped or seduced by hairy devils: the Communists or—in a popular reading of the October Revolution as a Jewish conspiracy—"the Jews."[206] Other popular tattoos from the 1950s and 1960s depict Russia itself as a beautiful naked woman harassed by Jews.[207] An example is an image in which two bearded devils ("the Jews," thus the accompanying text) penetrate a naked woman ("Russia") both vaginally and orally. One devil holds a flag with Lenin's portrait and the words "all power to the Soviets."[208] At the time, similar images abound in tattoos displaying citizens of the Caucasus or blacks in the role of Russia's rapists.[209]

In far-from-subtle pictorial terms, these Soviet-era tattoos reenact the gendered political metaphor explored here. That their makers were referring to Blok or Belyi—let alone Platonov or Pasternak—is not very likely. On the other hand, their renditions of a feminine Russia cannot be explained as mere variations on classic female allegories. Rather than representing the native land as a positive figure rendered temporarily inaccessible by external causes, their "brides Russia" portray a struggle between the country's internal authorities (the "Jews" or Soviets) and an imagined native Russian essence, which often eagerly partakes in the sexual abuse fraught upon it. As such, these popular representations of Russia have more in common with the texts we have been contemplating than with traditional gender-related political allegories.

Although an open intellectual debate was lacking in Soviet culture, the aforementioned analyses show that the tendency to represent the relationship Russia-state-intelligentsia as an amorous tragedy does not disappear during this period. The gendered view of Russia that prevailed in late-imperial discourse reemerges in a number of nonofficial texts (and images), all of which extend the metaphor to either the revolutionary period or Soviet Russia. In these texts, the idea underpinning the metaphor shifts from the problematic position of the pre-revolutionary intelligentsia within the triangle to newer relationships: one being that between the Soviet state and the former artistic intelligentsia, and the other being that between the Soviet state and the Soviet intelligentsia. At this point, however, the very categories of "state" and "intelligentsia" have become a complete blur.

Despite the change, the examples cited are solidly rooted in pre-revolutionary culture both thematically and linguistically. In addition, the authors all share with their predecessors a personal commitment to the theme of Russia's political fate. Feminine representations of Russia by Platonov, Pasternak, Andreev, and Grossman invariably draw inspiration from the authors' personal views on Russia's political or social destiny. Platonov feels "excessive anxiety" over the lot of the Soviet Union; Pasternak is said to "suffer from" and to "adore" Russia's fate; to Andreev, "Heavenly Russia" is a utopia whispered to him by spiritual predecessors; Grossman's work is considered a direct expression of its author's political opinions; and the "brides Russia" of prison tattoos are unlikely to refer to anything but their bearers' political views.

In this context of distinct authorial commitment, the metaphor preserves the political power of expression it possessed during the early twentieth century—a power that virtually vanishes when it reemerges as a prominent concept in postmodern culture. What follows is an in-depth discussion of the status of the metaphor within this new cultural environment.

Russia's Orgasm, or Marrying Putin:
Late Soviet and Post-Soviet Culture

WHEN INTERVIEWED IN 1991, the writer Vladi-
mir Sorokin wondered why he was always asked about ethical and social dimensions in his work: "I don't understand . . . aren't those just letters on a
piece of paper?"[1] His remark, which implies total indifference to any type
of social engagement, represents a giant leap from the attitude of distress
that authors like Blok and Pasternak conveyed when writing about the fate
of Russia.

Sorokin's statement appears less radical, however, when viewed as part
of a tendency that had gained substantial ground in the decades preceding
the interview in question, and that is generally known as the Russian variant
of postmodernism. In keeping with international trends, from roughly the
late 1960s on—and earlier, according to some—a new cultural-philosophical
mentality began taking shape in (mainly underground) Russian intellectual
circles.[2] The exact nature of this "postmodern" mentality is debated to this
day, but scholars more or less agree on what has become a well-known collection of its distinctive features: the conviction that all ideologies and hier-
archies are relative, which has led to the constant blending of cultures
traditionally labeled "high" and "low"; the pursuit of semantic pluralism,
transgression, play, and intertextuality (or an awareness that all has been said,
that is, "everything is quotation"); theoretical self-reflection on one's work; a
distrust of metanarratives or master narratives; and a tendency toward the
demythologization or deconstruction of cultural myths and stereotypes.[3]
When interviewed in 1991, Sorokin was a major and self-conscious representative of the Russian pendant of this new mode of thought.

It would be an exaggeration to label all the works discussed in this
chapter postmodern to the bone or to try fitting them neatly into theoretical
postmodern paradigms. Yet each author involved incorporates "bride Russia" metaphors into work that, in some way or another, displays several of
the features mentioned in the preceding paragraph.

The incorporation of these metaphors occurs in a Russian context where, as scholars have shown, postmodernism takes on a slightly different guise than it does in western-European-cum-American spheres.[4] One difference that has implications for "our" metaphor is the totalitarian context within which Russian postmodernism arises. If American postmodernism reacts in part to the commercial mass culture of late capitalism, Russian *postmodernizm* is born in a society that generates ideological content rather than consumer satisfaction. As a result, more than its American pendant, Russian postmodernism is "politicized," since one of the key languages to be deconstructed is that of socialist realism.[5] Not coincidentally, a recurring (postmodern) literary motif in the 1980s and 1990s, the decades pertinent to most of the texts discussed here, is that of "evaluating Soviet history, refracted through the prism of cultural history."[6] In general, Russian postmodernists are keen to travesty concepts that involve Russian history and national identity—the same concepts that have haunted Russian philosophers and writers from the outset.[7] As one might expect, the vision of Russia as unattainable bride is among their favorite objects of parody, and in 1990, when the Soviet Union collapses and censorship is abolished, gendered representations of Russia, intelligentsia, and state reemerge in literary and intellectual culture in unprecedented quantities.

For contemporary writers and thinkers, however, the metaphor no longer refers to political ideals in which they genuinely believe. It has become more of a cultural-literary cliché that begs to be unmasked. Never averse to relativistic play, postmodern authors have a particular appetite for "bride Russia" metaphors. The political factors that feed this appetite include the shift in sociopolitical categories that began influencing the metaphor in 1917. In late- and post-Soviet Russia, the state-intelligentsia-people tripod has lost its topicality even more than in the early Soviet years. Neither in Brezhnev's Soviet Union nor in post-Soviet Russia can an intelligentsia in the classic sense of the term be discerned. In late Soviet Russia, the group that identifies most strongly with "the intelligentsia" is the dissident movement, but this movement can hardly be said to share the "gnawing sense of moral obligation" toward "the dispossessed (the 'people')" that typified the traditional intelligentsia.[8] Russian dissidents concentrate more on exposing the crudities of the Soviet regime than on any personal relationship with "the people."

In addition, the very notion of preserving a native population or native essence had acquired too much of a *Blut-und-Boden* taste after the Second World War to retain its previous status of a burning social issue, in Russia as elsewhere. The same applies to the concept of defending the fate of an idealized (and feminized) "people": a concept virtually impossible to approach with authentic oppositional commitment after having been persistently exploited by the Soviet regime. Not coincidentally are those Russian writers and thinkers who *have* focused on populist and national ideologies in recent decades known as conservative and politically right-wing figures—think Aleksandr Solzhenitsyn or Valentin Rasputin. More postmodernistically inclined Russian intellectuals regard the classic intelligentsia's preoccupation with "the people" as a historical fact with which they cannot identify anymore.

The postmodern tendency to travesty former renditions of feminized metaphors for Russia is also fueled by a more pragmatic turn of events: renewed accessibility to the country's cultural heritage in post-Soviet society. After a brief and relative freedom of the press in the 1960s, the end of the century witnesses what Andrei Voznesenskii has tagged a "Renaissance in print."[9] Between approximately 1987 and 1990, a large number of formerly forbidden texts see the light of day, among which are most of the works and authors mentioned in the previous chapters. Whereas Blok had been reprinted in the Thaw era, Berdiaev had been out of print for decades in Russia before new editions of his work appeared in the 1990s.[10] The 1990s also witness reprints of and renewed interest in the *Milestones* collection, with its focus on the intelligentsia and the people. According to one scholar, "as soon as one could speak openly about Russia's national identity and future" after the initiation of perestroika, old political debates were resumed and "old terms such as Westernizers and Slavophiles cropped up again."[11] Solov'ev receives renewed attention.[12] And in the late 1980s and early 1990s, the previously discussed works of Platonov, Pasternak, Andreev, and Grossman are published in Russia for the first time (with the exception of *Blind Beauty*, which appeared earlier).

This is not to say that the works discussed in the preceeding chapters were wholly absent from public consciousness during the Soviet years. Not only do certain texts by Pasternak, Andreev, and Grossman circulate in samizdat from the 1970s on; also available in the private sphere are copies or old publications of works by Berdiaev, Solov'ev, and several of their contemporaries. Blok is never considered taboo. Crucial to the period of perestroika, however, is the shift in status of most of the texts discussed here: rather than being works that are secretly distributed and discussed, they are (renewed) objects of public debate that readers can obtain quite easily.

Given the interaction among the relevant factors—a playful return to cultural myths and stereotypes, renewed possibilities for critical discussion, and the reentry into public debate of texts reverting to national gender metaphors—it is not surprising that toward the end of the century, "bride Russia" once more occupies a central place in Russian literature and culture. In fact, the metaphor explored here already emerges in a distinctly postmodern context in several texts from the latter years of the Soviet regime. This chapter pauses to examine the adaptation of the metaphor in both postmodern works of this period and post-Soviet texts.

Heading the list is Venedikt Erofeev's *Moscow to the End of the Line.* Written in 1969 and circulating in samizdat from then until its official Russian publication in 1988–89, the novella marks a milestone in the history of the metaphor: in Erofeev's rendition, it appears first as a literary rather than as a politically motivated metaphor.[13] The author's genetically unrelated namesake, writer-cum-critic Viktor Erofeev, passes in review as well. Numerous coincidences meriting our attention are covered in a comparative analysis of Viktor Erofeev's novel *Russian Beauty,* written in 1980–82, and Vladimir Sorokin's novel *Marina's Thirtieth Love,* written in 1982–83.[14] Other works by Erofeev, Sorokin, and certain of their contemporaries are considered briefly. In addition, this chapter explores refigurations of the metaphor in the work of the popular post-Soviet writer Viktor Pelevin, in Mikhail Berg's novel "Ros and I," and in the poetry of the self-proclaimed "new sentimentalist" poet Timur Kibirov. In passing, the chapter reviews the metaphor's frequent occurrence outside literature, in contemporary philosophy, film, the visual arts, and in popular culture.

Thus, our focus is on the last two decades of the twentieth century. This division may seem arbitrary: from a strictly historical point of view, texts appearing in the 1980s qualify for analysis as products of the Soviet era. A more cultural-historically oriented approach, however, prompts their discussion as exponents of postmodern tendencies—tendencies that took flight only in post-Soviet Russia. The authors discussed here identify far more often with international postmodern developments than with Soviet culture. According to Sally Laird, they see Russian culture as "an object of phenomenological interest, not of political speculation."[15]

By implication, in spite of individual differences, they share a predominantly apolitical, ironic approach to the metaphor. They seek to deprive it of its original ideological function of expressing concern about Russia's future—a function that feminine representations of Russia still had in Pasternak's and Grossman's work. Instead, they approach the myth of Russia, the unattainable beloved, as one of many national clichés that clamor to be dismantled. That this interpretation does not always match with the reality of the text is a subject touched on later in this chapter.

Postmodernists' deconstructivist attitude to the metaphor coincides with a renewed focus on sexuality. Postmodern authors not only revive the fixation on gender issues that marked the early twentieth century but also turn sex into a thoroughly physical matter. Explicit sexual content now serves to underline the impossibility of any "deeper" moral or metaphysical thought behind visible reality.

This alleged impossibility brings us to a paradox that marks virtually all postmodern "bride Russia" texts: the contradiction between a claim that any moral or political commitment is alien to the Russian postmodernists' work, on the one hand, and the stated preference of the same group for issues of Russian identity, on the other. Such a predilection for "Russian themes" does suggest thematic commitment on behalf of the authors. So, too, do a number of utterances by the authors in question in interviews and essays.[16] This tension between pathos and apparent indifference is a cardinal concern of the analyses presented here.

VENEDIKT EROFEEV: IN LOVE WITH RUSSIA'S EYES

From the moment that Venedikt Erofeev's *Moscow to the End of the Line* begins circulating in samizdat in 1969, its cult status within Russian literature is sealed. Mark Lipovetsky speaks of the novel's solid impact "on the entire subsequent development of . . . contemporary Russian literature" and of a work that ushers the "postmodernist artistic paradigm . . . into the context of the Russian cultural tradition."[17] Postmodern irony—coupled with a healthy dose of Russian-national bias—also defines Erofeev's revision of the "bride Russia" metaphor.

As said earlier, in Erofeev's novella the association of Russia with an unattainable female beloved is literarily rather than politically motivated. The large number of intertextual references indicate that this association is, in fact, one of the key themes of the novel.

To start with, the novella is defined as a *poema,* a subtitle that recalls Gogol's *Dead Souls,* to which the text has been compared more than once.[18] Their kinship is reinforced by the plot, which, like that of *Dead Souls,* revolves around the "symbolic journey" of the hero's soul.[19] In Erofeev's case, this journey parallels the train trip that the hero-narrator Venichka tries to make from Moscow to the provincial town of Petushki to see his beloved. Getting steadily drunker as the narrative unfolds, Venichka muses on his alienation from society and from the people around him.

A significant background note to Erofeev's adaptation of this theme is the gender-informed view on intelligentsia and Russia of Blok and others of his like. The hero envisions his beloved in Petushki as a mystical feminine principle reminiscent of Solov'ev's World Soul and Blok's Beautiful Lady. According to Natal'ia Verkhovtseva-Drubek, Venichka literally "longs for the feminine hypostasis of the Trinity, for the fair-faced Sophia."[20] Like Solov'ev's poet, who "does not name" his muse, Venichka addresses his beloved as a nameless "you" or "she."[21] Where Solov'ev's "radiant friend" appeared to him surrounded by roses in the "purple of a heavenly glow" with eyes "filled with sky-blue fire,"[22] Venichka envisions his girl amidst "roses" dressed "in purple," with eyes like "clouds" (47, 88).[23] The emphasized reference to Venichka's mystical lover as "t h a t g i r l" and "s h e" (38, 43; double-space in original) also evokes Blok's hailing of the Beautiful Lady as You or She, capitalized. Blok resounds, too, in the hero's claim that he needs to "wait for her until dawn" (98)—the same time frame used by Blok's poet while awaiting the Beautiful Lady. Eduard Vlasov has reconstructed a number of additional elements in the lexicon used to describe Venichka's beloved that can be traced directly to Blok's feminine muse.[24]

The link with Blok's oeuvre is not surprising for readers familiar with Erofeev, who said he knew twenty-nine of Blok's poems by heart and that he was "in love with all those wonderful little Silver Age children."[25] Erofeev adapts not only the general outlines of the mystical feminine principle of these Silver Age children: he also recycles the concept of the mystical female beloved as a hypostasis of Russia. Throughout the work, Venichka's beloved is bracketed with Petushki, a place envisioned by the hero as the heavenly future utopia where his "liberation and happiness" lie (37; see also 54). This is not a universal utopia: even the title of the novella points out the contrast between this distinctly rural Russian space and the urban locus of Moscow. In Petushki, the girl said to be awaiting the hero embodies a classic Russian ideal of beauty, with her repeatedly glorified "ginger eyelashes," "braid from neck to bottom," and "gentle forms" (38, 45, 99). She is addressed repeatedly as "tsarina," a distinctly Russian title (41, 73, 113) which echoes the "national tsarina" designation that Blok lent his female muse. The "autumn day" on which the narrator hopes to see her evokes the title of a *Native Land* poem which equates Russia with a wife (99). In a more political context, Blok's concept of revolutionary Russia as a woman reverberates when the revolution is called "feverish, but beautiful [*prekrasna*]" (93).[26]

Erofeev reinforces the association of geographical space with a mystical bride through references to earlier sources. Venichka's longing to see Petushki is formulated in terms that parallel the apocalyptic vision of Jerusalem as Christ's bride (38).[27] He refers to his beloved as both exalted bride and "whore," using biblical designations for Jerusalem and Babylon (47).[28] A link between specifically Russian space and feminine categories is suggested when two characters argue—in an obvious allusion to the conclusion of Goncharov's *Precipice* (see chapter 1)—about whether or not "the Native land" is a grandmother (78).

But the early twentieth-century feminine concept of the poet as Russia's lover forms the most notable background for Erofeev's rendition of the metaphor. Blok emerges in several passages that center on the motif of meeting glances. Highlighted elements in the description of the narrator's beloved are her "whitish eyes," eyelashes, and glance (38, 44, 46, 113). The anxiety that Venichka experiences upon confronting her gaze is paralleled by his emotional reaction to glances directed at him by fellow travelers. Early in the story, he interprets such glances as the collective gaze of the "Russian people" (27–28). Somewhat later he elaborates on his observation.

> The one who looked at me, like the last time, with dozens of eyes—large, ready for anything, jumping from their sockets—the one who looked me in the eye was my native land, popping out of its sockets, ready for anything, large. Then, after a hundred and fifty grams of Russian vodka, I liked those eyes. Now, after five hundred grams of Kuban' vodka, I was in love with those eyes, in love like a madman. (58)

In this passage, the narrator's mistress, the Russian people, and his "native land"—the term that Blok used for Russia in its capacity as a beloved—symbolically coalesce. Apart from Blok's "bride Russia," who turned her "starry eyes" to the poet, the scene evokes a passage that supposedly inspired Blok—the "eyes filled with expectations" that Gogol's Rus' fixes on the narrator in *Dead Souls* (see chapters 1 and 2). In an ironic fashion, Erofeev thus reenacts the concept of the narrator-poet whose eyes meet those of a feminine Russia.

Erofeev also reiterates Blok's feminized Russia when depicting his exalted muse's inherent "darker" side. Verkhovtseva-Drubek sees Erofeev's heroine as part of the tradition of "profanation of an object of religious reverence" that is found in Dostoevsky and continues through Blok's female figures.[29] Venichka's beloved is indeed a divine-cum-profane figure. On the one hand, she is a "queen," "goddess," and "tsarina" (41, 44, 73, 113) who—like an unearthly being—possesses "bluish wings" (44). Pivotal to her depiction are the epithets "white" and "whitish," words traditionally associated with purity and saintliness (38, 41, 44–46); and she is literally called "saintly" (45). On the other hand, she appears as "unfaithful" and as a "temptress," "seductress," "whore," and "female demon" (38, 44–45, 47). Vlasov connects the "bliss and fragrance" and love of alcohol of Erofeev's heroine to the smell of "perfume and mists" of Blok's stranger, who moves "amidst drunkards."[30] In keeping with early twentieth-century—and, by extension, Gnostic—tradition, the exalted and the profane appear as two indissoluble sides of the same coin within Erofeev's heroine. The author's favorite means of expressing this indissolubility is the oxymoron: she is labeled a "shameless tsarina," a "favorite strumpet," and a "harmonious bitch" (41, 44).

Crucial to Erofeev's adaptation of the classic angelic-demonic paradigm is the overtly sexual dimension he gives it. Even though the "fallen woman" with whom Russia is associated in the works discussed in earlier chapters—from Blok to Grossman—is promiscuous, her physical dimension remains abstract (with the notable exception of Platonov's *Moscow*). Erofeev breaks with tradition by depicting the mystical beloved in Petushki in highly concrete terms. The physical pleasure that the narrator derives from his contact with her is underlined: he eulogizes her "gentle forms," "magnificent body," and "secret curves" (38, 45, 47). He pays detailed attention to a description of her body when they are first intimate: "like the heaven and earth was her belly. . . . And everything fused: roses, lilies, and that moist and quivering entry to Eden, curly all over . . . O, the sobbing of those bowels! . . . O, sweet navel!" (46–47). The beloved that Venichka links metaphorically to the earth is thus endowed with a tangible, sexually attractive body. This physical explicitness marks a crucial shift from modern to postmodern representations of Russia as bride-to-be. It is in *Moscow to the End of the Line* that such a shift can first be discerned.

So far, the association of the "Petushki girl" with Russia and the Russian people corresponds to Blok's and Solov'ev's female muses, in particular. A closer look at the hero-narrator reveals, however, that what sparks Erofeev's interest in these figures is the more politically oriented theme of people and intelligentsia that occupied so many minds at the beginning of the century. The central character, Venichka, exemplifies to perfection an intellectual who feels alienated from both the regime and ordinary people. His attitude toward the common people who surround him on his journey can hardly be understood as anything other than an ironic revision of the populist wish to merge with the people. If the narrator's idolizing of the eyes of his fellow Russians points in that direction, then Venichka literally blends with the people around him while being "absorbed" and "piled up inside" the "public's avalanche" at a minor train station near Petushki (87). In general, as Verkhovtseva-Drubek argues, the "joint drinking" of Venichka and his fellow travelers throughout the trip to Petushki can be read as his "merging with the people."[31] Andrei Zorin speaks of "slang and alcohol" as the "meeting place of the intelligentsia and the people" in Erofeev's novella.[32]

In *Moscow to the End of the Line,* intelligentsia and people do not really meet, though: the novella stresses the basic inability of "the poet" or hero to merge with the common people. Venichka, who refers to himself as a "poet" and as someone with a "delicate nature," accuses himself of thinking that he is "smarter and better than others" (45, 28, 98). His housemates interpret his refusal to notify them of his visits to the lavatory as a sign that he considers himself "higher than others" (29). He identifies with "the whole thinking part of Russia," whose futile efforts to "write about the simple man" and to "save him" have led to collective drunkenness "through despair" (65). As Zorin has shown, this statement might be linked to increasing interest, toward the end of the 1960s, in the Decembrist movement, "in which the oppositional intelligentsia that had formed at that time saw an analogy to its own social alienation from both regime and the masses."[33] The narrator does refer to the Decembrists in this passage (65); and he identifies with Dmitrii Pisarev, the Uspenskii cousins, and other artists linked to the populist movement (ibid.).[34]

Zorin rightly argues, then, that *Moscow to the End of the Line* revises "the eternal issues of Russian literature: the intelligentsia and the regime, the intelligentsia and the people."[35] It does so in terms that specifically evoke their discussion in the gendered terms of (pre-)revolutionary days. The novella reenacts the early twentieth-century accusation that the intelligentsia is excessively boyish and feminine, for example. The narrator is compared to a toddler and to women—Scheherazade, a "sweet female traveler," the woman in an Ivan Kramskoi painting, an "old granny," an "old bitch," Little Red Riding Hood—throughout the story (84, 96, 105, 109).[36] Although the typification of a hero as feminine and childish had marked Russian literature even in the nineteenth century, it can be assumed that Erofeev's protagonist is more a continuation of the early twentieth-century tradition. Erofeev is a devotee of the Silver Age, and Verkhovtseva-Drubek stresses Erofeev's affinity with the Symbolists, claiming that his "literary fever" lies with Belyi and Viacheslav Ivanov.[37] Erofeev's sympathy for Rozanov is well known. And we have witnessed how Vlasov reconstructed Venichka's bond with Blok's lyrical ego.

The link with the early twentieth century is intensified by Venichka's adoption of the hero's tendency—crucial to (post-)Symbolist debate—to envision himself, in relation to his "Russian muse," as a knight in search of his princess. At the beginning of the story, his dilemma at a fork in the road (18) has been read as a symbolic equivalent of the crisis of the folkloric knight.[38] He speaks of himself as an "idiot and brave knight": terms that evoke the image of Don Quixote and Wagner's Lohengrin (see 40, 72, 88).[39] That he poses specifically as the knight in the sleeping-beauty tale is suggested by his depiction of the search for his beloved as a journey "through the brushwood of dog roses" to a "Heavenly Princess" (95).

The novel travesties the alienation of this classic knightly hero from not only the people but also the regime. Venichka "spit[s] on the president's armchair" and defies the "enthusiasts" and "heroic deeds" of Soviet Russia (22, 92); in retrospect, he also criticizes the dogmas that such divergent characters as Peter the Great and the radical revolutionary Nikolai Kibal'chich "imposed" on the Russians as "not ours" (52). Thus, to Venichka—as to many an *intelligent* before him—the intelligentsia's antagonistic attitude to both the state and the West combine to form an entity. Vlasov has compared the language in which Erofeev's hero expresses that fusion to rhetorical devices used by Berdiaev and Rozanov,[40] but it might also allude to Soviet adaptations of Berdiaev's and Rozanov's ideas by Grossman (see chapter 3), whose work Erofeev claimed to admire.[41]

While Venichka compares the authorities that he despises with the "real" Russia of Petushki—where "our mission" lies (52)—the key to the story is found in his dual inability to break away from those authorities and to reach his utopia. On a symbolic level, the regime ultimately signs his death warrant when instead of finding Petushki's rural idyll he ends his journey near the ultimate symbol of state authority: the Moscow Kremlin. He is killed at the doorway of a nearby house by a violent foursome. In Vlasov's opinion, Venichka's observation that he has "seen those mugs" in newspapers suggests a reading of his killers as Marx, Engels, Lenin, and Stalin.[42] The final blow is dealt by "one of them, with the fiercest and most classic profile" (119). If Vlasov correctly interprets this character as the symbolic double of Stalin himself, then the story ends in a symbolic triumph of the Soviet system over the oppositional poet-*intelligent*.[43] His failure to reach the feminized Russian utopia of Petushki, together with his murder by representatives of the Soviet regime, inevitably forms an extension of the myth of Russia as the intelligentsia's unattainable bride.

As shown, Erofeev's adaptation of this myth does not remain unaffected by postmodern play. In *Moscow to the End of the Line*, the myth is presented in a highly ironic manner and in the context of the linguistic play and intertextual parody so typical of postmodernism. Here—to quote Andrei Zorin—the traditional oppositions of intelligentsia to "people" and state are "resolved in the linguistic sphere," above all else.[44] By implication, the metaphoric equating of Russia with the poet's unattainable bride has become an object of ironic-linguistic play.

Yet the novella can in no way be reduced to mere parody. Erofeev has been described as someone who "constantly oscillat[es] between seriousness and humour."[45] The same oscillation marks his attitude toward the issue of Russia's identity. His friend, the poet Ol'ga Sedakova, points to "acute national self-consciousness" as one of his features; according to her, Erofeev "had . . . a very strong Russian identification. Categories like 'we' and 'they' ('they' was Europe) remained real. He would say in all seriousness: '*We* taught *them* to write novels (Dostoevsky), music (Mussorgsky), and so on.'"[46] Referring specifically to *Moscow to the End of the Line*, Joost van Baak writes that "the (abstract) author's position is not that of a distantial postmodern collector of 'simulacra'"; instead it exemplifies "a continuous effort to occupy a moral position—that of the victimized individual against the immoral, repressive, and anonymous Soviet power."[47]

The following pages offer my argument that the tension between ironic distance and authentic pathos is a legacy left to Viktor Erofeev and Vladimir Sorokin. In their adaptation of the "bride Russia" metaphor, they echo several features of Venedikt Erofeev's revision of the myth, including the combination of a "detached" postmodern position and a genuine

fascination with "Russian" themes. This paradox, first made tangible in Erofeev's novella, is poised to mark most postmodern appropriations of the
metaphor.

VIKTOR EROFEEV AND VLADIMIR SOROKIN: RUSSIA'S ORGASM

In the summer of 2002, in conversations I had with each of them, Sorokin
referred to Viktor Erofeev as a "linguist" and to himself, by contrast, as an
"artist"; and Erofeev branded the Sorokin of the 1980s an "artistic Bohemian," in contrast to the "genuine literary dissident" he claims to have been
at the time.[48] While both are considered Russian postmodernists par excellence, they do not operate within the same literary circle. Sorokin began
his career as part of "Moscow conceptualism," a loosely connected underground movement that was pursuing a "deconstruction of Soviet ideological
language by presenting it as a language of a total metaphysical simulation."[49]
In radical literary experiments, he focused on random ideological linguistic
styles, from Soviet propaganda to nineteenth-century realist discourse. His
newer publications differ strongly from his early work, and in recent years
Sorokin has dissociated himself in no uncertain terms from postmodernism.[50] Until today, however, the majority of his texts still fall under Dagmar
Burckhart's 1999 definition of his work as a "tautological copying of styles,
jargons, and pretexts, as well as their combination into a supertext or mega-
text."[51] Crucial to this collage-like poetics are confrontations among sharply
contrasting styles, which serve to stress the relativity of each one involved.

Erofeev, by contrast, began his literary career as a critic. Although
he toys with random linguistic styles no less eagerly than Sorokin, the principle of collage is alien to his work. Clashes in his texts are not the result
of confrontations between individually coherent passages, but rather of a
stylistic or linguistic "dissonance that saturates the entire text," to quote
Mark Lipovetsky.[52]

The following sections concentrate on Erofeev's *Russian Beauty* and
Sorokin's *Marina's Thirtieth Love*. In these novels, the difference between
the two authors is counteracted by a highly similar thematic appropriation
of the "Russia bride" metaphor.[53] In our conversations, both claimed to have
written the novels in question independently—a remarkable disclosure,
given the many coincidences between the two narratives. In both works,
"our" gendered metaphor is not only implied in the opposition of a group
of Soviet dissidents to a sexually promiscuous heroine whose fate coalesces
with that of Russia; but both teem with inverted, sexualized allusions to ear-

lier versions of the metaphor: each uses an orgasm of mythical proportions to symbolize the hero's marriage to Russia; and both translate the social inadequacies of the intelligentsia into the theme of sexual impotence among Russian dissidents.

Irina and Marina: Russian Beauties

The resemblance between Erofeev's and Sorokin's novels manifests itself primarily in the profile of their heroines. Both are sexually promiscuous women who move to Moscow after growing up in provincial Russia. Erofeev's story focuses on Irina Vladimirovna Tarakanova, a prostitute with lesbian inclinations who has several sexual escapades with Soviet dissidents. In her search for true love, she becomes involved with the fictional éminence grise of political and cultural Moscow of the 1980s: Vladimir Sergeevich, alias Leonardik. In purposely contradictory terms, Erofeev creates the image of a mystical marriage between Irina and her lover and their possible conception of a son. Interwoven with this plot line is Irina's attempt to have a mystical "enemy" of Russia save that same Russia by penetrating her. Ultimately, the mystical marriage and resulting pregnancy seem to be realized through an equally mystical act of coitus between Irina and the then-deceased Leonardik—"seem to be" because the plot deliberately leaves room for multiple interpretations.

Sorokin's novel concentrates on the markedly similar story of Marina Ivanovna Alekseeva, a piano teacher who leads a sexually promiscuous life in 1980s Moscow, indulging in sexual excesses with lesbian lovers as well as prominent dissidents. Like Erofeev's story, Sorokin's centers on the notion of a mystical union between the heroine and her future Mr. Right. Envisioned by Marina as a messianic character, this bridegroom-to-be eventually turns up in the form of the prominent Communist Party official Sergei Nikolaevich Rumiantsev. Through him, Marina experiences her first orgasm with a man, a climax that marks her transformation from a flesh-and-blood individual to a cardboard character and model Soviet citizen. Marina's story ends even more inconclusively than that of her Erofeevian counterpart, with a newspaper item—stereotypical propaganda—from an old issue of *Pravda* that has nothing to do with the plot. The piece was randomly added to the tail end of the book by a friend of the author's who didn't mind doing the typing.[54]

As the summaries show, the stories of these two heroines progress along largely similar lines. In developing the plots, both authors turn to travesties of cultural myths that coalesce in equal detail.

"Very Russian"

In an essay on *Marina's Thirtieth Love,* David Gillespie speaks of Viktor Erofeev's heroine Irina as an "interesting point of comparison" with Marina: "For both Ir[in]a and Marina, the body is a text on which, in which, is decided in parodic terms the destiny of Russia."[55] As women whose fates are closely linked to that of Russia, both heroines deserve—without reservation—the label "Russian Beauty."

In Erofeev's text, the symbolic link that welds Irina to Russia is both implicit (through the plot) and explicit. The novel culminates in a scene in which Irina appoints herself Russia's mystical savior. She wants the act of liberation to take place on Kulikovo field—a setting that is inextricably interwoven with the gendered representation of Russia in Blok's poems, as explained in chapter 2 (304).[56] Reinforcing the poet's presence in this scene is Irina's assertion earlier in the story that she has "come to love Blok" and has learned his poems by heart (150). Not surprisingly, then, references to Blok resonate in her depictions of the struggle to liberate Russia from its alleged "enemy." Her elliptical description of the setting in which the enemy first appears—"Night. Street." (281)—evokes Blok's poem "Night, Street, Lantern, Drugstore . . ." ("Noch, ulitsa, fonar, apteka . . . ," 1912); on her way to Kulikovo field she literally echoes Blok's poem "Russia" when claiming that now "the impossible is possible" (333);[57] earlier, she has called the champagne she drinks "Blok-Gamaiun," a reference to an early Blok poem (29);[58] and the comparison of one of her lovers to a "kite" that "fell down" on her corresponds to the high-flier circling above Russia in "The Kite" (279).[59]

It is suggested throughout the novel that Irina not only operates as Russia's savior but also serves as its symbolic representative. She is described repeatedly as a patriot, a "Russian woman," and someone of "very Russian" and "national" beauty (58, 131, 188, 224, 256, 339, 362). Mimicking Pushkin's Tat'iana, she introduces herself to Vladimir Sergeevich as a "thoroughbred Russian girl" who "love[s] winter" (57–58). Irina refuses to emigrate, claiming she does not "know any languages, only folk verses" (257). She is praised for her "Slavic bravery and charm" (242). Irina explicitly identifies with Russia in the Kulikovo scene when asserting that "two fates require resolution: that of Russia and my own" (309). Deliberately dressed in the "national colors" of the Russian flag (309), she wants the setting to look like a painting "by Vasnetsov or something"; this artist's work was inspired by Russian history and folklore (332).[60] In a possible allusion to Pasternak and Blok, Vladimir Sergeevich first sees Irina in a "lilac dress" (50): as mentioned, the lilac dress of Pasternak's Lara linked her to the Russia of pre-revolutionary years, which Blok had called "lilac."

All in all, Erofeev is laying it on thick: his Irina is Russia's easily recognizable symbolic equivalent. Not unexpectedly, her status as such has been noted repeatedly in literary and scholarly criticism.[61]

Less discussed by critics—but perhaps even more obvious—is the identification of Sorokin's heroine with Russia. Sorokin himself defines Marina as one of many women in the late Soviet period "who identified with the body of Russia."[62] Like Irina, Marina refuses to emigrate from Russia (2:91, 161, 163).[63] Her conceptual connection with Russia is underlined through the plot development, in scenes that highlight her wish to alter her life. Marina has a recurring daydream of a man whom she envisages as both Russia's savior and the one to give her sexual fulfillment and true love (2:83–84, 120–22, 149, 182–83). Marina and Russia are paralleled in the outburst of the dream character, who says: "NOT YOU LOVE ME, BUT SHE!"—a gendered reference to the geographical contours of Russia (2:121; capitals in original).

The Marina-Russia parallel is intensified in two scenes in which Marina loses her temper with friends. In the first, she becomes so distressed when an American friend criticizes Russia that she hits him in the face (2:138–42). In the second, at a party, she overreacts to a reading of *Rose of the World* and boxes the ear of a friend who tries to prevent her from leaving (2:148–51).

Both scenes flirt with the idea of symbolically equating Marina with Russia. First, she reproaches the American for returning home and showing his "shitty friends slides—there she is, the wild Russia, admire it, guys, and now let's drink whisky. . . . You are a piece of shit" (2:142). The sexually loose Marina obviously identifies with the feminized "wild Russia" of her own tirade. Later, while leafing through *Rose of the World*, she is stirred by the passage about Russia's female Ecumenical Soul and its marriage to the demiurge; the passage feels "familiar, beloved, dear like . . . a first love, a first kiss" (2:149).

Possibly Sorokin is hinting that Marina also knows Grossman's "bride Russia" views when he has her say that "Grossman is, of course, nearer" to her than other samizdat authors (2:87). But the Marina-Russia parallel culminates in the turning point of the tale, which occurs when Marina meets Communist Party official Sergei Nikolaevich Rumiantsev. He merges with the long-awaited lover of her dreams when he gives her an orgasm that incites her spiritual transformation. Again, the personal and national levels merge: while coming, Marina envisions herself immersed in a sea of "millions of enlightened people" who sing the Soviet anthem (2:171–74). In this scene, Sorokin shifts back and forth between the anthem's propagandist thoughts on Russia and those of the sentimental Marina, who interprets the words of the anthem as signposts for her own life. Eventually, she occupies "her cell" and merges with the crowd (2:173). From this point on, Marina loses all desire to distance herself from Soviet society and transforms gradually into a model Soviet worker known only by the surname "Alekseeva." As Valentina Brougher argues, the transformation is articulated through her way of talking: after initially reflecting "the 'living' linguistic reality that seethes beneath the surface of the official language of the government organs," the speech of the new Marina "is in total harmony with the collective and the Party ideology that guides the collective."[64]

While he could not have read Platonov's novel before writing *Marina's Thirtieth Love,* Sorokin crafts an orgasmic scene reminiscent of the passage in *Happy Moscow* in which the heroine fuses with one suitor's "anticipation of socialism," appearing as a future wife amidst "the voices of millions of people," having found "contentment for her wandering heart."[65] To an even greater degree, Marina's orgasm mirrors Irina's sexual confrontation with "Russia's enemy" on Kulikovo field in *Russian Beauty.* Their meeting is accompanied by a mystical choir of "entirely Russian voices" in which Irina dissolves and which brings her to (religious) ecstasy (352–54). *Her* choir makes Marina cry (2:172), and Irina "melts into tears" upon hearing hers (352). Both scenes are couched in terms of a rebirth of the heroine (2:175; 354). Erofeev's Kulikovo scene is followed by a passage in which Irina experiences a physical orgasm with Leonardik; like Marina, who gradually dissolves into her surroundings from the orgasm moment on, Irina claims to be "not there anymore" (395). At the end of the novel, Irina varies on the same statement, claiming to "dissolve as a character" (461).

As stated earlier, Marina evolves from a woman with a highly individualized life led in dissident circles to a worker completely absorbed by the Soviet collective. Sorokin calls his consciously composed trajectory an "inside-out version" of "the classic Russian novel on the salvation of the hero."[66] To him, Marina "is 'released' from individuality, and . . . merges into the faceless 'collective.'"[67] Marina's affinity with that collective echoes the identification with the Russian people of classic nineteenth-century heroines—Pushkin's Tat'iana and Turgenev's Liza—and their twentieth-century heirs. Even when she tries to distance herself from ordinary Russian people after her initial encounters with Russian dissidents, Marina equates herself with those very people when she feels "sorry for them, sorry for herself" (2:83). In early reveries on a messianic bridegroom, she imagines him arriving at Vnukovo Airport and sees herself as part of the "sea" of Russian people that awaits him (2:84). Her eventual immersion in the collective is anticipated by Rumiantsev, who reproaches Marina in clichéd populist rhetoric for living "detached from the people. . . . You need to unite with the people. . . . You need to love your people" (2:166–67).

Erofeev's heroine also identifies with the common people. Like Marina, Irina moves primarily in dissident circles and is reproached for repudiating her common-folk roots (370); she also claims, however, to "love my people . . . one shouldn't bother and harass them!" (164). Glancing at the crowd in a provincial market square, she claims to have "indissolubly" "been T H E M" in her youth; she returns to this thought when urging herself to return to her "roots" and accept that "T H E Y are Y O U" (319–20, 370; emphasis in original). Repeatedly branding herself a savior of the Russian people, ultimately Irina says she is "simply happy to live and work in this land, amidst such a remarkable people" (295–98, 460).

The affinity of both heroines with the common people is motivated in part by their origins: like their nineteenth-century prototypes, they both grew up in the Russian provinces. Irina, in her youth, "lived and breathed the air of the steppe" (448); and Marina was raised in a village near Moscow "among the private barns and rare pines of an endless courtyard," in a house overgrown with "branches, thorns, and foliage," surrounded by the smell of "the earth, dog roses, and garbage" (2:28). Their move to Moscow reenacts the chronotope in Soviet film and painting, discussed in chapter 3, in which Moscow served as a metaphor for a new feminine fate. Both authors may well have harked back to that chronotope intentionally. Sorokin is a proclaimed fan of Grigorii Aleksandrov's and Ivan Pyr'ev's early Soviet comedies,[68] which include classic narratives of heroines from the Russian countryside who find their vocations and true love in Moscow.[69] Erofeev's novel, significantly, was initially titled *Moscow Beauty* (*Moskovskaia krasavitsa*).[70]

Sorokin's and Erofeev's "Moscow beauties" appear as hypostases of Russia in another respect: both impersonate the Russia-as-sleeping-beauty myth. The turning point in Marina's life—the moment of orgasm when she fuses with the Soviet collective—is described as a literal awakening: when her Party man penetrates her in her sleep, the sound of the national anthem wakes her. While in early twentieth-century poetry and philosophy it was often the revolution that was supposed to "awaken" a feminized Russia, here it is the Soviet utopia that rouses Marina, both literally and metaphorically. At the conclusion of the passage, she feels "born anew" (2:175). In a similar vein, Erofeev's Irina experiences her efforts to save Russia by allowing its "main enemy" to penetrate her as an "impossible resurrection" (354). The language used in the penetration scene evokes Belyi's "Green Meadow": where Irina seeks to end an "everlasting sorcery" of Russia, so that "the shroud will fall" (296, 321, 340), Belyi depicted Russia as a sleeping beauty "covered with the shroud of black death," whose "soul" has been stolen by a "sorcerer."[71]

Although the focus here has been on Sorokin's *Marina* and Erofeev's *Russian Beauty*, the myth of Russia as unattainable beloved has become a central theme in many more—literary and other—expressions of contemporary Russian culture. A recognition of its persistence in recent intellectual thought gets a substantial boost when one takes a brief look at some of these.

First of all, the metaphor can be and has been discerned in several other works by Erofeev and Sorokin. Oleg Dark sees the characters in Erofeev's story "Life with an Idiot" ("Zhizn s idiotom," 1990) as "direct personifications (the heroine—of Russia, her husband—of the intelligentsia)."[72] In *Men* (*Muzhchiny*, 1995), Erofeev not only states plainly that "Russia is feminine," but he also narrates how he "fell in love" with "the national symbol . . . of Russia"—a birch tree—in the same way that in the early twentieth century, "students fell in love with the proletariat."[73] Erofeev exploits similar gender metaphors in his "novel-cum-cyclopedia," *Encyclopedia of the Russian Soul* (*Entsiklopediia russkoi dushi*, 1999). Among a jumble of stereotypical qualifications, he defines the nation in terms that recycle familiar personifications of Russia, including those of Berdiaev. Russia is praised for its "softness and melodiousness" and for its "womanish [*bab'em*] appearance"; the nation's preoccupation with French culture is translated into gendered terms as the love of a "whore" who "gives herself" "selflessly" and "womanishly forgives" her male suitor for his mistakes.[74] In the autobiographically inspired *Good Stalin* (*Khoroshii Stalin*, 2004), Erofeev opposes himself as a dissident son to his father, who represents to him the Stalinist state. He does so in a narrative in which Russia once again stars as a femme fatale, appearing as a "beauty dressed in snow and furs" who "awaits her return to the warm womb of civilization."[75]

Sorokin toys with and travesties the "bride Russia" metaphor even more avidly than his colleague. The myth of Moscow as the heart of a feminine Russia figures prominently in both the telltale-titled essay "The Eros of Moscow" ("Eros Moskvy," 2001) and his screenplay for Aleksandr Zel'dovich's *Moscow* (*Moskva*, 2000). The two works—informed by the traditional Petersburg-Moscow opposition as a gendered pair, as Sorokin himself asserts[76]—were published together with *Marina's Thirtieth Love* in a collection that shares its name with the film (*Moscow/Moskva*, 2001). In the essay, a first-person narrator personifies Moscow as a sensual female beloved.[77] The sleeping-beauty myth pops up again when that lover is imagined as a "sleeping giantess," who lies "on her back in the middle of Russia," "dreaming a Russian dream."[78]

In "The Eros of Moscow," the narrator's goal is the penetration of a feminized Moscow. A similar sexual appropriation of feminized Moscow representations appears in the *Moscow* scenario. Its heroine, Masha, is penetrated by one of the heroes, Leva, through a world map: after cutting out a circle where Moscow is located, he makes love to her through the hole.[79] Ekaterina Degot' rightly remarks that the symbolic dimension of Moscow— which serves throughout the film "as legal stand-in for Russia in its . . . femininity"—is realized here "through the allegory of the vagina."[80]

What is more, Masha and her sister, Ol'ga, function as promoters of the beauty of Moscow and the Russian land: Masha recommends the city to Leva,[81] and the songs her sister sings as a nightclub artist are all variations on Soviet-era lyrics celebrating the glories of Moscow and Russia. At the very end of the film, Ol'ga's voice is heard singing and addressing a personified Moscow as "heart of the Russian earth."[82] Masha's role as future bride is stressed throughout the plot, which ends with Leva marrying both her and her sister.[83] In turn, he—as well as the film's other male characters, all of whom belong to the world of New Russians and the mafia—perfectly fits the paradigm of the Russian *intelligent* who is alienated from his native land. A gifted musician, he has returned to Russia after living as an emigrant in Berlin and Israel.

Sorokin plays not only with the myth of a feminine-bridal Moscow, but also with more traditional bridal conceptualizations of Russia. In *The Norm* (*Norma*, 1994), a classic hero-*intelligent* literally penetrates the Russian earth:

> Anton went out to the riverbank. Wet, clayey, it lay in front of the church and was called The Russian Earth. Anton fell on his knees and touched her with his hand.[84] She was warm, moist, trustful, and abundant. She awaited him; she waited like a woman, a mother, a sister, a beloved. He sank down on her, embraced her, feeling the blissful delights of her warmth. And she embraced him, embraced him tenderly and passionately, fervently and timidly, tenderly and commandingly. Nothing was more wonderful than this love, this nearness! It lasted endlessly, and when Anton's hot sperm gushed out into the Russian earth, the bell of the neglected church pealed above him. (1:166)

Echoing the scene in which Dostoevsky's Alesha ecstatically kisses the earth, this passage could hardly be more explicit in travestying and sexualizing the pagan notion of man as impregnator of the earth.[85] That motif keeps on recurring throughout Sorokin's oeuvre: not only is it central in descriptions of a sect known as the "Earthfuckers" (Zemleeby) in the novel *The Blue Lard* (*Goluboe salo,* 1999); it is also the theme of his joint project with photographer Oleg Kulik, revealingly titled *Deep into Russia* (*V glub' Rossii,* 1994); and it reemerges in the novel *23.000* (2006), in which a mysterious minor character describes in markedly sexual terms how he defends "Moist Mommy Earth" against invaders.

In *The Norm,* Sorokin links the "moist mother earth" myth to the modern metaphor of an intelligentsia alienated from an allegedly "authentic" Russia. The hero's erotic craving for the earth, among other things, coalesces with his love for a girl named Tania. The resemblance of this girl to Pushkin's Tat'iana—whose very name she carries—and her numerous nineteenth-century equals is exaggerated to the point of parody.

> Her face, eyes, hair, lips and shoulders . . . everything was equally charming, young, fresh, and harmonious with that same harmony, the appearance of which we call national beauty. In this case, it was Russian beauty in all its plenitude and appeal. . . . She couldn't possibly be from the city: her drawling accent was rural, and her whole look betrayed a rural origin. (1:160)

The Norm mimics not only nineteenth-century clichés, but also Blok's "bride Russia": Sorokin meticulously echoes the setting of *Native Land,* both in scenes with Tania and in the penetration passage. All are set in "fields," "rye," a wide "distance," "mist," and "smoke"—elements that figured prominently in Blok's writings on Russia (1:135–36). In the event that these elements alone do not instantly bring Blok to mind, Sorokin makes sure to complement them with more tangible links. Blok's "My Rus'! My Wife!" serves as the story's epigraph (1:135),[56] and repeated references to Russia in *Native Land* as a place "still the same" reverberate in Anton's recurrent attribution of the phrase "still the same" to himself and to his house (1:136, 137, 141).[57] Where the hero's head in one *Native Land* poem "disappears in the thick grass" on the way to his lover's "silent house," Sorokin's hero walks through "the thick grass" on the way to the "silent house" in which the story takes place (1:136).[58] Finally, the novel reiterates Blok's Kulikovo theme when the hero listens to passages from a study claiming that the Kulikovo battle "has become the symbol of the Russian people and its history" (1:139).[59]

Obviously, the "bride Russia" motif is not the main theme of *The Norm:* it is only one of several thematic clichés—along with the hero's love of Russian vodka, the Russian countryside, his Russian *niania,* and the pleasure of hunting with his father—that the text demythologizes. The same is true of Sorokin's elaboration on the metaphor in *Roman* (1994). Set up as a traditional Turgenevian or Tolstoyan novel, *Roman* describes the aristocratic hero's return to the estate of his youth. The classic tone of the story explodes only after hundreds of pages, when the model hero murders every character in the novel, including himself. Amidst what Karl-Heinz Kasper defines as "a catalog of wholly familiar realia from Russian literature," another copy of Pushkin's Tat'iana is introduced in *Roman.*[90] This Tat'iana appears after the hero has left his previous love because she did "not have a Russian soul" (2:357). By contrast, Tat'iana is blessed with "that silent charm which makes it easy to distinguish maidenly Russian beauty from any other" (2:464). Her depiction as "sincere," "simple," "natural," "pure," and "resolute" echoes in detail that of Pushkin's heroine and Turgenev's idealized "Russian" female characters (2:473, 485, 488, 492); and the very patronymic "Aleksandrovna"—coupled with her given name—alludes to her status as Aleksandr Pushkin's creation. To complete the picture, this "Russian heroine" acquires a manifestly Sophiological aura when the hero conceives of her "figure . . . cropping up on the riverbank, then at the church, then right nearby" as "the supernatural light that gives meaning to nature" and "permeates the Russian landscape" (2:480–81).

Among the many Russia-related clichés that Sorokin dismantles, the vision of Russia as a marriageable girl is particularly persistent. In his very first collection of stories, Sorokin's later Tanias are already foreshadowed in "Farewell" ("Proshchanie," 1977–84): this story's Turgenevian hero-*intelligent* muses on his "native land," wondering "what we mean by that word? A country? Its people?" (1:546). Or, thus the enumeration of possible answers significantly ends, would the term refer to his oh-so-Russian lover Tania—"that same girl with her mousy braid," whose hands "smelt of hay and field flowers" and whom he kissed, "pressing her against young smooth birches" (1:545–46)? In a more politicized context, the "bride Russia" motif reappears as recently as 2008, in the *Sugar Kremlin* collection (*Sakharnyi Kreml'*, 2008). The title story concludes with the eleven-year-old heroine kissing and licking a little Kremlin made of sugar: "and she dreamt of a sugar Ruler on a white horse."[91] The erotic tension between a feminized Russian people and its regime could hardly be expressed more graphically.

Besides Sorokin and Erofeev, a number of other contemporary writers, artists, and filmmakers have taken recourse to the metaphor. Many embroider on the stereotype of Moscow as the core of Russia's femininity. Programmatic is Andrei Bitov's assertion, in a recent essay, that "Moscow is feminine. Petersburg is another case! Masculine. As the proverb goes, 'Moscow poses as bride, Petersburg as groom.'"[92] In an essay written for the festival project *Moscow: Territory 2000*, the poet Ilia Kormil'tsev gives an explicit twist to the old saying by comparing the cityscape of Moscow to female genitalia.[93] Similarly, if less plastically, the artist-cum-critic Georgii Litichevskii writes in 2001 that Moscow "gives herself to the frivolous gaiety of her first meeting with the artist."[94] In a more negative tone, the "grand master of foul language"[95] Miroslav Nemirov addresses Moscow as a "randy whore" in a poetic response to the failed putsch of August 1991: "Why the fuck did you spread your legs for the Soviet regime? . . . You were the Politburo's bitch, weren't you, slut?"[96]

But the metaphor of Moscow as Russia's feminine heart is elaborated in particular detail in Ol'ga Mukhina's play *Iu* (1996), first performed in 2002 at Moscow's MKhAT Theater. Mukhina's Moscow is an object of masculine admiration whose "insane beauty" concurs with that of the heroine.[97]

> DMITRY: . . . MOSCOW ISN'T AS FAR AS YOU THINK. . . .
> ANDREI: But she does not love everyone. She does not wait for everyone. She does not forgive everyone.
> DMITRY: She waited for me. She smiled at me. She was happy to see me. . . .
> ANDREI: . . . This city will love others once again. HEY, MOSCOW, I want to yell right in her face . . . there will be a time when you will run after me! . . . But you despise my love. . . . All right, Moscow, come on, dance on my grave.
> SEVA: . . . LOVE, LOVE, LOVE. (*laughs*) What do you need Moscow for? . . .
> DMITRY: I love her.
> SEVA: There you go again! LOVE. . . . Don't believe her words; don't look her in the eye; otherwise you'll believe her—that's how she is![98]

Mukhina's feminized Moscow reverts to that other MKhAT production—*Three Sisters*—and to Soviet clichés, but it also recalls Blok.[99] His "bride Russia" resonates particularly in the facial references of male characters who want to "yell right in her [Moscow's] face" and refuse to "look her in the eye."

Blok also makes himself heard in Dmitrii Prigov's verse cycle "My Russia" ("Moia Rossiia," 1990), in which Moscow appears as a "young girl" in an "embroidered shawl."[100] Prior to the 1993 publication of this cycle in *Novyi mir*, Prigov had flirted with gendered stereotypes of the city in "Moscow and the Muscovites" ("Moskva i moskvichi," 1988), whose poet uses feminine metaphors in negation: "Moscow is not a girl . . . / It will not marry and will not run away / Neither is it a wife, nor a sister, nor a mother."[101]

Finally, the myth of a feminized Moscow vis-à-vis a male poet surfaces in Pavel Peppershtein's story "The Egg" ("Iaitso," 1983–97). In the epigraph, the poet greets Moscow with the words: "I love you. You also love me, I think. Embrace me then."[102] The epigraph corresponds to a fantasy, voiced later in the story, of a male hero who "embraces" Russia and who claims, in Blokian rhetoric: "I am happy that I can embrace my Native Land . . . . For the only true heaven is the merging with one's female beloved, and I have loved Russia all my life."[103]

If the works mentioned all revolve around the stereotype of Moscow as symbolic stand-in for a feminine Russia, perhaps an even larger number of contemporary texts and works of art embroider on the myth of Russia *as a whole* as a bridal or uxorial figure. A relatively early example is Vasilii Aksenov's novel *Island Crimea* (*Ostrov Krym*), written in the late 1970s and first published abroad in 1981. Greta Slobin has discussed how the "nationalist nostalgia for 'reunification'" of its hero—a man who "represents the traditions of Russian aristocracy"—is articulated in sexual terms through his romantic affairs with two female characters who balance "between the extreme aspects of the 'Mother Russia' myth, the virgin and the whore."[104]

Prigov relies on the same myth in his previously mentioned cycle, "My Russia." The maternal dimension prevails in a reference to "Russia / In a feminine sense, who needed to . . . bear a son"; but Russia is feminized in distinctly erotic phrases when the poet claims to "sleep on" Russia, recalling "her cold hands that stretch toward me at night abroad . . . either to embrace or . . . strangle me."[105] In the cycle "In the Sense Of" ("V smysle," 1990), Prigov reapplies the metaphor in a language that is redolent of Berdiaev and the Sophiological philosophers.

> Dasha's soul is an adagio
> In the sense of the charm of the feminine Russian character
> Fedor drifts with a bustard
> In the sense of the all-responsiveness of the Russian soul
> Iosif shows off to Sofiia
> In the sense of the intrusion of a foreign element.[106]

While resulting in euphonic patterns of sound, Prigov's combination of given names and characteristics also invites a symbolic reading. Together with Dostoevsky's name, the "feminine Russian character" of "Dasha" evokes the heroine in Dostoevsky's *Demons* and, more particularly, Berdiaev's interpretation of this Dasha as the future bride of Russia's "groom" Stavrogin.[107] Juxtaposed with this fragment and with "the all-responsiveness of the Russian soul," "Sofiia" conjures up pre-revolutionary Sophiological preoccupations. Seen in this light, the "intrusion of a foreign element" with which "Iosif" is connected prompts a reading of this name as Iosif Stalin, Russia's Caucasian or "foreign" dictator.

Separately, these interpretations may seem speculative, but their combination in the poetry of Prigov—a known "deconstructor" of "a variety of discourses"—renders random congruence unlikely.[108] Mere coincidence seems even less probable when one takes Prigov's later career into account. At the dawn of the twenty-first century, in commenting on his work he refers explicitly to feminized-Russia myths. Berdiaev and Rozanov loom large as he explains that "People . . . and State . . . form a gendered pair," and that "in mythopoetic representations . . . the People are endowed with some passive procreative force . . . while the state acquires a rough violent, instilling force."[109] Early twentieth-century debates echo, too, when he summarizes the "media opera" *Russia* (*Rossiia,* 2006, joint project with Aleksandr

Dolgin and Iraida Iusupova) as a conflict between himself, as representative of "the intelligentsia," and a feminized "Russia: a prediscursive creature," who appears in the unexpected guise of . . . the cat of the opera's coauthor Aleksandr Dolgin.[110]

In a slightly less ironic vein, in his 1998 collection of poems Vladimir Solov'ev—not to be confused with the philosopher—invites a feminized Russia to "remember with the two of us" its history and refers to it as an "enormous land" that refuses to "get up!" while complaining, "Oh, I am weary."[111] A year later, the playwright Rodion Beletskii has the hero of his short play *Nostalgia* (*Nostal'giia*) explain to another male character that "melancholy for your Native Land" is nothing but the erotic arousal experienced when confronted with a beautiful young girl.[112] Even more recently, the poet Aleksandra Petrova echoes the hero searching for his lost beloved in Chekhov's "House with a Mezzanine"—"Misius', where are you?"[113]—when, in her "Underground Rome" cycle ("Podzemnyi Rim," 2000), she assures Russia that

> I will return, I will find you,
> I will go to the courtyards,
> I will knock on the windows:
> Rus'-Misius',
> where are you?[114]

Apart from the explicit reference to Chekhov, Petrova reiterates the Shulamit motif that figured prominently in early twentieth-century representations of Russia (see chapter 2)—although, in Petrova's case, the lost nation-lover image is explained by an exile theme: Petrova wrote this cycle while an emigrant in Jerusalem.[115]

Contemporary Russian literature contains numerous examples of a gendered Russia-state-intelligentsia relationship; that much is clear. The same holds true for cultural expressions outside the strictly literary sphere. The more traditional myth of the Russian land as the ruler's wife emerges, for example, in a sci-fi novel by Evgenii Vitkovskii, *Pavel II* (2003), in which Russia awaits Emperor Pavel "as a bride a bridegroom."[116] And the vision of Russia as a sleeping beauty is central to a 1991 essay by Mikhail Epstein, a prominent theoretician of Russian postmodernism cited earlier in this study. Epstein describes the Russian "soul" as "a Sleeping Beauty and a sleeping *bogatyr'*, who seem to have been lost forever to the young hero, to the people, but are merely awaiting their hour . . . to awake and dazzle with their beauty, surprise with their strength."[117] Epstein echoes the motifs of the veil and the two faces that marked pre-revolutionary "bride Russia" metaphors when his sleeping beauty "turns away, she covers herself with her hands and scarf, she hides her shining face from all. . . . Hidden beauty, hidden strength, which are in need of a great reason to reveal themselves . . . to the sole promised one."[118]

The writer and critic Tat'iana Tolstaia also takes recourse to the nation-as-bride metaphor in her analysis of Andreï Makine's novel *The French Testament* (*Le testament français*, 1995). The very title of her review—"Russian Man at a Rendezvous" ("Russkii chelovek na randevu")—refers to Chernyshevskii's review of Turgenev, in which the former translated politico-national conflict with the use of amorous terms (see chapter 1). Tolstaia similarly interweaves amorous and national dimensions in her interpretation of Charlotte, Makine's Russian heroine.

> Time goes by, but . . . Charlotte does not change; she is still the same. . . . "If she is still so beautiful . . . ," the hero thinks, "it's because all those moments of light and beauty show through her eyes, face, and body. . . ." Toward the end of the novel, . . . Charlotte becomes an embodiment of Russia. . . . Her fate is the fate of Russia: Europe and Asia in one face . . . raped, but not killed . . . she accepts everything; the strongest emotion she's able to experience is "to be clouded by light tears". . . . She is the embodiment of Eternal Femininity and of the feminine principle that can be attributed, according to many, to "the Russian soul."[119]

It is difficult to miss the associations with Blok's and Berdiaev's feminized Russia in this reading of Makine. Apart from the obvious connection of Russia to an eternal feminine principle, Tolstaia invokes Blok through set phrases: relying on the novel's Russian translation,[120] she defines Charlotte in her symbolic capacity as "still the same" (*vse ta zhe*) and as "clouded" (*zatumanitsia*) by tears—words that Blok applied to his feminized Russia. The link is reinforced by the attribution to Charlotte of the epithet *prekrasna* (beautiful), which Blok reserved for his Beautiful Lady.[121] Tolstaia openly quotes Blok's poem "Scythians" ("Skify," 1918) later in the review.[122]

In the visual arts from the 1980s onwards, too, the myth of (specifically Soviet) Russia is a favorite subject of intellectual play. Vladislav Mamyshev embroiders on it by combining two supreme symbols of female sexuality and Soviet society in his "Marilyn Monroe in Moscow" ("Merilin Monro v Moskve," 1992). Creating a deliberately kitschy national icon, Mamyshev poses as a transvestite Monroe-in-billowing-white-dress, who holds the hammer and sickle in the position in which they appear on the Soviet flag.[123] A postmodern national icon also surfaces in *Natasha with Bust of Stalin* (1982–83), one of Vitalii Komar's and Aleksandr Melamid's many paintings of Stalin and Lenin surrounded by female muses.[124] Carter Ratcliff has pointed to Stalin's status in this painting as "unattainable lover" for the central female figure, who sits naked on a bed and stares at his bust.[125] Her "bountiful Russian femininity" is underlined by her quintessential Russian name: Natasha.[126]

The opposition of a feminized Russia and a masculine state features, too, in the installation *Sleeping Beauty* (*Spiashchaia krasavitsa,* 1990), by the contemporary-art hotshot Aleksandr Iakut. Having starred in the Russian pavilion at the 1990 Venice Biennale, the work was sold by Sotheby's in 1993 for the solid sum of $250,000. *Sleeping Beauty* consists of a life-size porcelain female figure lying in front of a limousine from Brezhnev's personal collection. When asked, Iakut explained that the woman "naturally" represents Russia and that she "naturally" refers to politically motivated visions of the "sleeping-beauty Russia" of (pre-)revolutionary times.[127]

If Iakut's "bride Russia" can be linked to the artist's publicly expressed conservative-nationalist views, then the same is true for the women in Aleksei Beliaev-Gintovt's "Serbian March" ("Serbskii marsh," 2008) series. Created by a renowned ultranationalist, "Serbian March" consists of photographs of a beautiful woman in traditional Slavic dress with a weapon, accompanied by texts banners reading "Absolute motherland!" or "Sevastopol' is a Russian city!" among other slogans. When Beliaev-Gintovt received the prestigious Kandinsky award for his series in December 2008, the images raised a great deal of dust, and his emphatically Slavic beauties were the talk of the town for weeks on end.[128]

Appropriations of the "bride-Russia" metaphor have also made their way into recent Russian films. This is not surprising if one takes account of Lynne Attwood's assertion that (post-)perestroika cinema has a tradition of "using women in particular to signify the motherland and morality."[129] Attwood herself plausibly interprets a scene in Sergei Snezhkin's film *An Extraordinary Incident on a Regional Scale* (*Chrezvychainoe proizshestvie raionnogo masshtaba,* 1989) in symbolic terms. When Snezhkin's hero, Shumilin, rapes his mistress against the background of a television-broadcast Brezhnev speech, Attwood says "the voice of Brezhnev, mingling with the victim's screams, indicates that what Shumilin is really 'fucking' is the Soviet system."[130]

The Snezhkin scene has its contemporary cinematic counterpart in female personifications of an "authentic" native Russia. An example of a movie whose female protagonist incarnates the capital is Zel'dovich's *Moscow,* mentioned earlier. Scholars have also interpreted the heroine of Petr Todorov's cinematic hit *Intergirl* (*Interdevochka,* 1989)—after Vladimir Kunin's novella of the same name (1988)—as a feminized Russia. According to Helena Goscilo, the story of Tania—who works as both prostitute and nurse—can be read as a "key metatext" for the trope of the "Whore as Motherland."[131]

176

Andrei Nekrasov's *Liubov' and Other Nightmares (Liubov' i drugie koshmary,* 2001), a favorite at several international film festivals, features a similarly allegorical heroine. The film centers on the figure of the narrator's beloved, a Dostoevskian criminal-cum-innocent heroine named Liubov'. In her love for the narrator, this distinctively Russian girl stands in sharp contrast to his wealthy, superficial English mistress. According to Nekrasov, he intended Liubov' to be a feminine allegory for Russia—one inspired by a Georgii Ivanov poem, which contrasts Stalin's prisoners, as the real Russia, with the Soviet state.[139] With his film, Nekrasov translated a political poem into yet another metaphoric representation of Russia as a female beloved.

Heavenly-Earthly

"Apart from unprecedented explicitness in physiological detail, then, the troping of nationhood along feminine lines as mother and whore—Body, Nature, Reproduction—has not undergone revolutionary change." This is Helena Goscilo's conclusion to an essay on feminine representations of Russia in contemporary Russian culture.[133] Goscilo's assumption holds true for most, if not all, of the heroines discussed here. Of pivotal importance to their depictions is the angelic-demonic antithesis, which, roughly speaking, can be considered a variation on the mother-whore dichotomy. Explicit physiological details matter more to contemporary feminine representations of Russia than Goscilo's conclusion might suggest, however.

This section of the study has provided a series of physically explicit examples of the metaphor. As pointed out, the psychological breakthrough in the stories involving Sorokin's Marina and Erofeev's Irina is established through an elaborately portrayed orgasm, and Sorokin varies repeatedly on the theme of Russia's sexual penetration in other works. Significant to my argument is that the radical focus on physicality is not irrelevant to the metaphor's status in Sorokin's and Erofeev's work—and that of contemporaries.

In Erofeev's *Russian Beauty* and Sorokin's *Marina,* the angelic-demonic characterization that marks most metaphoric "brides Russia" is taken to extremes. On the one hand, Irina and Marina are associated with religion and with an exalted mystical feminine principle. Both are emphatically religious,[134] both identify with Joan of Arc's selfless heroism,[135] and Marina, in addition, identifies with Andreev's mystical-esoteric creatures (2:148–49). Her lovers refer to her as an "angel," as "beautiful" (*prekrasna*), as a princess or tsarina, and as Venus (2:52–53, 74). In a similar vein, Irina is considered "beautiful" (*prekrasna*), incarnated "perfection," "an angel," and "a goddess" (162, 366, 381); "wings" are repeated elements in her portrayal (18, 73, 347–48). Her depiction parrots the stereotype of a saintlike feminine principle when she is compared to the Mother of God and told that, in the future, "angels will take off their halos for you, and you will become the tsarina of the Russian cosmos" (438, 132, 283). If, in addition, one remembers Irina's infatuation with Blok, then Galina Rylkova correctly views her as a "Soviet incarnation of the Solov'evian-cum-Blokian feminine ideal."[136]

Sorokin's and Erofeev's heroines do not simply reenact the exalted hypostasis of those feminine muses, however. Their inherent darker or "fallen" side, and that of their Gnostic predecessors, is played out as well. Marina claims to have "sinned all my life" (2:131); Sorokin labels her a "fallen soul."[137] As inspiration for the coupling of promiscuity to her allegorical-national dimension, Sorokin himself singles out Esenin's "Tavern Moscow" cycle ("Moskva kabatskaia," 1922–23), in which the city of Moscow is associated with female promiscuity.[138] Irina is no less a "fallen" woman. She claims to have been "spat upon" and "humiliated"; to have been called "scum" and to "have fallen" (134–35, 178, 422). According to Erofeev, she is "smart on one page, stupid on the next, a prostitute on the third, and a saint on the fourth."[139]

Within the two narratives, the heroines' sinfulness serves as a catalyst for drawing them closer to religion. Irina "felt like becoming a saint; sin is closer to sanctity," and Marina's wish to go to church is sparked by the feeling that she is "a simple sinner" (295; 2:130). For both, it is precisely the willingness to submit themselves sexually to anyone that links them to traditional saints, who sacrifice private lives for a higher goal. The link is manifest in Irina's will, which states: "Give my cunt to the poor, give it to invalids, cripples, workers in lowly positions, little men, bad students, to masturbators, old men, parasites, street urchins, butchers, to anyone" (443).

In both novels, the opposition saint-sinner is articulated through a play on the oppositional epithets "earthly" (*zemnaia*) and "heavenly" (*nezemnaia / nebesnaia*). Irina is called a "very earthy girl," but she and her groom, Leonardik, call each other "heavenly bride" and "heavenly bridegroom" (402, 163, 463). Combined with Irina's function as the embodiment of a feminine Russia who confronts a demonic enemy, these characterizations allude to Andreev's feminized "Heavenly Russia" and its "demons." Indeed, Erofeev claims that his novel contains a parodistic "play with concepts from *Rose of the World*."[140]

Sorokin's novel similarly plays with the earthly-heavenly dichotomy, in a context that can be traced even more directly to Andreev's feminized Russia. Marina consciously reflects on the opposition of an "earthly" to a "heavenly" feminine principle when she is introduced to a theory about the so-called "heavenly" and "earthly Mariia" in music (2:58–59). Sorokin emphasizes the phonetic link between Marina and Mariia by identifying his

178

heroine with her first love, Mariia, and by entitling a poem dedicated to his heroine "Ave Marina" (2:66, 90, 52). What is more, Marina is associated with a "heavenly" and an "earthly" hypostasis in the dream in which her Mr. Right reveals Russia's geographical contours. What she sees, he claims, is not contemporary Russia—"NOT THAT RUSSIA"—but "HEAVENLY RUSSIA" (2:121; capitals in original). Not only is this observation followed by patriotic lyrics sung by a choir, which prefigures the choir of her orgasm; it also convinces Marina that she is witnessing something "very important for her" (2:123). The setting of her dream unmistakably refers to the "fourth dream" in Chernyshevskii's *What Is to Be Done?* (*Chto delat'?* 1863), if only through Sorokin's playful imitation of the latter's bombastic language and overabundant use of capitals and exclamation points. Chernyshevskii's dream scene similarly features a "New Russia" that is shown to the heroine. Like the Russia that Marina faces in her dream, this "New Russia" is a utopian ideal rather than a concrete geopolitical unit. And like Marina, Vera is told to look to the future utopian Russia rather than to contemporary Russia.[141]

The connection between this "heavenly Russia" and another pretext— *Rose of the World*—becomes explicit when Marina runs across this treatise at a party. Having read the book in her youth, she responds emotionally particularly to the same "Heavenly Russia" concept that surfaced in her dream (2:148–50).

In short, we are dealing with two classic heroines of the angelic-demonic type. The kinship between these dualistic women and the feminized Russia of writers like Blok, Pasternak, and Andreev is obvious. In addition, Galina Rylkova links the bisexuality of Erofeev's Irina "together with her Solov'ëvian patronymic—Vladimirovna"—to Solov'ev's philosophy of androgyny.[142] The same assertion can be made for Sorokin's bisexual Marina.

Hitherto, I have highlighted the organic ties of Sorokin's and Erofeev's heroines with literary and philosophical predecessors. They differ from those earlier "Russian brides," however, in the explicit sexual detail with which their earthly dimension is portrayed. Like the "Petushki girl" in *Moscow to the End of the Line*, as incarnations of Russia both heroines are endowed with clear physical descriptions. The reader's very introduction to Irina takes place through a depiction of her vagina (5–7). Diametrically opposed to the abstract female principle that Blok's or Berdiaev's Russia represented, she appears as a sexually promiscuous figure—someone who makes love on a table to a foreign ambassador, who indulges in a threesome act, who plans to save Russia by letting its enemy penetrate her, and whose eventual fate is sealed with an endless orgasm (25, 39–43, 308–58, 393–95). Irina believes she is regarded "as a piece of succulent pink meat" that causes "ministers' and poets' trousers" to bulge (337). She articulates the captive heroine's traditional longing for a liberator-prince by asking: "Will you fuck me or not?" (41, 352)—and the heroine's traditional affinity with the poor and destitute is transposed to blatantly sexual spheres when Irina wishes to give her "cunt" to "masturbators" (443).

If the sexual-physical dimension is emphasized in Irina's portrayal, it is underscored even more strongly in Sorokin's novel. Given the pornographic character of roughly the first half of the book, an exhaustive description of the physical details of Marina's portrayal would exceed the scope of this study. Suffice it to say that virtually any imaginable part of her body, from toes to clitoris, and any imaginable sexual practice, from sadomasochism to group sex, pass before the reader in a description of her frivolous life.[143] As Valentina Brougher has asserted, in this part of the novel the heroine's "identity revolves largely around her sexual history."[144] Even Marina's transformation into an asexual Soviet worker is rendered in sexual terms, when she is penetrated and brought to orgasm by Party official Rumiantsev (2:170–74). Thus, Sorokin exploits to the full the sexual implications of the mystical connections envisioned by his predecessors between Russia and her "false" and "true" lovers. In her role as the symbolic equivalent of Russia, Marina is liberated not through any mystical union with a masculine principle, but through straightforward physical penetration.

In the other texts by Erofeev and Sorokin mentioned here, concrete physicality and sexuality play an equally vital role. In the former's *Encyclopedia of the Russian Soul*, Russia appears both as a "bottomless cunt" and an old spinster who, after a sexually promiscuous youth, "began to caress herself like an old woman" and whom the narrator advises to "masturbate, native land."[145]

But even more than Erofeev, Sorokin seems eager to translate his precursors' exalted representations of Russia into physical-sexual terms. Countering the near-saintly purity and perfection of the "Russian" Tanias in his *The Norm* and *Roman* (1:160, 163; 2:496, 542) is a glaringly physical dimension: *Roman*'s Tania reveals herself as the assistant of a murderous hero who ultimately severs and eats her various body parts (2:711–14); and *The Norm* recounts, in Romantic clichés, an encounter between Tania and the hero that can be read as nothing other than their first sexual encounter (1:162–63). The same hero concludes his musings on Tania and his youth with his literal penetration of the Russian earth (1:166).

As said, this concept—the sexual penetration of Russia by a male hero—is prominent throughout Sorokin's oeuvre. In *Moscow*, the heroine's vagina, penetrated through a map, symbolized the city of Moscow. In the aforementioned picture series with commentary by Sorokin, *Deep into Russia*, Oleg Kulik is depicted having vaginal, anal, and oral intercourse with a variety of animals.[146] Here the words "deep into Russia" refer to the artist's literal penetration of Russia and its primary rural representatives. *The Blue*

Lard similarly portrays coitus between men and the earth, this time enacted by members of the "Earthfuckers" sect. Designated specifically as "Russian," the earth in this novel is, like a tangible female body, "not soft, not crumbly . . . and it does not allow just any dick to enter" (3:135). The members' penetration of the earth is depicted with material-physical precision: whereas traditional marriage-with-Russia metaphors paid scarce attention to the whys and wherefores of the physical union, Sorokin addresses such matters in minute detail. The geographical disposition of suitable places for copulation with the earth is considered; statistics indicate time, place, and the number of penetrating sectarians involved; and the author elaborates on the number of ejaculations and the length of the Earthfuckers' penises (3:132–35). In *23.000,* the male character who guards the earth against intruders also engages in a distinctly sexual—and incestuous—relationship with his beloved "Moist Mommy Earth": he "licks" and "kisses" it "like a son, on the Face, the Breast and . . . in the Lap, her main moist aperture."[147] The heroine in *Sugar Kremlin* licks and kisses a small statue of the Kremlin "late at night . . . in her little bed."[148]

If each of these examples lends an explicit twist to elements of the "bride Russia" metaphor, then aside from *Marina,* Sorokin sexualizes that metaphor most recognizably in "The Eros of Moscow." The status of Sorokin's Moscow as female lover of the author-*intelligent* evokes several existing Russian texts, but in contrast to the largely abstract heroines in those earlier works, Sorokin's narrator treats his metaphoric mistress as a woman with strong physical desires. Claiming that Moscow, "like any other woman, needs genuine tenderness," he ascribes to the city seven "erogenous zones"—existing locations in Moscow, whose descriptions form the heart of the essay.[149] The contact between this feminized "city body" and the author is formulated in explicitly sexual terms: the latter wants to "grope for" and "touch" the city's "secret and tender spots."[150]

With "The Eros of Moscow," one might say that Sorokin maximalizes the erotic implications of Chekhov's three sisters' "Into Moscow, into Moscow"—the same implications that Eric Naiman first singled out in Platonov's *Happy Moscow.*[151] However, although the link between *Happy Moscow* and Sorokin's feminized Moscow is striking, the latter denies any influence and even denounces Platonov's heroine as artificial.[152]

In addition to Sorokin and Erofeev, the other authors and artists discussed in the previous section also appropriate "bride Russia" metaphors in highly concrete physical terms. It would be superfluous to discuss in detail each of the examples mentioned, but a brief selection indicates just how substantially they sexualize traditional visions of a feminized Russia. Prigov transforms snow into sperm when portraying a Russia that is sprinkled with a "white miracle" from the "living masturbation of the heavens";[153] the hero in Beletskii's *Nostalgia* compares feelings of longing for the "native land" to erotic arousal; the film historian Lynne Attwood speaks of a "cascade of sexual images" with a "symbolic function" after perestroika[154]—apart from the Snezhkin hero who literally "fucks" the Soviet system, one might think here of the heroine who symbolizes Russia in Nekrasov's *Liubov'*, who masturbates and indulges in lesbian love; Mamyshev's hammer-and-sickle self-portrait exploits the sexual connotations of the Monroe myth by imitating her low-cut dress and full red lips, puckered to kiss the viewer;[155] and Natasha in Komar and Melamid's *Natasha with Bust of Stalin* is a naked woman in an intimate, candlelit, bedroom setting.[156]

It is difficult to formulate a well-considered argument for this shift from largely abstract to concrete sexual imagery, but the erotic materialization of the metaphor is, in any case, more than merely a result of the abolition of censorship in the 1990s. Erofeev and Sorokin themselves point out a tendency among women in dissident circles in the 1980s, the decade in which their novels are set, to couple sexual promiscuity with anti-Soviet opposition in precisely the way that Irina and Marina do.[157] The son of David Samoilov—one of the dissident writers parodied in *Marina's Thirtieth Love*—more or less confirmed their observation recently, when he spoke in an interview of the dissidents' vision of "sexual laxity" as "a fight against totalitarianism and sanctimony. We thought that this lifestyle somehow had to do with ideology."[158] Thus a realistic social background does support the sexual bias of these novels, even though it may not account for the general preoccupation with sexuality in contemporary culture.

Nor is the post-Soviet authors' focus on explicit sexuality surprising on a grander scale: both in the Bible and in folkloric rituals, we have noted the sexually tinged relationship of man to a city or to the earth. However, these and other early instances of a focus on the body and on sexuality all share one feature: in each of them, from ritual to literary text, tangible physicality has an unmistakably ideological function. The sexual explicitness in biblical metaphors underlines the authors' political frustration and anger; rituals of copulation with the earth in folklore are supposed to increase the harvest.[159] Such a function is lacking in most of the post-Soviet works discussed here, in which an increased focus on physicality is connected with the authors' alleged abstinence from any ideologically motivated critique or personal authorial pathos. As Sorokin claims, his books "are only relationships with texts," as opposed to the work of "such figures as Evtushenko or Aitmatov," for whom "literature is partly an occasion for political activity."[160] Erofeev, in a renowned perestroika-era essay, proposed putting an "end to the literature that was burdened with social engagement."[161]

Further analysis of this apparent lack of ideological motivation appears later in this study. What matters here is its direct relationship to the overt sexuality of the texts mentioned. How that link functions is perhaps best explained through Sorokin's poetics. As shown, in Sorokin's work the intangibility of earlier feminine personifications of Russia is replaced by a highly palpable physicality: their sexual implications are realized to the full. His, as Slobodanka Vladiv-Glover asserts, is a "poetics of the body."[162] Sorokin defines his own work as "a debate about . . . the problem of the flesh, of bodiliness."[163] "My texts," he explains, "always focus on the issue of literary physicality. . . . I derive pleasure from the moment when literature becomes corporeal and nonliterary."[164] This pleasure makes itself unmistakably felt in Sorokin's revisions of the Russia-as-female-beloved metaphor.

A similar physical extension of abstract metaphors can be encountered many decades earlier, in the works of the futurist poet Vladimir Maiakovskii. Characteristic of his poetic "realization" of metaphors is the shift of attention from what Ivor Richards calls the "tenor" or underlying idea of the metaphor to its "vehicle," the metaphoric image through which the tenor is expressed. It is in Maiakovskii's poetry that such a transition of attention from the thematic meaning of a metaphor to its linguistic shell first appears as a conscious device. In this sense, the poet serves as the direct predecessor of Sorokin and Erofeev.

Ultimately, however, Maiakovskii—like most authors discussed in this study—does use metaphors to express social, political, or personal extraliterary themes that agitate him. In the poetics of Sorokin and Erofeev, metaphors largely lose this role. If we are to believe Sorokin's comments on his work, they principally lack a tenor (in the sense of a nonliterary meaning, or an underlying idea). In his texts, then, "our" gender metaphor comes to function as a literary phenomenon rather than as a purely political, extraliterary theme of concern to the author—as it was to Blok, or Pasternak, for example. Accordingly, in Sorokin's revisions of the metaphor of a bridal Russia, only the vehicle is left: what we encounter is a linguistic shell (the bride's body) without metaphysical content (ideological critique or political vision). The metaphor—to extend a comment on Sorokin's metaphors by Aleksandr Genis—"materializes to such a literal extent that it stops being one."[165]

It is not hard to see that the "materialized-metaphor" explanation of Sorokin's work is also true of Erofeev's novel. Does Irina not define herself as "a piece of succulent pink meat" for the novel's male characters rather than as a mystical beloved? This is not to say that Erofeev's attitude toward sexuality is identical to Sorokin's. Erofeev, as Robert Porter aptly states, is less interested in the "messy side of sex" that Sorokin tends to highlight: in Erofeev's work, "we are never overwhelmed with details."[166] A lack of detail notwithstanding, the shift from abstract to physical spheres, and from metaphor to "empty vehicle," is no less pivotal to Erofeev's poetics than it is to Sorokin's. In the words of one critic, in *Russian Beauty* "it is sex that blows up the moralizing mentality" and "reduces it to the level of parody."[167]

Summarizing, one could say that the level of physicality or sexuality of the metaphor in the works discussed in this and previous chapters is inversely proportional to the level of their ideological pathos. In the texts under consideration, when authorial commitment disappears, it tends to be replaced by a heightened orientation toward physicality.[168] The link between physicality and ideology has been singled out by the critic Slava Kuritsyn, who feels that postmodernism, with its distrust of ideological thought, is by definition marked by an "increased interest in problems of the body."[169]

The Dissidents: "No Balls"

In a 1997 article in *Novoe literaturnoe obozrenie,* Oleg Dark muses: "Is Irina Tarakanova in fact the female demon from Petushki? A brave idea to hand over the narrative to her, to turn her from an object of love into lover."[170]

Dark points out a relevant shift, from the female object of male adoration in *Moscow to the End of the Line* to the female subject of both Sorokin's and Erofeev's novels. Fully aware of this shift, Erofeev—Viktor, that is—claims that women in contemporary literature have gone from being "the object of culture . . . [to being] its subject. They used to be marveled at, judged, thrown under a train; everything was done for their sake."[171] Both *Russian Beauty* and *Marina* toy with this situation by tilting the narrative perspective from a masculine to a feminine point of view. Not surprisingly, in Sorokin's and Erofeev's novels it is the heroine rather than the men surrounding her who identifies with Russia.

Feminists point out that this shift in perspective does not necessarily imply that the heroine is no longer a foil for masculine ambitions. Helena Goscilo claims that *Russian Beauty,* "while parodying a host of Russian myths, nonetheless enthusiastically resorts to the malestream rhetoric that tropes nationhood as mother and, more recently, prostitute";[172] and according to Rosalind Marsh, in Erofeev's novel, as well as in many other recent films and literary texts, "woman is again being used as pure sign, albeit a sign which is now openly debased, rather than idealised as before."[173]

Whether or not one considers it problematic, the feminized Russia in the works discussed still appears, undeniably, as a product of masculine projections. Contrary to earlier periods, however, these projections can no longer be epitomized as fantasies of an idealized intelligentsia. Rather than identifying with the intelligentsia, Erofeev and Sorokin mock its modern equivalent: the dissident movement of the 1960s. Once again, they do so in parallel terms.

184

Intelligenty Versus *Dissidenty*

Erofeev's Irina and Sorokin's Marina are women who evolve from dissidents' sweethearts into lovers of strong masculine figures with close ties to the Soviet regime. As can be expected of true postmodernists, the authors characterize the dissident scene—initially adored by the two girls—in one long concatenation of clichés. Sorokin merges fiction with reality when he places Marina in the intimate company of prominent dissidents: the writers Vladimir Voinovich, Vladimir Bukovskii, and Lidiia Chukovskaia; historian Roi Medvedev; artist Oskar Rabin; physicist Andrei Sakharov; and literary scholar Efim Etkind (2:82, 85). In ambiguous terms, at the home of a dissident friend, Marina enjoys the thought of drinking from a cup that had been touched by "the lips of Sakharov, Orlov, Iakunin, Shcharanskii, Daniel', Sin'iavskii, Vladimov, Bukovskii, Kopelev, Roi and Zhores Medvedev" (2:87–88).[174] If this cross section of names qualifies Marina's surroundings as typically dissident, then the stereotype is reinforced by her reading material. The books she reads and loves form a highly impersonal blueprint of cult samizdat reads for the average oppositional Soviet intellectual. Apart from the Bible and Orwell's *1984*, they include works by Vasilii Grossman and Lidiia Chukovskaia, Sokolov's *School for Fools*, Solzhenitsyn's *Gulag Archipelago*, Georgii Vladimov's *Faithful Ruslan*, and the poetry of Boris Pasternak, Anna Akhmatova, Osip Mandel'shtam, Iosif Brodskii, Naum Korzhavin, David Samoilov, and Inna Lisnianskaia (2:87, 100–101).

While *Russian Beauty* contains less name-dropping, Irina's surroundings form an equally stereotypical—if not strictly underground-related—cross section of the Soviet intelligentsia. In a curious mixture of fiction and reality, Irina's admirers include the poet Bella Akhmadulina and the bard Vladimir Vysotskii (25, 36); she visits the gathering places of "all of intellectual Moscow," and her beaus vary from famous writer Vladimir Sergeevich and foreign diplomat Carlos to "hereditary *intelligent*" Iurochka and "playwright" Egor' (36, 320, 284). In Rylkova's words, Irina's suitors can be summarized as "prominent men of letters . . . striving underground writers and official Soviet journalists."[175] As Rylkova rightly points out, "the problems of what to write and how to write are at the core of the motivations and ambitions of many characters" in the novel.[176]

Both novels whimsically embroider on the identification with the traditional intelligentsia that typified dissident self-consciousness in late Soviet Russia. Because dissidents in the later period take a stance similar to that of imperial Russia's revolutionary intelligentsia—members of both groups are intellectual opponents of the regime—the former begin to identify fiercely with the latter.[177] Many a dissident, as research shows, believed that "they, the dissidents, were the contemporary repository of the moral principles of the intelligentsia, and that they, not the Soviet government, were its rightful heirs and successors."[178]

Not surprisingly, given their real-life identification with the traditional intelligentsia, Sorokin's and Erofeev's *dissidenty* fulfill a role similar to that of the intelligentsia in works discussed earlier in this study. Like their pre-Soviet prototypes, they are allocated the role of a weak masculine force that revels in eloquence rather than in concrete acts. In highly parodistic passages, Irina's friends eagerly discuss their attitude to art, morality, and, eventually, to "T H E M"—the common Russian people (287–89, 320–21; emphasis in original). Illustrative is the assertion of the *intelligent* Iurochka that "in some way T H E Y are better [than we]" (320; emphasis in original). Here as elsewhere, Iurochka and his friends echo the talk-rather-than-do mentality that dominated the classic intelligentsia's self-view. This irritates Irina, who—evoking the rhetoric of nineteenth- and early twentieth-century assaults on the intelligentsia—blames them for merely sitting and talking.

> You listen to shitty plays, but time is passing, you moan and don't understand why it all just goes on and goes on with no sign of it coming to an end, there's no way out, you say, and people are all tangled up in depression and misery, and all you do is tell jokes and amusing anecdotes, but if someone asks you: what is to be done? you're silent, or else you think up such a cock-and-bull story that everyone squirms with embarrassment, as if you just farted, you're so busy dismantling and grieving . . . you drink defiant toasts to your hopeless cause and you bad-mouth the establishment, you hoard your anger, you write satires on something that's already a satire. (290–91)

Plainly hinting at the title of Chernyshevskii's programmatic novel, Irina confronts "her" dissidents with the same question that has been troubling Russian intellectuals since the nineteenth century: What Is to Be Done?

In Sorokin's novel, the ineffectuality of the contemporary "intelligent-sia's" role is stressed on the very first page, which opens with one more "Russian man at a rendezvous": Valentin, a pianist and self-proclaimed "aging aristocratic offspring." He meets Marina, has sex with her, and complains about his inability to experience genuine emotion or love (2:10, 20). A contemporary descendant of that most famous sluggard of Russian literature, Oblomov, Valentin enters the scene—which takes place in his apartment—in a dressing gown, blaming (Soviet) society for his amorous failings. "All my life I have dreamt of loving someone," he complains: "either it is impossible for us to realize that feeling in our Soviet circumstances, or I simply haven't met the right person" (2:20). A more sociopolitical passivity characterizes another of Marina's intellectual friends, Mitia, who wants to emigrate, claiming "I just don't see a point in doing anything" (2:91).

If initially empathizing with her dissident lovers, eventually Marina is convinced by Rumiantsev's critique of them—a critique that virtually echoes Irina's.

> Everything will end in anger, drinking bouts and gossip. That whole silly dissident movement of yours. . . . What good is it? Think about it! Scream, criticize, deride? The easiest thing, you see, is to criticize. It's harder to do something. Truly, practically. To do something. Instead of just guessing how to save Russia. (2:161)

Scoffing at Marina, the Party official borrows unashamedly from the rhetoric of traditional attacks on the intelligentsia. In his portrayal, the dissidents resemble those literary exponents of the intelligentsia who, in earlier days, were known as "superfluous men." Not fortuitously did a reviewer compare the novel's dissidents to "here the Turgenevian student circle from *Rudin* . . . there the revolutionaries from—again—Turgenev's *Smoke* and *Virgin Soil.*"[179]

In Sorokin's novel, Marina's—and, symbolically, Russia's—"salvation" lies in her denunciation of the dissident "in crowd" and her subsequent union with Sergei Nikolaevich, who condemns it so vehemently. In what would prove a wry anticipation of the future destruction of Sorokin's books by pro-Putinist youngsters, she takes her samizdat collection into the street and burns it in a bonfire (2:179).[180]

Sorokin's and Erofeev's portraits of the *intelligenty* of Soviet Russia echo those of the intelligentsia as reconstructed in the previous chapters in more than one respect. Apart from their opposition to the regime, the two authors' dissidents also resemble Russia's historical intellectual elite through their orientation toward Western, rather than Russian, culture. In *Russian Beauty,* one dissident friend gives Irina a subscription to the ultimate medium for Western literature in translation—the journal *Inostrannaia literatura* (23). She mingles with her intellectual friends at gatherings in the home of an Oxford-educated South American ambassador (36–37), and she meets Vladimir Sergeevich through his son, who has had an affair with her friend on a trip to Paris (39).

Even more explicit is Sorokin's reenactment of the "alienated intellectual" paradigm. Emigration—a popular social coping strategy in Jewish Soviet circles—is a major issue for many of Marina's *bohème* friends. She witnesses "embassies bursting with grub, drinks, and *dissida* . . . with monstrous numbers of underground artists, poets, and writers who were obsessed with the idea of emigration, but who nevertheless did not emigrate" (2:137–38). In Rumiantsev's words, these "parasites'" estrangement from "native" Russian culture equals "living in your own country and hating your own people. And gaping open-mouthed at the West" (2:167).

The prototype of the pro-Western *dissida* is Mitia, a dissident-to-the-fingertips figure who fervently wants to emigrate to the United States (2:85, 88, 91). In a more traditional vein, orientation toward foreign cultures epitomizes the aristocratic Valentin: his language is interspersed with literary and cultural allusions, especially with reference to the ancient Greeks and Romans (2:10–14). Valentin's foreign orientation is contrasted openly with Marina's Russianness when the latter accuses him twice of speaking French to her instead of Russian (2:14–15).[181] In conclusion, the young pop singer Shit (Govno) and his friends are keen to keep up with the latest trends in Western music, film, and fashion (2:144–47). A foreign prism colors the attitude of all three men to Marina: they label her a Venus, a Hollywood girl, and—in Russified English—a "gerla" or "girl," respectively (2:12, 86, 146).

In addition, both novels travesty the tendency to characterize the intelligentsia as unmasculine in relation to the heroine. In sexual escapades with Marina, both Valentin and Mitia repeatedly seem "helpless" and passive, whereas she "decidedly" takes initiative (2:12–13, 89–90). Marina thinks of Valentin as a "little fat boy" with "puffed" lips, "round" eyes, and "blossoming" cheeks; Mitia equates himself and his friends in their attitude toward the state with naive "children" (2:12, 94).

In *Russian Beauty,* the comparison of Irina's dissident friends to children is even harder to miss. The two "bandit-*intelligenty*" who accompany Irina to the Kulikovo scene are referred to at least six times as "boys," three times as "kids" or "kiddies," and once as crying "children" who look to Irina as "their own mother" (320–21, 335, 340, 346, 352, 358). The contrast between these "immature" (male) dissidents and the (female) Irina in her role of Russia incarnate recalls Berdiaev's vision of the intelligentsia as Russia's excessively weak and boyish lover. In Oleg Dark's reading the novel, in general, recycles classic ideas on the "earth's dichotomy" as the "impossibility for a 'feminine' and a 'masculine' element to merge and reconcile."[182]

Thus, Sorokin and Erofeev parody and reapply the qualification of the intelligentsia discussed in previous chapters—as superfluous, Western-oriented, and unmasculine—with tangible parodistic pleasure to the dissident movement. A similar ironic revision characterizes several of the other postmodern works mentioned in this section.

Probably the most over-the-top heirs of nineteenth-century *intelligenty* are found in Sorokin's oeuvre. A clone of Onegin and of Turgenevian heroes, his Roman—in the novel of the same name—is branded a talented artist-intellectual with the smile "of a child" who is still in search of a goal in life (2:273–74, 76, 290–91). In an abundantly clear reference to traditional populist discourse, his love for Tania blends with a desire to bridge the "wall between the Russian common man and the Russian *barin*" (2:422).[183] His position of aristocratic westernized intellectual is emphasized at every opportunity: through comparisons of his looks to those of a western European (2:273–74); his love of foreign fashion (2:284, 318); his orientation toward Western culture; and, worthy of a Pushkinian or Turgenevian hero, his identification with a panoply of Western intellectuals and literary icons.[184] When, immediately after meeting Tania—the "Russian" heroine—he is referred to as "St. George the dragon slayer," the Symbolist myth of the artist as the savior of a feminized Russia looms large (2:467).

The hero in Sorokin's *The Norm* is a similar stereotypical westernized intellectual. The great-grandson of Fedor Tiutchev and burdened with a face that expresses "the joyous eccentricity of a Russian *intelligent*" (1:145), Anton ponders, in nationalist clichés, the "long-suffering earth" and the "path of the Russian soul" (1:145, 152, 159). He revels in Tania's "Russian beauty" and eagerly reflects on his own Russian origins (1:152).

While in both *The Blue Lard* and *23.000* the penetration of the Russian earth is not linked directly to a discourse on the role of the intelligentsia, this discourse does resonate in the album *Deep into Russia*. In a physical explication of Berdiaev's admonition to "impregnate" the native soil with masculine spirit (see chapter 2), *Deep into Russia* presents Oleg Kulik as a masculine force that penetrates rural Russia or Russian animals (apart from one ape, the artist is shown with Russian domestic animals or cattle). Sorokin's accompanying texts allude to classic nineteenth-century heroes and heroines and to the "Russian heroines" of Village Prose.[185]

"The intelligentsia" also stars in "The Eros of Moscow," where Moscow is proclaimed a female beloved by a narrator who poses as a downright classic *intelligent*. He doesn't refrain from the cliché pose of a Romantic poet when appearing in a cemetery "on a little bench next to some artist's grave," reading "Nabokov until dawn."[186] A self-proclaimed pivot of the city's intellectual life, this narrator "courts" Moscow while enjoying the company of other—nonfictional—contemporary artists and writers such as Andrei Monastyrskii, Igor' Vinogradov, and Dmitrii Prigov.[187]

Sorokin's works preserve the concept of the intelligentsia or the poet as Russia's (or Moscow's) future lover; they tend to speak of this love as something desired but not yet present at the moment of speaking. Within his oeuvre, however, the concept of the intelligentsia as an *ineffectual* lover of Russia is limited to *Marina's Thirtieth Love*. This ineffectuality does play a key role in Erofeev's *Encyclopedia of the Russian Soul*. Its narrator—portrayed as the author's double—asserts that "playing the good unhappy 'people' and the bad 'state' has ended in the defeat of the intelligentsia itself," whose "cycle of existence has come to an end."[188] He parrots the traditional attack on the intelligentsia as "weak," "helpless," and lacking initiative in its relationship to Russian society.[189] Berdiaev's critique of the intelligentsia as "womanish" or *bab'e* reverberates when the narrator's emigration from Russia is compared to a sex change—from *baba* to boy.[190] Alluding both to the myth of the intelligentsia and to the real-life Erofeev, a diplomat's son, the narrator poses as an "enemy of the people" and as someone who looks at Russia as a "stranger" views a "foreign state."[191] At times he has "worried passionately about the fate of the native land; I didn't sleep for nights; I was thinking only of how to save her."[192] That he identifies specifically with the role of a feminized Russia's male suitor is shown in designations of Russia as a whore and a young girl, as well as in an explicit declaration of love: "I am one of the happy few who can allow themselves to love this land with a strange love. She is mine."[193]

The other postmodern artists considered here tend to hark back to similar images in their portrayal of the male hero. In Peppershtein's "Egg" and Prigov's "My Russia," a male writer-poet is both in love with and slightly intimidated by a feminized Moscow/Russia;[194] in the latter's media opera, it is the poet as "intellectually articulated cultural subject"—"I, as the intelligentsia," explains the author—who "tortures" a "soft, complaisant" feminized Russia.[195] Nekrasov's *Liubov'*—advertised as a film about the "generations of the 1970s' and 1980s' dissident youth, which unconsciously identified hatred of the system with love for the Native Land"[196]—opposes a feminized Russia to a "bohemian egoist and intellectual" hero.[197] And Moscow's symbolic lovers Dmitrii and Andrei in Mukhina's *Iu*, both acting the role of the classic cultural *intelligent*, appear as childlike, effeminate creatures.[198]

Superfluity Sexualized

If, for Sorokin and Erofeev, the "bride Russia" is a distinctly physical figure, then physicality equally marks their depiction of the intellectual elite. The lack of masculinity with which religious philosophers of the early twentieth century charged the intelligentsia, the childishness and weakness of Iurii Zhivago, the female figures to whom Venedikt Erofeev's Venichka is compared—Erofeev's and Sorokin's novels maximize the implications of such accusatory analogies by depicting the dissidents as helpless children in distinctly bedroom terms. "Relying on my own experience," Irina claims in *Russian Beauty*, "I must say that writers are a shallow bunch, and as men even shallower . . . they are always sort of agitated, they fuss and they come very quickly" (14). To Irina, dissidents are "men with no balls" who are "useless at fucking" (291, 294). Again, the physicality can become glaringly concrete, as when Irina sighs that some of her "new friends . . . have the pathetic, whipped look of men who can't get it up,

Chapter Four

[while] others . . . are those live-wire types who twitch around convulsively if briefly" (294–95).

Marina's experiences with dissidents do not differ greatly from Irina's. Unlike Irina, who consciously complains about her lovers' sexual incompetence, Sorokin's heroine has no comment on their sexual activity. That their behavior matches that of Irina's lovers becomes painfully clear, however, in certain descriptive scenes: in bed with Marina, Valentin becomes a "helpless pink lump" overcome by a "shiver," whose hands touch her "convulsively" and who turns "deathly pale" (2:13–14). Another "pale" lover, Mitia, also seized by a "shiver," moves "impatiently and quickly" and utters a "powerless groan" while making love (2:89–90). Govno tries to kiss Marina with "a pale flabby face" and "drunken eyes" (2:151).

From the start, Marina associates the arrival of her true love with the orgasm that no dissident can offer her (2:100); ultimately, it is Party official Sergei Nikolaevich who triggers the climax she's been anticipating. In *Russian Beauty,* Irina's dissatisfaction with her friends' sexual incapacity is likewise contrasted to the unprecedented succession of orgasms she eventually experiences with Leonardik (395).

Sorokin reenacts the same sexualized opposition in "The Eros of Moscow," whose narrator depicts a group of "writers of the 1960s" as Moscow's incapable lovers. Comparing their street protests to efforts to make the feminized Moscow "come as soon as possible," Sorokin has the police—the Soviet regime incarnate—ruthlessly interrupt their failed act.[199] In *The Norm* and *Deep into Russia,* we have also seen the relationship of artists-*intelligenty* to the Russian earth rendered in sexual terms.[200]

In the work of the other artists discussed here, the relationship of the hero or poet to Russia is portrayed in sexual terms as well. In many of these cases, however, the sexualization of the metaphor is limited to a feminized Russia onto whom the hero's or poet's desires and frustrations are projected. Seldom are the physical qualities of the masculine figure discussed explicitly. An exception is a 1995 speech on fascism by the scandalous writer Eduard Limonov. Limonov transplants Berdiaev's concept of the "womanish intelligentsia" to the sexual sphere when he declares:

The landlady-intelligentsia, completely confused in her womanly caprices and in despair over her inability to please everybody—will suddenly find relief. A boss will come, will grab her by the hair, bow, and will use her for his own purposes. . . . No court, no democratic procedure or communist prison will satisfy her [the intelligentsia's] craving for punishment. They languish in their longing for the whip, for a thrashing, for crude blows to the liver, and it's only the fascists who can arrange these delights for them.[201]

191

Here the notion of a feminine intelligentsia changes from a gendered metaphor with implicit sexual connotations into an explicitly sexual-sadomasochistic image.

To Sorokin and Erofeev, the sexualized conceptualization of the contemporary "intelligentsia" is vital to a proper understanding of Russia's dissident movement. Asked about the sexual element in his depiction of dissidents, Erofeev links it directly to a wish to expose issues of power: in his words, the dissident hierarchy "rested upon the principle of the phallus. . . . There was a principal dick, a small dick. . . . Everything there was very rigid. . . . There was no less sexuality there than in any other power."[202] He tags *Russian Beauty* "the first anti-dissident novel" and the first to expose this mechanism.[203]

Erofeev claims that whereas he drew on personal experiences as a Soviet dissident to write his novel, Sorokin lacks such experience and is unable to understand the sexual principle underlying the dissident movement.[204] In *Marina,* however, Sorokin not only transfers dissident "superfluity" to the sexual sphere but does so in terms that do not differ substantially from Erofeev's. He agrees with one interviewer that "the dissident movement [fails] less from a social lack of expression than from a sexual one" and says that "looking at the dissidents" from a sexual rather than a sociopolitical perspective is a "big theme" in his work.[205]

In parodistic and sexually explicit scenes, then, both novels express the feeling that "underground" Soviet intellectuals, while claiming moral purity, in fact display the same hierarchical thinking that characterizes the Soviet regime itself. The two authors articulate this idea in terms reminiscent of earlier critical debate on the role of the intelligentsia. In their hands the concept of the intelligentsia as Russia's ineffectual bridegroom is transformed radically: stripped of its ideological charge, it morphs from an abstract into a highly concrete, sexual image—or, as the authors would have it, into empty metaphor.

The Rival Revisited

In both *Russian Beauty* and *Marina's Thirtieth Love,* the depiction of dissidents is diametrically opposed to that of Mr. Right. The latter functions simultaneously and paradoxically as an embodiment of the anti-establishment milieu of Soviet dissident artists and as a representative of that very establishment and of the Soviet regime.

Thus, one face of Erofeev's Vladimir Sergeevich is that of the prototypical independent artist: Irina refers to him as Leonardik, after Leonardo da Vinci, *homo universalis* of Europe's Renaissance (232). Defining their relationship as the predestined "merging" of "artist and heroine," she says Sergeevich enters her life "from the world of art, in a necklace of laurels and esteem" (48, 385). Leonardik himself identifies more with Pushkin and Tiutchev (58, 159),[206] and Galina Rylkova mentions his role as the spiritual heir of his namesake, Vladimir Sergeevich Solov'ev.[207] As an artist, he is branded "a giant" and contrasted against "the masses of society" (170–71).

The other face of this stereotypical man of the arts reveals a man of power who is at home among the political and artistic Soviet elite. Called a "hybrid of Tiutchev and a shaggy colonel" (161), Leonardik has a "reputation of being a serious man who hymns heroic deeds and labor" (132–33). His legacy to Russia is ominously compared to "a steel bayonet" (170). In his depiction, fiction and reality again blur: adorned with a war medal and familiar to Irina "from television," Vladimir Sergeevich is personally acquainted with giants of Soviet culture, such as Marshal Konstantin Rokossovskii, writer Aleksandr Fadeev, actor Nikolai Cherkasov, composer Dmitrii Shostakovich, and, to top it all off, Stalin himself (48, 51). That he occupies a pivotal role in this environment suggests his knowledge of state secrets and his presence at Stalinist parties (267, 327). After his death, there is a strong suggestion that the deceased Leonardik is the double of Russia's "main enemy," whom Irina confronts on Kulikovo field.

Sorokin's Rumiantsev forms a similar "hybrid" of artistic opposition and state authority. Outwardly, he is a match for the unspecified messianic "HE" of Marina's amorous reveries (capitals in original).[208] As the reader soon finds out, HE is a prominent dissident whose portrait adorns the wall of Marina's apartment (2:99). Clearly indicated by his description—a "wedge-shaped face with a fringe beard and a small, barely noticeable scar on his wrinkled forehead"—the man is none other than the famous dissident writer Aleksandr Solzhenitsyn (ibid.).[209]

Eventually, HE enters Marina's real life in a very different guise: as Sergei Nikolaevich Rumiantsev. In the flesh, her dream prince looks like Solzhenitsyn, but he reveals himself as a Party secretary—and one who devotes all his energy to the creation of a Soviet utopia (2:155). In a mockery of Russia's most famous dissident, Sorokin unites the man whose portrait asks "What have you done to be called HUMAN?" (2:99; capitals in original) with the Soviet system incarnate.[210]

The paradoxical Solzhenitsyn–Party man combination seems unexpected at first, but a closer look shows that Marina's fantasies have anticipated this confluence from the outset. HE is introduced in her dreams as a "great man who gave himself totally to the service of Russia" and who is received by a "sea of people" at Moscow's Vnukovo Airport, where he arrives "in tears" after a transatlantic flight (2:84). The scene—to which Marina attributes an "utterly cinematographic character" (2:84)—is an overt variation on a famous passage in Sergei Eisenstein's film classic *October* (*Oktiabr'*, 1927), in which Lenin's arrival is announced in a textual intermezzo with the same capitalized HE. Eisenstein's Lenin emerges as the long-awaited father of the revolution—and Russia's savior—from an international train that has pulled into St. Petersburg's Finland Station. The masses awaiting him are filmed as no less ecstatic than the "sea of people" in Marina's dream.

Ironically, the arrival scene in the novel would be echoed almost literally when the real Solzhenitsyn returned to Russia from the United States in 1994. Arriving on a transatlantic flight to Russia, an emotional Solzhenitsyn expressed the wish to dedicate himself to a "social and moral role" within contemporary Russia; at Magadan Airport, he was greeted, in the words of BBC News, by an excited "sea" of two thousand sympathizers.[211]

But this happened eleven years after Sorokin finished his book. In the novel, HIS ambiguous status is maximized from the moment the face on the portrait enters Marina's life as Rumiantsev. The man's physical resemblance to Solzhenitsyn is contradicted by his typical Soviet manner. He uses stock expressions from Soviet propaganda and identifies with the Soviet hero Vasilii Chapaev and "the proletariat" (2:176–78, 180). Arguing that he "loved, loves, and will love" the Russian people (2:162), he uses the three verb tenses that resound in a paramount Soviet phrase: "Lenin lived, lives, and will live." Vehemently rejecting the world of art (2:160), he claims to belong to Soviet Russia's "new people," who need to "retransfer everything onto state rails" (2:164, 166). He speaks "not for myself" but on behalf of the "force" of this state (2:167).

What we see is Rumiantsev assuming the same sort of paradoxical role that is fulfilled by Erofeev's Leonardik—a role that can be explained by each author's wish to dismantle dissident hypocrisy. Both characters personify the idea that the dissident movement, in its preoccupation with authority, does not differ substantially from the Soviet regime. According to Erofeev, Leonardik and the dissidents in his novel are not a pair marked by clashing contrasts. The latter "are constructed . . . as an alternative force, which theoretically takes on the power of a shadow cabinet—in other words, the power that takes over, which is what actually happened within a few years."[212] Discussing *Marina*, Sorokin says the artistic circles in which he moved in his early years "ironized both the Soviet regime . . . *and* the dissidents."[213]

But coincidences between Rumiantsev and Leonardik extend further than their characterization as dissident-cum-Soviet idols. In the "orgasm scenes" that form the key to both novels, the status of the two men is strikingly similar. They each assume a role that alludes to that of the fairy-tale sorcerer who appeared as Russia's symbolic seducer in the early twentieth century.

194

Chapter Four

Sorcerers: Symbolist Echoes

As mentioned previously, both Sorokin's and Erofeev's novels pivot around a scene in which the heroine experiences an orgasm of mythical proportions. In *Marina's Thirtieth Love,* this is the scene with Rumiantsev that represents the turning point between Marina's "dissident life" and her existence as a model Soviet heroine. Rendered as an awakening, the moment simultaneously marks a transition to the "dream level," which—as Valentina Brougher convincingly argues—defines the rest of the plot.[214] Not only does the transition itself take place in a dream; Marina's earlier visions of her savior also occur in daydreams or while sleeping (2:84, 99, 118–23). She experiences her merging with the choir in the orgasm scene as *obvorozhitel'no,* an adjective that means both "fascinating" and "bewitching" (2:173). If one adds Marina's status as a symbolic stand-in for Russia to Rumiantsev's role in the scene, the sum of the two conjures up an image of the metaphoric sorcerer—or false bridegroom of Russia—who was so popular in early twentieth-century culture. Significantly, Sorokin himself brands Rumiantsev, in his capacity as Solzhenitsyn's double, as a "werewolf" (*oboroten'*)[215]—the same term that Belyi uses for the foreign sorcerer who bewitches "sleeping beauty Russia" in "The Green Meadow."[216] A later Sorokin hero calls Gogol's "Terrible Vengeance," the story on which Belyi grafts this essay, "the world's most frightening tale."[217]

Rumiantsev's looks were inspired by a Solzhenitsyn portrait that Sorokin saw as a child, in which the writer looked "like an absolutely Western face."[218] This foreign dimension is reflected in the story in the arrival of the mysterious HE on a transatlantic flight and in HIS affinity with Western-oriented dissident circles. Revealing himself as Rumiantsev, the same HE turns out to be a Communist whose speech is a blend of Soviet and populist-Slavophile clichés. That Sorokin chooses Solzhenitsyn to fulfill the role of "werewolf" is not surprising. Like his fictional ego, the real-life Solzhenitsyn combines two contradictory images: that of the dissident who identifies with the traditional liberal intelligentsia, and that of the conservative thinker who asserts "that in countries such as Russia an authoritarian state was the only one in which . . . individual emancipation could be achieved."[219] The orgasm scene in which Sorokin places him was practically foretold by Solzhenitsyn himself in a 1975 article in *Kontinent.* In this emigrant journal Solzhenitsyn, probably paraphrasing Blok's "Twelve," quotes a popular verse from the early Soviet years: "We have shot the fat-assed *baba* Russia, / So that Communism could crawl across her body as a Messiah."[220] Whether or not this quotation inspired Sorokin is uncertain, but it is easy to picture Rumiantsev, the Communist par excellence, "crawling across" the body of Marina, alias Russia. In Sorokin's rendition, however, Solzhenitsyn becomes the very embodiment of the Communist regime that is criticized in his own poem.

The association of Rumiantsev with classic sorcerers is not limited to the "werewolf" image, however. It is reinforced when Mitia characterizes the dissident attitude toward the state as that of "children" who "approached a sleeping dragon . . . and tickled it under the nose" (2:94). Given Rumiantsev's status as the Soviet state incarnate, in this passage it is he who is compared symbolically to a dragon—a traditional equivalent of the sorcerer.

This reference to a dragon highlights yet another dimension of the classic sorcerer that Sorokin reiterates: that of maturity, as opposed to the intelligentsia's childishness. Without explicitly labeling Rumiantsev old or mature, he indirectly ascribes to him the role of father. The capitalized HE with which Marina refers to her Mr. Right first appears in the novel as a designation for her father's penis (2:45). Then, too, several details in the orgasm scene echo an earlier passage in which Marina is touched intimately and penetrated for the first time, by her father (2:43–48). When Rumiantsev enters her—while she is asleep and unwilling, as she was back then—she remembers the seaside setting of the incestuous act (2:171–74).

Thus, in a complex play involving intratextual and intertextual references, the novel not only *reenacts* the folklorist antithesis of hero—sorcerer as young son—old father, but ultimately *reverses* that opposition. In the end, in *Marina's Thirtieth Love* it is not the young intelligentsia or *dissida,* but the paternal sorcerer-like Rumiantsev, who symbolically liberates the heroine. In Sorokin's words, her story "is something like an inside-out version of Tolstoy's *Resurrection.* . . . Marina is 'released' from individuality. . . . It is a monstrous salvation—but a salvation."[221] The incestuous implications of that salvation are not concealed: if in Belyi's "Green Meadow" the sorcerer is merely said to be so old that he could have been the feminized Russia's father, then Rumiantsev literally merges with Marina's father in distinctly incestuous imagery.

All in all, Rumiantsev's character can be linked in more than one way to traditional symbolic sorcerers. Although that link must be reconstructed in *Marina,* Erofeev alludes to the same figure in glaringly overt terms. The deceased Leonardik discloses himself as a potential double of the "enemy of Russia" whom Irina confronts on Kulikovo field. Afterward, he seems to know about the confrontation (376–83). Irina asks, "If you appeared [on the field] . . . does that mean He exists?" whereupon Leonardik revealingly answers, "It means I exist" (383).

To an even greater extent than Rumiantsev, the demon with whom Leonardik is associated evokes early twentieth-century seducer-sorcerer paradigms. Irina conceives of the confrontation with the demon in terms that rely heavily on Belyi and Blok. She claims that by letting the demon penetrate her, she will end a long period of "sorcery" (*koldovstvo*) holding Russia in its grip (269). By contrast, the demon double Leonardik states that "sorcery actually preserves this country" (382). As we have seen, Belyi and Blok used the related term "sorcerer" (*koldun*) for evil forces that held a feminized Russia captive.

Even more reminiscent of "The Green Meadow" is Irina's repeated prediction that Russia will be liberated from the demon's sorcery when "the shroud falls" (*spadet pelena*) (321, 340). Her assertion corresponds to Belyi's claim that the "sleeping beauty Russia" was draped in a "shroud [*pelena*] of black death," which needed to be "lifted" (*snesena*).[222] Irina's appearance on the autumnal Kulikovo field, her quintessentially Russian looks, and her Blok-saturated speech also plainly evoke Blok's "Russia" poem, with its opposition of female Russia and male sorcerer.[223]

Like Sorokin's text, Erofeev's also gives an incestuous twist to the fatherly role that this sorcerer traditionally plays. If Irina's dissident friends are compared to children, Leonardik is associated with a father figure from the start: he and Irina first meet at the house of Leonardik's son, with whom she has just slept, and Leonardik is introduced by his son's exclamation, "Father!" (57). Irina—who has known Leonardik's name since childhood and has studied his books at school—repeatedly refers to him as an old man (121, 136, 162, 164, 231). As in Sorokin's novel, their incest-like affair echoes the bond between the heroine and her parent: Irina claims that, in her youth, her beauty gave her father an erection (337).

Again, "The Green Meadow" reverberates. According to Erofeev, however, rather than reviving Blok and Belyi, the novel toys with concepts from Andreev's *Rose of the World*.[224] The characterization of Russia's "main enemy" as a demon echoes the term that Andreev uses for the captivator of Russia's "Ecumenical Soul."[225] In terms that would not seem misplaced in Andreev's treatise, he is branded an "evil spirit" and a "voluptuous flesh-devouring demon, usurper and autocrat" (159, 296). Like Andreev, who branded Peter the Great and Stalin as two of Russia's key demons, Erofeev presents Russia's "main enemy" in terms that combine a mystical and a political vocabulary. That, via Andreev, these terms can be traced to early twentieth-century gender metaphors is beyond doubt.

Thus both novels revel in a playful deconstruction of well-known plots and ideas. That the resulting postmodern quilts are defined by strong preferences for certain themes over others is implied by their detailed coincidences. These suggest that the myth of the state as the evil captivator of a feminized Russia is a favorite concept of both authors.

This impression is reinforced by the recurrent use of the same myth elsewhere, by Sorokin and Erofeev as well as by other Russian postmodernists. In Sorokin's *The Norm,* the hero's father reads him a passage from a history study. It gives an account of the Kulikovo battle, albeit without the gendered dimension of interest here, in the same religio-mystical terms that mark *Russian Beauty:* "On Kulikovo field . . . a collision took place between a beneficial spiritual force . . . and filth and an evil force, which embodied . . . the ominous face of Satan" (1:140). In a 2005 interview, Sorokin himself would claim—in referencing Putin's increasingly authoritative regime—that "Russia remains totalitarianism's faithful mistress."[226]

Erofeev repeats the "false bridegroom" myth, too, when he describes a failed flirtation between foreign forces and a feminized Russia in *Encyclopedia of the Russian Soul:*

> If Russia ever loved anyone, it must be France. She gave her whole Slavic soul for France. . . . In her hankering after France, she stopped meeting anyone, looking at anyone; the Germans, Dutch, and Swedes remained on the roadside without the needed attention. . . . She lived promiscuously. . . . She loved Napoleon, who wanted to ram her, and she secretly dreamed of giving herself to him, like the last whore, behind the Mozhai, on the Borodino field, anywhere, anytime. . . . She was offended: the love was not mutual; she protested against her own love, . . . made a vow not to speak French, laughed bitterly at herself, mocked her own *prononce,* did not sleep for nights . . . but still she loved selflessly, devotedly, as never before.[227]

By opposing Russia to Napoléon as a "submissive" woman to her male seducer, Erofeev effectively travesties both the Slavophile-inspired language of Berdiaev and his contemporaries, and nineteenth-century conceptualizations of Moscow.

As we have seen, Prigov also recycles the concept of a masculine force intruding upon a feminine Russia with his Iosif-Sofiia opposition in "In the Sense Of." In "Moscow and the Muscovites," he contrasts a feminine Moscow in the form of an "innocent and pure" "white swan" with the less innocuous image of a "black raven, expert on European Wisdom."[228] That the feminized Moscow is really a bride is suggested not only by the image of a swan—a folkloric symbol for a bride—but also by her position elsewhere in the cycle as a maiden whose hand is sought by "Chinese and Mongols, and Georgians, Armenians, Assyrians, Israelites."[229]

Finally, Eduard Limonov—albeit in a piece of military rather than Silver Age rhetoric—represents Russia and fascism as wife and husband. In his speech on fascism, he claims that "Russia awaits it with fear and trembling, as one awaits the only strong and beautiful—if 'dangerous'—bridegroom in a ravaged house."[230]

Savior-Undoer: Romantic Echoes

In her essay on *Russian Beauty,* Rylkova rightly calls the "cultural renaissance" of the Silver Age a crucial prism for "cultural revitalization" in (post-) perestroika Russian literature.[231] Such emphasis notwithstanding, the panoply of cultural periods travestied by postmodernism ranges far beyond the twentieth century. For the metaphor examined here, the nineteenth century forms a crucial touchstone.

Apart from the traditional opposition of "Russian" heroines to a socially alienated "intelligentsia," postmodernists also revise the myth of the hero as both "savior" (*spasitel'*) and "undoer" (*pogubitel'*). As noted in chapter 1, this myth was crucial to several nineteenth-century novels whose heroines to be "saved" (or "undone") were associated with Russia. Iurii Lotman has shown that the savior-undoer paradigm also affected the depiction of the hero in twentieth-century variations on the "bride Russia" metaphor.[232]

In contemporary literature, Sorokin and Erofeev are particularly sensitive to ironic reproductions of this myth. The concept resonates with particular force in Erofeev's novel. Explaining the work, he says that *Russian Beauty* adapts "the dilemma of the undoer-savior . . . in a super-ironic key."[233] In a jumble of clichéd nineteenth-century designations of the hero, Irina refers to Leonardik as "a savior [*spasitel'*] after all," a "subtle thinker" (*tonkii myslitel'*), a "sovereign" (*povelitel'*) and, at the same time, a "traitor" (*predatel'*) and her "future avenger" (*budushchii mstitel'*) and "tormenter" (*muchitel'*) (120, 144–45, 154, 345, 463). If the terms used evoke nineteenth-century heroes,[234] the association is intensified by the resurrection of the deceased Leonardik, who takes Irina with him to the realm of the dead (375, 379–81). Deceased-groom motifs epitomize the Lenore plot that captured the imaginations of several nineteenth-century Russian poets, and they color the depiction of the most renowned savior-undoer of Russian literature: Eugene Onegin. His story offers an important source for the novel in general, as we saw: the heroes consciously identify with Tat'iana and with Pushkin.

Leonardik's depiction echoes the Lenore motif not only in terms of his appearance as a deceased lover. He is also labeled "bridegroom" (*zhenikh*) and "guest" (*gost'*), characteristic designations for the groom in Russian versions of Lenore (205, 207, 379).[235] What is more, Erofeev echoes the ritual prediction of future bridegrooms that appears in these works and in *Onegin:*

he has Irina break her mirror in anger over the deceased Leonardik's visit, after which a friend wonders whether Irina has seen her dead lover "in the mirror, or what?" (389–90, 399).

Sorokin ironically revises the savior-undoer paradigm as well, most clearly in *Roman*, whose hero—initially glorified as a "savior [*spasitel'*]" (2:504, 506)—literally transforms into an undoer by killing everyone around him, including himself. That Rumiantsev is also a hero of the savior-undoer type need not be explained here; however, Sorokin does not refer explicitly to the concept in his novel. He does parody other nineteenth-century clichés. Apart from the young-old (or child-father) opposition, these include the antithesis of Rumiantsev as powerful doer vis-à-vis the dissidents as weak thinkers. As Rumiantsev claims, referring to the latter: "One needs to do things, instead of guessing how Russia can be saved" (2:161). Rumiantsev's belief "in reality, in real concrete tasks" is in sharp contrast to the dissidents' faith in an abstract, distant future (2:94, 166). The strength and energy of this *homo Sovieticus* are expressed most emphatically—as is the dissidents' superfluity—on a sexual level. Contrary to their boyish helplessness in bed are Rumiantsev's "masculine motion" during lovemaking and his "body that smelled strongly of . . . masculinity" (2:170–71). Giving Marina the orgasm that her dissident friends failed to deliver, he is admired by her for his "strong fingers," the "elastically muscular knobs" of his jaws, his "strong," "rough and decided" movements, and his "concentrated" gaze (2:176).

A similar strong-doer–weak-thinker contrast is created in *Russian Beauty*. Whereas Irina's dissident friends are part of an underground crowd of social outcasts, Leonardik's face shines "with precisely that infallible light which indicates success in life" (49). Irina labels him "a soldier and a husbandman, a tiller of the soil and a standard-bearer" (170–71). He walks into her life "out of the December frost, with the firm step of a successful and famous man" (47).[236] As in the case of Rumiantsev, social success and sexual prowess collide: Leonardik's ability to give Irina an orgasm of mystical proportions stands in stark contrast to the sexual incapability of the dissidents (394–95). Radiating masculine eros and energy, he and Rumiantsev take the nineteenth-century antagonist into manifestly physical spheres.

Letters or Themes?

"I have no style of my own."[237] "All my books are only relationships with text."[238] "Aren't those just letters on a piece of paper?"[239] These are Sorokin's comments on his (early) work. Erofeev defines his oeuvre in terms that differ little from those of his younger colleague. As major goals he names the "laying bare of the devices of any discourse"[240] and "the rejection of all the Russian novel's concepts" so as "to show that a novel is like a trap."[241]

A similar dismissal of authorial pathos tints the authors' characterizations of the novels discussed here. As noted earlier, Sorokin calls *Marina* a travesty of Tolstoy's *Resurrection.*[242] Erofeev dubs *Russian Beauty* a "protest against the genre of the novel."[243] Most distinctly, this protest is expressed through the status of the heroine. According to the author, "instead of a Russian beauty" his novel "contains only a hole" and "no personage."[244] Toward the end of the story, Irina herself claims, "I'm not there anymore," "now we [Irina and Leonardik] will both cease to exist," and "I dissolve as a character" (395, 461).

"No personage" is a term that equally characterizes Sorokin's Marina, who begins to "disappear" gradually after her orgasm with Rumiantsev, albeit mainly in a linguistic sense. In Olga Khrustaleva's words, in *Marina's Thirtieth Love*

> through . . . clichés of ideological language, the disappearance of the depersonalized hero takes place just as naturally and logically as the absorption of literary styles. At first the girls at the factory call friends by first name, then by last name . . . until finally, by the end, the personal attachment of utterances disappears.[245]

Like the other "girls at the factory," Marina dissolves into the collective and literally vanishes from view toward the end of the novel, to make way for the impersonal style of Soviet propaganda.

Hence, both Irina and Marina can be read as random elements in a play with literary styles, rather than as central characters in a story. The same randomness marks the dissident motif. In my conversations with Erofeev and with Sorokin, both stressed the thematic "emptiness" of this concept and the arbitrariness of their decision to mock Soviet dissidents. As Erofeev put it, the dissident movement is comparable to "any other power."[246]

In general, for each of the two authors it is the literary experiment that is central and not an extraliterary "real world." Though today Sorokin dissociates himself from postmodern experimentation, the majority of his work under discussion here is defined by his earlier, radically postmodern view on writing. Both he and Erofeev focus on "the destruction of myths and clichés of collective observation" (Sorokin)[247] and "protest against all stereotypes," including "national stereotypes" (Erofeev).[248] Not surprisingly, then, a thematic approach to their work aggravates both authors. When I interviewed them, they reacted with irritation to questions suggesting the existence of central themes or key motifs in their oeuvres. As Sorokin repeatedly argued, "all that is shallow."[249]

Indeed, one can hardly read their texts—as one would any of those discussed in previous chapters—as thematically or sociopolitically motivated works. Dissecting the myth of a bridal Russia is what interests these authors, but that myth no longer functions as an expression of their personal attitude toward Russia.

Yet that is not the whole story. A distinct field of tension can be felt between the alleged thematic arbitrariness of their poetics and their literary practice. The sheer number of parallels between the two novels suggests that, when they were (virtually simultaneously) written, the topic on which both centered was of vivid interest to the authors. Moreover, while Irina and Marina function as random elements in a play of styles and stereotypes, each also forms the undeniable core of the plot in which she is involved. The very titles of both novels stem from *their* (nick)names; it is *their* perspectives that the reader follows; and the dramatic culminations, ironic or not, center on transitions in *their* lives. It is hard to believe, therefore, that the metaphoric representation of Russia as a beloved woman is merely a random national cliché to be parodied. Randomness seems even less likely when one takes into account the numerous other postmodern revisions of the metaphor, both inside and outside the literary sphere.

In light of the postmodern focus on sexuality, the shift of attention from nurturing-mother to sexy-woman imagery is not surprising. Not entirely un-expected either is these authors' preoccupation with nationalist clichés. As mentioned earlier, a preference for national-identity issues is quintessential to Russian postmodernism, as it has been to most Russian cultural-literary movements. An orientation toward national themes marked Venedikt Ero-feev's *Moscow to the End of the Line,* and the same focus on national clichés typifies the poetics of Sorokin and Erofeev, whose work can be read as one long string of Russian cultural stereotypes.

In the existent scholarship, the tension between the view that "these are only letters" and the thematic preference for issues of Russian iden-tity has not gone unnoted. Ekaterina Degot' argues that Sorokin is unique among his peers in focusing on the "pathos of positivity and nationalism" that characterized the Russian avant-garde; in her view, his attitude toward this pathos is less "external" and detached than Sorokin would have us be-lieve.[250] Sally Laird calls his work "for all its claims to detachment . . . a pas-sionate response to a society that lived on hypocrisy and sham."[251] Sorokin's statements in interviews, albeit never unambiguous or free of irony, attest to an indefatigable, intense preoccupation with "Russian mentality," "Russian metaphysics," and the "unpredictable zone" that he believes Russia, "the West's antipode," represents.[252] In outlining *Marina* and other works, he re-fers to them as quintessentially Russian, "local" texts.[253] That he attributes topical potential to the bridal metaphor is suggested in his recent assertion that Russia "remains totalitarianism's faithful mistress," to which he adds: "I respect but do not share that choice."[254]

A similar discrepancy between ironic distance and thematic involvement characterizes Erofeev's works. Deming Brown points to a paradox between an alleged lack of ideological commitment in his—and several of his colleagues'—texts and their "particular fascination with the peculiarities of 'Russianness.'"[255] Erofeev himself summarizes one of his anthologies of contemporary prose as a "novel on the wanderings of the Russian soul."[256] In a preface to another anthology, he speaks of the literary need to "observe the dynamics of Russia."[257] Characterizing *Russian Beauty* as strictly literary play, he simultaneously defines it, in sociological terms, as an attempt to create a "portrait" of "Soviet society . . . on the edge of perestroika."[258] As we have seen, *Russian Beauty* criticizes not only such manifestly literary categories as "the novel," but also the hierarchy within the historical Russian dissident movement.

Close examination reveals, in addition to the contradiction between thematic randomness and the fascination with national and social themes, a tension between a relativizing irony and genuine pathos in the writings of both authors. Relatively recent analyses of Sorokin's work linking the author to such anti-postmodern tendencies as the "new sincerity" (more on this subject later)[259] build on Laird's arguments about his early writings, in which she says that Sorokin's character depictions betray a distinct "pathos" and "unmistakable tenderness."[260] I have already mentioned the observation by Degot' that Sorokin is less detached from the nationalist-positive "pathos" that he mimics than he would have us believe. According to Mark Lipovetsky, Erofeev's poetics of "postmodern play" is "indivisible from pain."[261] In his "downright obsessive craving for blasphemic provocation" Birgit Menzel hears "the voice of a disillusioned Romantic," who commiserates "the loss of humanist values."[262] Sorokin speaks of his Marina as "very dear" to him and calls his attitude toward the dissident movement a fusion of irony "with pathos."[263] These observations are in line with Linda Hutcheon's view of postmodern irony, in which she detects "an affective 'charge' . . . that cannot be ignored."[264]

Obviously, the friction between thematic randomness and a genuine preference for particularly "Russian" themes should not lead to the conclusion that Erofeev's and Sorokin's works are ideologically motivated. Nor does it make their treatment of the "bride Russia" metaphor less different from the more engaged approach of a Blok or a Pasternak. Clearly, the metaphor of Russia, state, and intelligentsia as an amorous intrigue has experienced a shift: it has evolved from a politically expressive image into a clichéd object of literary play. This very status as cliché, however, reveals how the metaphor has gradually but firmly taken root in contemporary Russian intellectual culture.

VIKTOR PELEVIN: FLIRTING WITH
SCHWARZENEGGER

If *Marina* and *Russian Beauty* suggest that the "bride Russia" myth has taken solid root in contemporary culture, Viktor Pelevin's work reinforces this impression. "One of the youngest and most popular Russian postmodernists,"[265] Pelevin is particularly in vogue among Russian students and has been since the late 1990s. In his work, the image of Russia as an unattainable bride-to-be emerges in an ironized, sexualized version reminiscent of Erofeev's and Sorokin's heroines. This is perhaps not remarkable, given Pelevin's preoccupation with the topic of Russia, which is no less persistent than that of his contemporaries. As Keith Gessen writes, with reference to his early works, "Even when he wasn't allegorizing about Russia, Pelevin was turning it into metaphor."[266]

Pelevin's approach to national themes differs from that of his previously mentioned colleagues, however. Whereas their novels are set in Soviet society, Pelevin stages most of his "bridal Russias" in post-Soviet reality—and playfully incorporates the metaphor into settings of New Russians, soap series, and TV commercials.

Another difference is Pelevin's refusal to identify with postmodernism, although critics often label him a postmodernist.[267] Indeed, the combination of "metafiction," "intellectual playfulness," and focus on "contemporary popular entertainment" marks his works as distinctly postmodern products, as does his rejection of any socially or nationally motivated literature.[268] According to Pelevin, "there is no society,"[269] and "Russian subject matter does not exist. Neither does any other."[270] But at the same time Pelevin distances himself from postmodernism. He argues that it is "like eating the flesh of a dead culture,"[271] and claims that "people like Sorokin I don't care for."[272] More than one observer has argued that Pelevin makes use of postmodern devices only to create literature that is thoroughly ideological.[273]

One can hardly deny such an underlying thematic-ideological layer in the author's works. In the words of Aleksandr Genis—who calls Pelevin's fiction a "sermon"—Pelevin "does have a 'message,' a credo that he exposes in his works and that he wants to communicate to his readers."[274] The theme of an unattainable feminized Russia is vital to that message, as a closer look reveals.

Pelevin's Russia: From Natasha to Tat'iana

Pelevin avidly travesties the concept of Russia as the intelligentsia's unattainable beloved in several of his works. In contrast to authors like Erofeev and Sorokin, rather than giving center stage to this concept in one particular work, he weaves its key elements into a number of narratives.

Pelevin's play with the metaphor is informed particularly by the feminized Russias of Berdiaev, Blok, and their contemporaries. Berdiaev is of topical importance to Pelevin, as his repeated appearance in the latter's oeuvre indicates. In *Chapaev and Pustota,* the philosopher features as the hero's drunken conversation partner,[275] and in *Generation "P" (Pokolenie "P,"* 1999) a commercial slogan states that

> Neither icons, nor Berdiaev,
> nor the program *Third Eye*[276]
> will save you from the villains
> who have taken hold of oil and gas![277]

But even more clearly than Berdiaev, Blok is vital to Pelevin's take on the "bride Russia" concept. The writer's prose brims with references to Blok's poetry, and he devoted an essay to Blok while a student at Moscow's Literary Institute. "The Theme of the Native Land in the Poetry of S. Esenin and A. Blok" ("Tema rodiny v poezii S. Esenina i A. Bloka"), as he called the piece, juxtaposes motifs of sorcery in Blok's and Esenin's "Rus'" poems and concludes that "their most important shared feature was love for their land."[278] Grigorii Nekhoroshev rightly argues that "if one neglects the patriotic rhetoric that is necessary for all introductory compositions . . . then the accents that the university entrant places are distinctly visible: mysticism, sorcerers."[279] The poems that he picks are telling: "Rus'" is the poem in which Blok first stages a feminized sleeping-beauty Russia.

Allusions to the metaphor in question first resound in *The Life of Insects* (*Zhizn' nasekomykh,* 1994), an early collection of stories dealing with Kafkaesque man-insect transformations. One story line focuses on two male Russian gnats whose gray color is linked to the image of the feminized Russia in Blok's "Russia."[280] In an ironic revision of Berdiaev's gendered characterizations of intelligentsia and (foreign) state, the two weak, shy, "simple" gnats with a "womanish wing-beat" are contrasted to an authoritative and powerful American gnat.[281] The play with concepts of a feminine Russia and a masculine West is expanded when the American gnat plans to sting a Russian's body and explains to his Russian congeners—who merely sit and watch—that "every landscape has its charm . . . here everything is closer to unassimilated nature . . . we simply forgot how she smells, moist mother skin."[282] As Keith Livers has claimed, this scene openly "deconstructs . . . the Slavophile myth of an originary Russian identity."[283]

The allusion to a penetration of "moist mother earth" is extended in later stories in the collection, one of which describes an amorous liaison

between the American gnat and a fly, Natasha. The latter acts as an insec-
tile double of traditional Russian heroines in a number of respects. Apart
from sharing their "simple-hearted" and "open" character, Natasha bears
the distinctly Russian name of Tolstoy's most patriotic heroine. Today that
name perfectly represents the external male gaze on Russian femininity:
"Natashas" is what post-Soviet prostitutes working abroad are called.[284]
Within the story, the fly foregrounds her national-symbolic status herself by
inversion, when claiming that "I am not Russia after all. I am Natasha."[285]
That this comment creates rather than denies a metaphoric link is also pos-
ited by Livers, in whose words Natasha is "mark[ed] as Russian through
and through."[286] In his relationship with this quintessentially Russian fly, the
American gnat literally fulfills the role of a foreign parasite when he is said
to be sponging on the blood of a "sold-out" and "sucked-dry" Russia.[287]

Thus, more than one element of the classic "bride Russia" metaphor
reemerges in *The Life of Insects*. If such elements appear here as separate
motifs that cannot be traced to one plot line, then that situation changes
in *Chapaev and Pustota (Chapaev i Pustota,* 1996).[288] In this novel, Pelevin
stages a meeting between the Hollywood actor Arnold Schwarzenegger and
"simply Maria," the female star of a Mexican soap opera that was popular in
1990s Russia. Embedded in the novel as a mental patient's fantasy to which
the hero listens, the rendezvous is anticipated as the "tragic alchemic marriage with the West" that Russia tries "again and again to accomplish."[289] The
scene leaves little doubt that, within this marriage, Russia and the West are
embodied in the Mexican soap star and the Hollywood actor, respectively.
Following Maria's "unconscious identification with Russia," her encounter
with Schwarzenegger is envisioned as a marital union with a bridegroom
who needs to "appear from" the West.[290]

In an analysis of the novel, Viacheslav Desiatov highlights the link
between Pelevin's alchemic marriage and traditional alchemic imagery.[291]
Pivotal to both is the category of androgyny, while travesty is crucial to Pelevin's story. Pelevin literally "travesties" the concept of Russia as a female
beloved in a number of references to transgender transformations.[292] Maria
is, in fact, the alter ego of a male mental patient.[293] A delirious reverie, her
story is diagnosed as a deviation with "anal dynamics"; she has a voice that
sounds "more like that of a tall man than of a small woman"; and she is introduced as a "woman with broad masculine shoulders, looking more like
a cross-dressed man."[294] In an allusion to the Hollywood comedy *Junior*
(1994), in which Schwarzenegger bears a child, Pelevin's story envisions him
as pregnant by Maria.[295]

Having written his story in the mid-1990s, Pelevin is unlikely not to
have had another Maria in mind as well: in 1993, the post-Soviet media devoted massive attention to a religious cult surrounding a Ukrainian woman

who conceived of herself as "Mariia Devi Khristos," aka "the Mother of the World." In creating his mystical Maria-Russia, Pelevin may well have had *this* Mariia's "decidedly Slavic features" (I am quoting Eliot Borenstein) and the cult's reliance on, among other traditions, the Divine Sophia concept in mind.[296]

But whether parodying the "Devi Khristos" cult or not, Pelevin depicts the relationship between the two androgynous characters in terms that lead us straight back to the Silver Age. Redolent of Berdiaev's concept of an "active" masculine stimulus for a "passive" Russia are the terms in which Maria—in her role as Russia incarnate—fantasizes about her groom. In Maria's view, "a force was needed, stern and unbending," and that "all-triumphant force" should be combined "with her gentle love."[297] Desiatov argues that since Maria is really a man, her character cannot help but evoke Rozanov's and Berdiaev's debate about the "eternally womanish" aspect of the "Russian soul."[298]

Apart from recalling Berdiaev's pronouncements, the passage in question consciously evokes Blok's representations of Russia. The first reference to Blok's gendered view of Russia and the Russian revolution is found in the hero's simultaneous observations that "all revolutions" have a "feminine nature" and that he is influenced by "some of Aleksandr Blok's new moods."[299] These "moods" certainly dominate the scene in which Maria appears. Her characterization as "simply Maria" and "maiden [*deva*] Maria"—who hasn't "been anywhere until this"—echoes the words of the Stranger in Blok's play of the same name (*Neznakomka*, 1906).[300] In introducing Maria, Pelevin maximizes the invisibility motif that epitomizes Blok's feminized Russia:

> Like an unsteady painting: an embankment, enclosed in swirls of smoke, and a woman who walked along it . . . she began to be dashed by waves of smoke that looked like mist, becoming denser and denser until it covered everything around her, except for the cast-iron barrier of the embankment and a few meters of surrounding space.[301]

Blok's Faina and the feminized nation in his "Russia" were likewise invisible or "covered with clouds." In addition, the setting of an as-yet-unknown woman walking along an embankment again evokes *The Stranger*, whose heroine enters the scene in similar surroundings.[302]

In the encounter between Maria and Schwarzenegger, allusions to Blok resonate even more palpably. Maria anticipates his arrival, in a

> whirlwind of concepts that revealed itself to her . . . "beautiful lady" (here it was clear who was being referenced), "stranger" (likewise), then glimmered the word "Bridegroom" (capitalized for some reason), then the word "Guest"

(also capitalized), followed by the incomprehensible phrase "alchemic marriage," then the totally obscure "rest is in vain; I knock on the gates."[303]

A more overt reference to Blok's poetry—to his "beautiful lady," his "stranger," and the opening poem of *Verses on the Beautiful Lady,* "Rest Is in Vain . . ."—is difficult to imagine.[304] Moreover, the passage cited evokes the Romantic motif of the deceased bridegroom through obvious allusions to Pushkin's "Bridegroom" and Lermontov's "Guest"—the same allusions that color the depiction of Russia-cum-Irina's groom in *Russian Beauty,* as we saw.

The passage is reminiscent of Erofeev's, as well as Sorokin's, novels in other respects, too. Maria is said to appear once millions of Russians switch on the TV to watch *Simply Maria* and begin identifying with her vicissitudes. In other words, she emerges as a female embodiment of the fantasies of ordinary Russian people. Maria herself suggests that she is "woven from thousands of Russian consciousnesses."[305] In yet another allusion to Blok—this time to "You are with millions," the famous opening words of his poem "Scythians"[306]—Maria wonders about all those

> Russian consciousnesses that remembered her and thought about her. How many were there: millions? Dozens of millions? Maria . . . was convinced that were all those hearts in which her fate was inscribed to strike in unison, their combined noise would be much louder than the deafening explosions across the river.[307]

Similar unions of a symbolic "Russian" heroine with a Russian collective mark the orgasm scenes featuring Sorokin's Marina and Erofeev's Irina, as well as the emergence of Platonov's Moscow from a crowd of "millions of people" as socialism incarnate. Whereas in these novels the heroines become one with Soviet mass culture, however, Pelevin's heroine appears rather as a product of post-perestroika popular culture. *Simply Maria* was no less a Russian hit than was its predecessor, *The Rich Also Cry,* which 70 percent of Russians regularly watched in the early 1990s.[308] Desiatov could hardly be more right, therefore, in labeling Maria the "'hyperreal' personification" of 1990s' Russia.[309]

After *Chapaev and Pustota,* Pelevin again reverts to the concept of a feminized Russia in *Generation "P."* Set in a stereotypically post-Soviet world of advertising agencies and nouveau riche, this novel enthusiastically mocks clichés about the "Russian idea" and the "Russian soul." These appear in the form of commercial catchphrases: Tiutchev's illustrious lines "Russia cannot be understood with the mind, / . . . / One can only believe in Russia" are transformed, for example, into a slogan for a Smirnoff ad.[310]

Among a series of other national stereotypes, *Generation "P"* travesties—as did *Marina* and *Russian Beauty*—Andreev's concept of Russia's
feminine "Ecumenical Soul." This time Andreev appears when a colleague
retells his drug-inspired vision of Russia to the hero.

> I reread *The Rose of the World*, the passage about the soul of the nation. An-
> dreev wrote that it is a woman called Navna. Afterward, I had this vision—
> she's lying there as though asleep on this white rock, and leaning over her is
> this vague black figure, with short little wings; you can't see his face, and he's
> just giving it to her. . . .[311]

If openly referring to Andreev, the passage also evokes another political
metaphor: that of Pobedonostsev as a sorcerer with short owl's wings who
captivates the sleeping-beauty Russia in Blok's *Retribution*.[312] The sorcerer
myth resounds, again, when another minor character envisions the "naked
girl . . . Russia" as assaulted by a man whose "face cannot be seen," dressed
in "an army coat with epaulettes."[313]

In the early twentieth century Pobedonostsev acted as the captivator
of a feminized Russia; Pelevin presents wholly different characters as its vio-
lators. Later in the story, the oligarch Boris Berezovsky and the Chechen
rebel leader Salman Raduev "plan to pierce the mystical body of Russia in
its most sacred places with their banal television towers."[314] Pelevin's choice
is not fortuitous. "One of the richest and most influential men in Russia"
and "known enemy of the 'young reformers' in the government" of the
late 1990s, Berezovsky is today's ideal heir to the legacy of the powerful
reactionary Pobedonostsev.[315] He is known to have had close ties with
Raduev's network.

In *Generation "P,"* Pelevin tightly weaves the allegories mentioned
into the story of the hero, Tatarskii, whose resemblance to "Lermontov's
demon" and status as a young writer mark him as a contemporary example
of the classic hero-*intelligent*.[316] The symbolic representations of Berezovsky
and Raduev are specifically the product of *his* imagination; the depiction of
Russia as a girl who is violated makes *him* vomit.[317]

The personal link between Tatarskii's fate and that of a feminized Russia, as suggested by such reactions, intensifies as the novel draws to a close.
In a mystical-surreal turn of events, he is proclaimed the "new husband"
whom the Mesopotamian goddess of war and sexual love, Ishtar, is supposed to find in Russia.[318] Characterized as the "sum of all the images used
in commercials,"[319] Ishtar serves as a suitable alter ego for the "girl Russia"
in earlier passages; as mentioned above, in Pelevin's novel a commercial is
no more than a paraphrased cliché about a "Russian idea" or "Russian soul."
In a parodistic play on messianic-nationalist views, Tatarskii is told that "a

special responsibility rests on us in Russia" and that he and Ishtar need to "mystically unite."[320] An earlier reference to the "sexual union" between the "essence of the goddess's body" and her chosen one indicates that this union should be understood as another alchemic marriage with transformational powers.[321] From a jumble of elements from pop and esoteric culture, the poet-adman Tatarskii thus emerges as the mystical husband of a feminine "soul of Russia."

A few years later, Pelevin travesties the metaphor even more radically in his prose collection *Dialectics of the Period of Transition from Nowhere to Nowhere* (*Dialektika perekhodnogo perioda iz niotkuda v nikuda*, 2004). The novel with which the collection opens, "Numbers" ("Chisla"), revives and revises the feminized-Russia paradigm. Here Pelevin maximizes the latent homoerotic and transvestite dimensions of *Chapaev* through a mystical battle between the hero, Stepa, and his antipode, Srakandaev. A clash between two big names in the banking world of Yeltsin's and Putin's Russia, their combat is portrayed as an archetypal struggle between good and evil. Stepa, associated with the sun, is a "Savior" (*Spasitel'*) and a "sacred being"; he is a Saint George–like "warrior" who fights an evil "beast." By contrast, Srakandaev is not only portrayed as that "beast," but is also linked to the moon and "the anti-world" and is described as a "mystical enemy" and "the spirit of evil."[322]

The battle between hero and foe symbolizes more than a general conflict between good and evil forces. This is a politically charged clash. Stepa identifies with the Russian people and with messianic Eurasian views on Russia's future;[323] Srakandaev is a socially successful New Russian who spends "his nights in elitist nightclubs."[324] Both are involved in a complicated relationship of protection and intimidation with the ultimate embodiment of the Russian state today, the FSB.

Then, too, the Stepa-Srakandaev antithesis is rendered in terms that satirize gendered debates on Russia from the early twentieth century—debates that enter the novel in the form of academic enunciations by Stepa's mistress, an English linguist called Mius. According to her,

> what happens right now in Russia affects a deep, archetypal layer, so to speak. . . . The theme . . . is the clash of two primordial principles in the Russian soul. One is kind, trustful, not very bright, even a little daft—in short: *iurodivoe*.[325] The other, by contrast, is mighty, fierce, and mercilessly triumphant. Merging in a symbolic marriage, they fertilize each other and give the Russian soul its inexhaustible force and depth.[326]

This passage, which could have been copied from Berdiaev, is transferred into the sphere of the grotesque when Mius compares the two principles to a "wonky Zaporozhets" and to the absolute symbol of new Russian wealth, a "gangster Mercedes 600," respectively.[327] Mius argues that the marriage between the two principles occurs at an intersection where the Zaporozhets crashes into the Mercedes from behind.[328] She asserts that, in contemporary Russia, their "marriage" is subject to a "mental revolution."[329] Her theory makes an indelible impression on Stepa, who interprets the "mental revolution" as a personal revolt.[330]

That Mius's theory does indeed anticipate an inner revolution within Stepa becomes clear when he faces his "mystical enemy," Srakandaev. Their encounter is anticipated in national-symbolic terms: it is associated with the 1943 battle at Kursk between Soviet and German forces, and the two men are compared to screws in a modern-day Gogolian troika.[331] A link between this encounter and Mius's concept of the Zaporozhets-Mercedes collision is first suggested by the opponents' contrasting cars: as opposed to Stepa's "solid-patriotic Rusich-700V," Srakandaev drives a James Bond–inspired Aston Martin.[332] In a rather extravagant reenactment of his mistress's analysis, Stepa eventually "crashes into" his opponent from behind as prophesied: he anally penetrates Srakandaev—whose *nomen est omen*—during a nightclub tête-à-tête.[333] To make the situation yet more preposterous, in this scene Stepa mentally transforms into "Tat'iana"; that this name refers to Russian literature's best-known Tat'iana is suggested when it is explained as "Tat'iana," "the 'Russian soul' type."[334] The coitus of this Stepa-alias-Tat'iana and Srakandaev occurs in front of a smiling portrait of none other than the state incarnate, President Putin.[335]

It would be superfluous to review all the other surreal turns and intertextual motifs in the Stepa-Srakandaev plot line. Suffice it to say that Stepa eventually recognizes Srakandaev as his (or her?) bridegroom and that he interprets their sexual confrontation as a direct analogy to the symbolic marriage outlined by Mius.[336] Again, Pelevin shifts traditional gendered metaphors of Russia-intelligentsia-state to the homoerotic sphere, using a transvestite as the modern-day double of the mystical "bride Russia." He offers an inverted version of the Russia of Berdiaev, Grossman, and several other authors discussed here: if their representations of Russia focus on its passivity and weakness, Pelevin's "Russian soul" takes the initiative and "fertilizes" the West itself. Significantly, in the end, Srakandaev dies and Stepa emerges as the winner of the symbolic battle that forms the core of the novel.

Though not in a Russian context, the metaphor reappears in Pelevin's play *Helmet of Fear* (*Shlem uzhasa*, 2005). This time it is the "Japanese national soul" that is represented as a girl raped by a "demon." The cliché association of the "raping demon" with the West is not hidden behind any allusions here: if the (manga) girl represents post–World War II Japan, then "the monster . . . [symbolizes] contemporary corporative economics of the Western sort"—or so one of the play's characters thinks.[337]

Naked Girl: Physicality

In Pelevin's work, the metaphor appears in perhaps an even more farcical adaptation than it does in Sorokin's and Erofeev's texts—surfacing in post-Soviet pop culture against a backdrop of Hollywood films, soap operas, drugs, fast Western cars, and nightclubs. Within this unexpected setting, the "bride Russia" is as physically tangible a figure as in the novels by Sorokin and Erofeev. *The Life of Insects* contains a vividly painted lovemaking scene between the American gnat and Natasha, symbol of Russia;[338] in *Generation "P,"* Russia appears as a "naked girl" on the brink of sexual abuse and penetration; and in "Numbers," the reader is spared little detail as the "Russian soul type" Stepa-Tat'iana penetrates Srakandaev's anus.

In *Chapaev and Pustota,* however, Pelevin transposes the abstract "Russia-bride" myth into physical spheres most elaborately. To start with, the marriage between Maria and Schwarzenegger—the respective symbolic embodiments of Russia and the West—is conveyed in unequivocally sexual terms. Maria muses: "What, after all, is that alchemic marriage? . . . Won't it hurt me? I mean, afterwards?"[339] She imagines "with sweet terror" how the alchemic marriage will occur "quickly and somewhat clumsily."[340] Her mystical bridegroom is, at the same time, a thoroughly physical being: Maria is not only curious about the size of Schwarzenegger's penis; but in an unequivocal reference to the actor's most famous role—that of the cyborg Terminator—she also envisions "the most tender parts of her body sprawled on the angular hips of a metallic person lying on his back."[341] As in Erofeev's and Sorokin's novels, the sex appeal of the heroine's true love diametrically opposes his rivals' sexual superfluity: sexy Schwarzenegger is set off against Maria's previous lovers—"dirty Lenias and drunken Ivans."[342]

The material palpability of Maria is emphasized by her vulnerability to physical damage. Not only does she fear that the mystical marriage will cause her pain; ultimately she complains—with bruised face and bleeding lips—to Schwarzenegger that "the way you want it, it hurts!"[343] In Maria, then, Pelevin replaces traditionally abstract feminized-Russia metaphors with the distinct physicality seen in the work of his two contemporaries. Like Erofeev and Sorokin, he exchanges the transcendent "bride Russia" in texts from Blok to Grossman for a woman of flesh and blood with sexual desire and physical substance.

While focusing on the sexual dimension of the metaphor, Pelevin denies any interest in its social or ideological charge. If such a stance again links him with Sorokin and Erofeev, so does his persistent preference for "Russian themes." Pelevin's parody of the Russia-as-female-beloved metaphor is, like theirs, more than merely one stereotype among many. With the exception of *The Life of Insects* and *Helmet of Fear*, it forms the very heart of the texts mentioned. "To reach an alchemic trinity of Russia with West and East" is, in the words of one reviewer, "the problem over which the crazy heroes" of *Chapaev and Pustota* "vainly rack their poor heads."[344] The culmination of *Generation "P"* lies in the hero's mystical marriage with Ishtar, the commercialized "Russian idea" incarnate. The central theme of "Numbers" is the confrontation between the hero and his antipode—a confrontation which evolves into a symbolic marriage between the "Russian soul" Tat'iana and a Western counterforce. Pelevin's literary universe, in other words, revolves to a substantial extent around distorted, derided "bride Russia" metaphors.

MIKHAIL BERG: LAND OR WOMAN?

If Russian postmodernists eagerly revert to the metaphor under discussion, then Mikhail Berg's short novel "Ros and I" ("Ros i ia") represents a prime example of that eagerness. First published in 1990, "Ros and I" offers readers a typically postmodern play with genres and intertextual references. Berg presents it as the monograph of a fictive literary scholar, F. Erskin. Erskin's pseudo-academic literary study includes a number of stories and poems, several of which retell the incestuous relationship between a sister and brother, the "Ros" and "I" of the title. A native reader is unlikely to miss the pun that this title provides: together, the two names form the Russian word for "Russia."

Most likely the title alludes to Khlebnikov's poem "I and Russia" ("Ia i Rossiia," 1921–22): not only is "Ros i ia" a variation on Khlebnikov's title, but it also echoes the poem's personified physical relationship between a poet-hero and Russia.[345] As Irina Skoropanova has argued,

> On a cultural-philosophical level, the images of [Berg's] brother and sister can be regarded as the embodiment of the West and of Russia, respectively, or, to be more precise, as the embodiment of two hypostases of Russia: its Europeanized hypostasis (cultural, enlightened, but also degenerate, having absorbed foreign vices together with foreign virtues) and its organic, "earthly" hypostasis (uncultured, virginal-undeveloped, but independent, with an enormous submissiveness, a huge potential for spiritual-cultural growth).[346]

In the portrayal of Ros, the national-allegorical layer that Skoropanova sketches practically leaps off the page. The hero, akin to the traditional westernized and morally depraved Russian hero-*intelligent,* asks his sister in a poem, "Ros, my Ros, / . . . who are you, a land or a woman?"[347] In an overt play on earlier texts and authors, he addresses her in a modern-day ode:

> O, rus, Horace once said.
> O Rus', thus Pushkin supported him.
> O Ros, you repeat after him.[348]

Interestingly, the feminine ending of the existing terms for Russia (Rossiia and Rus') has been replaced by a masculine ending in Ros's name. Her gender is further confused in a poem in which she is addressed as the hero's (or lyrical ego's) *"father*land" (my italics).[349]

This gender mix-up suggests that Berg precedes Pelevin in endowing the bridal metaphor with transvestite connotations. In "Ros and I" the gender reversal is less prominent, however: dominant is Ros's status as the very embodiment of femininity—*and* as a contemporary counterpart of Blok's, Berdiaev's, and Andreev's feminized Russias.[350] Besides her status as a female allegory for Russia, she is related to these figures through her duality: her "pure heavenly profile" in contrast to her description as "devil" and "prostitute."[351] She is redolent of Berdiaev's Russia when the fictive author attributes to her such qualities as "weakness," "slavishness," and "indetermination."[352] Given the story's distinctly metaphoric context, Ros's tendency to copy and blindly obey her brother reads as an allusion to the traditional aspersions cast on Russia as an uncritical imitator of the West.[353] Likewise, as Skoropanova observes, Ros's eventual rejection of her brother's love alludes to symbolic representations of a "Russia [that] truly becomes aware of herself and [that] herself becomes an object of Western admiration."[354]

Berg's novel thus provides an unusually explicit postmodern revision of the myth of Russia and the intelligentsia as a tragic amorous pair. In a number of respects, his revision resembles those of previously discussed authors. Consider, for example, Berg's maximization of the incestuous implications of the metaphor. While Sorokin and Erofeev alluded to a sexual relationship between their "brides Russia" and their fathers, and Pelevin transferred this union to the homoerotic and transvestite sphere, Berg places it in an incestuous brother-sister context. In Skoropanova's view, here the incest motif underscores the "native link that exists between the two Russias" and expresses "the anomaly of the national archetype's inner disunity."[355]

Berg shares with the authors mentioned, moreover, a focus on the physical dimension of the metaphor. In his novel, the bodies and amorous activities of Ros and her brother receive the same detailed sexual depiction that typifies the postmodern texts discussed earlier. To mention but two examples, the hero ejaculates on his sister's breasts and makes her masturbate in his presence.[356]

In contorting and inverting the traditional metaphor in a postmodern text, Berg does not rob it of genuine pathos. We are talking here, after all, of the tragic image of an *unattainable* bride Russia. Just as in the novel as a whole "tragedy shows through the laughable mistakes, absurdities, contradictions," so the doomed passion between Ros and her brother acquires a sense of dramatic tension in spite of its ironic charge.[357] Berg's novel thus epitomizes the postmodern tendency to whimsically travesty the gendered myth of Russia and its intelligentsia, without overlooking its force as a dramatic topical image.

TIMUR KIBIROV: DZHUGASHVILI'S FAITHFUL WIFE

The introduction to this study opens with a quotation from Timur Kibirov on the current trivialization of feminized-Russia metaphors. Kibirov's attitude toward the metaphor is emblematic of a reaction to postmodernism that arose in the late 1980s and that is referred to in Russia as a "new sincerity," "new sentimentalism," or "critical sentimentalism."[358] Without entering into the subtleties of the different terms, one can borrow Mark Lipovetsky's words to summarize these recent developments as "an attempt to *reconstruct the edifice of humanism in the space of chaos.*"[359] Artists who adhere to the "new sincere" or "new sentimental" philosophy claim to share with postmodernists an awareness of the limitations of language and ideology—but, they say, rather than dismantling them, they seek to accept these limitations and to use nostalgic irony as a strategy for infusing them with new life.

If speaking of "new sincere" artists is an awkward affair—there is no such thing as a "new sincere" manifesto to which a concrete group of authors subscribes—then Kibirov is one of the few Russian poets who consciously poses as its representative. Kibirov's purported "new sincere" stance clearly makes itself felt in his poems on Russia. Unlike the authors of novels such as *Russian Beauty*, Kibirov's adaptations of the gendered myth of Russia revive a distinct lyrical ego.

He first turns to the metaphor in a poem from the collection *Sentiments* (*Santimenty*, 1989), "Russian Song: Prologue" ("Russkaia pesnia: Prolog"), in which the poet greets Russia with "Hello, my earth. Hello, my wife," and anticipates their "fatal meeting."[360] Although Blokian overtones color this poem, in the juxtaposition of land to wife and the adjective "fatal," which Blok ascribed to his feminized Russia, Blok's poetry reverberates particularly in a related poem, "Russian Song" ("Russkaia pesnia"). Informed by eighteenth-century odes to Russia, as Kibirov related in conversation, this poem is fashioned like a contemporary hymn to the nation.[361] Its poet sings the praises of Russia in lines that abound in intertextual references. Invoking "Russia, Russia, Russia, / the Russian SFSR!" the poet openly refers to Blok when he exclaims, "Aleksandr Aleksanych called / You a wife—well, well!"[362] An amorous intrigue develops involving this poet, who identifies with Blok, "dear mama" Russia, and "father Stalin."

> Russia found itself a better
> Suitor [than Blok], and our dear mama
> was faithful to only one man,
> Dzhugashvili is a father to us all.[363]

Incestuous implications (the contemporary author's hobbyhorse, it seems) emerge once again when the poet describes the struggles with his problematic dual role of son and lover. In his view, "It is time for Freud to intervene . . . / It is time to play this Oedipal drama / to an end."[364] He advises the feminized Russia to turn away from the Soviet state and to "play marriage" with him instead.[365]

Amidst a hodgepodge of literary and cultural reminiscences, the feminized Russia in "Russian Song" appears in terms that rely heavily on Blok. Represented as a promiscuous female, Russia is "You" who "can dance until you fall," who behaves "scandalously" and "fights" but represents, at the same time, "another" land: "our invisible Russia," whose "dear traits" the poet sees "for the first time."[366] The analogy with the exalted-debased duality and the hidden-face motif that epitomize Blok's "bride Russia" could scarcely be more apparent.

In subsequent poems, Kibirov repeatedly returns to the concept of the poet as Russia's male suitor. It is touched upon in the collection *Message to Lenka* (*Poslanie Lenke,* 1990), in which the poet links "my wife" and "my land";[367] in *Ostrovitianov Street* (*Ulitsa Ostrovitianova,* 1999), where "my native land" indicates a female "you" with whom the poet seems to be amorously involved;[368] in *Notations* (*Notatsii,* 1999), in which the poet addresses a feminized Russia and complains of the "total misunderstanding between you and me";[369] and in the *Sfiga* cycle (2000), which hears him call his female beloved "Italy," "like Blok his wife: O Rus'!"[370]

Obviously, the fragments mentioned here can be traced to Blok's gendered view of the gap between the intelligentsia and the (Russian) people. Kibirov expounded on his fascination with this issue in an interview, explaining that he discovered his vocation as a poet at the age of thirteen, thanks to a collection of Blok's poems that plunged him into a state of "physical nar-

cotic drunkenness."[371] To Kibirov, "the banality . . . that the intelligentsia is
terribly far away from the people" is "one of the biggest age-old catastrophes
of Russia."[372]

The terms that Kibirov uses to describe the theme in question illustrate how he strives to return to major themes in Russian cultural history
through a combination of ironic distance ("banality") and authorial commitment ("age-old catastrophes"). In his attitude to the metaphor discussed
here, this striving is never absent, but it emerges as a conscious theme only
in 2000, in the cycle "Upon Reading the Almanac *Rossiia-Russia*" ("Po
prochtenii al'manakha *Rossiia-Russia*").

"Upon Reading the Almanac *Rossiia-Russia*" opens with the poet's
complaint about the inevitable "platitudes" and "connotations" evoked by
the word "Russia."[373] His complaint is followed by an ironic revision of classic odes to Russia. In *his* ode, the poet attempts to give his country a new
name in addition to existing labels. As we have seen, Blok's "wife" passes in
review as one of the clichés that he seeks to evade:

> To Blok a wife.
> To Isakovskii a mother.
> To Dolmatovskii a mother.
> What do you want me to call you?
> A grandmother? No way![374]

Kibirov contributes to the list by comparing Russia to a "mother-in-law"; to
himself he assigns the role of "neglected son-in-law" and husband of what
he calls Russia's "excessively beautiful" "daughter." In yet another intratextual reference, he says this "daughter" is the result of a marriage between
Blok and Russia.[375]

Hence Kibirov's lyrical "I" presents itself both figuratively and literally
as an heir of Blok and his gendered vision of Russia. A principal difference
between their treatments of Russian themes, however, lies in the heavily
self-conscious irony of Kibirov's stance—a stance made explicit in the next
poem. Echoing Gogol's famous apostrophe to the troika, this work opens
with a poet who accuses Russia of "not answer[ing]" his questions about its
identity.[376] The depiction of "the writer" parodies writers in general, but it
also serves as self-mockery, specifically of Kibirov's lyrical "I."

> And the writer is writing and writing . . .
> And with floods of vague prophecies
> he overwhelms mother earth.
> This and that, he claims. Nothing else.

> Having had his fling, he goes to his tavern
> . . . and finally collects his answer:
> his very own horror and gibberish.[377]

In other words, "the writer" doesn't realize that his metaphors for Russia reveal more about him than about the female principle onto which he projects his fantasies. A child of postmodern and (post-)feminist times, Kibirov is ironizing the paradigm of a male author who revels in emotional musings on the fate of Russia. And yet at the same time, his lyrical ego's awareness of his own triviality does not diminish his sentimental attitude to Russia in the least. Significantly, the cycle concludes with a gruff but benevolent confession to his Russian-Blokian muse: "But to love . . . oh, I love you all right; come on."[378]

Thus, Kibirov tries reverting to myths of Russia as the poet-*intelligent*'s beloved without allowing their clichéd connotations to dominate. He openly acknowledges that the view of Russia as the poet's unattainable bride has become a literary stereotype but chooses, nevertheless, to approach it as an emotionally powerful image.

POP CULTURE: DUMPING ZIUGANOV, MARRYING PUTIN

From Sorokin to Pelevin, from Erofeev to Kibirov: the "bride Russia" metaphor seems indispensable for contemporary Russian authors. It is popular not only in "highbrow" cultural expressions, however, as numerous references to "bridal Russias" in mass-culture and mass-media spheres attest.

The metaphor pops up in poetry created outside the professional literary scene, for one. If in the professional sphere it remains a hobbyhorse of male authors mainly, then the concept of Russia as Christ's bride is reiterated in amateur verses by two girls, who claim to live in Novosibirsk and decided to post their writing online.

> There is no place for the Native Land here.
> But soon a time will come—there will be a voice:
> . . . "The Bridegroom cometh from the Heavens
> . . . Arise, Russia, from your dream,
> Wake up, dear one, you are the bride."[379]

Moreover, the metaphoric representation of Russia as a bride or another female character is part of a tendency in late Soviet and post-Soviet rock music to "return to thoughts about Russia."[380] Written by Fedor Chistiakov, the lyrics of a song by the rock group Nol', "It's Just That I Live on Lenin Street" ("Prosto ia zhivu na ulitse Lenina"), contain the words:

> How I hate and love my Native Land.
> . . . No matter what a deaf, blind, ugly monster she is
> But I simply have nothing else to love.[381]

If this passage evokes Blok's ambivalent attitude toward a feminized Russia, the rock group DDT's sing-along "Native Land" ("Rodina") does so even more openly. Patently alluding to Blok's *Native Land*, the vocalist-composer Iurii Shevchuk sings:

> Native land,
> I am going to my native land.
> Let them scream that she is ugly:
> We like her.
> Sleeping Beauty,
> Trustful of scoundrels,
> But to us . . .[382]

Julia Friedman and Adam Weiner have claimed, and rightly so, that "more than an underhand compliment to one's motherland, these verses constitute a confession of love by someone who is fully aware of his beloved's flaws."[383] Blok's status as a key source in this context is suggested not only by the amorous feelings expressed here for Russia; it can also be deduced from the title of the song, which literally repeats that of Blok's collection of Russia-related poems, and by the *Retribution*-like reference to Russia as a sleeping beauty. In the pop song, Blok's "sorcerer," Pobedonostsev, is replaced by the "scoundrels" to whom the "native land" relates so "trustfully." The couplets show a singer-poet who is opposed to these "scoundrels" in his love for Russia.[384]

Other lyrics by Shevchuk reinforce the impression that he is inspired by Blok's views on Russia. In "Russians" ("Rossiiane"), for example, the singer openly echoes the poet-hero in the Kulikovo cycle and *Song of Fate* when he identifies with a Kulikovo warrior who has become "*intelligentnei*";[385] as used here, that term means not only "smarter" or "more educated," but also "more like an *intelligent*" or a member of the intelligentsia. Sergei Shnurov, lead singer of the popular punk-rock band Leningrad, recycles similar metaphors when claiming, with reference to Russia, "We are like a 'Sleeping Beauty,' and when we wake up, it makes a big impression on everyone."[386]

But even more stubbornly than in contemporary pop lyrics, metaphors of Russia as bride or virgin reappear in visually oriented cultural spheres.

In 1990s tattoos, for instance, Russia is again portrayed as a woman who is sexually molested, this time by post-Soviet Russia's favorite whipping boys: citizens of the Caucasus.[387] Political cartoons also reenact and revise the metaphor examined here. In the 1990s, post-Soviet Russia is depicted as a sleeping beauty, an attractive naked girl, and a fallen woman in cartoons in a number of newspapers.[388] Later, Putin operates as Russia's violator in a caricature that shows him forcibly penetrating a kneeling "Russian people," represented by a woman in the colors of the national flag.[389] Although "the intelligentsia" does not appear in these images, the cartoons do focus on tension between the current regime and an "authentic" feminine Russia.

In the mass media, similar gendered constructions can be discerned in political rhetoric. Tat'iana Riabova has demonstrated how, in public political discourse, the president—whether it be Gorbachev, Yeltsin, or Putin—is opposed as a masculine force to a feminine Russia or Russian people. One example is the Yeltsin slogan cited in the introduction to this study. If you enter "Vova rulit" on YouTube, you are treated to another: an animated music video by Ukrainian rappers who ironically laud Putin—both in words and in sexually suggestive moves by female dancers—as a hypermanly hero who makes "women blush." Yet another is the sexualized take on Russian history of Russia's most colorful ultranationalist, Vladimir Zhirinovskii: to him, "the October Revolution raped the people, the Stalin era can be compared to homosexuality, the Khrushchev years to masturbation, and Brezhnev to impotence."[390] In less harsh words, the famous actress Natal'ia Krachkovskaia has recourse to similar metaphors when she sees Russia as "a feminine country," adding that "at the moment she is like a bride to be given away."[391] At the time of speaking, Krachkovskaia suggested General Lebed' as a perfect husband for the bride-to-be.

If Krachkovskaia's words seem to have been lifted from a Berdiaev text, the satirical TV show *Puppets* (*Kukly*) harks back to more traditional metaphoric rituals when portraying the results of the 2000 presidential elections in marital terms. The happy groom Putin is coupled with a passive bride, "the Federation," while Georgii Ziuganov and Grigorii Iavlinskii co-star as the bride's rejected lovers.[392] Ironically, in real life Ziuganov endorses the metaphor by speaking of Russia as being "raped" by today's rulers.[393] By this time, the metaphor has reached the State Duma—literally—in the form of an enormous canvas by the artist Sergei Bocharev, which was exhibited in the parliamentary hall in 1998. The art historian Marina Koldobskaia explains Bocharev's *Uneven Marriage* (*Neravnyi brak*)—whose title partly echoes that of another political allegory, Evdokiia Rostopchina's poem "Nasil'nyi Brak"[394]—in satirically drenched terms: "The intelligentsia, that is, all sorts of Sakharovs, Likhachevs, and Rostropoviches," marries off a "girl in red *sarafan,* that is, Russia" to no one less than the first President Bush.[395]

In 2007, while in Moscow working on this manuscript, I encountered similar rhetoric (but from the other camp) as witness to a demonstration against the war in Chechnya. Demonstrators handed out a verse by the poet and writer Igor' Guberman that depicts Russia within the familiar paradigm of the false groom's bride: "Sadly, Russia is married / to a nonexistent fiend. / . . . / But the piper is near."[396]

The Internet plays an active role in the dissemination of the metaphor in these types of mass contexts. Chistiakov's and Shevchuk's lyrics, for instance, can be found on densely trafficked websites, where visitors browse the texts of their favorite groups free of charge. In 2001 the journal *Afisha,* which published Sorokin's "Eros of Moscow," extended Sorokin's literary writing to the popular sphere by inviting online readers to describe their own "eros of Moscow."[397] On the site of the electronic journal *Samizdat,* a "punk version" of his essay appeared shortly after its first publication.[398]

A particularly prominent digital space for the circulation of the metaphor is the chat room. To mention but two examples: referring to political developments under Yeltsin, the webmaster of one forum calls Russia an aging sleeping beauty vainly awaiting a prince to wake her with a kiss;[399] another chatter concludes a critique on contemporary politicians, and Zhirinovskii in particular, by labeling Russia a sleeping beauty who needs to "wake up, get rid of its assholes," and find itself a normal leader.[400] In pre-digital days, such discussions would not have been recorded and accessed on such a broad scale; now they form part of a regularly visited panoply of virtual discussion sites.

Why the metaphor is still so vital in chat rooms, whose younger participants are not always familiar with authors like Blok and Pasternak, is perhaps best explained by a look at post-Soviet history books. Galina Zvereva has shown that these textbooks rarely present Russia as a gender-neutral entity: "Russia is the beautiful, proud, majestic, suffering heroine who is subjected to humiliation and assaults. . . . 'National History' looks like the personal path followed by a personified woman—Russia."[401] In an earlier publication, I pointed to the fact that similar personifying rhetoric marks the reception of the painter Viktor Vasnetsov's work.[402] A lack of proof that allegorical motifs underpin Vasnetsov's Russian fairy-tale figures takes nothing away from their interpretation, throughout the twentieth century, as political symbols. Within the discursive context of the Soviet era, Vasnetsov's sleeping or captive princesses supposedly symbolize the poor people, waiting to be freed from the tsarist regime; but in post-Soviet Russia, they are read just as easily as a (feminized) Russia in the "cruel grip" of "Kashchei," alias the

Bolsheviks.[403] People who grow up with such a personified conception of history are likely, when the time comes to express their own political views in print, to replicate the same rhetorical devices.

A beloved subject in literary texts—as well as in artworks, films, journals, history books, online chat rooms, mass media, cartoons, tattoos, pop lyrics, and amateur poetry—"Russia as bride" has taken an indisputable hold in contemporary Russian intellectual *and* popular culture. Today, however, the status of this metaphor differs from what it was in the early twentieth century. Although still incorporating a political power of expression for some, for many others the metaphor is nothing more than an object of playful irony. It often occurs in examples that distort the concept and highlight its sexual or violent implications. Accordingly, in contemporary culture the "unattainable bride Russia" is very much a physical being, whether a sexually desirable daughter, a lesbian prostitute, or a transvestite.

In other words, the once politically motivated metaphor has today turned into a literary-cultural stereotype. It is its very status as a favorite object of mockery, however, that reveals the topical importance of the bridal myth in contemporary Russian culture—an importance that authors' comments and interviews confirm more often than not. The paradox is not surprising when one considers Linda Hutcheon's notion that "the authority of clichés sometimes rests precisely on the fact that there may be something in them that still speaks to us."[404] In a Russian context, Slava Kuritsyn expresses a similar thought. Referring to postmodern deconstructions of stereotypes of Russia, he claims that rather than random linguistic play, "this is also a variation on a 'lamentation on Russia.'"[405] A contemporary "lamentation on Russia": that is, perhaps, the best way to read the postmodern adaptations of the metaphor discussed here.

Conclusion

WHEN DISCUSSING KIBIROV'S POEMS on Russia at a conference in Amsterdam in 2003, I was asked whether poetic efforts to transcend irony are not doomed to failure in today's "post-postmodern" society. One could indeed say that the texts of a "new sincere" poet such as Kibirov are unable to avoid an all-pervading sense of irony. The affective tone with which his poems address a feminized Russia cannot prevent their author from struggling with the knowledge that his view of the subject inevitably reverts to "trivial nonsense." This type of struggle is not yet present in Blok's gendered view on Russia. Nor can it be found in any of the other works discussed here that predate the era of postmodernism.

Whether the affective or indeed the ironic prevails in Kibirov's poetry is not the issue here, however. What does matter is the sheer impossibility of using gendered representations of the Russia-state-intelligentsia triangle without acknowledging their status as a "secondhand" concept—historically as well as literarily.

The sociopolitical reality of an oppositional relationship involving "native people," "ruling class," and "intelligentsia"—from which the metaphor departs—no longer bears any relation to contemporary reality. After the atrocities of Nazi Germany and the Stalinist regime, the notion of a people or native essence seeking future protection can no longer be considered without irony. Nor does the traditional near-mystical view of an intellectual elite destined to fulfill a nationalist role make much sense these days.

These social changes aside, the vision of Russia as the unattainable bride of the intelligentsia has also become outmoded, thanks to its very persistence throughout twentieth-century literature and intellectual thought. Kibirov's poems illustrate the impossibility of regarding the metaphor as a "fresh" addition to the current literary scene. It is one of those prominent myths of Russian intellectual tradition that have evolved from a startling poetic creation into a cultural stereotype.

Among other things, this study has attempted to show that the metaphor of a bridal Russia can now rightly be considered such a stereotype or cliché. If nothing else, the previous analyses have demonstrated that, from Blok's first drafts of *Native Land* in 1907 to Kibirov's recent poems, the twentieth century saw a range of representations of Russia as a bride-to-be. As a rule, such representations refer, in some way or another, to the sociopolitical triangle summarized here as Russia-state-intelligentsia. The tendency to conceive of these three categories as a problematic tripod has its roots in the nineteenth century, when Russia's intellectual elite began to experience its social status as problematic, but it was early twentieth-century Russian culture that provided the conditions for the transformation of this sociopolitical emotion into a prominent gender metaphor.

As we have seen, the definition of the social categories within that metaphor varies significantly from text to text. "The state" can refer to the tsarist regime, to Soviet authorities, or, ultimately, to Pelevin's benevolently smiling Vladimir Putin. In the works discussed here, the state stands in symbolic opposition to a (representative of a) westernized intellectual elite, which is even harder to reduce to a simple definition: what began in the prerevolutionary period as the intelligentsia or the Social Democrats became the dissident movement of the late Soviet years and, in post-Soviet Russia, a posh elite of admen and New Russians. Feminized Russia, by contrast—an imaginary native essence in the form of a woman—remains more or less unchanged throughout the works discussed here. Its transformation from a politically to a predominantly literarily motivated concept notwithstanding, this "Russian soul" is relatively constant, from Berdiaev's feminized Russian earth to the consummate Russian beauties that populate the novels of Viktor Erofeev and Vladimir Sorokin.

As we have seen, the "bride Russia" metaphor was affected substantially by the transition from imperial Russia to the Soviet Union and, finally, to today's Russia, but its presence in Russian literature from 1900 to the present has also been marked by more artistically motivated changes. Most importantly, it has evolved from a topic of sociopolitically motivated debate at the beginning of the century into a rewarding object of literary-cultural play in contemporary culture. This shift is driven partly by the sheer frequency with which the metaphor appeared in previous decades, but it is also in keeping with the postmodern approach to cultural myths in general. Where "modern" authors used the metaphor to express various views on the social or political situation in Russia, their postmodern colleagues see it as more of a cultural cliché that they can embed in an ironic treatment of historical styles and stereotypes. The metaphor has gone from being the "theme of life and death" that it was to Blok in 1908 into what Sorokin called a "shallow theme" in 2002.

And yet, despite the assertions of postmodern authors that the metaphor is of no thematic interest to them as a sociopolitical or nationalist device, their work tells another story. Contrary to their claims that the gendered metaphor under discussion is significant solely as an object of aesthetic play, these authors' texts—as well as some of their statements in interviews—suggest it is more than a random stereotype in need of being dismantled. Its frequent and salient occurrence in a large number of postmodern texts implies that the metaphor is more vital and more topical than many of those who take recourse to it are willing to admit.

The transformation from modernism to postmodernism coincides with yet another major change in the rendition of the metaphor throughout the century. Consider for a moment its metamorphosis from an abstract image into a blatantly concrete, physical form. As opposed to the perhaps promiscuous, but always physically indistinct, metaphoric "bride Russia" of Blok, Berdiaev, or Pasternak, the postmodern Russian beauty is described in minute detail, from head to toe. Characteristic is the contrast—to mention but two extremes—between Lara's vague physical profile in *Doctor Zhivago* and Sorokin's precisely worded description of Marina's limbs and genitals. The other two components of the triangle are sexualized no less in contemporary literature and culture: illustrative examples are Berdiaev's intelligentsia, charged rather abstractly with a "lack of masculinity"; and Erofeev's dissidents, who, in a much more physical vein, are "useless at fucking." The very notion of a failed union between the intelligentsia and the people has shifted, metaphorically speaking, from an impossible mystical marriage in pre-revolutionary years to frustratingly unachieved orgasms in some of today's texts.

I have argued that the evolution from an abstract to a physical-sexual sphere relates directly to the anti-ideological premises of postmodernism. The level of carnality in the works examined appears to be inversely proportional to the level of ideological pathos; in other words, the disappearance of the author's sociopolitical commitment tends to be replaced by a heightened orientation toward physicality. It is not a coincidence that Sorokin, a radical postmodernist, claims to "derive pleasure from the moment when literature becomes corporeal."[1]

In addition to tracing the development of gendered metaphors throughout the twentieth century, this study has sought to illustrate the extent to which they have become rooted in intellectual and public consciousness today. The previous two chapters have shown that the metaphor at issue continues to occupy a prominent place in present-day Russian intellectual and pop culture.

It might prove fruitful, therefore, to explore the possible existence of a similar metaphor in other Russian art forms of the twentieth century. This study has shed light on a number of paintings and musical works in passing. Given the prominent place held by the metaphor in literary, philosophical, and journalistic spheres, an investigation of its appearance in the areas of art and music seems like the natural step to take at this point. Sources that spring to mind are the many musical and visual artworks of the early twentieth century that focus on the fairy tale of a prince who sets out to free a princess held captive by a sorcerer. Apart from *Kashchei,* the aforementioned opera by Rimsky-Korsakov, these works include another of his operas, *Tsar's Bride* (*Tsarskaia nevesta,* 1899); Igor Stravinsky's ballet *Firebird* (*Zhar-ptitsa,* 1910); and drawings and paintings of fairy tales by Ivan Bilibin. During the same period, in terms of literature and philosophy, fairy-tale intrigues of this nature figured so often as an allegory of the Russia-intelligentsia-state relationship that one could assume they fulfilled a similar function in other art forms. Unfortunately, the testing of this hypothesis falls outside the scope of my analysis.

The same applies to postmodern visual art, music, and film. This study touches briefly, but not systematically, on a handful of contemporary pop lyrics, cinematic scenarios, and artworks that reenact "bride Russia" metaphors in one way or another. The prominence of such metaphors in contemporary literature and intellectual thought suggests that a closer examination of its presence in these and other creative or rhetorical disciplines today could yield further valuable results.

These or similar queries would constitute a new chapter, however. For now, it suffices to conclude that, in the course of the twentieth century, the view of Russia, state, and intelligentsia as a tragic amorous intrigue took firm root as a major constituent of intellectual thought in Russia. By today, unattainable as she may be, the "bride Russia" has become a highly tangible ingredient of Russian culture.

Notes

ACKNOWLEDGMENTS

1. See on this paradox, among others, Groys, *Die Erfindung Russlands,* 8ff.
2. Buruma and Margalit, *Occidentalism,* 75ff.

INTRODUCTION

1. Kibirov, *"Kto kuda,"* 481. Throughout this book, translations of Russian and other non-English texts are mine unless otherwise indicated. In discussing Russian titles (such as those of literary texts, artworks, and films), I provide the reader with an existing or self-devised English translation and show the original Russian title within parentheses. I use the ALA-LC Romanization standard for the transliteration of Cyrillic letters, except where a different spelling is common: e.g., "Tolstoy" rather than "Tolstoi."
2. Ibid., 482.
3. Among many others, see on this trend Hosking, *Russia,* 293–94.
4. Leerssen, "Imagology: History and Method," 26.
5. See, for example, Kurz, *Metapher,* 5: "Metapher und Symbol sind Binnenelemente literarischer Texte, die Allegorie dagegen ist auch eine Gattungsform."
6. Richards, *Philosophy of Rhetoric,* 97, 117.
7. Quotations from ibid., 96.
8. See on this, among others, Riabov, *Matushka-Rus',* 46.
9. Anderson, *Imagined Communities,* 6.
10. See the authoritative collection of essays edited by Pipes (*The Russian Intelligentsia*); Kemp-Welch's list of sources on the theme (*Stalin and the Literary Intelligentsia,* 269 n. 1); Confino, "On Intellectuals"; Wirtschafter, *Social Identity,* 88–91; and—for an extensive list of predominantly Russian publications on the topic—Mogil'ner, *Mifologiia "Podpol'nogo cheloveka,"* 5–6.
11. Erlich, *Modernism and Revolution,* 9.
12. If, for practical reasons, I stick to the term "protagonist," then one cannot apply that term without reserve to all the works under consideration. In

Berdiaev's nonfictional texts, rather than with a protagonist we are dealing with a "masculine element," for instance; in Blok's poems, the central male character is, strictly speaking, a "lyrical ego."

13. Goscilo and Lanoux, *Gender and National Identity*, 6, 8.

14. The same reservations as for the term "protagonist" (n. 12) apply here.

15. Groys, *Die Erfindung Russlands*, 8.

16. Notable examples include Andrew, *Women in Russian Literature;* Andrew, *Narrative and Desire;* Andrew, *Narrative, Space;* Ashwin, *Gender, State and Society;* Barta, *Gender and Sexuality;* Borenstein, *Men Without Women;* Cheauré and Haider, *Pol, gender, kul'tura;* Chester and Forrester, *Engendering Slavic Literatures;* Clements et al., *Russian Masculinities;* Costlow et al., *Sexuality and the Body in Russian Culture;* Ebert, *"Die Seele hat kein Geschlecht";* Edmondson, *Gender in Russian History;* Engel and Reck, *Frauen in der Kultur;* Goscilo, *Dehexing Sex;* Goscilo and Lanoux, *Gender and National Identity;* Heldt, *Terrible Perfection;* Kaganovsky, *How the Soviet Man Was Unmade;* Kay, *Men in Contemporary Russia;* Khotkina et al., *Zhenshchina: Gender: Kul'tura;* R. Marsh, *Gender and Russian Literature;* R. Marsh, *Women and Russian Culture;* Morozov, *Muzhskoi sbornik;* Riabov, *Zhenshchina i zhenstvennost';* Riabov, *Russkaia filosofiia zhenstvennosti;* Ushakin, *O muzhe(N)stvennosti;* Ushakin, *Pole pola;* and Van Leeuwen-Turnovcová et al., *Gender-Forschung in der Slawistik.*

17. See Hubbs, *Mother Russia;* Barker, *The Mother Syndrome;* and Riabov, *Matushka-Rus'.*

18. Ebert, *"Die Seele hat kein Geschlecht,"* 150.

19. Bethea ("Literature," 173–74) and Iurii Lotman ("Siuzhetnoe prostranstvo," 98) mention the trend to represent nineteenth- and twentieth-century Russian heroines as Russia incarnate and the hero-*intelligent* as their ineffectual lover. Irina Sandomirskaia (*Kniga o rodine,* 59) and Elizabeth Cheauré ("'Vater Sowjet,'" 138–99ff.) consider examples of an "erotic attitude" toward Russia from the first half of the twentieth century. Hubbs halts at the myth to be analyzed here in *Mother Russia,* 213–16.

20. See Riabov, *Zhenshchina i zhenstvennost'; Russkaia filosofiia zhenstvennosti;* and *Matushka-Rus'.*

21. Brouwer, "The Bridegroom"; and Makushkinskii, "Otvergnutyi zhenikh."

22. Makushinskii, "Otvergnutyi zhenikh," 43.

23. For an introduction, see Veeser, *The New Historicism.* For a list of Slavonic studies that can be related to a "New Historicist" perspective, see Etkind, *Khlyst,* 6 n. 2.

24. These include Iurii Lotman's *Besedy o russkoi kul'ture,* Etkind's *Khlyst,* Irina Paperno's *Semiotika povedeniia,* and Christopher Ely's *This Meager Nature.*

25. White, *Metahistory*, ix and 2.

26. Leerssen, "Imagology: History and Method," 27.

27. Strictly speaking, *Moscow to the End of the Line, Russian Beauty*, and *Marina's Thirtieth Love* are also Soviet texts. Since they can be considered precursors of post-Soviet literary developments, however, I discuss them in the chapter on contemporary culture.

28. Bonnell, *Iconography of Power*, 73. See also 66.

29. Tertz, *On Socialist Realism*, 44.

30. Lezhnev quoted in Kornienko, "Na kraiu sobstvennogo bezmolviia," 59.

31. Hansen-Löve, "Zur Mythopoetik des russischen Symbolismus," 65.

32. Blok, *Sobranie sochinenii*, 8:265.

33. Ibid., 5:688; italics in original.

34. Richards, *Philosophy of Rhetoric*, 100.

35. Hosking, *Russia*, 286.

36. Pasternak paraphrased in Berlin, *Personal Impressions*, 180.

37. Sorokin, *Sbornik rasskazov*, 121.

38. Cixous, "Sorties," 90.

39. Ibid., 91.

40. Fetterly, *The Resisting Reader*, 28–29.

41. R. Marsh, *Women and Russian Culture*, 9. On the same issue, see also Heldt, *Terrible Perfection*, 13; and Andrew, *Narrative and Desire*, 8, among others.

42. Heldt, *Terrible Perfection*, 12.

43. R. Marsh, *Women and Russian Culture*, 9.

44. Goscilo, "Negotiating Gendered Rhetoric," 32.

45. Avdeev and Monnier, "Marriage in Russia," 29.

46. Engel, *Women in Russia*, 3.

47. Lotman, "Siuzhetnoe prostranstvo," 98.

48. For a list of feminist studies dealing with the impact of gender on nationality discourses, see Mayer, "Gender Ironies," 5.

49. Ibid., 16.

50. See on this topic, among others, Mosse, *Nationalism and Sexuality;* Goscilo and Lanoux, *Gender and National Identity;* Tolz and Booth, *Nation and Gender in Contemporary Europe;* Yuval-Davis, *Gender and Nation;* and Mazurana et al., *Gender, Conflict, and Peacekeeping*. See also Oleg Riabov's website *Matushka-Rus': Natsiia, Gender, Voina*, http://www.ivanovo.ac.ru/alumni/olegria/index.html.

51. See Mayer, "Gender Ironies of Nationalism," 10.

52. See Sluga, "Identity, Gender, and the History of European Nations," 101.

53. Mosse, *Nationalism and Sexuality*, 99.

54. Zaitseva, "National, Cultural, and Gender Identity in the Russian Language," 31, 44. See also Babenko, "Moskva zhenskogo roda," 25–30; and Riabov, *Zhenshchina i zhenstvennost'*, 111.

55. See Pettman, *Worlding Women,* 49; and Goscilo and Lanoux, *Gender and National Identity,* 9 and 25 n. 15.

56. See Wenke, "Gendered Representations," 69; and Mosse, *Nationalism and Sexuality,* 31.

57. Mosse, *Nationalism and Sexuality,* 17 and 23.

58. Böröcz and Verdery, "Gender and Nation," 249.

59. See Mosse, *Nationalism and Sexuality,* 90–114. Additional examples are Czechia's Libuše and Vlasta (Malečkova, "Nationalizing Women"); the *suomi neito* or Finnish Maid (Valenius, *Undressing the Maid*); the *Nederlandse maagd* or Dutch Virgin (Becker, "'Zoo praalt ook Nêerlands maagd'"); and Fjallkonan, the Icelandic Mountain Woman (Bjørnsdottir, "They Had a Different Mother").

60. See Von Plessen, *Marianne und Germania 1789–1889.*

61. For a reproduction, see Goscilo, "Negotiating Gendered Rhetoric," 32.

62. On the popularity of this concept in nationalist rhetoric, see Hubbs, *Mother Russia,* 207–28; Riabov, *Matushka-Rus',* 109–10; Ely, *This Meager Nature,* 209–10; and Edmondson, "Gender, mif i natsiia."

63. Examples include Mother Ireland (Martin, "Death of a Nation," 67); Sweden's Moder Svea (Tornbjer, *Den nationella modern,* 71–88); Mother Finland (Valenius, *Undressing the Maid,* 114, 116, 122, 143, 146–48); Poland's Matka Polka (Packalén, "The Polish Mother Figure"); the "Deutschland, bleiche Mutter" myth (Ruppert, *"Deutschland, bleiche Mutter"*); nationalist discourses modeling Iceland as mother (Bjørnsdóttir, "They Had a Different Mother," 95); Mother India (Mayo, *Mother India*), and the Mauritian national hymn, which honours the nation as "Mère Patrie."

64. Such a division can be reconstructed from nineteenth- and twentieth-century philosophical and political texts by Nietzsche (Nietzsche, *Werke,* 136); Madame de Staël (see Sluga, "Identity, Gender," 106); Otto von Bismarck (quoted in Rozanov, *Sochineniia,* 322); Comte de Gobineau (see Sluga, "Identity, Gender," 105); Zionism's founding father Theodor Herzl (Mayer, *Gender Ironies of Nationalism,* 285–86); Adolf Hitler and the leader of the Baltic Germans, Carl Schirren (Riabov, *Matushka-Rus',* 135–36); and, in Russia, Kiukhel'beker, Herzen, Khomiakov, and Kavelin (Riabov, *Matushka-Rus',* 58–59) and the historian Pogodin (Pogodin, *Istoricheskie aforizmy,* 13–14).

65. Pryke, "Nationalism and Sexuality," 537.

66. In nationalist discourse, it has been reconstructed for Belgium (Valenius, *Undressing the Maid,* 149), Finland (ibid., 16, 47–48, 131, 163), France (Pryke, "Nationalism and Sexuality," 538), Germany (Hermand, *Sieben Arten,* 128), Iran (Najmabadi, "The Erotic *Vatan,*" 459–60), Romania (Böröcz and Verdery, "Gender and Nation," 248), and former Yugoslavia (Mostov, "Sexing the Nation," 90–92). The Dutch writer Jan Wolkers asserted in the 1960s–1970s that American multinationals raped the Dutch virgin (personal communication with the author).

67. Hussein, *Zabiba and the King*.

68. Rostopchina, "Nasil'nyi brak," 99–102; and Valenius, *Undressing the Maid*, 131ff.

69. Mickiewicz, *Dzieła poetyckie*, 219.

70. For studies on this theme, see Layton, *Russian Literature and Empire*, 175 n. 1.

71. Layton, *Russian Literature and Empire*, 175–210. See also Aleksandr Odoevskii's poem "Georgia's Marriage with the Russian Empire" ("Brak Gruzii s russkim tsarstvom," 1838, in Odoevskii, *Polnoe sobranie*, 226–27).

72. Layton, *Russian Literature and Empire*, 186 and 188.

73. Valenius, *Undressing the Maid*, 99–110.

74. Böröcz and Verdery, "Gender and Nation," 243–49.

75. Najmabadi, "The Erotic *Vatan*."

76. Hermand, *Sieben Arten*, 130.

77. Seifert, *The Plague Column* (unnumbered).

78. *Binnenstad*, "Burgemeester Wallage," 1.

79. Chester, "The Landscape of Recollection," 59.

80. Tchaikovsky, *O Rossii*, 109 and 169.

81. Tsvetaeva quoted in Bal'mont, *Stikhotvoreniia*, 11.

82. Shklovskii, *Sobranie sochinenii*, 230.

83. Chagall quoted in Figes, *Natasha's Dance*, 567.

84. Nabokov, *Speak, Memory*, 18. Nabokov's first novel, *Mashen'ka* (1926), focuses on a fictive double of his first love (*Mashen'ka*, 7), who equally "embodies Russia" for the novel's Russian-emigrant hero (Desiatov, "Arnol'd Shvartsenegger," 192).

85. Najmabadi, "The Erotic *Vatan*," 452–53.

86. See Valenius, *Undressing the Maiden*, 105–6.

87. Nabokov, *Speak, Memory*, 193.

CHAPTER ONE

1. Griboedov, *Polnoe sobranie*, 276–77.

2. Lotman, *Besedy o russkoi kul'ture*, 109.

3. See Toporkov, "Materialy po slavianskomu iazychestvu," 222; Domnikov, *Mat'-zemlia i tsar'-gorod*, 60–104; or Dieterich, *Mutter Erde*.

4. Zazykin, "Zemlia kak zhenskoe nachalo," 61 and 70.

5. Domnikov, *Mat'-zemlia i tsar'-gorod*, 97.

6. Hubbs, *Mother Russia*, 76.

7. Levinton, "Zametki o fol'klorizme Bloka," 179.

8. Hubbs, *Mother Russia*, 83.

9. Lotman and Uspenskii, "'Izgoi' i 'izgoinichestvo,'" 222.

10. Ibid., 227–28.

11. Pliukhanova, *Siuzhety i simvoly moskovskogo tsarstva*, 75; Riabov, *Matushka-Rus'*, 101–2.

12. Apocalypse 12, 13:2, 19:11–20.

13. Senderovich, *Georgii Pobedonosets*, 76.

14. Meletinskii, "Zhenit'ba v volshebnoi skazke," 308.

15. Russian versions of this plot replace the traditionally female wicked fairy with the male sorcerer or dragon who dominates in the Saint George legend and Russian folktales.

16. Senderovich, *Georgii Pobedonosets*, 50 and 293; Finkelstein, *Der Ritter und der Kult der Schönen Dame*, 38–45.

17. Propp, *Istoricheskie korni volshebnoi skazki*, 341.

18. Senderovich, *Georgii Pobedonosets*, 55–80.

19. Hubbs, *Mother Russia*, 146–47.

20. *Kashchei* is opposed as the captor of a young princess to a prince who must free her in the folkloric "Self-Playing Gusli" tale ("Gusli-samogudy"), which was published in a *lubki* anthology around 1830 (Taruskin, *Stravinsky and the Russian Traditions*, 565). Taruskin links this tale to what became one of Russia's most popular narratives of a tsar-*kashchei*, an enchanted princess and a hero who needs to free her, Iakov Polonskii's poem "Winter Road" ("Zimnii put'," 1844) (ibid., 556–58). For the plot of a captive princess in need of liberation from evil forces, see also Vasilii Zhukovskii's poem "Sleeping Princess" ("Spiashchaia tsarevna," 1831); Pushkin's "Ruslan and Liudmila" ("Ruslan i Liudmila," 1819); and his "Tale of Tsar Saltan" ("Skazka o tsare Saltane," 1831). Scholars have discussed these works as pretexts for Blok's representation of Russia and the intelligentsia (Schahadat, *Intertextualität und Epochenpoetik*, 332–33; Mints, *Aleksandr Blok*, 314). Crucial to the politicized version of the sorcerer–captive-heroine–hero triangle in the early twentieth century are Gogol's story "Terrible Vengeance" ("Strashnaia mest'," 1832) and Dostoevsky's "Landlady" ("Khoziaika," 1847).

21. See, for instance, the Borodin reference in the online *Bol'shoi Entsiklopedicheskii Slovar'*: http://shp.by.ru/spravka/encyclop/bes/2q/2j.shtm.

22. Abraham, *On Russian Music*, 173.

23. Borodin, *Romansy i pesni*, 20–21.

24. Mints, *Aleksandr Blok*, 314.

25. Konstantinov, *Spiashchaia krasavitsa*, 116.

26. Nadson, *Polnoe sobranie*, 159–61.

27. Solov'ev, *Sochineniia*, 2:235.

28. On this trend, see Pliukhanova, "Kompozitsiia pokrova bogoroditsy," 89; Nekliudov, "Telo Moskvy," 23; Billington, *The Icon and the Axe*, comments to illus. 1.

29. Pliukhanova, *Siuzhety i simvoly*, 77.

30. Pliukhanova, "Kompozitsiia pokrova bogoroditsy," 89.

31. For examples of the use of this expression, see Mokeev, "Sud'ba zlatoglavoi sviashchennoi Moskvy."

32. See Wisdom 8:2, 8–19.

33. On the history of the Sophia concept, see Tokarev, *Mify*, 464–65, or Averintsev, *Sofiia-Logos*, 162; on its role in Gnosticism, see Jonas, *The Gnostic Religion*, 42–91 and 174–99.

34. Domnikov, *Mat'-zemlia i tsar'-gorod*, 68–70.

35. See Riabov, *Russkaia filosofiia zhenstvennosti*, 33; Averintsev, *Sofiia-Logos*, 162. On Sophia's role as patroness and female embodiment of Novgorod, see Onasch, *Gross-Nowgorod*, 64 and 187.

36. Averintsev, *Sofiia-Logos*, 162.

37. Mystical texts propagating a marriage between man and Sophia include Jakob Boehme's *Weg zu Christo* (1620), John Pordage's *Sophia* (1675), and Gottfried Arnold's *Geheimnis der Göttlichen Sophia* (1700).

38. Billington, *The Icon and the Axe*, 245–46. For examples, see Kliucharev in *Poety XVIII veka*, 308; Lopukhin quoted in Vaiskopf, *Siuzhet Gogolia*, 497; and Novikov quoted in Odesskii, "Ob 'otkrovennom' i 'prikrovennom,'" 83.

39. Quoted in Odesskii, "Ob 'otkrovennom' i 'prikrovennom,'" 83.

40. See Vaiskopf, *Siuzhet Gogolia*, 24.

41. Brouwer, "The Bridegroom," 58.

42. Karamzin, *Polnoe sobranie*, 308–9.

43. Vaiskopf, *Siuzhet Gogolia*, 25.

44. Odoevskii, *Polnoe sobranie*, 141–42.

45. In 1610 Russia was in the midst of the "Time of Troubles" (1598–1613), when several false pretenders aspired to the throne and Muscovy was in political chaos.

46. Odoevskii, *Polnoe sobranie*, 133–34.

47. Mann, *V poiskhakh zhivoi dushi*, 318. Gogol is rendered here in the account of Archimandrite Feodor of the Holy Trinity–St. Sergius Lavra, with whom he discussed the book.

48. Vaiskopf, *Siuzhet Gogolia*, 416.

49. Brouwer, "The Bridegroom," 58.

50. Ibid., 276.

51. See Hansen-Löve, *Der Russische Symbolismus*, 10.

52. See in this context the academic comments to his work (Dostoevsky, *Polnoe sobranie*, 7:343), as well as Syrkin, *Spustit'sia, shtoby voznestis'*, 199; Bem, *O Dostojevskem*, 277; Passage, *Character Names*, 60 and 96; Toporov, *Sviatost' i sviatye*, 83; Averintsev, *Sofiia-Logos*, 163; and Zander, *Taina dobra*, 64ff.

53. Among others, see Averintsev, *Sofiia-Logos*, 163; and Zander, *Taina Dobra*, 65 and 81.

54. Dostoevsky, *Polnoe sobranie*, 14:99.

55. Ibid., 14:99, 14:383, and 15:129.

56. Ibid., 14:328.

57. Ibid., 15:186.

58. Ibid., 10:117.

59. Ibid., 5:322 and 405.

60. On the influence of Gnosticism on Solov'ev, see Cioran, *Vladimir Solov'ev*, 17ff.; and Losev, *Vladimir Solov'ev*, 157; on his reliance on Russian Orthodoxy, see Losev, *Vladimir Solov'ev*, 171 and 222; on Solov'ev and German mysticism, see Solov'ev quoted in Florenskii, "Pis'mo desiatoe," 331. For an extensive discussion of all three, see De Courten, *History, Sophia and the Russian Nation*, 242–68.

61. De Courten, *History, Sophia and the Russian Nation*, 215.

62. See on this also Mochul'skii, "Vladimir Solov'ev," 748; Losev, *Vladimir Solov'ev*, 222.

63. Solov'ev, *Sochineniia* (1990), 2:576–77.

64. Copleston claims that to Solov'ev, Sophia variously represents "the substance of God, of the Trinity, . . . the archetype of Creation, . . . the substance of the Holy Spirit . . . the 'eternal Feminine' and . . . the Theotokos, Mary the Mother of God" (Copleston, *Philosophy in Russia*, 224–25). The "woman clothed with the sun" must have called Sophia to mind for Solov'ev, given her close relation to the hypostases that Copleston mentions, both in biblical origin and content.

65. Solov'ev, *Sochineniia* (1990), 2:318.

66. Solov'ev, *La Russie et l'église*, 264.

67. Solov'ev, *Sochineniia* (1989), 2:167.

68. Ibid., 2:165.

69. Ibid.; and Solowjew, *Una Sancta*, 52.

70. Solov'ev, *Sochineniia* (1989), 2:169–70.

71. The tendency to conceive of Russia as a bride also reverberates in Solov'ev's depiction of Russia in "The Russian Idea" as a girl experiencing first love (Solowjew, *Una Sancta*, 46); and, in another essay, as a "lonely" "person" who should be joined "in a union with what she lacks" (Solov'ev, *Sochineniia* [1989], 1:249–50).

72. Solov'ev, *Sochineniia* (1989), 2:169.

73. Ibid.

74. Groys, *Die Erfindung Russlands*, 42.

75. Ibid., 43.

76. See Losev, *Vladimir Solov'ev*, 205; Bulgakov quoted in Burlak, *Solov'ev*, 535.

77. On this worldview, see also De Courten, who claims that Solov'ev's "self-perception as a prophet" was directed primarily by his view of Russia as the future incarnation of Sophia (*History, Sophia and the Russian Nation*, 215).

78. Losev, *Vladimir Solov'ev*, 380–81. Solov'ev is referring here to the reac-

tionary politicians Konstantin Pobedonostsev, Dmitrii Tolstoi, and M. N. Katkov (ibid., 380).

79. Averintsev, "K uiasneniu smysla nadpisi," 49.

80. *Die Stadt als Frau*.

81. See Apocalypse 17:1–6, 19:7, 21:9–27; Isaiah 54:5–10; Ezekiel 16; Jeremiah 3:7–20; and Hosea 2:4–25. The cities of Nineveh and Tyre are also typified as whores (Nahum 3:4; Isaiah 23:16–17). In the Song of Songs the bride Shulamit is equated to the cities of Tirzah and Jerusalem; she refers to herself as "a city where one finds peace" (6:4, 8:10).

82. Ezekiel 16:25–26.

83. See Lamentations 1.

84. Kantorowicz, *The King's Two Bodies*, 212–27.

85. See Nekliudov, "Telo Moskvy," 370.

86. Hubbs, *Mother Russia*, xiv.

87. Domnikov, *Mat'-zemlia i tsar'-gorod*, 259. On the marital connotations of the relationship between the Kievan or Russian ruler and the land, see also ibid., 309–12.

88. Hubbs, *Mother Russia*, 170.

89. Vereecken, "Jaroslavna" (unpublished).

90. See Brouwer, "The Bridegroom," 56–57; and Hubbs, *Mother Russia*, 188–89.

91. Andrew, *Women*, 12–13; and Brouwer, "Tema samozvanchestva," 60–63.

92. See, for instance, Maikov, *Izbrannye proizvedeniia*, 193 and 198; and Lomonosov, *Izbrannye proizvedeniia*, 85 and 101.

93. Tatishchev, *Imperator Aleksandr II*, 88.

94. See Riabov, *Matushka-Rus'*, 48.

95. Pliukhanova, *Siuzhety i simvoly*, 190–203.

96. Nekliudov, "Telo Moskvy," 369.

97. See *Argumenty i fakty*, no. 50 (1999).

98. Quoted in Nekliudov, "Telo Moskvy," 370.

99. Ibid.

100. Ibid.

101. Among others, see Nekliudov, "Telo Moskvy"; Isupov, "Dialog stolits"; Vanchugov, *Moskvosofiia i Peterburgologiia;* and Babenko, "Moskva zhenskogo roda."

102. Fedotov, *Sud'ba i grekhi Rossii*, 1:51.

103. Zagoskin, "Dva kharaktera," 127 and 130.

104. Tolstoy, *Polnoe sobranie*, 11:324.

105. Grois, *Utopiia i obmen*, 360–61.

106. Gogol, *Sobranie sochinenii*, 6:160.

107. Groys, *Die Erfindung Russlands*, 8.

108. Tucker, "The Image of Dual Russia," 588 and 592.

109. See Khomiakov's "Thoughts" ("Dumy," 1831), "Russian Song" ("Russkaia pesnia," 1830s), his two "To Russia" poems ("Rossii," 1839 and 1854), and "To Repenting Russia" ("Raskaiavsheisia Rossii," 1854).

110. Khomiakov, *Stikhotvoreniia i dramy,* 97.

111. Danilevskii, *Rossiia i Evropa,* 480.

112. Ibid., 265.

113. Gogol, *Sobranie sochinenii,* 5:207.

114. Vaiskopf, *Siuzhet Gogolia,* 547.

115. Zagoskin quoted in ibid.

116. See, for instance, Maikov, *Izbrannye proizvedeniia,* 185 and 187; Derzhavin, *Ody,* 25; and Lomonosov, *Izbrannye proizvedeniia,* 86.

117. On the attitude of the Russian intellectual elite toward Western influences in the course of the eighteenth century, see Rogger, *National Consciousness.*

118. Tucker, "The Image of Dual Russia," 588.

119. Billington, *The Icon and the Axe,* 233.

120. On the "parting of ways" between "government and the educated public" in the early nineteenth century, see Riasanovsky, *A Parting of Ways.*

121. Literally "people of sundry ranks," in the nineteenth century the Russian term *raznochintsy* referred to intellectuals who did not bear a noble title or were not registered within a particular class. On its problematic historical definition, see Hosking, *Russia,* 263.

122. Ibid., 265.

123. See Lotman, *Besedy,* 51–53.

124. McDermid, "The Influence of Western Ideas," 23. On the coincidence of venerations of femininity and the ordinary people, see also Lotman, *Besedy,* 52–53.

125. Atkinson, "Society and the Sexes," 28.

126. Paperno, *Semiotika povedeniia,* 80.

127. Herzen, *Sobranie sochinenii,* 16:77.

128. Ibid., 6:68.

129. Makushinskii, "Otvergnutyi zhenikh," 37.

130. Lotman, "Siuzhetnoe prostranstvo," 98.

131. The parallel between the social and amorous spheres also characterizes the late eighteenth- and early nineteenth-century French novel. In Rousseau's *Julie ou la nouvelle Héloïse* (1761) or Stendhal's *Le rouge et le noir* (1830), the hero's position in society is raised through his romance with a girl from a higher social class (see Brouwer, "The Bridegroom," 56). In *Julie,* the link between the hero's social and amorous strivings also consists in his wish to free the heroine through education. This idea would influence the Russian radical intellectuals of the 1860s and their fictive marriages.

132. Examples include Tat'iana's husband—Prince N.—in Pushkin's *Eugene Onegin,* a second Prince N. in Turgenev's "Diary of a Superfluous Man" ("Dnevnik lishnego cheloveka," 1850), and the "successful lawyer" in Turgenev's "Torrents of Spring" ("Veshnie vody," 1872).

133. Pushkin, *Polnoe sobranie,* 6:5 stanza 4.

134. Herzen, *Sobranie sochinenii,* 4:49.

135. Goncharov, *Sobranie sochinenii,* 5:342 and 6:446.

136. Tolstoy, *Polnoe sobranie,* 10:266 and 11:84.

137. Turgenev, *Polnoe sobranie,* 7:234.

138. Ibid., 7:85.

139. Zander, *Taina dobra,* 81.

140. Herzen, *Sobranie sochinenii,* 4:120 and 4:122.

141. Turgenev, *Polnoe sobranie,* 6:349 and 8:243.

142. Gheith, "The Superfluous Man," 230. For an extensive discussion of the superfluous-man type, see Chances, *Conformity's Children.*

143. See Turgenev, *Polnoe sobranie,* 6:133; 7:166, 171, 268, and 269; and 11:37.

144. See Pushkin, *Polnoe sobranie,* 6:1 stanzas 23–25; Goncharov, *Sobranie sochinenii,* 4:5, 235, 260, and 281; Turgenev, *Polnoe sobranie,* 7:40; and Tolstoy, *Polnoe sobranie,* 10:22.

145. On this cult see, among others, Wessling, "Smert' Nadsona."

146. Dobroliubov, "Kogda zhe pridet," 224.

147. Dostoevsky, *Polnoe sobranie,* 26:137–38 and 143.

148. Chernyshevskii, "Russkii chelovek," 207.

149. Ibid. Sander Brouwer has shown that Chernyshevskii's and Pavel Annenkov's *Asia* reviews both "treat the hero's indecisiveness in establishing an amorous relationship as the expression of his social superfluity"; Brouwer links both interpretations to the westernized-hero-versus-Russian-heroine plot ("The Bridegroom," 54).

150. Chernyshevskii, "Russkii chelovek," 210.

151. Pisarev, "Zhenskie tipy," 188.

152. Mathewson, *The Positive Hero,* 61.

153. Lotman, "Siuzhetnoe prostranstvo," 98.

154. Bethea, "Literature," 173.

155. Brouwer, "The Bridegroom," 52.

156. Makushinskii, "Otvergnutyi zhenikh," 35. On the status of nineteenth-century heroines as Russia incarnate for heroes-*intelligenty,* see also Andrew, *Women in Russia,* 27, 38, 47–48, and 143–44; R. Marsh, *Women in Russian Culture,* 9; and Markovich, "'Russkii Evropeets,'" 86–87.

157. Brouwer, "The Bridegroom," 49; and Makushinskii, "Otvergnutyi zhenikh," 35.

CHAPTER TWO

1. Throughout this chapter, references to the collected works of Berdiaev (*Sobranie sochinenii*) appear in the text and contain only volume and page numbers.

2. Jager, *Tussen Rusland en Europa*, 253.

3. Döring and Smirnov, "Realizm," 11–12.

4. Ibid., 1 and 11.

5. Pipes, *The Russian Intelligentsia*, 56.

6. See Riabov, *Zhenshchina i zhenstvennost'*.

7. Matich, "Androgyny," 168.

8. Bershtein, "Tragediia pola," 219.

9. See on this Elkin, "The Russian Intelligentsia," 43; and Terras, *Handbook*, 463.

10. Blok and Belyi, *Perepiska*, 263.

11. See Jager, *Tussen Rusland en Europa*, 40.

12. Fedotov, *Sud'ba i grekhi Rossii*, 1:115.

13. Belyi, *Simvolizm*, 333; and Bal'mont, *Stikhotvoreniia*, 398. See also Rozanov, *Russkaia gosudarstvennost'*, 241; Ivanov, "Dostoevsky," 389–90, and "Osnovnoi mif," 510–11; and Berdiaev, *Sobranie*, 3:108–9.

14. Merezhkovskii, *Atlantida-Evropa*, 295–96.

15. Popov, "The Russian Oedipus," 591–93.

16. Rozanov, "Zhenshchina," 189.

17. Nesterov, *Pis'ma*, 114.

18. Nesterov, *Vospominaniia*, 101.

19. See Rutten, "Mikhail Nesterov and Aleksandr Blok."

20. For more examples, see ibid., 255.

21. For the impact of Solov'ev's thought on the authors discussed here, see, among others, Belyi, *Vospominaniia o Bloke*, 23–44; Berdiaev, *Sobranie*, 1:43 and 181; and, for a scholarly view, Losev, *Vladimir Solov'ev*, 575–94. For his influence specifically on Blok, see, among others, Mints, *Aleksandr Blok*, 389–425; Pyman, *The Life*, 1:71–73 and 103–4; and Chukovsky, *Alexander Blok*, 64–71. Related to the Symbolist trend of "nationalizing" Sophiology might be the glorification of Empress Elizabeth in the memoirs and art of Alexandre Benois. It has recently been argued that Benois' "Elizabethan cult" possibly harks back to Solov'ev's Sophia ideal (Krasnov, "Khudozhestvennyie obrazy,"). Given Elizabeth's status as empress and thus ultimate representative of the Russian state in her time, such an interpretation suggests a link between Russia and a Sophiological female figure in Benois' art.

22. Belyi, *Vospominaniia o Bloke*, 23–29.

23. Merezhkovskii, *Voskresshie bogi*, 387.

24. Gippius, *Stikhotvoreniia*, 158.

25. Belyi, *Simvolizm*, 328.

26. Andrew, *Narrative, Space and Gender*, 157–85. See especially 179.

27. Burgin, *Sophia Parnok*, 40.

28. Ibid., 21.

29. Domnikov, *Mat'-zemlia i tsar'-gorod*, 643.

30. Mints, *Poetika russkogo simvolizma*, 208.

31. Belyi, *Serebrianyi golub'*, 287–88.

32. Belyi, *Simvolizm*, 329 and 333.

33. As a rule, in this chapter references to Blok's work appear in the text and only contain volume and page numbers. These references refer to the 1960–63 collection of his works (*Sobranie sochinenii*). The edition of his collected work (*Polnoe sobranie*), as yet incomplete, is occasionally used for comments.

34. Sargeant, "*Kashchei the Immortal*," 22–43.

35. Belyi, *Vospominaniia*, 87.

36. On Blok's political involvement around 1905, see Azadovskii, "Stikhiia i kul'tura," 13–15. On his gendering of the revolution in the poems in question, see Mints, *Poetika Aleksandra Bloka*, 430–31.

37. Kruk, "Blok i Gogol," 88.

38. Rozanov, *Russkaia gosudarstvennost'*, 241.

39. Rozanov, *O pisatel'stve*, 261. In colloquial speech, the term *baba* refers to a married peasant woman, wife, or old woman. "Muzhik" means peasant, bumpkin, or husband.

40. From October 1907 date drafts for the *Native Land* poem "Densely Forested Slopes . . ." ("Zadebrennye lesom kruchi . . ."), which oppose the poet to a young girl, in terms which he applies to a feminized Russia in later poetry (*Polnoe sobranie*, 3:500–501).

41. Orlov, *O Rodine*, 14.

42. This cycle and poem were later included in *Native Land*, but first appeared independently in 1909 and 1910, respectively (see Blok, *Polnoe sobranie*, 3:910 and 929).

43. Blok, *Zapisnye knizhki*, 117–18.

44. Blok, *Polnoe sobranie*, 3:934.

45. See ibid, 3:929–30 and 4:579.

46. See, for instance, Rozanov, *O pisatel'stve*, 262–72, 330–33; and Blok, *Sobranie sochinenii*, 5:118, 211, and 511; 8:127–29, and 273–78.

47. Voronova, *Knigi*, 46–47.

48. Vadimov, *Zhizn' Berdiaeva*, 81.

49. Ibid., 68.

50. Blok, *Sobranie sochinenii*, 5:742–44; and Pyman, *The Life*, 2:28.

51. Blok, *Sobranie sochinenii*, 5:744; and Blok, *Polnoe sobranie*, 3:913–16 and 930.

52. Among others, this is the case in Viacheslav Ivanov's review "O russkoi

idee," *Zolotoe runo,* no. 1 (1909); Sergei Gorodetskii's "Blizhaishaia zada-cha russkoi literatury," *Zolotoe runo,* no. 4 (1909), and his review of "Noch-nye chasy" in *Rech',* no. 320 (1911); Nikolai Gumilev's "Pis'ma o russkoi poezii: Aleksandr Blok: 'Nochnye chasy,'" in *14-yi sbornik stikhov* (Moscow, 1911); E. V. Anichkov's "'Nochnye sny' Aleksandr Bloka," *Zaprosy zhizni,* no. 2 (1911); G. Khitrovo's "Rus' moia, zhizn' moia! . . . ," *Sankt-Peterburgskie vedomosti,* no. 176 (1913); A. A. Gizetti, "O Bloke," *Vestnik literatury* 10, no. 34 (1921); Andrei Belyi, in *Poezia slova* (Petrograd, 1922); Iurii Aikhenval'd, "Aleksandr Blok," in *Poety i poetessy* (Moscow, 1922); Viktor Zhirmunskii, *Poezia Aleksandra Bloka* (Petrograd, 1922), chaps. 3, 8; Kornei Chukovskii, *Aleksandr Blok kak chelovek i poet* (Petergof, 1924); Georgii Fedotov, "Na pole Kulikovom," *Sovremennye zapiski,* no. 32 (1927); and, somewhat later, in Nikolai Berdiaev, "Russkaia literatura XIX veka i ee prorochestva" in his *Istoki i smysl russkogo kommunizma* (London, 1937).

53. Contemporary discussions on Blok's "bride Russia" can be approached as secondary material—or, given their essayistic and poetic nature, as part of the discourse on a gendered Russia. I examine them in both capacities.

54. Quoted in Blok, *Polnoe sobranie,* 3:935.

55. See the comments to Belyi, *Serebrianyi golub',* 312.

56. Ibid., 310.

57. On their connection, see Carlson, "The Silver Dove," 74; and Belyi, *Serebrianyi golub',* 6.

58. Belyi, *Simvolizm,* 368.

59. Belyi, *Serebrianyi golub',* 312.

60. Carlson, "The Silver Dove," 61.

61. Ivanov, "Antichnyi uzhas," 61–65.

62. *Vekhi,* 5.

63. Carlson, "The Silver Dove," 90.

64. See Belyi in *Vekhi,* 457; and Bulgakov in the comments to Belyi, *Serebrianyi golub',* 312.

65. Rozanov, *Sochineniia,* 327–29.

66. See Berdiaev, *Sobranie,* 1:161, 171, 179, 181, 183, 187, 217–19, 221, 223–25, 229–30; and Vadimov, *Zhizn' Berdiaeva,* 60, 77–78, 81, 82, 84, 88, 94, 103, 120–21, 126, 146, and 168–70.

67. See Berdiaev, *Sobranie,* 1:157, 160–61, 174, 167–71, 176–79, 181, 183–87, 196, 212–15, 220, 235; and Vadimov, *Zhizn' Berdiaeva,* 61, 70–72, 78, 80–81, 84, 101–2, 104, 109, 125–26, 129–33, 159–60, 168–70, 173, 190–91.

68. To Blok's "your [Russia's] windy songs / Are like the first tears of love" (*Sobranie,* 3:254) corresponds the question to Russia "Should I believe your songs" in Kliuev's cycle (*Sochineniia,* 1:244); the "traits" of Kliuev's feminized Russia "are clouded" by the snow of the "sorcerer January" (ibid., 1:225), where Blok labeled it a woman whose "beautiful traits" are "clouded" by sorrow after it

gave itself to a "sorcerer" (3:254). See also Kliuev's poem "Risings of the Steppe Fire" ("Kostra stepnogo vzvivy," 1910). For an online Russian version of this poem, see, for instance, http://az.lib.ru/k/kljuew_n_a/text_0040.shtml.

69. Kliuev, *Sochineniia,* 1:244.

70. Ibid., 1:225.

71. Ibid., 1:456–57.

72. Pyman, *The Life,* 2:139–40.

73. Blok and Belyi, *Perepiska,* 264 and 312–13.

74. Chulkov, *Imperatory,* 343–44.

75. Severianin, *Sochineniia,* 4:20.

76. See Blok, *Polnoe sobranie,* 3:951.

77. Bal'mont, *Stikhotvoreniia,* 398.

78. Ibid., 452.

79. For a reproduction, see Bonnell, *Iconography of Power,* fig. 2.3.

80. *Novyi satirikon,* no. 24 (1915). For this and similar cartoons and posters, see Oleg Riabov's site, http://www.ivanovo.ac.ru/alumni/olegria/nation2/iww _russia1.htm.

81. Norris, *A War of Images,* fig. 7.4.

82. Sologub, *Sobranie sochinenii,* 245.

83. Voloshin, *Sobranie,* 221.

84. Ibid., 511. The Galician Retreat was a notorious military defeat of the Russians by the Germans and Austrians during World War I.

85. Solntseva, *Strannyi eros,* 39.

86. Kliuev, *Sochineniia,* 1:455.

87. They include the cycle *Rus',* published in the journal *Severnye zapiski,* nos. 7 and 8 (1915) (parts had been published earlier in *Novyi zhurnal dlia vsekh,* no. 5 [1915]); the poems "Only for You I Twine a Wreath . . ." ("Tebe odnoi pletu venok . . ."), and "Whirl By as a Fleeting Little Bird . . ." ("Zaneslisia zaletnoiu ptashkoi . . ."), both published in the literary-scientific supplement of the journal *Niva,* no. 12 (1915); "I Am Tired of Living . . ." ("Ustal ia zhit' . . ."), published in *Severnye zapiski,* no. 9 (1916); "You Didn't Believe in My God . . ." ("Ne v moego ty boga verila . . ."), published in the newspaper *Petrogradskii vecher* on February 7, 1916; and "The Trimmed Roads Began to Sing . . ." ("Zapeli tesanye dorogi . . ."), published in the *Ezhemesiachnyi zhurnal,* nos. 7 and 8 (1916).

88. Esenin, *Sobranie sochinenii,* 1:224–25.

89. Kusikov quoted in McVay, *Isadora and Esenin,* 82.

90. See Timenchik, "Khram Premudrosti," 298; and Khoruzhii, *O starom i novom,* 167.

91. Trubetskoi, "Natsional'nyi vopros," 359–62.

92. Ibid., 370.

93. Florenskii, *Sochineniia,* 357–59.

94. Ivanov, "Zhivoe predanie," 345.

95. Berdiaev, *Sud'ba Rossii*, 14.

96. Rozanov, *Poslednie list'ia*, 339.

97. Ibid., 340.

98. Ern, "Nalet Val'kirii," 260.

99. The latter appears in *The Fate of Russia* as "Nationality and Messianism" ("Natsional'nost' i messianizm").

100. See Riabov, *Matushka-Rus'*, 145.

101. See Erlich, *Modernism and Revolution*, 9–10.

102. See Thomson, *The Premature Revolution*, 25–28; Erlich, *Modernism and Revolution*, 17–24; Chukovsky, *Alexander Blok*, 135–36; Maiakovskii, *Sobranie sochinenii*, 148–49; and Azadovskii, "Stikhiia i kul'tura," 71–72.

103. Chukovsky, *Aleksandr Blok*, 132; and Belyi, *Vospominaniia*, 407.

104. Hackel, *The Poet and the Revolution*, 78–79.

105. Chulkov, "Metel'," 4.

106. Blok, *Polnoe sobranie*, 5:301–2 and 364.

107. Ibid., 5:382 and 400–402.

108. Ibid., 5:405.

109. Christa, *The Poetic World*, 109.

110. Belyi, *Stikhotvoreniia*, 440 and 444.

111. Shpet, *Esteticheskie fragmenty*, 14.

112. Esenin, *Sobranie*, 1:273; 2:8, 20, and 44–45.

113. Ibid., 2:47, 58, and 97.

114. Kliuev, *Sochineniia*, 2:161.

115. Ibid., 2:303 and 152. A *zurna* is a Caucasian wind instrument; *Zyriane* is an ancient term for the Komi people.

116. Voloshin, *Sobranie*, 257–58 and 525.

117. See "Peace" ("Mir") and "Deaf-and-Dumb Rus'" ("Rus' glukhonemaia"), both published in *Slovu-svoboda!* on December 10, 1917; "Native Land" ("Rodina"), published in *Ialtinskii golos*, November 17, 1918; "Invocation of the Russian Earth" ("Zakliat'ie o Russkoi zemle"), published in *Iuzhnoe slovo*, no. 3 (1919); "On the Station" ("Na vokzale"), published in *Pomoshch*, no. 1 (1922); "On the Bottom of the Inferno" ("Na dne preispodnei"), published in Berlin in *Novaia russkaia kniga*, no. 2 (1923); and "Streetwalker Rus'" ("Rus' guliashchaia"), published in *Nakanune* on February 18, 1923.

118. In addition to the poems, see the comments in Voloshin, *Sobranie*, 259 and 527.

119. B. Antonovskii, "Roman Lenina i Rossii," *Novyi Satirikon*, no. 27 (1917).

120. See Rutten, "Kashchei the Immortal."

121. C. Marsh, *M. A. Voloshin*, 140.

122. Voloshin, *Stikhotvoreniia*, 257.

123. Ivanova, "Trudnaia lira."

124. Shkapskaia, *Stikhi*, 69–70 and 80.

125. Ibid., 81–83.

126. Ibid., 80. On Shkapskaia's female perspective, see also Heldt, *Terrible Perfection*, 243.

127. I refer here to "The Religious Bases of Bolshevism" ("Religioznye osnovy bol'shevizma"), published in *Russkaia svoboda* 16–17, no. 3 (1917); "German Influence and the Slavic Peoples" ("Germanskoe vlianie i slavianstvo"), published in *Narodopravstvo* 6, no. 2–4 (1917); "The Recovery of Russia" ("Ozdorovlenïe Rossïi"), published in *Nakanune* 6, no. 1–2 (1918) (these essays are all included in *The Spiritual Bases of the Russian Revolution*); and "On Sanctity and Honesty" ("O sviatosti i chestnosti"), published in *The Fate of Russia*.

128. Kliuev, "Razrukha."

129. Bulgakov, "Moia rodina," 364 and 373.

130. See Fedotov, *Sud'ba i grekhi*, 1:2, 4, 102–22, 178; and 2:104, 143, and 252.

131. Makushinskii, "Otvergnutyi zhenikh," 43.

132. Among others, see Blagoi, *Tri veka*, 288–89; Dolgopolov, *Aleksandr Blok*, 25, 57, 93, and 110; Gorbaneva, *Khudozhnik i mir*, 14; Mints, *Poetika Aleksandra Bloka*, 224, 360, 543, and 545; Mints, *Aleksandr Blok*, 129; P'ianykh, *Aleksandr Blok*, 8; Pravdina, "Iz istorii formirovaniia," 22; Iakovlev, *Sud'ba Rossii*, 9–10; and Schahadat, *Intertextualität*, 297ff. On the link between Blok's feminized Russia and the state-intelligentsia-people debates, see Mints, *Poetika Aleksandra Bloka*, 160, 491; and her *Aleksandr Blok*, 104; Thomson, *The Premature Revolution*, 22–23; Rodina, *Aleksandr Blok*, 174–77; Medvedev, *Dramy i poemy*, 60; Gromov, *Geroi i vremia*, 494–95 and 503–4; Orlov, *O Rodine*, 14; and the academic comments to Blok's *Polnoe sobranie*, 3:901 and 3:916. See also Terras, *Handbook*, 417; and Moser, *Cambridge History*, 56.

133. Etkind, *Khlyst*, 312.

134. Khodasevich, *Sobranie sochinenii*, 7–8.

135. Azadovskii, "Stikhiia i kul'tura," 18.

136. Mints, *Poetika Aleksandra Bloka*, 350–51.

137. Chukovsky, *Alexander Blok*, 28.

138. Among others, see Belyi and Ivanov-Razumnik, *Perepiska*, 108; Belyi quoted in P'ianykh, *Aleksandr Blok*, 439 and 448–49; and Voloshin, *Sobranie*, 537–38, 557.

139. Mints, *Poetika Aleksandra Bloka*, 351.

140. On this, see also Pravdina, "Iz istorii formirovaniia," 23.

141. Mints, *Poetika Aleksandra Bloka*, 351.

142. Gromov, *Geroi i vremia*, 519.

143. See in this respect Berberova, *Aleksandr Blok*, 86; Medvedev, *Dramy i poemy*, 57–61; Rodina, *Aleksandr Blok*, 190–91; and Westphalen, *Lyric Incarnate*, 90–98 and 101.

144. Mints, *Poetika Aleksandra Bloka,* 282; italics in original.

145. Shortly before writing "Russia," "Autumn Day," and the people-and-intelligentsia article, Blok defines "Shchedrin, Belinskii, Dobroliubov" as "delicious *intelligentskaia* candy"; he repeatedly mentions "Dobroliubov on the people" as a source of inspiration (Blok, *Sobranie,* 7:114–15). In the same period, he repeatedly refers to his rereading of Turgenev's novels, and calls attention to nineteenth-century classics that focused on national issues, such as *Eugene Onegin* and *Dead Souls* (ibid., and 5:288–89). He credits the Slavophiles and Westernizers for having "started the discussion concerning the people and the intelligentsia" (5:332). In 1908 he also asserted that "if today you open a random page of the history of our nineteenth-century literature . . . everything will seem interesting, urgent and topical to you; . . . at the moment there is not . . . one question among the questions raised by the great Russian literature of the previous century, which does not burn in our minds" (5:334–35).

146. Blok and Belyi, *Perepiska,* 34; italics in original.

147. Blok, *Pis'ma k zhene,* 68. The word *narodnyi* was translated here as "national"; additionally, the adjective refers to the (common) people.

148. See Blok, *Sobranie,* 3:254–55, 268, and 586; and 4:115–16, 142, 145–46, and 149.

149. Gromov, *Geroi i vremia,* 503; see also Mints, *Aleksandr Blok,* 129; and Pravdina, "Iz istorii formirovaniia," 21.

150. Schahadat, *Intertextualität,* 269–70.

151. On this link, see Mints, *Aleksandr Blok,* 362–88; Schahadat, *Intertextualität,* 310–27; and Blagoi, *Tri veka,* 288–89.

152. Mints, *Aleksandr Blok,* 350.

153. See ibid., 385; and Blagoi, *Tri veka,* 289.

154. See Blok, *Sobranie,* 8:208, 210; and Blok, *Polnoe sobranie,* 3:909–10; on this, see also Azadovskii, "Stikhiia i kul'tura," 20–26.

155. Blok, *Zapisnye knizhki,* 131.

156. See the comments to the poem in Blok, *Sobranie,* 3:586–87.

157. The characterization as nun may also have been inspired by a role played by the actress Natal'ia Volokhova, with whom Blok was romantically involved in 1906–8 and whom he declared to be the prototype for Faina's character (Blok, *Sobranie,* 7:187). Blok first declared his love for Volokhova at a dress rehearsal of Maurice Maeterlinck's play *Sister Beatrice (Soeur Béatrice,* 1901), in which she fulfilled the part of abbess (see Pyman, *The Life,* 2:262).

158. Brouwer, "De Oudgelovige," 34.

159. Etkind, *Khlyst,* 5.

160. Blok, *Zapisnye knizhki,* 103. Whereas Pecherskii's heroine is mostly referred to as Flenushka, she is baptized as Faina (Pecherskii, *V lesakh,* 198).

161. On this, see Rutten, "Mikhail Nesterov."

162. Blok elaborated on this antithesis in the essay "Literary Results of

1907" ("Literaturnye itogi 1907 goda") (Blok, *Sobranie*, 5:210–11); see also Mints, *Poetika Bloka*, 491.

163. For the association of the feminized Russia with a river (slope), see Blok, *Sobranie*, 3:249, 254, 296, 586, 590; 4:115–16, 139, 142–45, 149, 161; with the steppe: 3:249, 268–70; 4:135; forests: 3:254, 268; 4:115, 142, 149; fields and meadows: 3:254, 281; 4:115, 117, 142, 144; villages, huts, and decrepit village houses: 3:254, 257, 281, 586, 590–91; 4:116, 117, 149–50; mist, smoke, and open fire: 3:249, 254, 269, 586, 590; 4:115–16, 135, 142–44; the wind: 3:254, 268–69; 4:115, 139, 142–45, 149, 151, 159–63, 166; and with the distance, or open spaces: 3:249, 255, 268–69; 4:115, 135, 142–43, 146, 155.

164. See Valerii Parnok in Burgin, *Sophia Parnok*, 21; Belyi, *Serebrianyi golub'*, 122–23; Kliuev, *Sochineniia*, 1:457; Shkapskaia, *Stikhi*, 82; Berdiaev, *Sobranie*, 3:351–52; Voloshin, *Sobranie*, 221; Chulkov, *Imperatory*, 343.

165. Sologub, *Sobranie*, 245.

166. Shkapskaia, *Stikhi*, 70, 80, and 81.

167. Merezhkovskii, *Antikhrist*, 387.

168. Belyi, *Simvolizm*, 333.

169. Belyi, *Serebrianyi golub'*, 180.

170. Ibid., 123 and 188.

171. Voloshin, *Sobranie*, 289.

172. Ibid., 221, 257, and 364.

173. Kliuev, *Sochineniia*, 1:225 and 244; and Kliuev, "Razrukha."

174. Kliuev, *Sochineniia*, 2:143–44. Worth noting is the source of inspiration that Kliuev's correspondence with Blok provided for the latter's turn to religious dissent in the years 1907–9 (see Azadovskii, "Stikhiia i kul'tura," 8–9, 20–23).

175. Esenin, *Sobranie*, 1:224.

176. Ely, *This Meager Nature*, 213.

177. Belyi, *Serebrianyi golub'*, 68. The translation used is George Reavey's: *Andrei Biely, The Silver Dove* (New York: Grove, 1974). On Katia's link with nineteenth-century heroines, see also Mochulsky, *Andrei Belyi*, 143.

178. See, for instance, Mints, *Aleksandr Blok*, 129.

179. See Levinton, "Zametki o fol'klorizme," 177. For "swan," see Blok, *Sobranie*, 3:591; 4:104, 108, 137–38, 144–45, and 149–50; Blok particularly reverts to the swan motif in the context of the Kulikovo battle, in the Old Russian accounts of which the same image occurs repeatedly, albeit not in the context of marital imagery (*Polnoe sobranie*, 3:928). For "princess," see 3:247 and *Polnoe sobranie*, 3:506; for "prince," see 3:247, 4:114, 144, and 149; and *Polnoe sobranie*, 3:506. For the hero's depiction as foreign guest, see 4:121 and 138.

180. Kravtsov and Kulagina, *Slavianskii fol'klor*, 61 and 73.

181. Esenin, *Sobranie*, 1:224.

182. For an extensive discussion of this link, see Schahadat, *Intertextualität*, 301–7.

183. See Zhukovskii, *Sochineniia*, 17–18, 22, 23; and Pushkin, *Polnoe sobranie*, 6:101.

184. Mints, *Poetika simvolizma*, 254.

185. Pravdina, "Iz istorii formirovaniia," 21; and Orlov, *Aleksandr Blok*, 58 and 362.

186. Belyi, *Simvolizm*, 329 and 333.

187. Ibid., 329.

188. Ibid. The image of the "veil of black death," as well as the title of the essay, are borrowed from Valerii Briusov's poem "Orpheus and Eurydice" ("Orfei i Evridika," 1903–4) (see Briusov, *Sobranie*, 385–87).

189. See Carlson, "The Silver Dove," 75; and the comments to Belyi, *Serebrianyi golub'*, 6.

190. Belyi, *Simvolizm*, 368.

191. The link between these fragments and Belyi's essay has been observed in Gromov, *Geroi i vremia*, 512–13; Kruk, "Blok i Gogol," 88 and 92; Mints, *Poetika Bloka*, 494; Mints, *Aleksandr Blok*, 62; Hackel, *The Poet and the Revolution*, 79–82; and Pravdina, "Iz istorii formirovaniia," 31; see also Blok, *Polnoe sobranie*, 2:682.

192. See Orlov quoted in Blok, *Polnoe sobranie*, 5:427; Mints, *Aleksandr Blok*, 77–78; Kruk, "Blok i Gogol," 88, 92.

193. See Billington, *The Icon and the Axe*, 484; Hansen-Löve, "Zur Mythopoetik," 69.

194. See Gorodetskii quoted in P'ianykh, *Aleksandr Blok*, 540.

195. Kliuev, *Sochineniia*, 1:225.

196. Esenin, *Sobranie*, 1:200; 2:58.

197. Voloshin, *Sobranie*, 286.

198. Blok, *Zapisnye knizhki*, 37.

199. Blok, *Polnoe sobranie*, 2:80.

200. Ibid., 3:911.

201. Milner-Gulland, *The Russians*, 2.

202. For "still the same," see Blok, *Sobranie*, 3:249, 254, 259, and 268–69; for the "primordial" motif, see 3:254, 269, and 281. The phrase "still the same" is also applied to Blok's exalted muse in the poems "The Years Have Passed . . ." ("Proshli goda . . . ," 1906), "When Despair and Anger Fade . . ." ("Kogda zamrut otchaian'ie i zloba . . . ," 1908), and, with reference to Russia, in the short essay "The Sun over Russia" ("Solntse nad Rossiei," 1908).

203. See Blok, *Sobranie*, 4:149; and Schahadat, *Intertextualität*, 277–78 and 298.

204. Nesterov, *Pis'ma*, 114.

205. Esenin, *Sobranie*, 1:194.

206. Kliuev, *Sochineniia*, 1:225.

207. Fedotov, *Sud'ba i grekhi*, 2:41–42.

208. Hansen-Löve, "Zur Mythopoetik," 62.

209. Chukovsky, *Alexander Blok*, 61.

210. Belyi, *Vospominaniia*, 39.

211. On this, see, for example, Blok, *Polnoe sobranie*, 3:171, 923, 925, and 927.

212. On this, see Pravdina, "Iz istorii formirovaniia," 22.

213. See Gippius, *Zhivye litsa*, 33.

214. See, for instance, Gippius, *Zhivye litsa*, 33; Belyi, Ivanov-Razumnik, and Shteinberg, *Pamiati*, 22; Chukovsky, *Alexander Blok*, 132–37; and Fedotov, *Sud'ba i grekhi Rossii*, 107.

215. Carlson, "The Silver Dove," 75.

216. Kliuev, *Sochineniia*, 1:244 and 225.

217. Voloshin, *Sobranie*, 221.

218. Esenin, *Sobranie sochinenii*, 1:116–17, 157, and 224–25.

219. Voloshin, *Stikhotvoreniia*, 257.

220. Kliuev, *Sochineniia*, 2:204.

221. Mints, *Aleksandr Blok*, 359.

222. Belyi, *Simvolizm*, 333.

223. Ibid., 330.

224. Belyi, *Vospominaniia*, 169.

225. McVay, *Isadora and Esenin*, 10, 38, and 115.

226. Ibid., 129. See also Rutten, "Ot 'dushi Ameriki.'"

227. Seroff, *The Real Isadora*, 312; and Duncan and MacDougall, *Duncan's Russian Days*, 369.

228. McVay, *Isadora and Esenin*, 115 and 129.

229. Belyi, *Serebrianyi golub'*, 190.

230. Schahadat, *Intertextualität*, 315–19.

231. On this, see Mints, *Aleksandr Blok*, 92.

232. See Blok, *Sobranie*, 4:104–6, 112, and 127–30 for the black-versus-white antithesis; and 4:104, 115–16, and 119–20 for city versus shelter.

233. Clowes, "*Doctor Zhivago*," 64–65.

234. Kliuev, *Sochineniia*, 1:456–57.

235. See Esenin, *Sobranie sochinenii*, 1:135, 193–94, 224–25, 273; and 2:20.

236. Ibid., 1:116, 132, and 135. Esenin would later marry the same Isadora Duncan upon whom Belyi grafted his metaphor; but when he wrote the poems in question, they had not yet met in person.

237. Voloshin, *Sobranie*, 221.

238. Ibid., 257–59, 263, 289, 364.

239. Masing-Delic, "The Mask Motif," 81.

240. Among others, Friedrich Schiller ("Das verschleierte Bild zu Sais," 1795) and Novalis ("Die Lehrlinge zu Sais," 1798–1800) refer to the legend of

Isis's veil; on the impact of these works and their authors on Russian Symbolism, see Wachtel, *Russian Symbolism*, 117–19, 121–22, and 157ff.

241. Revealing are the titles of Ivanov's essay "The Face and Masks of Russia" ("Lik i lichiny Rossii," 1917) and Fedotov's article "The Face of Russia" ("Litso Rossii," 1918).

242. The terms used are *pokryvalo* (shawl, veil, cover); *fata* (a bridal veil); *pelena* (shroud, veil [also figuratively], or altar cloth); *platok* (shawl, scarf, kerchief); and *pokrov* (cover, coat, sheath, hearse cloth, funeral pall, mantle, or shroud).

243. Savinova and Zimina, "Kitezh," 283. According to this legend, based on the vicissitudes of a Russian village near Suzdal', the legendary town of Kitezh mysteriously disappeared—either under the ground or in the water of the Svetoiar lake—upon a threatening Tatar invasion. Its invisibility allegedly preserved it from destruction (see ibid).

244. Voloshin, *Sobranie*, 279 and 221.

245. See Blok, *Sobranie*, 3:254–55, 268; 4:117, 125, 141, 147, and 150.

246. Fedotov, *Sud'ba i grekhi*, 1:178; see also 1:4.

247. Chulkov, "Metel'," 4.

248. See Blok, *Sobranie*, 3:255 and 4:164. See also Kliuev, *Sochineniia*, 1:244; Belyi, *Serebrianyi golub'*, 39; and Fedotov, *Sud'ba i grekhi*, 1:4.

249. Gogol, *Sobranie*, 5:201; Blok, *Zapisnye knizhki*, 117–18.

250. Solov'ev, *Stikhotvoreniia*, 169.

251. See Blok, *Sobranie*, 3:268, 586, 590; and 4:116, 141, and 162. In 1917, Esenin similarly proclaims his "beloved Rus'" to "burn many . . . with your face" (Esenin, *Sobranie sochinenii*, 1:235). Here the connotation of the "burning face" (*ognennyi lik*) of Divine Wisdom in traditional Russian iconography undoubtedly plays a role as well.

252. Shkapskaia, *Stikhi*, 69.

253. Belyi quoted in Blok, *Polnoe sobranie*, 3:938.

254. Fedotov, *Sud'ba i grekhi*, 1:116.

255. See Sosnina and Shangina, *Russkii traditsionnyi kostium*, 205; and Kirsanova, *Russkii kostium*, 153.

256. Levinton, "Zametki," 175–78.

257. Kliuev, *Sochineniia*, 1:225.

258. Esenin, *Sobranie sochinenii*, 1:303.

259. Bal'mont, *Stikhotvoreniia*, 398.

260. Belyi, *Serebrianyi golub'*, 290.

261. Esenin, *Sobranie sochinenii*, 2:44.

262. Fedotov, *Sud'ba i grekhi*, 1:117.

263. Shkapskaia, *Stikhi*, 70, 81.

264. Belyi, *Simvolizm*, 329.

265. Belyi, Ivanov-Razumnik, and Shteinberg, *Pamiati*, 33.

266. Panchenko quoted in Azadovskii, "Stikhiia i kul'tura," 24.

267. See Blok, *Sobranie*, 8:141 and 144; and Pyman, *The Life*, 1:213–17.

268. Mints, *Aleksandr Blok*, 273.

269. Azadovskii, "Stikhiia i kul'tura," 47–53.

270. Kliuev, *Pis'ma*, 6 and 122.

271. Ibid.

272. See, in this respect, Blok, *Sobranie*, 7:101; 8:215, 219, 252, and 258–59.

273. Erlich, *Modernism and Revolution*, 19.

274. Thomson, *The Premature Revolution*, 28.

275. Quoted in Pyman, *The Life*, 36.

276. Quoted in Blok, *Polnoe sobranie*, 5:401.

277. Mints, *Poetika Bloka*, 351.

278. On this, see also Medvedev, *Dramy i poemy*, 60.

279. Rodina, *Aleksandr Blok*, 181.

280. Medvedev, *Dramy i poemy*, 60.

281. See Blok, *Sobranie*, 4:133–34; and Schahadat, *Intertextualität*, 268. A similar figure will appear later in "The Twelve": here, a long-haired "writer" and "orator . . . says with half-loud voice: Traitors! They have ruined Russia!" (*Sobranie*, 3:348).

282. Mints, *Aleksandr Blok*, 103.

283. See Rodina, *Aleksandr Blok*, 177. Pushkin's Germann is a Russian foreigner par excellence: the son of a Russified German, he is introduced as "*nemets!*"—"a German!"—and compared twice to Napoléon (Pushkin, *Polnoe sobranie*, 8:227, 235, and 244–45).

284. Belyi, *Serebrianyi golub'*, 284–87, and 24, 83, 169, 216. For a discussion of Dar'ial'skii's role as such, see the comments in ibid., 389–92; and Carlson, "The Silver Dove," 84, 90, 93.

285. Belyi, *Serebrianyi golub'*, 37, 167.

286. Belyi, *Stikhotvoreniia*, 441.

287. Chulkov, "Metel'," 6.

288. Voloshin, *Sobranie*, 347.

289. See Blok, *Sobranie*, 4:161, 163, 438, 440, 441, and 444.

290. For "passivity," see Blok, *Sobranie*, 4:121, 156, 149; "fear," 4:141, 147, 150, 162, 450; "childishness," 4:120, 162, and 436–37.

291. Lotman and Uspenskii, "'Izgoi,'" 226–28.

292. Pushkin, *Polnoe sobranie*, 8:244.

293. Belyi, *Simvolizm*, 328; see also Lotman and Uspenskii, "'Izgoi,'" 227.

294. Belyi, *Serebrianyi golub'*, 285–90.

295. Ibid., 37, 123–24, and 196.

296. Belyi, *Stikhotvoreniia*, 441.

297. Chulkov, "Metel'," 4.

298. Voloshin, *Sobranie*, 347.

299. Levinton points in this context to the folkloric identification of marriage with a battle (Levinton, "Zametki," 179).

300. In addition, in 1910 Blok depicted Vladimir Solov'ev as a "poor knight" and "knight-monk" in his essay of the same name ("Rytsar'-monakh"). He proclaimed Solov'ev as destined to save the "captive princess, the World Soul" from the "dragon" of Chaos (*Sobranie sochinenii*, 5:451); the national dimension is not prominent here, though.

301. Mints, *Poetika Bloka*, 359.

302. Bal'mont quoted in Blok, *Polnoe sobranie*, 3:905; Gippius, *Zhivye litsa*, 33; and Belyi, *Vospominaniia*, 414.

303. See Blok, *Sobranie sochinenii*, 5:88–89; and Mints, *Poetika Bloka*, 50 and 173.

304. It might prove interesting to examine the intelligentsia's metaphoric representation as Don Quixote, a myth which Vsevolod Bagno has identified as a "key to events in Russian intellectual and social life" from the eighteenth century onwards; in this context, the role of Dulcinea-Aldonza tended to be projected either on humanity as a whole, or on Russia or the Russian people (Bagno, "Russkoe donkikhotstvo," 217 and 222).

305. Blok, *Polnoe sobranie*, 3:927.

306. Senderovich, *Georgii Pobedonosets*, 233–37. The Saint George story functioned in a political context in Blok's 1904 poem "Duel" ("Poedinok"), which depicts the relationship between Moscow and Petersburg as a struggle over a mystical female figure between Moscow's patron Saint George and Peter the Great (ibid., 235; and Blok, *Sobranie sochinenii*, 2:144, 415). In *Native Land*, a dragon-slayer plot is reenacted in "Dreams"; given its placement in this collection and its thematic link with the poems discussed earlier, an interpretation of this poem as a political allegory does not seem unlikely.

307. For an interpretation of German in this vein, see Gromov, *Geroi i vremia*, 512; and Mints, *Poetika Bloka*, 360. By contrast, Senderovich argues that Blok associated Saint George with state power (*Georgii Pobedonosets*, 235–36).

308. Belyi, Ivanov-Razumnik, and Shteinberg, *Pamiati*, 26.

309. Mints, *Poetika Bloka*, 360.

310. On this, see Mints, *Poetika simvolizma*, 254; Riabov, *Zhenshchina*, 58–59 and 113–14.

311. Belyi, *Simvolizm*, 328, 333.

312. Voloshin, *Sobranie*, 257–58, 262.

313. Severianin, *Sochineniia*, 4:20.

314. Kliuev, "Razrukha."

315. Propp, *Istoricheskie korni*, 222.

316. Significantly, in *The Idiot* Rogozhin features as the symbolic opponent

of Myshkin, with whom the knightlike hero of Blok's works can be associated, as said above.

317. Erlich, *Modernism and Revolution,* 19.

318. Belyi, *Simvolizm,* 329.

319. See Lotman and Uspenskii, "'Izgoi,'" 222–23.

320. Belyi, *Simvolizm,* 329.

321. Ibid.

322. Ibid., 329 and 333.

323. Propp, *Istoricheskie korni,* 218 and 245.

324. These two poems have repeatedly been linked to "The Green Meadow"; see Belyi, *Vospominaniia,* 407; Kruk, "Blok i Gogol," 88 and 92; Mints, *Aleksandr Blok,* 62; Blok, *Polnoe sobranie,* 3:932. Mints treats the sorcerer and kite in *Native Land* as symbolic equivalents (Mints, *Poetika Bloka,* 360).

325. Propp, *Istoricheskie korni,* 218.

326. Mints, *Aleksandr Blok,* 62.

327. See Blok, *Polnoe sobranie,* 3:950.

328. Belyi, *Vospominaniia,* 435–36.

329. Dostoevsky, *Polnoe sobranie,* 1:471 and 484. On the status of the political figures mentioned as the Companion's prototypes, see also Mints, *Aleksandr Blok,* 64.

330. See Medvedev, *Dramy i poemy,* 67.

331. Given the previously discussed link between *Song of Fate* and Pushkin's "Queen of Spades," this depiction evokes allusions to the figure of Count St. Germain (1710–84), a French adventurer who came to Russia and helped Catherine II in her power struggle with Peter III. Interested in alchemy, he is still a popular character in occult philosophies today. In "Queen of Spades," St. Germain appears as a mysterious rich "charlatan" who is said to have told the countess the card secret around which the plot evolves (Pushkin, *Polnoe sobranie,* 8:229).

332. See Gromov, *Geroi i vremia,* 513; and Mints, *Aleksandr Blok,* 62.

333. Belyi, *Peterburg,* 24, 32, 49, 51, 78. On the Pobedonostsev-Ableukhov link, see the editorial comment to Belyi, *Peterburg,* 643, 655, 650.

334. Belyi, *Peterburg,* 78.

335. Ibid., 16, and 644 n. 14.

336. On this, see Orlov, *O Rodine,* 117; Pravdina, "Iz istorii formirovaniia," 31; Mints, *Aleksandr Blok,* 77–78; and Gromov, *Geroi i vremia,* 513.

337. Dolgopolov, *Aleksandr Blok,* 104.

338. Ibid., 104–5.

339. Mints, *Aleksandr Blok,* 737.

340. Quoted in Sargeant, *"Kashchei the Immortal,"* 31.

341. Belyi, *Peterburg,* 643 n. 11, and 650 n. 58.

342. For a reproduction, see Orlov, *Aleksandr Blok v portretakh,* 40, 362.

For a comprehensive list of 1905–6 cartoons of Pobedonostsev, see Belyi, *Peterburg,* 643 n. 11, and 650 n. 58.

343. Belyi, *Peterburg,* 650 n. 58 The source quoted here is Maksim Gorky's "The Life of Klim Samgin" ("Zhizn' Klima Samgina," begun in 1925), in which the author mentions a postcard of "Pobedonostsev in the guise of a bat" (M. Gor'kii, *Polnoe sobranie sochinenii* [Moscow, 1974], 22:159, and 25: 254).

344. Bonnell, *Iconography of Power,* 66.

345. Examples include the cartoons "Russia" ("Rossiia"), *Nagaechka,* no. 2 (1905); "Russia's Evil Genius" ("Zloi genii Rossii"), *Strely,* no. 1 (1905); "He Seems Quiet Now" ("Kazhetsia, uspokoilsia"), *Vampir,* no. 1 (1906); and the nameless cartoon on the back cover of *Pchela,* no. 1 (1906). For these and other relevant images, see King and Porter, *Images of Revolution,* or the visuals on Oleg Riabov's website, http://www.ivanovo.ac.ru/alumni/olegria/nation2/russia1.htm.

346. Hackel, *The Poet and the Revolution,* 82.

347. Ibid., 81–82.

348. Kliuev, *Sochineniia,* 1:225.

349. Kliuev, "Razrukha."

350. Severianin, *Sochineniia,* 4:20.

351. Quoted in Burgin, *Sophia Parnok,* 40.

352. Voloshin, *Sobranie,* 222, 257–58, and 262.

353. Ibid., 527.

354. Berdiaev, "Russkaia literatura," 220.

355. Ibid.

356. Quoted in Berdiaev, *Sobranie,* 4:5.

357. Androgyny is central to Solov'ev's view of "godmanhood" that was exemplified in chapter 1; and Blok speaks of his "spirit" in distinctly androgynous terms in a diary entry of June 1902 (Blok, *Sobranie,* 7:48).

358. Berdiaev, *Sud'ba Rossii,* 22.

359. See Berdiaev, *Sobranie,* 1:10, 43, 76, 133, and 233; on Berdiaev's status as an aristocrat, see also Vadimov, *Zhizn' Berdiaeva,* 11, 52, 101, and 103.

360. See Berdiaev, *Sobranie,* 1:227–33; and Vadimov, *Zhizn' Berdiaeva,* 105–7 and 116–18.

361. Quoted in Vadimov, *Zhizn' Berdiaeva,* 106.

362. Aizlewood, "Berdiaev and Chaadaev," 125–28 and 135.

363. Ibid., 135.

364. For the quotations mentioned, see, respectively, Berdiaev, *Sobranie,* 3:414, 352; Berdiaev, *Sud'ba Rossii,* 33; Berdiaev, *Sobranie,* 4:270.

365. Rozanov, *Russkaia gosudarstvennost',* 241.

366. Rozanov, *Sochineniia,* 328–29.

367. Ivanov, "Antichnyi uzhas," 65.

368. Ivanov, "Dostoevsky," 389; and Ivanov, "Osnovnoi mif," 51.

369. See Berdiaev, *Sobranie,* 3:108, and Bulgakov, "Russkaia tragediia," 4 and 12.

370. Ivanov, "Dostoevsky," 413; and Ivanov, "Osnovnoi mif," 510.

371. Ivanov, "Zhivoe predanie," 345.

372. Florenskii, *Sochineniia,* 357–59. Florenskii already conceived of a Russia-Sophia link in his *Pillar and Confirmation of Truth (Stolp i utverzhdenie istiny,* 1908–12) and in a 1912 letter to Samarin (Florenskii, "Pis'mo," 774).

373. Trubetskoi, "Natsional'nyi vopros," 359–61 and 370.

374. Bulgakov, "Moia rodina," 373.

375. "Spontaneity" is an imperfect translation of the Russian philosophical term *stikhiinost',* from the noun *stikhiia,* which can, in philosophy, refer either to one of the elements of nature; a natural phenomenon that reveals itself as an irrefutable destructive force; or an unorganized force within social surroundings.

376. For examples, see, for "spontaneity," Berdiaev, *Sud'ba Rossii,* 17, 29, 106, and Berdiaev, *Sobranie,* 3:415; for "chaos," *Sud'ba Rossii,* 24, 28; and *Sobranie,* 3:423; for "weakness," *Sud'ba Rossii,* 79, and *Sobranie,* 3:354, 4:247, 249; for "servitude," *Sud'ba Rossii,* 12, 21–23, 25, 34, and *Sobranie,* 3:352, 354; for "passivity," *Sud'ba Rossii,* 12, 14, 24, 31, 34, 79, 106, and *Sobranie,* 3:418, 4:147, 243, 249; and for the desire to "dissolve" in the collective, *Sud'ba Rossii,* 13, 24, 34, and *Sobranie,* 3:354, 418.

377. See Berdiaev, *Sud'ba Rossii,* 29 and 79; and Berdiaev, *Sobranie,* 3:356, 361.

378. See Berdiaev, *Sud'ba Rossii,* 12–13, 17, 28–29, 36, 79, 106, 191; and Berdiaev, *Sobranie,* 3:108, 351, 352, 361, 414–15, 4:147, 270, 273, and 5:324.

379. For accusations of "the people" for their submissive attitude toward (a) the Russian earth or "national element," see Berdiaev, *Sud'ba Rossii,* 13, 24, and Berdiaev, *Sobranie,* 3:354; and (b) the Russian state, see *Sud'ba Rossii,* 12, and *Sobranie,* 3:352–53.

380. See Riabov, *Matushka-Rus',* 140.

381. See Riabov, *Zhenshchina,* 117 and 121–22; and Ivanov, "Zhivoe predanie," 344.

382. Ivanov, "Dostoevsky," 389; and Ivanov, "Osnovnoi mif," 510.

383. Rozanov, "Zhenshchina," 122.

384. Ibid., 189.

385. Rozanov, *Sochineniia,* 323–24 and 329–30.

386. Ibid., 323 and 328–29.

387. Berdiaev, *The Russian Idea,* 266.

388. See Riabov, *Matushka-Rus',* 127.

389. Ivanov, "Dostoevsky," 389–91; and Ivanov, "Osnovnoi mif," 510–11.

390. Ivanov, "Dostoevsky," 403 and 414. In another paradoxical twist, Ivanov also regarded several male literary characters as embodiments of Russia (see Ivanov, "Osnovnoi mif," 417 and 442).

391. Rozanov, *Sochineniia*, 330; and Rozanov, *O pisatel'stve*, 260–61.

392. Ivanov, "Dostoevsky," 413.

393. Rozanov, *Poslednie list'ia*, 339.

394. Rozanov, *Sochineniia*, 324.

395. Berdiaev, *Sud'ba Rossii*, 17, 79; and Berdiaev, *Sobranie*, 3:361, 4:270.

396. Rozanov, *O pisatel'stve*, 261.

397. Berdiaev, *Sud'ba Rossii*, 16.

398. Ibid., 33.

399. Ibid., 11, 30.

400. Ibid., 25.

401. Ibid., 34.

402. Ibid., 29.

403. Ibid., 79.

404. Ivanov, "Antichnyi uzhas," 61.

405. Ivanov, "Dostoevsky," 390.

406. See Riabov, *Matushka-Rus'*, 134.

407. Berdiaev, *Sud'ba Rossii*, 31, 12; and Berdiaev, *Sobranie*, 4:248–49.

408. Berdiaev, *Sud'ba Rossii*, 33.

409. Ivanov, "Antichnyi uzhas," 61 and 65.

410. Vadimov, *Zhizn' Berdiaeva*, 105–7.

411. Berdiaev, *Sud'ba Rossii*, 23. See also, for instance, ibid., 35, 106; and Berdiaev, *Sobranie*, 3:418.

412. For examples, see, for "active," Berdiaev, *Sud'ba Rossii*, 17, 31, 35, 79, 106, and Berdiaev, *Sobranie*, 3:361, 418; for "creative," *Sud'ba Rossii*, 25, 31, 35, and 106; for "form-endowing," *Sud'ba Rossii*, 23, 33, and *Sobranie*, 3:418–19; for "light-bearing," *Sud'ba Rossii*, 23, 25, 33, 106, and *Sobranie*, 3:418–19; for the association of the masculine force with "logos," *Sud'ba Rossii*, 33, and *Sobranie*, 3:418–19; for "consciousness," *Sud'ba Rossii*, 23, 106; for "the spirit," *Sud'ba Rossii*, 18, 25, 29, 33, 106, and *Sobranie*, 3:361. The term "strong" coincides with the term for "manly" (*muzhestvennyi*) in Russian; in this context, it appears in combination with practically all the other terms on most pages mentioned. On these dichotomies in Silver Age thought, see also Riabov, *Matushka-Rus'*, 14–15.

413. Ivanov, "Antichnyi uzhas," 61 and 65.

414. Ivanov, "Dostoevsky," 414, 417, 389; "Osnovnoi mif," 510.

415. Bulgakov, "Russkaia tragediia," 7.

416. Florenskii, *Sochineniia*, 359.

417. Riabov, *Zhenshchina*, 9–10.

418. See Berdiaev, *Sud'ba Rossii*, 23 and 33–34.

419. Bulgakov, "Russkaia tragediia," 7.

420. Ivanov, "Dostoevsky," 510; and Ivanov, "Osnovnoi mif," 389.

421. Florenskii, *Sochineniia*, 359.

422. For Berdiaev's attribution to the intelligentsia of "weakness," see *Sobranie*, 3:108, 415–17, 4:153, 228, and 269; of "passivity," *Sobranie*, 3:415–16, 424; of "chaos" or "formlessness," *Sud'ba Rossii*, 106, and *Sobranie*, 3:108, 415, 4:274; of "darkness," *Sud'ba Rossii*, 106, and *Sobranie*, 3:415–16, 4:277, 281, and 283. For its identification with paganism or sectarianism, see *Sobranie*, 3:422 and 361; with nature or anti-culture, ibid., 4:277–78; and with "spontaneity" or unreflected submission to the elements, ibid., 3:415–17 and 423–24.

423. See, for example, Berdiaev, *Sobranie*, 3:427; 4:152, 273, 284; and 5:324.

424. Rozanov, *Mimoletnoe*, 112.

425. Ivanov, "Zhivoe predanie," 347.

426. See Berdiaev, *Sobranie*, 1:159–60 and 87.

427. Riabov, *Matushka-Rus'*, 22.

428. Ivanov, "Dostoevsky," 391–392; and Ivanov, "Osnovnoi mif," 511–12.

429. Bulgakov, "Russkaia tragediia," 4–5.

430. Bulgakov in *Vekhi*, 83.

431. Riabov, *Zhenshchina*, 114–15.

432. See Berdiaev, *Sud'ba Rossii*, 111; and Berdiaev, *Sobranie*, 4:34–35.

433. On the lack of chivalric tradition, see Berdiaev, *Sud'ba Rossii*, 34, and Berdiaev, *Sobranie*, 3:417, 4:36, 271; for "boundlessness," see *Sud'ba Rossii*, 4:36, and *Sobranie*, 272.

434. Rozanov, *Russkaia gosudarstvennost'*, 241.

435. Ivanov, "Zhivoe predanie," 344–45.

436. Florenskii, *Sochineniia*, 358.

437. See Gertsyk, "N. A. Berdiaev," 43; and Belyi, "Tsentral'naia stantsiia," 59.

438. Berdiaev, *Sud'ba Rossii*, 22.

439. Ibid., 29; and Berdiaev, *Sobranie*, 4:268.

440. Ibid.

441. See Berdiaev, *Sobranie*, 3:423, 4:274; and Berdiaev, *Sud'ba Rossii*, 22.

442. Berdiaev, *Sobranie*, 4:276, 36–37.

443. Berdiaev, *Sud'ba Rossii*, 12, 14; and Berdiaev, *Sobranie*, 3:361, 4:270, and 274.

444. See Berdiaev, *Sud'ba Rossii*, 14; and Berdiaev, *Sobranie*, 4:274.

445. Berdiaev, *Sud'ba Rossii*, 25.

446. Rozanov, *Sochineniia*, 323 and 327.

447. Ibid., 327; italics in original. See also ibid., 329.

448. Ibid.

449. Ibid., 328.

450. Berdiaev, *Sud'ba Rossii*, 12.

451. See, for instance, ibid., 22; and Berdiaev, *Sobranie*, 3:356, 423, 426, 4:37, 148, 270, 274.

452. Berdiaev, *Sud'ba Rossii*, 23 and 35.

453. Rozanov, *O pisatel'stve*, 261.

454. Rozanov, *Poslednie list'ia*, 340.

455. Rozanov, *Sochineniia*, 323, 327, 329.

456. Bulgakov, *Svet nevechernii*, 425.

457. Quoted in Riabov, *Zhenshchina*, 123. On Ern's interpretation of the German people as excessively masculine, see also Riabov, *Matushka-Rus'*, 135.

458. Quoted in Riabov, *Matushka-Rus'*, 135.

459. Ebert, *Symbolismus in Russland*, 137.

460. Merezhkovskii, *Antikhrist*, 26, 24.

461. Ibid., 26.

462. Shkapskaia, *Stikhi*, 81–83.

463. Berdiaev, *Sud'ba Rossii*, 25.

464. Ibid.

465. Rozanov, *Russkaia gosudarstvennost'*, 241–42.

466. Bulgakov in *Vekhi*, 83–84. It could prove fruitful to study the link between the highly similar metaphors of demonic captivity in Bulgakov's essay and Voloshin's 1918 poem "Deaf-and-Dumb Rus'" ("Rus' glukhonemaia"), parts of which were discussed earlier in this chapter.

467. Bulgakov in *Vekhi*, 83–84.

468. Rozanov, *Poslednie list'ia*, 339.

469. Ivanov, "Zhivoe predanie," 344–45.

470. Ivanov, "Dostoevsky," 413.

471. Ibid.

472. See ibid., 390; and Ivanov, "Osnovnoi mif," 510.

473. Ivanov, "Dostoevsky," 389; and Ivanov, "Osnovnoi mif," 510.

474. Ern quoted in Riabov, *Zhenshchina*, 113–14.

CHAPTER THREE

1. Billington, *The Icon and the Axe*, 532.

2. Clark, *The Soviet Novel*, 15.

3. Ibid., 20–24.

4. Ibid., 23.

5. Günther, "'Schastlivaia Moskva,'" 172.

6. Attwood, "Sex and the Cinema," 70.

7. Simpson, "Soviet Superwoman," 99.

8. Clark, *The Soviet Novel*, 114.

9. Günther, "'Stalinskie sokoly," 126–28; Günther, "Poiushchaia rodina"; and Günther, "'Schastlivaia Moskva,'" 171.

10. Tatarinov, *Znakomye pesni*, 4.

11. Clark, *The Soviet Novel*, 4.

12. Sholokhov, *Sobranie*, 294.

13. Gor'kii quoted in M. Epstein, *After the Future*, 184.

14. Brooks, *Thank You, Comrade Stalin*, xv.

15. Dunham, *In Stalin's Time*, 27.

16. Du Plessix-Gray, *Soviet Women*, 126.

17. Kimball, *Intelligentsia*. For an extensive discussion of the social role and structure of the Soviet intelligentsia, see also Churchward, *The Soviet Intelligentsia*.

18. Dunham, *In Stalin's Time*, 16.

19. Parthé, *Russian Village Prose*, 3.

20. Gillespie, "Is Village Prose Misogynistic?" 235.

21. Solzhenitsyn, *Rasskazy*, 130.

22. Blok, *Sobranie sochinenii*, 3:254 and 268.

23. Clark, *The Soviet Novel*, 7.

24. See also Malia, "What Is the Intelligentsia?" 17.

25. See Olesha, *Zavist'*, 36, 37, 67, 68, 98, 101.

26. Gachev, *Natsional'nye obrazy mira*, 290–94.

27. *Blind Beauty* was published in 1969 in *Prostor* (no. 10). *Happy Moscow* was first published in 1991 in *Novyi mir* (no. 9); *Doctor Zhivago* (in Russia) in *Novyi mir* in 1988 (no. 1–4); *Forever Flowing* in *Oktiabr'* in 1989 (no. 6); and (fragments of) *Rose of the World* in *Novyi mir* in 1989 (no. 2).

28. On samizdat distribution, see Brown, *The Last Years*, 62 (for Pasternak); Epshtein, *Vera i obraz*, 205 (for Andreev); and Garrard, "A Conflict of Visions," 57 (for Grossman).

29. Grossman did read *Doctor Zhivago* while writing *Forever Flowing*, as will be discussed.

30. Platonov, *Kotlovan*, 120. On Nastia's status as a symbol of the new Russia, see also Bullock, *The Feminine*, 94, 97, 98.

31. As Pia Berger-Bügel claims, the allegorical link between the heroine and the city of Moscow—or, by extension, Soviet Russia in general—is undisputed in research on the novel (*Andrej Platonov*, 118). It is discussed by, among others, Berger-Bügel in *Andrej Platonov*, 118–19; Kostov, *Mifopoetika*, 123; Walker, "Unmasking the Myths," 120; Walker, "Journey from St. Petersburg"; Naiman, "Introduction," xxii–xxiii; Drubek-Maier, "Rossiia—'pustota,'" 252, 256, 265; Iablokov, "Schast'ie i neschast'ie," 222; and Matveeva, "Simvolika obraza," 314–15.

32. Berger-Bügel, *Andrej Platonov*, 109.

33. Livingstone, "Danger and Deliverance," 411. On the absence of a "superiority of one given perspective, one given estimative reference point" (Van Baak) in Platonov's texts, see Van Baak, "Paradoks i psevdologika," 291–93; Hodel, *Erlebte Rede*, 1–2; and Tolstaia-Segal, "Ideologicheskie konteksty," 250–51.

34. "Unsettling" is quoted from Livingstone, "Danger and Deliverance," 409.

35. Platonov's poetics were repeatedly associated with postmodernism.

Thomas Seifrid claims that "if the style of Platonov's later works resembles anything, it is . . . the postmodernist manner of the paintings of Komar and Melamid or Dmitrii Prigov's verse, in which irony similarly protrudes from beneath a posture of feigned naïvety and an ostensibly accepting, domesticated depiction of the Soviet world" (*Andrei Platonov*, 201). See also Natasha Drubek-Maier's use of the term "deconstruction" in relation to the Sophia myth in *Happy Moscow* ("Rossiia—'pustota,'" 253).

36. This is not to say that the conceptualization of Russia as a bride is wholly absent from *The Foundation Pit*. In one scene, partying workers refer to the U.S.S.R. as an unmarried "gal" to whom they want to "pay court" (*Kotlovan*, 127).

37. For quotations in this section, I have relied on the English edition of *Happy Moscow*, translated by Robert and Elizabeth Chandler, Angela Livingstone, Nadia Burova, and Eric Naiman (Platonov, *Happy Moscow*). Page numbers refer to the original Russian text as printed in the third volume (*Schastlivaia Moskva*) of Platonov, *"Strana filosofov."*

38. Drubek-Maier, "Rossiia—'pustota,'" 251–69. On this link, see also Kostov, *Mifopoetika*, 116–17 and 126; Walker, "Journey from St. Petersburg"; Barsht, *Khudozhestvennaia antropologiia*, 45; Berger-Bügel, *Andrej Platonov*, 121; Malygina, *Andrei Platonov*, 298 and 302; Matveeva, "Simvolika obraza," 316–17; and Livers, *Constructing the Stalinist Body*, 29. On the link of the heroine in *Chevengur* with a feminine World Soul, see Geller, *Andrei Platonov*, 246–47; Drubek-Maier, "Rossiia—'pustota,'" 252; and Tolstaia-Segal, "Literaturnyi material o proze Andreia Platonova," 194.

39. See comments in *Kotlovan*, 149; Kostov, *Mifopoetika*, 116–17; Matveeva, "Simvolika obraza," 317; Borenstein, *Men Without Women*, 112–17; and Bullock, *The Feminine in the Prose of Andrey Platonov*, 63.

40. Borenstein, *Men Without Women*, 212.

41. Walker, "Journey from St. Petersburg"; Kostov, *Mifopoetika*, 116; and Barsht, *Khudozhestvennaia antropologiia*, 45.

42. For a discussion of the relation between erotic and platonic love in Platonov's work in general and in *Happy Moscow* in particular, see Kostov, *Mifopoetika*, 152–63.

43. On this, see Berger-Bügel, *Andrej Platonov*, 117; and Drubek-Maier, "Rossiia—'pustota,'" 263.

44. Seifrid, *Andrei Platonov*, 36. If this is not the place to consider the complexity of Platonov's attitude to the physical as opposed to the transcendental, then Thomas Seifrid's Platonov study and Kostov's analysis of the novel discuss this theme in detail (Seifrid, *Andrei Platonov*, 25, 36, 38, 57, 63, 107, and 144; Kostov, *Mifopoetika*, 163–80; see also Barsht, *Khudozhestvennaia antropologiia*, particularly 45 and 117).

45. Kornienko, "Na kraiu," 60.

46. As Drubek-Maier and others have pointed out, Moscow literally "falls" or descends from heaven in the scene where she jumps with a parachute from an airplane. For a close reading of this passage in the light of the Sophia concept, see Drubek-Maier, "Rossiia—'pustota,'" 253–55; and also Iablokov, "Schast'ie i neschast'ie," 224–25.

47. Drubek-Maier, "Rossiia—'pustota,'" 253 and 256–58.

48. Walker, "Journey from St. Petersburg"; Matveeva, "Simvolika obraza," 316.

49. Exceptions are an article which discusses Moscow as a "symbol of nature" (Matveeva, "Simvolika obraza," 318–20), and Berger-Bügel's mention of a "direct connection" between Moscow's body and nature (*Andrej Platonov*, 116).

50. While this link did not generate excessive scholarly attention, Clint Walker ("Journey from St. Petersburg") and A. Evdokimov ("Obrazy romana," 276–77) do discuss analogies between Moscow, on the one hand, and Pushkin's Tat'iana and Blok's female figures, on the other.

51. Naiman, "Introduction," xxii. Naiman emphasizes Moscow's function within the narrative as "a kind of Every Citizen": "repeatedly she is introduced to the reader obliquely—a woman is described in a particular situation and then—presto!—that woman turns out to be Moscow Chestnova" (ibid.).

52. Seifrid, *Andrei Platonov*, 69.

53. Borenstein, *Men Without Women*, 3. Borenstein returns to this idea on p. 237.

54. Bullock, *The Feminine*, 116, 186.

55. The link between Moscow and socialist Russia intensifies elsewhere in the novel, when the former is designated as the feminine embodiment of the Red Army (Platonov, *Schastlivaia Moskva*, 22).

56. Drubek-Maier, "Rossiia—'pustota,'" 256; Matveeva, "Simvolika obraza," 315.

57. On this context, see Walker, "Unmasking the Myths," 120 and 123; Naiman, "Introduction," xix; and Günther, "'Schastlivaia Moskva,'" 172.

58. Günther, "'Stalinskie sokoly,'" 134–35; see also Fomenko, "Kraski i zvuki," 176.

59. Kornienko, "Na kraiu," 65.

60. Hans Günther discusses the link between this cult and Stalinist Moscow myths in "Poiushchaia rodina," 58 and 49.

61. See Nekliudov, "Telo Moskvy."

62. I thank Robert Chandler for directing me toward this link between the two texts and sharing his e-mail correspondence with Olga Meerson on the topic.

63. Khlebnikov, *Sobranie sochinenii*, 2:581.

64. Ibid., 337. The typification of a feminized Moscow as "enchanted" or "enslaved" might be understood as another political appropriation of the

sleeping-beauty tale that was so popular in the early twentieth century— this time with Moscow as enchanted beauty and the early Soviet state as the sorcerer.

65. Zamiatin, "Moskva—Peterburg," 106–13. For a juxtaposition of this and Gogol's text, see Babenko, "Moskva zhenskogo roda," 26–27.

66. See Günther, "'Stalinskie sokoly,'" 125–27. On masculine-feminine dichotomies in Soviet-era representations of Petersburg/Leningrad and Moscow, see also Grois, *Utopiia i obmen,* 361.

67. For examples, see Tatarinov, *Znakomye pesni,* 17, 28–29, 73, 81. See also Cheauré, "'Vater Sowjet,'" 34; Günther, "Poiushchaia rodina," 58; and Fomenko, "Kraski i zvuki," 176–77.

68. Fomenko, "Kraski i zvuki," 176.

69. See Günther, "Poiushchaia rodina," 58; and Günther, "'Schastlivaia Moskva,'" 172.

70. Günther, "Poiushchaia rodina," 53.

71. See Tatarinov, *Znakomye pesni,* 76; see also ibid., 44–45; and Tret'iakova, *Nashi liubimye pesni,* 246–47.

72. B. Antonov, "Boets Krasnoi Armii! Ty ne dash' liubimoe na pozor i beschestie gitlerovskim soldatam," reprinted on Oleg Riabov's *Natsiia i gender* site at http://www.ivanovo.ac.ru/alumni/olegria/nation2/iiww_russia2.htm.

73. Goscilo and Lanoux, *Gender and National Identity,* 14–16.

74. Naiman, "Introduction," xxii–xxiii. Naiman links this image to the famous expression "[in]to Moscow, [in]to Moscow" from Chekhov's *Three Sisters (Tri sestry,* 1901), which allegedly gained renewed popularity among Soviet readers at that time (Naiman, "Communism and the Collective Toilet," 97).

75. Berger-Bügel, *Andrej Platonov,* 115.

76. Kostov, *Mifopoetika,* 124.

77. On this, see also Fomenko, "Kraski i zvuki," 177.

78. Berger-Bügel, *Andrej Platonov,* 133.

79. Kornienko, "Proletarskaia Moskva," 360.

80. Ibid., 367.

81. Kostov, *Mifopoetika,* 140–42.

82. See ibid., 143–44.

83. Iablokov, "Schast'ie i neschast'ie," 236.

84. Blok, *Sobranie sochinenii,* 4:137.

85. Ibid., 4:129.

86. Eric Naiman has reconstructed a link between Platonov's work and the gender philosophy of Solov'ev, Berdiaev, and Rozanov ("Historectomies," 270–71).

87. Blok, *Sobranie sochinenii,* 4:149.

88. Evdokimov, "Obrazy romana," 278.

89. Walker, "Unmasking the Myths," 121.

90. On this, see Berger-Bügel, *Andrej Platonov*, 171. In her view, Bozhko is an exception, being a "man of the people" rather than a Soviet elite member (ibid., 140).

91. Drubek-Maier, "Rossiia—'pustota,'" 265.

92. Ibid.

93. B. Pasternak, *Sobranie sochinenii*, 5:453.

94. E. Pasternak and E. Pasternak, *Zhizn' Borisa Pasternaka*, 413.

95. The symbolic Lara-Russia parallel is mentioned and discussed in, among others, Siniavskii, "Nekotorye aspekty," 363–64; Gifford, *Pasternak*, 183, Rowland and Rowland, *Pasternak's Doctor Zhivago*, 44, 51, 72, 73, 77; Billington, *The Icon and the Axe*, 557–58; Payne, *The Three Worlds*, 182–83; and Siegel, *Revolution and the Twentieth Century Novel*, 189.

96. Cornwell, *Pasternak's Novel*, 87. The novel's hero-antagonist-heroine triangle has also been discussed as a political allegory by Steussy, "The Myth," 194; and, in more associative terms, in Rowland and Rowland, *Pasternak's Doctor Zhivago*, 45–46 and 72–77; and Siegel, *Revolution*, 189.

97. B. Pasternak, *Sochineniia*, 266–67. English translation by Christopher Barnes (Pasternak, *The Voice of Prose*).

98. In autobiographical sketches and letters, Pasternak extensively discussed Blok's influence on his person and work (B. Pasternak, *Sochineniia*, 14–17; B. Pasternak, *Sobranie sochinenii*, 5:439 and 5:442–43). For scholarly analyses of Blok's impact on Pasternak, see Barnes, *Boris Pasternak*, 1:111, 142, 260, 290–91, and 2:214–15, 252–53; E. Pasternak and E. Pasternak, *Zhizn' Borisa Pasternaka*, 384; Lesnaia, "Blokovskie traditsii"; and Gifford, "Pasternak."

99. Gerschenkron quoted in Cornwell, *Pasternak's Novel*, 19.

100. Billington, *The Icon and the Axe*, 556.

101. Barnes, *Boris Pasternak*, 1:94.

102. Ibid.,111.

103. Quoted in Livingstone, *Pasternak on Art*, 206.

104. For an overview of the discussion, see Cornwell, *Pasternak's Novel*, 18–19.

105. B. Pasternak, *Sochineniia*, 25.

106. Barnes, *Boris Pasternak*, 1:111.

107. Ibid., 415.

108. Berlin, *Personal Impressions*, 179.

109. Ibid., 180–81.

110. B. Pasternak, *Sobranie sochinenii*, 5:433. Angela Livingstone observed in this context that in his novel Pasternak, "'poet for poets' and man of high culture, 'steps . . . on the throat of his own song' . . . in order to become clear and loud and noticed" (see Livingstone, "Gamlet: Dvanov: Zhivago").

111. B. Pasternak, *Sobranie sochinenii*, 5:536–37.

112. E. Pasternak, *Boris Pasternak*, 621.

113. Barnes, *Boris Pasternak*, 2:227.

114. Pasternak quoted in Barnes, *Boris Pasternak*, 2:227.

115. Throughout this section, references to *Doctor Zhivago* (vol. 3 of Pasternak, *Sobranie sochinenii*) consist only of page numbers and appear in the text. For English translations, the translated version by Hayward and Harari (Pasternak, *Doctor Zhivago*) was used. Since their translation often deviates considerably from the original, it is not always followed literally.

116. B. Pasternak, *Sobranie sochinenii*, 5:460.

117. Heldt, *Terrible Perfection*, 46–47; and Clowes, "*Doctor Zhivago*," 34–36.

118. Harris, "Pasternak's Vision," 390.

119. Clowes, "*Doctor Zhivago*," 74. See also ibid., 21–22; and Tengbergen, *Klassieken*, 408.

120. On Lara's symbolic coalescence with nature, see also Clowes, "*Doctor Zhivago*," 69; Livingstone, "Unexpected Affinities," 195.

121. See Harris, "Pasternak's Vision," 389; Billington, *The Icon and the Axe*, 557; Cornwell, *Pasternak's Novel*, 38; Kelly, "Eternal Memory," 2610; Clowes, "*Doctor Zhivago*," 32–33; Spencer, "Soaked in *The Meaning*," 83–84; and Zander, "Filosofskie temy," 37ff. and 42.

122. On Solov'ev's influence on Pasternak, see also Witt, *Creating Creation*, 114–21.

123. B. Pasternak, *Sobranie sochinenii*, 2:48; see also ibid., 3:651.

124. Rowland and Rowland, *Pasternak's Doctor Zhivago*, 51–55.

125. Quoted in De Mallac, *Boris Pasternak*, 196; my italics.

126. For a discussion of Lara as a female representation of Russia's historical fate in the revolutionary period, see also Billington, *The Icon and the Axe*, 558 and 560; Cornwell, *Pasternak's Novel*, 86–87; Siegel, *Revolution*, 189; and Rowland and Rowland, *Pasternak's Doctor Zhivago*, 51, 72–77. Lara has also been regarded as the embodiment of the October Revolution (see Steussy, "The Myth," 194), a reading which can be motivated by a comparison with Pasternak's "The Russian Revolution" ("Russkaia revoliutsia," 1918). In this early poem, Pasternak addresses the revolution as a female figure and calls it a "foreign girl" who came to Russia and "found shelter with us" (B. Pasternak, *Sobranie sochinenii*, 1:620). The poet's initial joy over the "beauty" of the feminized Revolution is followed by his disappointment in its bloody outcome. In connection with this poem, the French origin of foreign girl Lara in *Doctor Zhivago* might allude to the French Revolution. Like the poem's lyrical ego, Zhivago revels in Lara's beauty, but she is at the same time associated with (sexual) degeneration.

127. E. Pasternak, "Otrazhenie Blokovskoi poezii," 355. The link between the Beautiful Lady and Pasternak's feminized Russia is also noted in E. Pasternak

and E. Pasternak, *Zhizn' Borisa Pasternaka*, 413; De Mallac, *Boris Pasternak*, 181; Rowland and Rowland, *Pasternak's Doctor Zhivago*, 44–45; Billington, *The Icon and the Axe*, 557; and Zander, "Filosofskie temy," 45–46.

128. See E. Pasternak, *Sobranie sochinenii*, 3:703. Pavel Florenskii's philosophy of color could be mentioned here as a possible additional source. According to Florenskii, the Divine Sophia appeared specifically in the colors violet, lilac, and azure in her capacity as "the dark of pettiness that advances to meet the light" (*Sochineniia*, 414 and 417).

129. B. Pasternak, *Sochineniia*, 14–15.

130. B. Pasternak, "K kharakteristike Bloka," 452.

131. B. Pasternak, *Sochineniia*, 15.

132. De Mallac, *Boris Pasternak*, 52.

133. Pasternak quoted in Barnes, *Boris Pasternak*, 2:105.

134. See B. Pasternak, *Sobranie sochinenii*, 3:51; and Blok, *Sobranie sochinenii*, 2:185–86.

135. See Blok, *Sobranie sochinenii*, 2:140; and B. Pasternak, *Sobranie sochinenii*, 3:47 and 97.

136. Rowland and Rowland, *Pasternak's Doctor Zhivago*, 49–51.

137. Clowes, "*Doctor Zhivago*," 70–74.

138. Cornwell asserts that a "number of commentators" interpreted Zhivago as a "superfluous" hero (Cornwell, *Pasternak's Novel*, 16). See, for some examples, Rühle quoted in ibid., 16; Billington, *The Icon and the Axe*, 557; Tengbergen, *Klassieken*, 409; and E. Pasternak and E. Pasternak, *Zhizn' Borisa Pasternaka*, 414.

139. Pasternak's very characterization of the novel in a letter as a "novel in prose" (*Sobranie sochinenii*, 5:452) calls forth *Eugene Onegin's* subtitle, "a novel in verse."

140. Kelly, "Eternal Memory," 2610. The juxtaposition of Hamlet and Zhivago has by now become commonplace in research on the novel; see, among others, Glazov-Corrigan, "A Reappraisal"; Cornwell, *Pasternak's Novel*, 42; Clowes, "*Doctor Zhivago*," 16–17; and Livingstone, "Gamlet: Dvanov: Zhivago."

141. Here again, one can discern a parallel between the fate of Lara and Russia: in the passage where Russia is called a marriageable girl, her admirers fail to regain her "lost love" by hard work and indulge merely in "speeches and good wishes"; Zhivago similarly revels in "speeches" and poetic creation instead of trying to keep his "lost" love (Pasternak, *Sobranie sochinenii*, 3:446).

142. Gifford, *Pasternak*, 183.

143. See B. Pasternak, *Sobranie sochinenii*, 3:282–83. See also Gifford, *Pasternak*, 191.

144. Clowes, "*Doctor Zhivago*," 31.

145. Cornwell, *Pasternak's Novel*, 86. Zhivago is also discussed as a representative of the pre-revolutionary intelligentsia and its vestiges in Soviet society

in, among others, Gimpelevich-Schwartzmann, *Boris Pasternak*, 42–43; Siegel, *Revolution*, 189; Lesnaia, "Blokovskie traditsii," 110; De Mallac, *Boris Pasternak*, 196; and Clowes, "*Doctor Zhivago*," 16–17.

146. Billington, *The Icon and the Axe*, 557.

147. Clowes, "*Doctor Zhivago*," 34.

148. De Mallac, *Boris Pasternak*, 17.

149. On Pasternak and Esenin, Ivanov, and Bal'mont, see B. Pasternak, *Sochineniia*, 17; Barnes, *Boris Pasternak*, 1:258 and 329; and De Mallac, *Boris Pasternak*, 51 and 75. On his contact with Shklovskii and Belyi, see De Mallac, *Boris Pasternak*, 105; and B. Pasternak, *Sochineniia*, 24.

150. De Mallac, *Boris Pasternak*, 104.

151. Ibid., 104–5.

152. See Kelly, "Eternal Memory," 2610; Fleishman, *Boris Pasternak*, 259; and De Mallac, *Boris Pasternak*, 306. Pasternak quoted in Carlisle, *Voices in the Snow*, 196.

153. B. Pasternak, *Sobranie sochinenii*, 2:68–69. On this, see also Fleishman, *Boris Pasternak*, 260.

154. See Wilson, "Doctor Life," 442 and 448–51; Lamont, "Yuri Zhivago's 'Fairy Tale,'" 517–21; B. Pasternak, *Sobranie sochinenii*, 3:699; Senderovich, *Georgii Pobedonosets*, 255–94; Gasparov, "Vremennyi kontrapunkt," 246; Gifford, *Pasternak*, 193; and E. Pasternak and E. Pasternak, *Zhizn' Borisa Pasternaka*, 431.

155. See B. Pasternak, *Sobranie sochinenii*, 3:699.

156. Gimpelevich-Schwartzmann, *Boris Pasternak*, 60. In this respect, the novel offers grounds for comparison with Platonov's feminized Moscow.

157. Senderovich, *Georgii Pobedonosets*, 264.

158. For a psychoanalytical perspective on this trend, see Popov, "The Russian Oedipus."

159. Rowland and Rowland, *Pasternak's Doctor Zhivago*, 67.

160. Cornwell, *Pasternak's Novel*, 73. Lara and Zhivago, in the latter's death scene, are read as symbolic equivalents of Andromeda and Perseus by Boris Gasparov ("Vremennoi kontrapunkt," 246).

161. Zander also views Lara as a sleeping beauty enchanted by Komarovskii ("Filosofskie temy," 47).

162. Siegel, *Revolution*, 189.

163. E. Pasternak and E. Pasternak, *Zhizn' Borisa Pasternaka*, 476–77.

164. Carlisle, *Voices in the Snow*, 202.

165. Ibid., 208.

166. B. Pasternak, *Sobranie sochinenii*, 4:873.

167. Ibid., 4:595.

168. Carlisle, *Voices in the Snow*, 205.

169. B. Pasternak, *Sobranie sochinenii*, 4:541.

170. Ibid., 4:588.

171. E. Pasternak and E. Pasternak, *Zhizn' Borisa Pasternaka*, 477.

172. B. Pasternak, *Sobranie sochinenii*, 4:547.

173. E. Pasternak and E. Pasternak, *Zhizn' Borisa Pasternaka*, 477. Karen Evans-Romaine also links the play to Tchaikovsky's ballets *Sleeping Beauty* and *Iolanta*—a connection which confirms that besides Belyi's "sleeping beauty Russia," the traditional sleeping-beauty plot functions as a key "subtext" for the play ("Pasternak and Tchaikovsky," 107ff.).

174. Billington, *The Icon and the Axe*, 564.

175. Epshtein, *Vera i obraz*, 205.

176. M. Epstein, "Daniil Andreev," 329.

177. Epshtein, *Vera i obraz*, 206.

178. Ibid., 205–6.

179. Ibid., 326.

180. Ibid., 207.

181. Andreev, *Roza mira*, 188.

182. See M. Epstein, "Daniil Andreev," 337–38.

183. Andreev, *Roza mira*, 135, 329.

184. Ibid., 322–29, 473–505.

185. Andreev, *Sobranie sochinenii*, 1:270.

186. M. Epstein, "Daniil Andreev," 339.

187. Andreev, *Roza mira*, 409.

188. For a more elaborate summary of Andreev's views on femininity, see M. Epstein's "Daniil Andreev," 332–46.

189. Ellis, *Vasilii Grossman*, 1.

190. Garrard, "A Conflict of Visions," 57–58.

191. See, for instance, Ellis, *Vasilii Grossman*, 205–11; Lanin, *Idei "otkrytogo obshchestva,"* 9; Garrard, "A Conflict of Visions," 57–58; and Garrard, "The Original Manuscript," 285. One critic goes so far as to state that the whole work is "a historico-sociological analysis rather than a novel" (Pospelovskii quoted in Tökés, *Dissent in the USSR*, 346).

192. Grossman, *Vse techet . . .* , 173.

193. Ibid., 173–75.

194. Ibid., 176.

195. Ibid.

196. Ibid.

197. Ibid.

198. Ibid., 173–79.

199. See Blok, *Sobranie sochinenii*, 3:328; and Grossman, *Vse techet . . .* , 176.

200. Grossman, *Vse techet . . .* , 173.

201. Ibid., 105.

202. See, for instance, Markish, "Liubil li Rossiiu Vasilii Grossman?" 12.

203. Lipkin, "'Istinnaia sila—Dobrota,'" 270–71.

204. Baldaev, *Russian Criminal Tattoo Encyclopaedia*, 2:175.

205. Ibid.

206. Ibid., 2:186 and 3:102, 250.

207. Ibid., 2:226 and 3:188.

208. Ibid., 2:226.

209. Ibid., 2:225. For the image of Russia as female sex object, see also 2:175 and 279.

CHAPTER FOUR

1. Sorokin, *Sbornik rasskazov*, 121.

2. According to Boris Groys (*The Total Art of Stalinism*) and Mikhail Epstein ("The Origins and Meaning"), for instance, Russian postmodernism can be traced back as far as socialist realism.

3. In its treatment of (Russian) postmodernism, this study has benefited from analyses by Hans Bertens and Douwe Fokkema in *International Postmodernism;* Mark Lipovetsky's approach, rooted in chaos theory and Bakhtinian polyphony (*Russian Postmodernist Fiction*); Irina Skoropanova's overview in *Russkaia postmodernistskaia literatura;* Mikhail Epstein's discussions of Moscow conceptualism and Sots Art (*After the Future,* "The Origins and Meaning," and—together with Alexander Genis and Slobodanka Vladiv-Glover [eds.]—*Russian Postmodernism*); and from panoramic overviews by Sergei Kuznetsov ("Postmodernism in Russia") and Sven Spieker (*Figures of Memory*).

4. Among other analyses, a helpful exploration of Russian versus non-Russian notions of postmodernism is found in Birgit Menzel's *Bürgerkrieg*, 328–35.

5. See, for example, Skoropanova, *Russkaia postmodernistskaia literatura,* 71.

6. Ibid., 356.

7. On this, see also—apart from Skoropanova—Lipovetsky, who claims that Russian postmodernism is "first and foremost, a question of Russian culture's identity" (*Russian Postmodernist Fiction,* 233); and Brown, *The Last Years,* 169.

8. Erlich, *Modernism and Revolution,* 9.

9. Quoted in Makeeva, "Geroi V. Pelevina."

10. See Lipovetsky, *Russian Postmodernist Fiction,* 7; and Laird, *Voices of Russian Literature,* xxiv.

11. Jager, *Tussen Rusland en Europa,* 64.

12. Laird, *Voices of Russian Literature,* xxiv.

13. The novella's manuscript was published in Jerusalem in 1973, followed by a French publication in 1977. In 1988–89 the text appeared in the journal *Trezvost' i kultura.*

14. *Marina's Thirtieth Love* appeared in France in 1987 (Paris), in Switzerland in 1991 (Zürich), and in Russia in 1995. Erofeev's *Russian Beauty* appeared in Russia in 1990.

15. Laird, *Voices of Russian Literature*, xxii.

16. Without explicitly distinguishing between the status of interviews, essayistic texts, and literary texts, in my analysis of these varying genres I rely on Pierre Bourdieu's theory of *literary position-taking* (see Bourdieu, *The Field of Cultural Production*, 30).

17. Lipovetsky, *Russian Postmodernist Fiction*, 67.

18. See in this respect, among others, Tolstaia quoted in Shmel'kova, *Poslednie dni Venedikta Erofeeva*, 258; Lipovetsky, *Russian Postmodernist Fiction*, 66–67; and Terras, *Handbook of Russian Literature*, 130. On Erofeev's indebtedness to Gogol as a writer, see Shmel'kova, *Poslednie dni*, 28.

19. Altshuller quoted in Lipovetsky, *Russian Postmodernist Fiction*, 67.

20. Verkhovtseva-Drubek, "'Moskva-Petushki,'" 91.

21. The quotation stems from the programmatic Solov'evian-muse poem "Three Meetings" ("Tri svidaniia," 1898).

22. Solov'ev, *Stikhotvoreniia*, 177–78.

23. Throughout this chapter, references to Erofeev's novella—from the 2000 Vagrius *Moskva-Petushki* edition—appear in the text and contain only page numbers.

24. See Vlasov, "Bessmertnaia poema," 256, 268, 281, and 452.

25. Venedikt Erofeev, "Sasha Chernyi i drugie," 116.

26. Vlasov, "Bessmertnaia poema," 487.

27. Ibid., 243.

28. Apocalypse 21:2, 17:1. Erofeev chose the archaic term for "whore" (*bludnitsa*) used in the Russian Bible translation instead of more current Russian designations for the term.

29. Verkhovtseva-Drubek, "'Moskva-Petushki,'" 91–92.

30. Vlasov, "Bessmertnaia poema," 281.

31. Verkhovtseva-Drubek, "'Moskva-Petushki,'" 92.

32. Zorin, "Opoznavatel'nyi znak," 121.

33. Ibid.

34. On this, see also Vlasov, "Bessmertnaia poema," 346–52.

35. Zorin, "Opoznavatel'nyi znak," 122.

36. In this respect, see Vlasov, "Bessmertnaia poema," 518.

37. Verkhovtseva-Drubek, "'Moskva-Petushki,'" 91.

38. Vlasov, "Bessmertnaia poema," 140.

39. Ibid., 253.

40. Ibid., 299–302.

41. Shmel'kova, *Poslednie dni*, 28.

42. Vlasov, "Bessmertnaia poema," 544.

43. Ibid., 557.

44. Zorin, "Opoznavatel'nyi znak," 122.

45. Pawlikowski quoted in Robert Porter, *Russia's Alternative Prose*, 74.

46. Sedakova, "Monolog o Venedikte Erofeeve," 101; italics in original.

47. Van Baak, "Where Did Venička Live?" 44–45.

48. Transcripts of the conversations are available upon request from contact@ ellenrutten.nl.

49. Lipovetsky, *Russian Postmodern Fiction*, 312.

50. For an anti-postmodern statement from his hand, see Sorokin, "Mea Culpa?"

51. Dagmar Burkhart, "Vorwort," 5.

52. Lipovetsky, *Russian Postmodernist Fiction*, 165.

53. Tat'iana Rasskazova and David Gillespie also point to the similarities between the two novels; see Rasskazova's "Tekst kak narkotik" in Sorokin, *Sbornik rasskazov*, 124; and Gillespie, "Sex and Sorokin," 165.

54. Personal conversation.

55. Gillespie, "Sex and Sorokin," 165.

56. Throughout this chapter, references to Erofeev's *Russian Beauty*—in the ZebraE *Russkaia krasavitsa* edition—appear in the text and contain only page numbers. Andrew Reynold's translation (Erofeev, *Russian Beauty*) has been used for the translations, albeit not always literally.

57. See Blok, *Sobranie sochinenii*, 3:254.

58. The poem in question is "Gamaiun, Prophetic Bird" ("Gamaiun, ptitsa veshchaia," 1899); see Blok, *Sobranie sochinenii*, 1:19.

59. See Blok, *Sobranie sochinenii*, 3:281.

60. Irina's idea of what the scene should look like—clover strewn with white bones, skulls, arrows, lances, and carrion crows against a setting of "peaceful" "autumn gold"—alludes to Viktor Vasnetsov's painting *Knight at the Crossroads* (*Vitiaz' na rasput'e*, 1878). The same Vasnetsov inspired Blok to write the Gamaiun poem to which Irina refers, with his canvas *Gamaiun, Prophetic Bird* (*Gamaiun, ptitsa veshchaia*, 1895).

61. For a discussion of Irina as the embodiment of (the) Russia(n people) see, among others, Dark, "Chernovoe pis'mo," 184; Goscilo, "The Gendered Trinity," 78; Porter, *Russia's Alternative Prose*, 151; and Dalton-Brown, "Ludic Nonchalance," 224.

62. Personal conversation.

63. Throughout this chapter, references to texts from Sorokin's collected works (*Sobranie sochinenii*) will appear in the text and contain only volume and page numbers.

64. Brougher, "Demythologising Socialist Realism," 100 and 112.

65. Platonov, *Schastlivaia Moskva*, 52–53.

66. Sorokin, "Tekst kak narkotik," 124–25.

67. Ibid.

68. Laird, *Voices of Russian Literature*, 161.

69. Prime examples are Aleksandrov's *Volga-Volga* (1934), which Sorokin

considers a "work of genius" (Laird, *Voices of Russian Literature*, 161); and Pyr'ev's *The Pig-Herd and the Shepherd* (*Svinarka i pastukh*, 1941). I thank Professor Igor Smirnov for guiding me to *The Pig-Herd* as a source for Sorokin's take on the metaphor.

70. Personal conversations with Arie van der Ent. The "Moscow variant" was preserved in Dutch and German translations of the novel as *Een Schoonheid uit Moskou* (Amsterdam: Arena, 1990) and *Die Moskauer Schönheit* (Frankfurt am Main: Fischer, 1993), respectively.

71. Belyi, *Simvolizm*, 329.

72. Dark, "Chernovoe pis'mo," 178.

73. Viktor Erofeev, *Muzhchiny*, 96 and 37.

74. Viktor Erofeev, *Entsiklopediia russkoi dushi*, 35 and 67–69.

75. Viktor Erofeev, *Khoroshii Stalin*, 140.

76. Personal conversation.

77. Sorokin, *Moskva*, 9ff.

78. Ibid., 9.

79. Ibid., 391.

80. Degot', "Kinostsenarii Vladimira Sorokina," 224. Conversely, one could argue that the symbolical axis around which the film revolves is not the vagina, but the anus—as Helena Goscilo has done in a more recent analysis of the film (Goscilo, "Re-Conceptualizing Moscow").

81. Sorokin, *Moskva*, 388.

82. Ibid., 431.

83. Leva's and Masha's first talk concerns her status as another man's bride-to-be (ibid., 387–88). One of the last scenes shows Masha in bridal costume at her wedding. At the festive ballet for this occasion, her groom is shot. The scene is followed directly by her and her sister's marriage with Leva.

84. Given its marked femininity, I adopt the feminine grammatical gender for "the Earth" in my translation. In Russian, the feminine adjective and noun are motivated partly by the feminine gender of the word "earth" (*zemlia*).

85. For both Dostoevsky and the pagan view of the earth, see chapter 1.

86. See Blok, *Sobranie sochinenii*, 3:249.

87. See ibid., 3:254, 269, and 281.

88. Ibid., 3:247.

89. Ibid., 3:249–53.

90. Kasper, "Das Glöckchen und die Axt," 107.

91. Sorokin, *Sakharnyi Kreml'*, 44–45.

92. Bitov, "Vol'naia ptitsa," 472. For an extensive analysis of this essay's rendition of urban gender metaphors, see Babenko, "Moskva zhenskogo roda," 28–29.

93. Kormil'tsev, "Moskva: Opyt urbanisticheskogo analiza."

94. Litichevskii, "Pesnia o Moskve."

95. Viacheslav Kuritsyn on Nemirov, as quoted in Guseinov, "Five Poets," 16.

96. Nemirov, *Nekotorye stikhotvoreniia,* 84. The translation used is Misha Gabovich's.

97. Mukhina, *Iu,* 1:7.

98. Ibid., 1:7 and 2:3; capitals in original.

99. Apart from the examples mentioned in chapter 3, one could think of the lyrics to "Aleksandra," the title song of the 1979 film hit *Moscow Does Not Believe in Tears (Moskva slezam ne verit).* These portray Moscow as a female figure whose "maternal love" is "stronger than any other kind of love," who "did not believe in tears, but in love," who "did not hide her worries," and who needs to be "looked in the face" (Sukhareva and Vizbor, "Aleksandra," 21).

100. Prigov, *Napisannoe s 1990 po 1994,* 38.

101. In addition, the poet speculates on Moscow's "maidenly walk" (Prigov, *Sovetskie teksty,* 183, 186). The fragments evoke both the Russia that "will not marry" in drafts of Blok's "Russia" and the "mother, sister and wife" Russia in his "People and the Intelligentsia" (*Sobranie sochinenii,* 3:591 and 5:321).

102. Peppershtein, *Dieta starika,* 181.

103. Ibid., 191.

104. Slobin, "Revolution Must Come First," 248–50.

105. Prigov, *Napisannoe s 1990 po 1994,* 32, 34, and 22.

106. Prigov, *Piat'desiat' kapelek krovi,* 97.

107. Berdiaev, *Sobranie,* 3:108–9.

108. Lipovetsky, *Russian Postmodernist Fiction,* 303.

109. Prigov, "Narod i vlast'."

110. Cinefantom, *Pamiati Dmitriia Aleksandrovicha Prigova.* A YouTube video of the opera is available at http://ru.youtube.com/watch?v=If_PhfzjBak.

111. Solov'ev, *"Umom Rossiiu ne ponyat' . . . ,"* 18–19 and 105.

112. Beletskii, "Nostal'giia" (unpublished).

113. Chekhov, *Polnoe sobranie,* 9:191.

114. Petrova, *Vid na zhitel'stvo,* 85.

115. Ibid., 5–6.

116. Vitkovskii, *Pavel II.*

117. Epshtein, *Bog detalei,* 215.

118. Ibid., 214–15.

119. Tolstaia, "Russkii chelovek na randevu," 360–61.

120. Andrei Makin, *Frantsuzskoe zaveshchanie,* trans. Iu. Iakhnina and N. Shakhovskaia, in *Inostrannaia literatura,* no. 12 (1996).

121. Tolstaia, *Den',* 360.

122. Ibid., 362. See Blok, *Sobranie sochinenii,* 3:360.

123. On this, see Obermayr, "Russland: Konzept: Frau," 149.

124. Here one can think of their *Stalin and the Muses* (1981–82), *Lenin*

Lived, Lenin Lives, Lenin Will Live! (1982), and *The Origins of Socialist Realism* (1982–83).

125. Ratcliff, "Prologue," 137.

126. Ibid.

127. Personal conversation with the artist, May 2007.

128. For online reproductions and an account of the December 2008 scandal, see Openspace.ru, "Mozhet li ul'trapravyi pochvennik"; and Degot', "Mog li ul'trapravyi natsionalist."

129. Attwood, "Sex and the Cinema," 70.

130. Ibid., 69.

131. Goscilo, "The Gendered Trinity," 78–90.

132. Ibid. For the poem in question—"Russia Lives in Prison for Thirty Years . . ." ("Rossiia tridtsat' let zhivet v tiur'me . . . ," 1948–50)—see Ivanov, *Sobranie stikhotvorenii,* 269–70.

133. Goscilo, "The Gendered Trinity," 80.

134. For Sorokin, see *Sobranie sochinenii,* 2:22, 83, 84, 94, 130–31, 142–43; for Viktor Erofeev, *Russkaia krasavitsa,* 18, 73–74, 94, 154, 175, 407–12.

135. See, for Sorokin, *Sobranie sochinenii,* 2:82; for Viktor Erofeev, *Russkaia krasavitsa,* 24, 28, 60, 283, 295, 483.

136. Rylkova, *The Archeology of Anxiety,* 191.

137. Personal conversation.

138. Ibid. Sorokin would litter "The Eros of Moscow" with the same "heavenly" to "earthly" opposition in a manifestly Moscow-related context: quoting Prigov, the essay's narrator claims that "everyone has his Heavenly and his Earthly Moscow" (Sorokin, *Moskva,* 16).

139. Personal conversation. Robert Porter points to Irina's repeated typification as a "genius of pure beauty" (*genii chistoi krasoty*), a phrase borrowed from Pushkin's "To °°°" poem ("K °°°," 1825). Pushkin, thus says Porter, related to his poem's subject, Anna Kern, with the same ambiguity that typifies Irina's portrait—he referred to her in a letter to his brother as a "whore of Babylon" (Porter, *Russia's Alternative Prose,* 156).

140. Personal conversation.

141. Nikolai Chernyshevskii, *Shto delat'?* 321.

142. Rylkova, *The Archeology of Anxiety,* 190.

143. See, among other pages, Sorokin, *Sobranie sochinenii,* 2:11–14, 31, 37–38, 43–48, 51–52, 65–66, 73–76, 89–90, 101–18, 169–73.

144. Brougher, "Demythologising Socialist Realism," 98–99.

145. Viktor Erofeev, *Entsiklopediia russkoi dushi,* 208 (see also 141), and 70.

146. Sorokin and Kulik, *V glub' Rossii.*

147. Sorokin, *Trilogiia,* 622, 626. For additional quotations, see the entire scene, 622–26.

148. Sorokin, "Sakharnyi Kreml'."

149. Sorokin, *Moskva,* 9, 15.

150. Ibid., 9, 10. Moscow is similarly turned into a sexually tangible feminine body in Il'ia Kormil'tsev's Moscow sketch, which ranges from a description of the Boulevard Ring as its labia to the Kremlin as its clitoris ("Moskva"). The metaphor of a feminine city is today sexualized outside of the Russian context too. The contemporary Indian poet Makarand Paranjape refers to the city of Bhopal as a woman who "opens her soft things" to the poet, and whom he "enter[s] as lover-tourist" (here quoted in Nekliudov, "Telo Moskvy," 371). A 1991 marketing campaign to promote Hamburg included a poster of a seated woman between whose opened legs a tunnel was depicted, with the comment "Welcome to Hamburg!" (ibid.).

151. See the Platonov section in chapter 3. On this link, see also Degot', "Kinostsenarii Vladimira Sorokina," 223; and Elena Stishova, "Zvuk lopnuvshei struny." In fact, Sorokin's screenplay for *Moscow* consciously alludes to *Three Sisters:* not only do the names of its three heroines—Irina, Masha, and Ol'ga—repeat those of Chekhov's sisters, but the film's very setting and the composition of its dialogues as an exchange of empty cliché phrases unmistakably call to mind Chekhov's plays.

152. Personal conversation.

153. Prigov, *Napisannoe s 1990 po 1994,* 25.

154. Attwood, "Sex and the Cinema," 64–65.

155. Obermayr, "Russland: Konzept: Frau," 149.

156. Reproduction in Ratcliff, *Komar and Melamid,* 139.

157. Personal conversations with both.

158. Davydov quoted in Shevelev, "All of This Looks Like a Parable . . . ."

159. Zazykin, "Zemlia kak zhenskoe nachalo," 70.

160. Sorokin, "Tekst kak narkotik," 121 and 125. The writer-poets Evgenii Evtushenko and Chingiz Aitmatov are representatives of the generation of "men of the 1960s" which postmodern Russian authors criticize.

161. Erofeev, "Pominki po sovetskoi literature," 433.

162. Vladiv-Glover, "Sorokin's Post-Avant-Garde Prose," 30.

163. Sorokin quoted in Laird, *Voices of Russian Literature,* 155.

164. Sorokin quoted in Roll, *Postmodernisty o postkul'ture,* 123.

165. Genis, "Beseda deviataia," 224.

166. Porter, *Russia's Alternative Prose,* 149.

167. Sokolov, "Russkii bog," 186. On the one hand, this makes both authors worthy heirs of de Sade and his explicit sex scenes, intended to undermine society's moral rigor. Erofeev is a known admirer of de Sade, as his scholarly work shows (Erofeev, "Metamorfoza"). On the other hand, the socially critical element of de Sade's prose is alien to the poetics of both, and Sorokin distinctly distances himself from him in an interview (Sorokin, "Nasilie nad chelovekom").

168. From a feminist perspective, Helena Goscilo describes a similar move from traditional idealizing perceptions of femininity toward the (non-idealizing) physical sphere in contemporary women's prose: "women's earlier corporeal self was generalized and sanitized into the classical body . . . and permitted only two forms of effluvia: picturesque tears of sorrow . . . and maternal milk. . . . The fluids now entering and exiting women's orifices, by contrast, are blood, semen, mucus, bile, urine, and alcohol" (*Dehexing Sex,* 89).

169. Kuritsyn, "TELO TEKSTA," 63.

170. Dark, "V.V.E.," 258.

171. Viktor Erofeev, "Russkie tsvety zla," 14.

172. Goscilo, *Dehexing Sex,* 43.

173. R. Marsh, *Women and Russian Culture,* 23.

174. Apart from those mentioned, the names in this list refer to the following famous dissidents: physicist Iurii Orlov; Orthodox priest Father Gleb Iakunin; Sakharov's English interpreter and spokesman for the Soviet Jewish movement, Natan Shcharanskii; poet and translator Iulii Daniel'; writers Andrei Sin'iavskii, Georgii Vladimov, and Lev Kopelev; and biologist Zhores Medvedev (Roi Medvedev's brother).

175. Rylkova, *The Archeology of Anxiety,* 189.

176. Ibid..

177. See Bergman, "Soviet Dissidents," 16ff.

178. Ibid., 23.

179. Zamost'ianov, "Pristrastie k anekdotam," 227.

180. In the summer of 2002, Moving Together (Idushchie Vmeste)—a youth group that claims to be affiliated with President Putin—protested against allegedly amoral contemporary novels, with Sorokin's *The Blue Lard* as a key target, by tearing them up in public. In March 2005, the Moving Together group again protested against Sorokin's work at the premiere of the opera *Rosenthal's Children (Deti Rozentalia),* for which he wrote the libretto. Again, copies of *The Blue Lard* were publicly ripped up in the process.

181. This reproach not only evokes the "which-language-to-speak" question which was parodied by Tolstoy and other nineteenth-century authors; it also links Marina to Dostoevsky's Grushen'ka, who is offended "as if touched on a very painful spot" by a stranger's Polish speech: "Speak Russian, speak Russian . . . !" she screamed. . . . She turned red from anger" (Dostoevsky, *Polnoe sobranie,* 14:387–88).

182. Dark, "Chernovoe pis'mo," 178.

183. See also Sorokin, *Sobranie sochinenii,* 2:365–66, 378, 382, 413–14, 421, and 396–403.

184. These include Lancelot, Byron's Childe Harold, Shakespeare's Hamlet, Dante, and Raphael; see Sorokin, *Sobranie sochinenii,* 2:280, 281, 284, 305, 308, 318, 329, 331–32, 334, 378, 382, 408.

185. Sorokin and Kulik, *V glub' Rossii* (unnumbered). In an interview, Kulik represents the project in stereotypical rural-idyll terms (Bavil'skii, "Dialogi")—terms that, as I have written elsewhere, could have come straight from the mouth of a Turgenevian hero (Rutten, "Where Postmodern Provocation Meets Social Strategy," 166).

186. Sorokin, *Moskva*, 13.

187. Ibid., 11–12, 15.

188. Viktor Erofeev, *Entsiklopediia russkoi dushi*, 179, 193.

189. Ibid., 160.

190. Ibid., 52.

191. Ibid., 12, 166, 237.

192. Ibid., 42.

193. Ibid., 165.

194. Prigov, *Napisannoe s 1990 po 1994*, 22; Peppershtein, *Dieta starika*, 181.

195. Prigov quoted on Cinefantom.

196. See, for instance, http://www.ozon.ru/context/video_detail/id/1712844/.

197. Quotation from Timasheva, "'Kinotavr.'"

198. In stylized photographs, their milieu is depicted as that of the well-to-do in turn-of-the-century Russia. Classical typifications of the weak *intelligent*-hero resonate when Andrei is compared to "a little child" and, because of his impatience, to Napoléon, and when he is said to cry over a tender letter from his grandmother (Mukhina, *Iu*, 1:2). Dmitrii enters the novel as the hero who returned to Moscow from abroad; he feels a populist-like "physical love" for and wish to "kiss" all the people he sees on the street; he is called a "boy" and claims defensively that he is not "a little one"; and he loves philosophical conversations (ibid., 1:2, 3 and 7). The repeated claim that Dmitrii "looks like a hero" hints at the same combination of predestination for a messianic role—a "hero"—and the inability to live up to it—he merely "looks" like one—that epitomizes the traditional nineteenth-century hero (ibid., 1:2 and 2:7).

199. Sorokin, *Moskva*, 15.

200. See Sorokin, *Sobranie sochinenii*, 1:166; and Sorokin and Kulik, *V glub' Rossii* (unnumbered).

201. Limonov quoted in Rancour-Laferriere, *Russian Nationalism*, 204–5.

202. Personal conversation.

203. Ibid.

204. Ibid.

205. Sorokin, "Tekst kak narkotik," 124.

206. See also Rylkova, *The Archeology of Anxiety*, 189 and 194.

207. Ibid., 190.

208. Significantly, Erofeev's Irina likewise refers to the male force which

she confronts on Kulikovo field with a capitalized "HE" (*Russkaia krasavitsa*, 344–45).

209. His status as such is made explicit when Marina muses on how "HE" looked "when writing Denisych" (Sorokin, *Sobranie sochinenii*, 155), in reference to Solzhenitsyn's novella *A Day in the Life of Ivan Denisovich* (*Odin den' Ivana Denisovicha*, 1962). In our conversation Sorokin emphasized that Sergei Nikolaevich is, in fact, Solzhenitsyn.

210. A similarly negative role is attributed to Solzhenitsyn in *Russian Beauty*: here he is staged as a "well-known informer" within his labor camp, and as an "old blockhead" whose negative reports on Russia are embarrassing (Viktor Erofeev, *Russkaia krasavitsa*, 22, 33).

211. BBC News, "Dissident Writer."

212. Personal conversation.

213. Ibid.

214. Brougher, "Demythologising Socialist Realism," 104, 110–11.

215. Personal conversation.

216. Belyi, *Simvolizm*, 333.

217. I am referring to *Bro's Way* (*Put' Bro*, 2004), in Sorokin, *Trilogiia*, 33.

218. Personal conversation.

219. Bergman, "Soviet Dissidents on the Russian Intelligentsia," 29–30.

220. Solzhenitsyn, "Sakharov i kritika," 221.

221. Sorokin, "Tekst kak narkotik," 124–25.

222. Belyi, *Simvolizm*, 328.

223. Blok, *Sobranie sochinenii*, 3:254.

224. Personal conversation.

225. See *Russkaia krasavitsa*, 296; and Daniil Andreev, *Roza mira*, 134.

226. Sorokin, "Rossiia ostaetsia liubovnitsei."

227. Viktor Erofeev, *Entsiklopediia russkoi dushi*, 67–69.

228. Prigov, *Sovetskie teksty*, 186.

229. Ibid., 182.

230. Limonov quoted in Rancour-Laferriere, *Russian Nationalism*, 205.

231. Rylkova, *The Archeology of Anxiety*, 180.

232. On this, see Lotman, "Siuzhetnoe prostranstvo," 98.

233. Personal conversation.

234. See, for example, the reference to the (*-itel'*) rhymes in Onegin's description in Brouwer, "The Bridegroom," 53.

235. Here one can think of Zhukovskii's *Svetlana* ballad (1812), Pushkin's poem "The Bridegroom" ("Zhenikh," 1825), and Lermontov's "Guest" ("Gost' [Klarisu iunosha liubil . . .]," 1832).

236. This links him from the start with Pasternak's Komarovskii, whose abduction of Lara is preceded by his similar introduction as a powerful figure "in a

fur coat to the ground," who enters from the winter frost into the country house where Lara and Zhivago are staying (Pasternak, *Sobranie sochinenii,* 3:440).

237. Sorokin quoted in Laird, *Voices of Russian Literature,* 161.

238. Sorokin, "Tekst kak narkotik," 121.

239. Ibid.

240. Erofeev quoted in Lipovetsky, *Russian Postmodernist Fiction,* 165.

241. Personal conversation.

242. Sorokin, "Tekst kak narkotik," 124.

243. Personal conversation.

244. Ibid.

245. Khrustaleva, "New Literature," 203.

246. Personal conversation.

247. Sorokin and Wituchnowskaja, "Nichts leichter," 68.

248. Personal conversation.

249. Ibid.

250. Degot', "Kinostsenarii Vladimira Sorokina," 225.

251. Laird, *Voices of Russian Literature,* 160.

252. Ibid., 153; Sorokin and Wituchnowskaja, "Nichts leichter," 67.

253. Laird, *Voices of Russian Literature,* 153; personal conversation.

254. Sorokin, "Rossiia ostaetsia liubovnitsei."

255. Brown, *The Last Years,* 169.

256. Viktor Erofeev, "Russkie tsvety zla," 6.

257. Viktor Erofeev, "Vremia rozhat'," 6.

258. Erofeev quoted in Meier, "Obvenchavshiisia so svobodoi," 220.

259. See, for instance, Bavil'skii, "Znaki prepinaniia"; Bondarenko, "Roman V. Sorokina"; and Iur'ev, "Tri postmodernizma."

260. Laird, *Voices of Russian Literature,* 148.

261. Lipovetskii, "Mir kak tekst," 65.

262. Menzel, *Bürgerkrieg,* 343.

263. Personal conversation.

264. Hutcheon, *Irony's Edge,* 15.

265. Lipovetsky, *Russian Postmodernist Fiction,* 296.

266. Keith Gessen, "Subversive Activities," 68.

267. See ibid., 68; Lipovetsky, *Russian Postmodernist Fiction,* 296; or Ishimbaeva, "'Chapaev i Pustota,'" 314. To Sally Dalton-Brown, Pelevin's work is "the most essentially 'postmodern' of contemporary Russian prose" (Dalton-Brown, "Ludic Nonchalance," 216).

268. Lipovetsky, *Russian Postmodernist Fiction,* 296.

269. Pelevin, "Vdali ot kompleksnykh idei zhivesh."

270. Pelevin, "Lev Kropyv'ianskii."

271. Laird, *Voices of Russian Literature,* 184.

272. Ibid., 184.

273. See Kornev, "Stolknovenie pustot," 248; Gessen, "Subversive Activities," 68; Lipovetsky, *Russian Postmodernist Fiction,* 196; and Genis, "Beseda desiataia," 230.

274. Genis, "Beseda desiataia," 231.

275. Pelevin, *Chapaev i Pustota,* 173.

276. A Russian TV show dealing with supernatural phenomena.

277. Pelevin, *Generation "P,"* 223.

278. Pelevin quoted in Nekhoroshev, "Nastoiashchii Pelevin."

279. Ibid.

280. Pelevin, *Zhizn' nasekomykh,* 10.

281. Ibid., 10–15.

282. Ibid., 14.

283. Livers, "Bugs in the Body Politic," 4.

284. I am grateful to Helena Goscilo for pointing this link out to me.

285. Pelevin, *Zhizn' nasekomykh,* 77.

286. Livers, "Bugs in the Body Politic," 10.

287. Pelevin, *Zhizn' nasekomykh,* 76–77.

288. I thank Sander Brouwer for numerous helpful suggestions concerning political gender metaphors in this novel.

289. Pelevin, *Chapaev i Pustota,* 49; see also 111.

290. Ibid., 54, 60–61.

291. Desiatov, "Arnol'd Shvartsenegger," 192. Desiatov also mentions Belyi's *Peterburg* and Pil'niak's *The Naked Year* (*Golyi god,* 1921) as pre-texts for Pelevin's rendition of the relation Russia–the West (Desiatov, "Arnol'd Shvartsenegger," 195–96).

292. Earlier in the story, an actor who plays Marmeladov in a variété version of *Crime and Punishment* turns out to be a cross-dressed woman; and the beauty of the hero's beloved Anna "can hardly be called feminine" (Pelevin, *Chapaev i Pustota,* 33, 101).

293. Ibid., 55, 111–12.

294. Ibid., 54, 55, 56.

295. Ibid., 80.

296. Borenstein, "Articles of Faith," 251. For an analysis of the Mariia Devi Khristos cult and its resonance in the Ukrainian and Russian press, see ibid.

297. Ibid., 58–59.

298. Desiatov, "Arnol'd Shvartsenegger," 193.

299. Pelevin, *Chapaev i Pustota,* 25.

300. Ibid., 55, 62; Blok, *Sobranie sochinenii,* 4:85, 99–100. Desiatov also observes a link between Pelevin's Maria and Maria in Blok's *Stranger* (Desiatov, "Arnol'd Shvartsenegger," 192–93).

301. Pelevin, *Chapaev i Pustota,* 56.

302. See Blok, *Sobranie sochinenii,* 4:82, 90.

303. Pelevin, *Chapaev i Pustota,* 59–60.

304. "Rest is in vain," "I knock on the gates . . ." are lines from "Rest Is in Vain . . ." ("Otdykh naprasen . . . ," 1903), the opening poem of the *Verses on the Beautiful Lady* (Blok, *Sobranie sochinenii,* 1:74). Desiatov points to an additional link with "New America"; in his view, "the union between Maria and Schwarzenegger is prepared, to some extent, by Blok's hopes on the future appearance of an 'artist-man' . . . and a forceful industrial Russia" ("Arnol'd Shvartsenegger," 194).

305. Pelevin, *Chapaev i Pustota,* 64.

306. Blok, *Sobranie sochinenii,* 3:360.

307. Pelevin, *Chapaev i Pustota,* 57.

308. Andaly, "Love, Tears, Betrayal . . . ."

309. Desiatov, "Arnol'd Shvartsenegger," 191.

310. Pelevin, *Generation "P,"* 77; see Tiutchev, *Polnoe sobranie,* 2:165.

311. Pelevin, *Generation "P,"* 76.

312. The association with *Retribution* is reinforced by the packaging of the drug that evokes the vision, "with a dragon—dragon-slayer" logo (ibid., 79); one of the Russian qualifications for Saint George, *pobedonosets* or "triumphator," almost converges with Pobedonostsev's name. Ironically, here and in the Silver Age "man of power" Pobedonostsev would fulfill the role of the dragon rather than Saint George.

313. Pelevin, *Generation "P,"* 164.

314. Ibid., 262.

315. BBC News, "Flamboyant Businessman."

316. Pelevin, *Generation "P,"* 13, 93.

317. Ibid., 262, 77, respectively.

318. Ibid., 293.

319. Ibid., 296.

320. Ibid., 290, 296.

321. Ibid., 40–41.

322. For Stepa, see Pelevin, *Dialektika,* 25, 29, 33, 42, 45; for Srakandaev, ibid., 33, 124–25, 152, and 190.

323. Ibid., 67–68, 104.

324. Ibid., 127.

325. A *iurodivyi* is a "God's fool," an idiot believed to possess the divine gift of prophecy.

326. Pelevin, *Dialektika,* 36.

327. Ibid.

328. Ibid., 36–37.

329. Ibid.

330. Ibid., 54.

331. Ibid., 125–27.

332. Ibid., 127.

333. Pelevin, *Dialektika,* 192–93.

334. Ibid., 193, 258.

335. Ibid., 193. In view of this outcome of the symbolic battle, it is tempting to read the book's cover illustration as a portrait of the two heroes (ibid., cover). Marrying two core figures of Russian art history, it represents Valentin Serov's *Girl with Peaches* (*Devochka s persikami,* 1887), who is embraced by Mikhail Vrubel's demon (*Demon Seated* [*Demon (sidiashchii),* 1890]). Wearing sunglasses on the book cover, the innocent girl calls to mind Stepa—the "sacred being," associated with the sun, who turns out to be a girl; by implication, who else could the dark, intimidating demon represent but the "spirit of evil" and "moonbrother" Srakandaev?

336. Pelevin, *Dialektika,* 194–95, 230.

337. Pelevin, *Shlem uzhasa,* 20–21.

338. Pelevin, *Zhizn' nasekomykh,* 150–56.

339. Pelevin, *Chapaev i Pustota,* 65.

340. Ibid., 67.

341. Ibid., 70, 73.

342. Ibid., 72.

343. Ibid., 76.

344. Ishimbaeva, "'Chapaev i Pustota,'" 323.

345. Khlebnikov, *Sobranie sochinenii,* 2:216.

346. Skoropanova, *Russkaia postmodernistskaia literatura,* 323. Skoropanova's stress on the "potential for . . . growth" can be linked to yet another wordplay in the title, linked with the concept of maturing: "Ros i ia" can in Russian also be read as "I grew (up), too" in allusion to the hero's development in the course of the story.

347. Erskin, "Ros i ia," 78–79. Since Berg published "Ros i ia" as a work by F. Erskin, quotations from the novel will refer to the latter here.

348. Ibid., 79–80.

349. Ibid., 40.

350. On this, see also Skoropanova, *Russkaia postmodernistskaia literatura,* 323, 326.

351. Erskin, "Ros i ia," 71, 76.

352. Ibid.

353. Ibid., 77.

354. Skoropanova, *Russkaia postmodernistskaia literatura,* 325.

355. Ibid., 323.

356. Erskin, "Ros i ia," 74–77.

357. Skoropanova, *Russkaia postmodernistskaia literatura,* 310.

358. The terms in question were coined in Prigov, "Preduvedomlenie k sborniku" (new sincerity); Gandlevskii, "Razreshenie ot skorbi" (critical sentimentalism); and Epshtein, "O novoi sentimental'nosti" (new sentimentality).

359. Lipovetsky, *Russian Postmodernist Fiction,* 247; emphasis in original.

360. Kibirov, *"Kto kuda,"* 108.

361. Personal communication.

362. Kibirov, *"Kto kuda,"* 115. A similar sympathetic-ironic stance toward Blok's Russia view appears as early as 1974 in Iurii Kuznetsov's epic poem "Gold Mountain" ("Zolotaia gora"), where the poet envisions how "An airy Blok flashed by in the crowd, / The one who called Rus' his wife, / And he couldn't think of anything better / Musing on his land." (Kuznetsov, *Izbrannoe*, 353).

363. Kibirov, *"Kto kuda,"* 116.

364. Ibid.

365. Ibid., 119–20.

366. Ibid., 118–19, 121.

367. Ibid., 176.

368. Ibid., 396.

369. Ibid., 413.

370. Ibid., 488.

371. Kibirov, ". . . I spokoino zanimat'sia," 169.

372. Ibid., 172.

373. Kibirov, *"Kto kuda,"* 481–82.

374. Ibid., 482.

375. Ibid., 482–83.

376. Ibid., 483. In the conclusion to *Dead Souls*, the narrator asks the metaphoric troika-Russia: "Rus', where are you heading? Answer. It does not answer" (Gogol, *Sobranie sochinenii*, 5:233).

377. Kibirov, *"Kto kuda,"* 483.

378. Ibid., 484.

379. Eliseevy, "V serdtsakh i t'ma."

380. Friedman and Weiner, "Between a Rock," 134.

381. Chistiakov, "Prosto ia zhivu." As stated earlier, in Russian Russia is referred to with the personal pronoun "she" by default of a separate pronoun for inanimate objects; however, Chistiakov emphasizes this femininity by rhyming "native land" (*rodina*) with the emphatically gendered term *urodina* ("female monster")—a female pendant of the Russian word for "monster" (*urod*).

382. Shevchuk, "Rodina."

383. Friedman and Weiner, "Between a Rock," 119.

384. Shevchuk, "Rodina."

385. Shevchuk, "Rossiiane."

386. Shnurov quoted in Koldobskaya, "Sleeping Beauty-2."

387. See Baldaev, *Russian Criminal Tattoo Encyclopaedia*, 224 and 225, for two examples and comments on the commonness of this motif in criminal circles.

388. Examples includes Tat'iana Poliakova's "Who Are You, Russia?" ("Tak kto zhe ty, Rossiia?") in *Sovetskaia Rossiia*, August 29 and September 19, 1992; Larisa Emelina, "Russia" ("Rossiia"), in *Novaia Rossiia*, no. 3–4, 1992; and the

anonymous cartoons "More Socialism!" ("Bol'she sotsializma!") in *Iskra*, February 18, 1990, and "This is our native land, my son" ("Eto nasha rodina, synok"), in *Imperiia*, 1997 (number unknown). For these and more examples, see Guseinov, *Karta nashei rodiny*, 222, 224–26, and 228.

389. The cartoon in question has circulated since the early 2000s on http://ww.pridurki.org and on http://www.vladimirvladimirovich.com/photojoke .php.

390. Zhirinovskii quoted in Kartsev and Bludeau, *!Zhirinovsky!* 93.

391. Krachkovskaia quoted in Riabova, "Maskulinnost' kak faktor," 446.

392. Riabova, "Maskulinnost' kak faktor," 447.

393. Ibid.

394. Rostopchina's 1846 poem represents the relationship between Russia and Poland as that between a male aggressor and his female victim, respectively; I refer to it in my introduction (see n. 68).

395. Koldobskaia, *Iskusstvo v bol'shom dolgu,* 119. For a reproduction, see the image on the artist's website, http://www.botcharov.ru/galpic/neravnyj_brak.

396. Translated from the demonstration leaflet, collected on May 24, 2007, in Moscow.

397. *Afisha*'s original ad has been removed from the Internet, but a relatively extended description of the project can be found on http://diy.boom .ru/bookarchiv.html, under contribution no. 53.

398. Blinov, "Pank eros moskvy."

399. G. Kuznetsov, "Spiashchii krasavits."

400. Psaik, "A cho za gundesh' . . . "

401. Zvereva, "Formy reprezentatsii russkoi istorii," 174.

402. See Rutten, "Kashchei the Immortal."

403. Polynskii, "Vasnetsy s podvoria novgorodskogo."

404. Hutcheon, *Irony's Edge,* 27.

405. Kuritsyn, "Zhizn' s kokainom," 216.

CONCLUSION

1. Sorokin quoted in Roll, *Postmodernisty,* 123.

Bibliography

Abraham, Gerald. *On Russian Music.* London: Reeves, 1939.

Afanas'ev, E. L. "Moskva v razdum'iakh russkikh myslitelei poslepetrovskogo vremeni." In *Moskva v russkoi i mirovoi literature,* ed. N. D. Bludilin, 42–51. Moscow: Nasledie, 2000.

Aizlewood, Robin. "Berdiaev and Chaadaev, Russia and Feminine Passivity." In *Gender and Sexuality in Russian Civilisation,* ed. P. Barta, 121–40. London: Routledge, 2001.

Andaly, Paula. "Love, Tears, Betrayal . . . and Health Messages." *Perspectives in Health Magazine* 8, no. 2 (2003): available online at http://www.paho .org/English/DD/PIN/Number17_article2_5.htm.

Anderson, Benedict. *Imagined Communities: Reflections on the Origin and Spread of Nationalism.* Rev. ed. London: Verso, 1991.

Andreev, Daniil. *Roza mira.* Moscow: Mir Uranii, 2002.

———. *Sobranie sochinenii v trekh tomakh.* Vol. 1. Moscow: Moskovskii rabochii, 1993.

Andrew, Joe. *Narrative and Desire in Russian Literature, 1822–49: The Feminine and the Masculine.* New York: St. Martin's, 1993.

———. *Narrative, Space and Gender in Russian Fiction, 1846–1903.* Amsterdam: Rodopi, 2007.

———. *Women in Russian Literature, 1780–1863.* New York: St. Martin's, 1988.

Ashwin, Sarah. *Gender, State and Society in Soviet and Post-Soviet Russia.* London: Routledge, 2000.

Atkinson, Dorothy. "Society and the Sexes in the Russian Past." In *Women in Russia,* ed. D. Atkinson, A. Dallin, and G. Warshofsky Lapidus, 3–39. Stanford, Calif.: Stanford University Press, 1977.

Attwood, Lynne. "Sex and the Cinema." In *Sex and Russian Society,* ed. I. Kon and J. Riordan, 64–89. Bloomington: Indiana University Press, 1993.

Avdeev, Alexandre, and Alain Monnier. "Marriage in Russia: A Complex Phenomenon Poorly Understood." *Population: An English Selection,* vol. 12 (2000): 7–49.

Averintsev, S. S. "K uiasneniiu smysla nadpisi nad konkhoi tsentrasl'noi apsidy Sofii Kievskoi." In *Drevnerusskoe iskusstvo: Khudozhestvennaia kul'tura domongol'skoi Rusi,* ed. V. N. Lazarev, 25–50. Moscow: Nauka, 1972.

———. *Sofia-Logos: Slovar'.* Kiev: Dukh i Litera, 2001.

Azadovskii, Konstantin. "Stikhiia i kul'tura." In *N. Kliuev: Pis'ma k Aleksandru Bloku,* 3–109. Moscow: Progress-Pleiada, 2003.

Babenko, N. G. "Moskva zhenskogo roda, Peterburg muzhskogo." *Russkaia rech',* no. 1 (2007): 25–30.

Baehr, Stephen Lessing. *The Paradise Myth in Eighteenth-Century Russia: Utopian Patterns in Early Secular Russian Literature and Culture.* Stanford, Calif.: Stanford University Press, 1991.

Bagno, Vsevolod. "Russkoe donkikhotstvo kak fenomen kul'tury." In *Vozhdi umov i mody: Chuzhoe imia kak nasleduemaia model' zhizni,* ed. V. Bagno, 217–33. St. Petersburg: Nauka, 2003.

Baldaev, Danzig, ed. *Russian Criminal Tattoo Encyclopaedia.* Vols. 2 and 3. London: Fuel, 2006 and 2008.

Bal'mont, Konstantin. *Stikhotvoreniia.* Leningrad: Sovetskii pisatel', 1969.

Barker, Adele Marie. *The Mother Syndrome in the Russian Folk Imagination.* Columbus, Ohio: Slavica, 1986.

Barnes, Christopher. *Boris Pasternak: A Literary Biography.* Vol. 1, *1890–1928.* Cambridge, Eng.: Cambridge University Press, 1989.

———. *Boris Pasternak: A Literary Biography.* Vol. 2, *1928–1960.* Cambridge, Eng.: Cambridge University Press, 1998.

Barsht, Konstantin. *Khudozhestvennaia antropologiia Andreia Platonova.* Voronezh: VGPU, 2001.

Barta, Peter I. *Gender and Sexuality in Russian Civilisation.* London: Routledge, 2001.

Bavil'skii, Dmitrii. "Dialogi s Olegom Kulikom #7: Zhivotnoe: Brat'ia." *Topos,* September 23, 2002: available online at http://www.topos.ru/article/530.

———. "Znaki prepinaniia no. 45: Glavnaia kniga oseni—Vladimir Sorokin 'Put' Bro,' roman." *Topos,* September 14, 2004: available online at http://topos.ru/article/2746.

BBC News. "Dissident Writer Solzhenitsyn Returns." *BBC News,* May 27, 1994: available online at: http://news.bbc.co.uk/onthisday/hi/dates/stories/may/27/newsid_2495000/2495895.stm.

———. "Flamboyant Businessman Linked to Eltsin's Sackings." *BBC News,* April 29, 1998: available online at http://news.bbc.co.uk/1/hi/special_report/1998/03/98/russian_crisis/-69282.stm.

Becker, Jochen. "'Zoo praalt ook Nêerlands maagd in de achtbre rei der kunsten': Nationalisme in de Nederlandse kunst en kunstgeschiedschrijving in de 17e en 19e eeuw." In *Eigen en vreemd: Identiteit en ontlening in taal, literatuur en beeldende kunst (Handelingen van het 39ste Nederlandse Filolo-*

gencongres, Vrije Universiteit, Amsterdam, 18–19 december 1986), 171–79. Amsterdam: Vrije Universiteit, 1987.

Beletskii, Rodion. "Nostal'giia." Unpublished, 1999.

Beller, Manfred, and Joep Leerssen. *Imagology: The Cultural Construction and Literary Representation of National Characters: A Critical Survey*. Amsterdam: Rodopi, 2007.

Belyi, Andrei. *Peterburg*, ed. L. K. Dolgopov. Moscow: Nauka, 1981.

———. *Serebrianyi golub': Rasskazy*. Moscow: Respublika, 1995.

———. *Simvolizm kak miroponimanie*. Moscow: Respublika, 1994.

———. *Stikhotvoreniia i poemy*. Moscow: Respublika, 1994.

———. "Tsentral'naia stantsiia." In *N. A. Berdiaev: Pro et contra: Antologiia*, pt. 1, ed. A. Ermich, 53–61. St. Petersburg: RKhGI, 1994.

———. *Vospominaniia o Bloke*. Moscow: Respublika, 1995.

Belyi, Andrei, and Ivanov-Razumnik. *Perepiska*. St. Petersburg: Feniks, 1998.

Belyi, Andrei, Ivanov-Razumnik, and A. Z. Shteinberg. *Pamiati Aleksandra Bloka*. Petrograd: Vol'naia filosofskaia assotsiatsiia, 1922.

Bem, A. L., ed. *O Dostojevskem: Sbornik stati a materialu*. Prague: Edice Slovanské knihovny, 1972.

Berberova, Nina. *Aleksandr Blok et son temps: Biographie*. Paris: Actes Sud, 1991.

Berdiaev, Nikolai. *The Russian Idea*. Hudson, N.Y.: Lindisfarne, 1992.

———. "Russkaia literatura XIX veka i ee prorochestva." In *Russian Critical Essays: XXth Century*, ed. S. Konovalov and D. Richards, 213–26. Oxford: Clarendon, 1971.

———. *Sobranie sochinenii*. Paris: YMCA, 1983–.

———. *Sud'ba Rossii*. Moscow: Sovetskii pisatel', 1990.

Berger-Bügel, Pia Susan. *Andrej Platonov: Der Roman Sčastlivaja Moskva im Kontext seines Schaffens und seiner Philosophie*. Munich: Otto Sagner, 1999.

Bergman, Jay. "Soviet Dissidents on the Russian Intelligentsia, 1956–85: The Search for a Usable Past." *Russian Review* 51, no. 1 (1992): 16–35.

Berlin, Isaiah. *Personal Impressions*. London: Hogarth, 1980.

Bershtein, Evgenii. "Tragediia pola: Dve zametki o russkom veinengerianstve." *Novoe literaturnoe obozrenie*, no. 65 (2004): available online at http://magazines.russ.ru/nlo/2004/65/bern13.html.

Bertens, Hans, and Douwe Fokkema, eds. *International Postmodernism: Theory and Literary Practice*. Amsterdam: John Benjamins, 1997.

Bethea, David M. "Literature." In *The Cambridge Companion to Modern Russian Culture*, ed. N. Rzhevsky, 161–205. Cambridge, Eng.: Cambridge University Press, 1998.

Billington, James. *The Icon and the Axe: An Interpretive History of Russian Culture*. New York: Vintage, 1970.

Binnenstad. "Burgemeester Wallage: Groningen is meisje waar je direct verliefd op wordt." *Binnenstad beter* 5, no. 1 (2004).

Birnbaum, Henrik. "Further Reflections on the Poetics of *Doktor Zhivago:* Structure, Technique, and Symbolism." In *Boris Pasternak and His Times: Selected Papers from the Second International Symposium on Pasternak,* ed. L. Fleishman, 284–315. Berkeley, Calif.: Berkeley Slavic Specialties, 1989.

Bitov, Andrei. "Val'naia ptitsa." In *Puteshestvie iz Rossii,* 425–77. Moscow: Vagrius, 2003.

Bjørnsdóttir, Inga Dóra. "They Had a Different Mother: The Central Configuration of Icelandic Nationalist Discourse." In *Is There a Nordic Feminism? Nordic Feminist Thought on Culture and Society,* ed. D. von der Fehr, A. Jónasdóttir, and B. Rosenbeck, 90–104. London: UCL, 1998.

Blagoi, D. *Tri veka: Iz istorii russkoi poezii XVIII, XIX i XX vv.* Moscow: Sovetskaia literatura, 1933 (reprint 1969).

Blinov, Kirill. "Pank eros moskvy." *Samizdat* (2001): available online at http://zhurnal.lib.ru/b/blinow_kirill_alekseewich/punkeros.shtml.

Blok, Aleksandr. *Pis'ma k zhene (Literaturnoe nasledstvo, no. 89).* Moscow: Nauka, 1978.

———. *Polnoe sobranie sochinenii i pisem v dvadtsati tomakh.* Moscow: Nauka, 1997–.

———. *Sobranie sochinenii v vos'mi tomakh.* Moscow-Leningrad: Gosudarstvennoe izdatel'stvo khudozhestvennoi literatury, 1960–63.

———. *Zapisnye knizhki 1901–1920.* Moscow: Khudozhestvennaia literatura, 1965.

Blok, Aleksandr, and Andrei Belyi. *Perepiska.* Munich: Flink, 1969.

Boland, Eve. *Object Lessons: The Life of the Woman and the Poet in Our Time.* London: Vintage, 1995.

Bondarenko, Mariia. "Roman V. Sorokina 'Led': Siuzhet-attraktsion—ideologiia—novaia iskrennost'—katafaticheskaia dekonstruktsiia." *Literaturnyi dnevnik,* April 2002: available online at http://www.vavilon.ru/diary/020518.html.

Bonnell, Victoria E. *Iconography of Power: Soviet Political Posters Under Lenin and Stalin.* Berkeley: University of California Press, 1999.

Borenstein, Eliot. "Articles of Faith: The Media Response to Maria Devi Khristos." *Religion* 25, no. 3 (1995): 249–66.

———. *Men Without Women: Masculinity and Revolution in Russian Fiction, 1917–1929.* Durham, N.C.: Duke University Press, 2000.

Böröcz, József, and Katherine Verdery. "Gender and Nation." *East European Politics and Societies* 8, no. 2 (1994): 223–316.

Borodin, A. P. *Romansy i pesni dlia golosa v soprovozhdenii fortepiano.* Moscow: Muzyka, 1985.

Bourdieu, Pierre. *The Field of Cultural Production: Essays on Art and Literature.* Cambridge, Eng.: Polity, 1993.

Briusov, Valerii. *Sobranie sochinenii.* Vol. 1, *Stikhotvoreniia, poemy 1892–1909.* Moscow: Khudozhestvennaia literatura, 1973.

Brooks, Jeffrey. *Thank You, Comrade Stalin! Soviet Public Culture from Revolution to Cold War.* Princeton, N.J.: Princeton University Press, 2000.

Brougher, Valentina. "Demythologising Socialist Realism: Vladimir Sorokin's *Marina's Thirtieth Love.*" *Australian Slavonic and East European Studies,* no. 1 (1998): 97–113.

Brouwer, Sander. "The Bridegroom Who Did Not Come: Social and Amorous Unproductivity from Pushkin to the Silver Age." In *Two Hundred Years of Pushkin.* Vol. 1, *"Pushkin's Secret": Russian Writers Reread and Rewrite Pushkin,* ed. J. Andrew and R. Reid, 49–65. Amsterdam: Rodopi, 2003.

———. "De Oudgelovige en de Populist: Reli-politiek drama in enkele bedrijven." *Tijdschrift voor Slavische Literatuur,* no. 31 (2002): 32–40.

———. "Tema samozvanchestva v russkoi literature: Traditsii: Preemstvennost': Novatorstvo." In *Kanun: Al'manakh: "Chuzhoe imia v russkoi kul'ture,"* no. 6, 56–101. St. Petersburg: Rossiiskaia akademiia nauk, 2001.

Brouwer, Sander, and Ellen Rutten. "Rusland als onbereikbare geliefde: Een Russisch stereotype met Romantische wortels." *Tijdschrift voor Slavische Literatuur,* no. 30 (2001): 13–23.

Brown, Deming. *The Last Years of Soviet Russian Literature.* Cambridge, Eng.: Cambridge University Press, 1993.

Bulgakov, Sergei. "Moia rodina." In *Russkaia idea,* ed. M. A. Maslin, 363–74. Moscow: Respublika, 1992.

———. "Russkaia tragediia." In *Tikhie dumy,* 1–31. Paris: YMCA, 1976.

———. *Svet nevechernii.* Moscow: Folio, 2001.

Bullock, Philip Ross. *The Feminine in the Prose of Andrey Platonov.* London: MHRA, 2005.

Burgin, Diana Lewis. *Sophia Parnok: The Life and Work of Russia's Sappho.* New York: New York University Press, 1994.

Burkhart, Dagmar. "Vorwort." In *Poetik der Metadiskursitivät: Zum postmodernen Prosa-, Film- und Dramenwerk Sorokins,* ed. D. Burkhart, 5. Die Welt der Slaven 6. Munich: Otto Sagner, 1999.

Burlak, D. K., ed. *Solov'ev: Pro et contra: Antologiia.* St. Petersburg: RKhGI, 2000.

Buruma, Ian, and Avishai Margalit. *Occidentalism: The West in the Eyes of its Enemies.* New York: Penguin, 2004.

Cahoone, Lawrence, ed. *From Modernism to Postmodernism: An Anthology.* Oxford: Blackwell, 1996.

Carlisle, Olga. *Voices in the Snow: Encounters with Russian Writers.* London: Weidenfeld and Nicolson, 1962.

Carlson, Maria. "The Silver Dove." In *Andrey Bely: Spirit of Symbolism,* ed. J. E. Malmsted, 60–96. Ithaca, N.Y.: Cornell University Press, 1987.

Chances, Ellen B. *Conformity's Children: An Approach to the Superfluous Man in Russian Literature.* Columbus, Ohio: Slavica, 1978.

Cheauré, Elisabeth. "'Vater Sowjet' und 'Mutter Erde': Überlegungen zur Gender-Problematik in der sowjetischen Literatur (am Beispiel von Texten der 'Kolchoz-' und der 'Dorfliteratur')." In *Ordnungen der Landschaft: Natur und Raum technisch und symbolisch entwerfen,* ed. S. Kaufmann, 133–55. Würzburg: Ergon, 2002.

Cheauré, Elisabeth, and Karoline Haider, eds. *Pol, gender, kul'tura: Sex, Gender, Kultur.* Moscow: RGGU, 1999.

Chekhov, Anton. *Polnoe sobranie sochinenii i pisem.* Moscow: Nauka, 1983–88.

Chernyshevskii, N. G. "Russkii chelovek na rendez-vous." In *Izbrannye literaturno-kriticheskie stat'i,* 194–216. Moscow: Gosudarstvennoe izdatel'stvo detskoi literatury ministerstva prosveshcheniia, 1953.

———. *Shto delat'? Iz rasskazov o novykh liudiakh.* Moscow: Khudozhestvennaia literatura, 1985.

Chester, Pamela. "The Landscape of Recollection: Tolstoy's *Childhood* and the Feminization of the Countryside." In *Engendering Slavic Literatures,* ed. Pamela Chester and Sibelan Forrester, 59–83. Bloomington: Indiana University Press, 1996.

Chester, Pamela, and Sibelan Forrester, eds. *Engendering Slavic Literatures.* Bloomington: Indiana University Press, 1996.

Chistiakov, Fedor. "Prosto ia zhivu na ulitse Lenina" (2005): available online at http://www.lyricsworld.ru/lyrics/Nol-Fedor-CHistyakov/Prosto-ya-zgivu-na-ulice-Lenina-10799.html.

Christa, Boris. *The Poetic World of Andrey Bely.* Amsterdam: Hakkert, 1977.

Chukovsky, Kornei. *Alexander Blok as Man and Poet,* ed. and trans. D. Burgin and K. O'Connor. Ann Arbor, Mich.: Ardis, 1982.

Chulkov, Georgii. *Imperatory: Psikhologicheskie portrety.* Moscow: Moskovskii rabochii, 1991.

———. "Metel': Listki iz dnevnika." *Narodopravstvo,* no. 20 (January 8, 1918): 4–6.

Churchward, L. G. *The Soviet Intelligentsia: An Essay on the Social Structure and Roles of Soviet Intellectuals During the 1960s.* London: Routledge and Kegan Paul, 1973.

Cinefantom. *Pamiati Dmitriia Aleksandrovicha Prigova* (2007): available online at http://cinefantom.ru/?p=400.

Cioran, Samuel. *Vladimir Solov'ev and the Knighthood of the Divine Sophia.* Waterloo, Ont.: Wilfrid Laurier University Press, 1977.

Cixous, Hélène. "Sorties." In *New French Feminisms: An Anthology,* ed. E. Marks and I. de Courtivron, 90–99. Amherst: University of Massachusetts Press, 1980.

Clark, Katerina. *The Soviet Novel: History as Ritual.* Chicago: University of Chicago Press, 1981.

Clements, B. E., R. Friedman, and D. Healey, eds. *Russian Masculinities in History and Culture.* New York: Palgrave, 2002.

Clowes, Edith. "*Doctor Zhivago* in the Post-Soviet Era: A Re-Introduction" and "Characterization in *Doktor Zhivago:* Lara and Tonia." In *Doctor Zhivago: A Critical Companion,* ed. E. Clowes, 3–47, 62–76. Evanston, Ill.: Northwestern University Press, 1995.

Confino, Michael. "On Intellectuals and Intellectual Tradition in Eighteenth and Nineteenth-Century Russia." *Daedalus: Journal of the American Academy of Arts and Sciences* 101, no. 2 (1972): 117–51.

Copleston, Frederick C. *Philosophy in Russia: From Herzen to Lenin and Berdiaev.* Notre Dame, Ind.: University of Notre Dame, 1986.

Cornwell, Neil. *Pasternak's Novel: Perspectives on "Doctor Zhivago."* Keele, Eng.: Keele University, 1986.

Costlow, Jane T., Stephanie Sandler, and Judith Vowles, eds. *Sexuality and the Body in Russian Culture.* Stanford, Calif.: Stanford University Press, 1993.

Dalton-Brown, Sally. "Ludic Nonchalance or Ludicrous Despair? Viktor Pelevin and Russian Postmodernist Prose." *Slavonic and East European Review* 75, no. 2 (1997): 216–34.

Danilevskii, N. I. *Rossiia i Evropa.* Moscow: Kniga, 1991.

Dark, Oleg. "Chernovoe pis'mo." *Strelets,* no. 1 (1992): 177–87.

———. "V. V. E., ili krushenie iazykov." *Novoe literaturnoe obozrenie,* no. 25 (1997): 246–63.

De Courten, Manon. *History, Sophia and the Russian Nation: A Reassessment of Vladimir Solov'ëv's Views on History and His Social Commitment.* Bern: Peter Lang, 2004.

De Mallac, Guy. *Boris Pasternak: His Life and Art.* Norman: University of Oklahoma Press, 1981.

Degot', Ekaterina. "Kinostsenarii Vladimira Sorokina 'Moskva' v novorusskom i postavangardnom kontekstakh." In *Poetik der Metadiskursivität: Zum postmodernen Prosa-, Film- und Dramenwerk Sorokins,* ed. D. Burkhart, 223–28. Die Welt der Slaven 6. Munich: Otto Sagner, 1999.

———. "Mog li ul'trapravyi natsionalist ne poluchit' premiiu Kandinskogo?" Openspace.ru, December 11, 2008: available online at http://www.open space.ru/art/projects/89/details/6467/.

Derzhavin, G. R. *Ody.* Leningrad: Lenizdat, 1985.

Desiatov, V. "Arnol'd Shvartsenegger—Poslednii geroi russkoi literatury." In *Ekfrazis v russkoi literature,* ed. L. Geller, 190–99. Moscow: MIK, 2002.

Die Stadt als Frau: Hauptseminar, Universität Bonn (2004): introduction

available online at http://www.atfrauenforschung.uni-bonn.de/veranst/
ss2000hauptseminar.htm.

Dieterich, Albrecht. *Mutter Erde: Ein Versuch über Volksreligion.* Leipzig:
Teubner, 1913.

Dobroliubov, Nikolai. "Kogda zhe pridet nastoiashchii den'?" In *Literaturnaia kritika v shesti tomakh,* 2:206–41. Moscow: Khudozhestvennaia literatura, 1935.

Dolgopolov, Leonid. *Aleksandr Blok: Lichnost' i tvorchestvo.* Leningrad: Nauka,
1984.

———. *Poemy Bloka i russkaia poema kontsa XIX–nachala XX vekov.* Leningrad: Nauka, 1964.

Domnikov, Sergei. *Mat'-zemlia i tsar'-gorod: Rossiia kak traditsionnoe obshchestvo.* Moscow: Aleteia, 2002.

Döring, Renata, and Igor' Smirnov. "Realizm: Diakhronicheskii podkhod." *Russian Literature,* vol. 8 (1980): 1–39.

Dostoevsky, Fedor. *Polnoe sobranie sochinenii v tridtsati tomakh.* Leningrad:
Nauka, 1972–1990.

Drubek-Maier, Natasha. "Rossiia—'pustota v kishkakh' mira ('Schastlivaia Moskva'
A. Platonova kak allegoria)." *Novoe literaturnoe obozrenie,* no. 9 (1994):
251–69.

Du Plessix-Gray, Francine. *Soviet Women: Walking the Tightrope.* New York:
Doubleday, 1989.

Duncan, I., and A. Macdougall. *Isadora Duncan's Russian Days and Her Last
Days in France.* London: Victor Gollancz, 1929.

Dunham, Vera. *In Stalin's Time: Middleclass Values in Soviet Fiction.* Cambridge, Eng.: Cambridge University Press, 1976.

Ebert, Christa. *"Die Seele hat kein Geschlecht": Studien zum Genderdiskurs in
der russischen Kultur.* Frankfurt am Main: Peter Lang, 2004.

———. *Symbolismus in Russland: Zur Romanprosa Sologubs, Remisows, Belys.*
Berlin: Akademieverlag, 1988.

Edmondson, Linda. *Gender in Russian History and Culture.* Basingstoke, Eng.:
Palgrave, 2001.

———. "Gender, mif i natsiia v Evrope: Obraz matushki Rossii v evropeiskom
kontekste." In *Pol, gender, kul'tura: Sex, Gender, Culture,* ed. E. Cheauré
and K. Haider: 135–62. Moscow: RGGU, 2003.

Eliseevy, Mariia i Svetlana. "V serdtsakh i t'ma, i sueta . . ." (1998): available online at http://zhurnal.lib.ru/e/eliseewy_m_i/.

Elkin, Boris. "The Russian Intelligentsia on the Eve of the Revolution." In *The
Russian Intelligentsia,* ed. R. Pipes, 32–47. New York: Columbia University
Press, 1961.

Ellis, Frank. *Vasilii Grossman: The Genesis and Evolution of a Russian Heretic.*
Oxford: Berg, 1994.

Ely, Christopher. *This Meager Nature: Landscape and National Identity in Imperial Russia.* DeKalb: Northern Illinois University Press, 2002.

Engel, Barbara Alpern. *Women in Russia, 1700–2000.* Cambridge, Eng.: Cambridge University Press, 2004.

Engel, Christine, and Renate Reck, eds. *Frauen in der Kultur: Tendenzen in Mittel- und Osteuropa nach der Wende.* Innsbruck, Austria: Institut für Sprachwissenschaft, 2000.

Epshtein, Mikhail. *Bog detalei: Narodnaia dusha i chastnaia zhizn' v Rossii na iskhode imperii (Esseistika 1977–88).* Moscow: R. Elinina, 1998.

———. "O novoi sentimental'nosti." *Strelets* 2, no. 78 (1996): 223–31.

———. *Vera i obraz: Religioznoe bessoznatel'noe v russkoi kul'ture 20-go veka.* Tenafly, N.J.: Hermitage, 1994.

Epstein, Mikhail. *After the Future: The Paradoxes of Postmodernism and Contemporary Russian Culture.* Amherst: University of Massachusetts, 1995.

———. "Daniil Andreev and the Mysticism of Femininity." In *The Occult in Russian and Soviet Culture,* ed. B. Glazer Rosenthal, 325–57. Ithaca, N.Y.: Cornell University Press, 1997.

———. "The Origins and Meaning of Russian Postmodernism." In *Re-entering the Sign: Articulating New Russian Culture,* ed. E. Berry and A. Miller-Pogacar, 25–47. Ann Arbor: University of Michigan Press, 1995.

Epstein, Mikhail, Alexander Genis, and Slobodanka Vladiv-Glover, eds. *Russian Postmodernism: New Perspectives on Post-Soviet Culture.* New York: Berghahn, 1999.

Epstein, Thomas. "Introduction." In *Russian Postmodernism: New Perspectives on Post-Soviet Culture,* ed. M. Epstein, A. Genis, and S. Vladiv-Glover, vii–xii. New York: Berghahn, 1999.

Erlich, Victor. *Modernism and Revolution: Russian Literature in Transition.* Cambridge, Mass.: Harvard University Press, 1994.

Ern, Vladimir. "Nalet Val'kirii." In *N. A. Berdiaev: Pro et contra: Antologiia,* pt. 1, ed. A. Ermichev, 255–61. St. Petersburg: RKhGI, 1994.

Erofeev, Venedikt. *Moskva-Petushki.* Moscow: Vagrius, 2000.

———. "Sasha Chernyi i drugie." *Teatr,* no. 9 (1991): 116.

Erofeev, Viktor. *Entsiklopediia russkoi dushi.* Moscow: Podkova Dekont+, 1999.

———. *Khoroshii Stalin.* Moscow: ZebraE, 2004.

———. "Metamorfoza odnoi literaturnoi reputatsii: Markiz de Sad, sadizm i XX vek." *Voprosy literatury,* no. 6 (1973): 135–68.

———. *Muzhchiny.* Moscow: ZebraE, 2005.

———. "Pominki po sovetskoi literature." In *Strashnyi sud: Roman, rasskazy, malen'kie esse,* 424–34. Moscow: Soiuz fotokhudozhnikov Rossii, 1996.

———. *Russian Beauty,* trans. A. Reynolds. London: Hamish Hamilton, 1992.

———. *Russkaia krasavitsa.* Moscow: ZebraE, 2002.

————. "Russkie tsvety zla." In *Russkie tsvety zla,* ed. V. Erofeev, 5–31. Moscow: ZebraE / Eksmo, 2001.

————. "Vremia rozhat': Predislovie." In *Vremia rozhat',* ed. V. Erofeev, 15–27. Moscow: ZebraE / Eksmo, 2001.

Erskin, F. "Ros i ia." *Vestnik novoi literatury,* no. 1 (1990): 11–90.

Esenin, Sergei. *Sobranie sochinenii v piati tomakh.* Moscow: Khudozhestvennaia literatura, 1966–68.

Etkind, Aleksandr. *Khlyst: Sekty, literatura i revoliutsiia.* Moscow: Novoe literaturnoe obozrenie, 1998.

Evans-Romaine, Karen. "Pasternak and Tchaikovsky: Musical Echoes in Pasternak's *Blind Beauty."* In *Literature and Musical Adaptation,* ed. M. Meyer, 105–36. Amsterdam: Rodopi, 2002.

Evdokimov, A. "Obrazy romana na stranitsakh literaturnoi kritiki pisatelia." In *"Strana filosofov" Andreia Platonova: Problemy tvorchestva,* vol. 3, ed. N. Kornienko, 276–81. Moscow: Nasledie, 1999.

Fedotov, Georgii. *Sud'ba i grekhi Rossii: Izbrannye stat'i po filosofii russkoi istorii i kul'tury v dvukh tomakh.* St. Petersburg: Sofiia, 1991.

Fetterly, Judith. *The Resisting Reader: A Feminist Approach to American Fiction.* Bloomington: Indiana University Press, 1978.

Figes, Orlando. *Natasha's Dance: A Cultural History of Russia.* London: Penguin, 2003.

Finkelstein, Miriam. "Der Ritter und der Kult der Schönen Dame in der russischen Romantik und im Biedermeier." Doctoral thesis, Ludwix-Maximilians-Universität München, 1999.

Fleishman, Lazar. *Boris Pasternak: The Poet and His Politics.* Cambridge, Mass.: Harvard University Press, 1990.

Florenskii, Pavel. "Pis'mo desiatoe: Sofiia." In *Stolp i utverzhdenie istiny,* 318–92. Paris: YMCA, 1989.

————. *Sochineniia v chetyrekh tomakh.* Vol. 2. Moscow: Mysl', 1996.

Fomenko, Lidiia. "Kraski i zvuki 'Schastlivoi Moskvy.'" In *"Strana filosofov" Andreia Platonova: Problemy tvorchestva,* vol. 3, ed. N. Kornienko, 176–86. Moscow: Nasledie, 1999.

Friedman, Julia, and Adam Weiner. "Between a Rock and a Hard Place: Holy Rus' and its Alternatives in Russian Rock Music." In *Consuming Russia: Popular Culture, Sex and Society Since Gorbachev,* ed. M. Baker, 110–38. Durham, N.C.: Duke University Press, 1999.

Gachev, G. *Natsional'nye obrazy mira: Kosmo-Psikho-Logos.* Moscow: Progress, 1995.

Gandlevskii, Sergei. "Razreshenie ot skorbi." In *Lichnoe delo No.: Literaturno-khudozhestvennyi al'manakh,* ed. L. Rubinshtein, 226–32. Moscow: Soiuzteatr, 1991.

Garrard, John. "A Conflict of Visions: Vasilii Grossman and the Russian Idea." In

The Search for Self-Definition in Russian Literature, ed. E. Thompson, 57–76. Amsterdam: Benjamins, 1994.

———. "The Original Manuscript of *Forever Flowing:* Grossman's Autopsy of the New Soviet Man." *Slavic and East European Journal* 38, no. 2 (1994): 271–90.

Gasparov, B. M. "Vremennyi kontrapunkt kak formoobrazuiushchii printsip romana Pasternaka 'Doktor Zhivago.'" In *Literaturnye leitmotivy,* 241–74. Moscow: Nauka, 1993.

Geller, Mikhail. *Andrei Platonov v poiskakh schast'ia.* Moscow: MIK, 1000.

Genis, Aleksandr. "Beseda desiataia: Pole chudes: Viktor Pelevin." *Zvezda,* no. 12 (1997): 230–34.

———. "Beseda deviataia: 'Chuzn' i zhido': Vladimir Sorokin." *Zvezda,* no. 10 (1997): 222–25.

Gertsyk, E. K. "N. A. Berdiaev." In *N. A. Berdiaev: Pro et contra: Antologiia,* pt. 1, ed. A. Ermich, 39–52. St. Petersburg: RKhGI, 1994.

Gessen, Keith. "Subversive Activities." *New York Review of Books* 51, no. 20 (2004): 65–70.

Gheith, Jehanne M. "The Superfluous Man and the Necessary Woman: A 'Re-Vision.'" *Russian Review* 55, no. 2 (1996): 226–44.

Gifford, Henry. *Pasternak: A Critical Study.* Cambridge, Eng.: Cambridge University Press, 1977.

———. "Pasternak and the 'Realism' of Blok." In *Oxford Slavonic Papers,* vol. 13, ed. S. Konovalov and J. Simmons, 96–107. Oxford: Oxford University Press, 1967.

Gillespie, David. "Is Village Prose Misogynistic?" In *Women and Russian Culture: Projections and Self-Perceptions,* ed. Rosalind Marsh, 234–44. New York: Berghahn, 1998.

———. "Sex and Sorokin: Erotica or Pornography?" In *Poetik der Metadiskursivität: Zum postmodernen Prosa-, Film- und Dramenwerk Sorokins,* ed. D. Burkhart, 161–66. Die Welt der Slaven 6. Munich: Otto Sagner, 1999.

Gimpelevich-Schwartzmann, Zina. *Boris Pasternak: What M Is Out There?* New York: Legas, 1990.

Gippius, Zinaida. *Stikhotvoreniia.* St. Petersburg: Akademicheskii proekt, 1999.

———. *Zhivye litsa.* St. Petersburg: Azbuka, 2001.

Glazov-Corrigan, Elena. "A Reappraisal of Shakespeare's Hamlet: In Defence of Pasternak's *Doktor Zhivago.*" *Forum for Modern Language Studies* 30, no. 3 (1994): 219–38.

Gogol, Nikolai. *Sobranie sochinenii v semi tomakh.* Moscow: Khudozhestvennaia literatura, 1984–86.

Goncharov, Ivan. *Sobranie sochinenii v vos'mi tomakh.* Moscow: Khudozhestvennaia literatura, 1979–80.

Gorbaneva, A. I. *Khudozhnik i mir v liricheskikh tsiklakh A. Bloka 1907–1916 gg.* Moscow: MPGU, 1992.

Goscilo, Helena. *Dehexing Sex: Russian Womanhood During and After Glasnost.* Ann Arbor: University of Michigan Press, 1996.

———. "The Gendered Trinity of Russian Cultural Rhetoric Today—or The Glyph of the H[i]eroine." In *Soviet Hieroglyphics: Visual Culture in Late Twentieth-Century Russia,* ed. N. Condee, 68–91. Bloomington: Indiana University Press, 1995.

———. "Negotiating Gendered Rhetoric: Between Scylla and Charybdis." In *Representing Gender in Cultures,* ed. E. H. Oleksy and J. Rydzewska. Frankfurt am Main: Peter Lang, 2004.

———. "Re-Conceptualizing Moscow (W)hole/sale." *Slavic and East European Journal* 51, no. 2 (2007): 314–33.

Goscilo, Helena, and Beth Holmgren, eds. *Russia, Women, Culture.* Bloomington: Indiana University Press, 1996.

Goscilo, Helena, and Andrea Lanoux, eds. *Gender and National Identity in Twentieth-Century Russian Culture.* DeKalb: Northern Illinois University Press, 2006.

Griboedov, Aleksandr. *Polnoe sobranie sochinenii v trekh tomakh.* Vol. 2, *Dramaticheskie sochineniia: Stikhotvoreniia: Stat'i: Putevye zametki.* St. Petersburg: Notabene, 1999.

Gromov, Petr. *Geroi i vremia.* Leningrad: Sovetskii pisatel', 1961.

Grossman, Vasilii. *Vse techet . . .* Frankfurt am Main: Posev, 1970.

Grois, Boris. *Utopiia i obmen.* Moscow: Znak, 1993.

Groys, Boris. *Die Erfindung Russlands.* Munich: Carl Hanser, 1995.

———. *The Total Art of Stalinism.* Princeton, N.J.: Princeton University Press, 1992.

Grübel, Rainer Georg. *An den Grenzen der Moderne: Vasilii Rozanovs Denken und Schreiben.* Munich: Fink, 2003.

Gumilev, Nikolai. "Pis'ma o russkoi poezii: Aleksandr Blok: 'Nochnye chasy' (14-yi sbornik stikhov)." In *Aleksandr Blok, Andrei Belyi: Dialog poetov o Rossii i revoliutsii,* ed. M. F. P'ianykh, 546–48. Moscow: Vysshaia shkola, 1990.

Günther, Hans. "Poiushchaia Rodina: Sovetskaia massovaia pesnia kak vyrazhenie arkhetipa materi." *Voprosy literatury,* no. 4 (1997): 46–61.

———. "'Schastlivaia Moskva' i arkhetip materi v sovetskoi kul'ture 30-kh godov." In *"Strana filosofov" Andreia Platonova: Problemy tvorchestva,* vol. 3, ed. N. Kornienko, 170–76. Moscow: Nasledie, 1999.

———. "'Stalinskie sokoly': Analiz mifa 30-kh godov." *Voprosy literatury,* no. 6 (1991): 122–41.

Guseinov, Gasan. "Five Poets in the Russian Blogosphere." *Kultura: Language and Social Change: New Tendencies in the Russian Language,* ed. G. Guseinov, no. 10 (2006): 10–18.

Bibliography

―――. *Karta nashei rodiny: Ideologema mezhdu slovom i telom*. Helsinki: Institute for Russian and East European Studies, 2000.

Hackel, Sergei. *The Poet and the Revolution: Aleksandr Blok's "The Twelve."* Oxford: Clarendon, 1975.

Hansen-Löve, Aage. *Der Russische Symbolismus: System und Entfaltung der poetischen Motive*, vol. 2. Vienna: Verlag der Österreichischen Akademie der Wissenschaften, 1998.

―――. "Zur Mythopoetik des russischen Symbolismus." *Mythos in der Slawischen Moderne: Wiener Slawistischer Almanach: Sonderband*, ed. Wolf Schmid, no. 20 (1985): 61–105.

Harris, Jane Gary. "Pasternak's Vision of Life: The History of a Feminine Image." *Russian Literature Triquarterly*, no. 6 (1974): 389–423.

Heldt, Barbara. "Motherhood in a Cold Climate: The Poetry and Career of Maria Shkapskaya." In *Sexuality and the Body in Russian Culture*, ed. J. Costlow, S. Sandler, and J. Vowles, 237–55. Stanford, Calif.: Stanford University Press, 1993.

―――. *Terrible Perfection: Women and Russian Literature*. Bloomington: Indiana University Press, 1987.

Hermand, Jost. *Sieben Arten an Deutschland zu leiden*. Königstein, Ger.: Athenäum, 1979.

Herzen, Aleksandr. *Sobranie sochinenii v tridtsati tomakh*. Moscow: RAN SSSR, 1954–65.

Hodel, Robert. *Erlebte Rede bei Andrej Platonov: Von v zvezdnoj Pustyne bis Cevengur*. Bern: Lang, 2001.

Hosking, Geoffrey. *Russia: People and Empire 1552–1917*. London: HarperCollins, 1997.

Hubbs, Joanna. *Mother Russia: The Feminine Myth in Russian Culture*. Bloomington: Indiana University Press, 1988.

Hussein, Saddam. *Zabiba and the King*. Virtualbookworm.com (2004).

Hutcheon, Linda. *Irony's Edge: The Theory and Politics of Irony*. London: Routledge, 1994.

Iablokov, E. "Schast'e i neschast'e Moskvy ('Moskovskie' siuzhety u A. Platonova i B. Pil'niaka)." In *"Strana filosofov" Andreia Platonova: Problemy tvorchestva*, vol. 2, ed. N. Kornienko, 221–40. Moscow: Nasledie, 1995.

Iakovlev, M. Vl. *Sud'ba Rossii v poezii A. Bloka i M. Voloshina*. Moscow: MPU, 1995.

Irigaray, Luce. "This Sex Which Is Not One." In *Feminisms: An Anthology of Literary Theory and Criticism*, ed. R. Warhol and D. Herndl, 350–56. New Brunswick, N.J.: Rutgers University Press, 1991.

Ishimbaeva, G. "'Chapaev i Pustota': Postmodernistskie igry Viktora Pelevina." *Voprosy literatury*, no. 6 (2001): 314–23.

Isupov, K. G. "Dialog stolits v istoricheskom dvizhenii." In *Moskva-Peterburg: Pro et contra,* ed. D. K. Burlak, 6–81. St. Petersburg: RKhGI, 2000.

Iur'ev, Dmitrii. "Tri postmodernizma." *Russkii zhurnal,* February 9, 2007: available online at http://www.russ.ru/culture/kolonki/tri_postmodernizma.

Ivanov, Georgii. *Sobranie stikhotvorenii.* Würzburg, Ger.: Jal, 1975.

Ivanov, Viacheslav. "Antichnyi uzhas (po povodu kartiny L. Baksta 'Terror Antiquus')." *Zolotoe runo,* no. 4 (1909): 51–66.

———. "Dostoevsky: Tragediia—Mif—Mistika." In *Lik i lichiny Rossii: Estetika i literaturnaia teoriia,* 351–459. Moscow: Iskusstvo, 1995.

———. "Osnovnoi mif v romane 'Besy.'" In *Besy: Antologiia russkoi kritiki,* ed. L. I. Saraskina, 508–13. Moscow: Soglasie, 1996.

———. "Zhivoe predanie." In *Sobranie sochinenii,* 3:339–348. Brussels: Foyer Oriental Chrétien, 1979.

Ivanova, Svetlana. "Trudnaia lira." *Znamia,* no. 10 (2001): available online at http://magazines.russ.ru/znamia/2001/10/ivanova-pr.html.

Jager, Janine. *Tussen Rusland en Europa: Russische debatten over de intelligentsia, de staat en de natie in de jaren 1908–1912.* Amsterdam: Jan Mets, 1998.

James, C. Vaughan. *Soviet Socialist Realism: Origins and Theory.* New York: St. Martin's, 1973.

Jonas, Hans. *The Gnostic Religion: The Message of the Alien God and the Beginnings of Christianity.* Boston: Beacon, 1991.

Kaganovsky, Lilya. *How the Soviet Man Was Unmade: Cultural Fantasy and Male Subjectivity Under Stalin.* Pittsburgh, Pa.: University of Pittsburgh Press, 2008.

Kantorowicz, E. *The King's Two Bodies: A Study in Medieval Political Theology.* Princeton, N.J.: Princeton University Press, 1957.

Karamzin, Nikolai. *Polnoe sobranie stikhotvorenii.* Moscow-Leningrad: Sovetskii pisatel', 1966.

Kartsev, Vladimir, and Todd Bludeau. *!Zhirinovsky!* New York: Columbia University Press, 1995.

Kasper, Karlheinz. "Das Glöckchen und die Axt in Sorokins 'Roman.'" In *Poetik der Metadiskursivität: Zum postmodernen Prosa-, Film- und Dramenwerk Sorokins,* ed. D. Burkhart, 102–14. Die Welt der Slaven 6. Munich: Otto Sagner, 1999.

Kay, Rebecca. *Men in Contemporary Russia: The Fallen Heroes of Post-Soviet Change?* Hants, Eng.: Ashgate, 2006.

Kelly, Ian Crawford. "Eternal Memory: Historical Themes in Pasternak's *Doctor Zhivago.*" *Dissertation Abstracts International, A: The Humanities and Social Sciences* 47, no. 7 (1987): 2610.

Kemp-Welch, A. *Stalin and the Literary Intelligentsia, 1928–39.* London: Macmillan, 1991.

Kenez, Peter. "Soviet Cinema in the Age of Stalin." In *Stalinism and Soviet Cinema,* ed. R. Taylor and D. Spring, 54–69. London: Routledge, 1993.

Khlebnikov, Velimir. *Sobranie sochinenii.* Vol. 2. Moscow: IMLI RAN, Nasledie, 2001.

Khodasevich, Vladislav. *Sobranie sochinenii v chetyrekh tomakh.* Vol. 4. Moscow: Soglasie, 1997.

Khomiakov, A. S. *Stikhotvoreniia i dramy.* Leningrad: Sovetskii pisatel', 1969.

Khoruzhii, Sergei. *O starom i novom.* St. Petersburg: Aleteia, 2000.

Khotkina, Z. L., N. L. Pushkareva, and E. I. Trofimova. *Zhenshchina: Gender: Kul'tura.* Moscow: MTsGI, 1999.

Khrustaleva, Olga. "New Literature: A Polystylistics of Stereotypes." In *Re-entering the Sign: Articulating New Russian Culture,* ed. E. Berry and A. Miller-Pogacar, 189–208. Ann Arbor: University of Michigan Press, 1995.

Kibirov, Timur. ". . . I spokoino zanimat'sia svoim delom (Besedu vedet Elena Seslavina)." *Druzhba narodov,* no. 7 (1996): 167–74.

———. "*Kto kuda, a ia v Rossiiu . . .*" Moscow: Vremia, 2001.

Kimball, Alan. *Intelligentsia:* available online at http://www.uoregon.edu/~kimball/ntg.htm.

King, David, and Cathy Porter. *Images of Revolution: Graphic Art from 1905 Russia.* New York: Pantheon, 1983.

Kirsanova, R. M. *Russkii kostium i byt XVIII–XIX veka.* Moscow: Slovo, 2002.

Kliuev, Nikolai. *Pis'ma k Aleksandru Bloku 1907–1915,* ed. Konstantin Azadovskii. Moscow: Progress / Pleiada, 2003.

———. "Razrukha" (2004): available online at http://obretenie.narod.ru/txt/kluev/kluev_gamaun.htm.

———. *Sochineniia.* Munich: Neimanis, 1969.

———. *Stikhotvoreniia i poemy.* Leningrad: Sovetskii pisatel', 1977.

Koldobskaia, Marina. *Iskusstvo v bol'shom dolgu.* Moscow: NoMi, 2007.

Koldobskaya, Marina. "Sleeping Beauty-2." *New Times,* March 2004: available online at http://www.newtimes.ru/eng/detail.asp?art_id=817.

Konstantinov, M. *Spiashchaia krasavitsa.* Moscow: Iskusstvo, 1990.

Kormil'tsev, Il'ia. "Moskva: Opyt urbanisticheskogo analiza." In *Moskva—Territoriia 2000* (2000): available online at http://www.guelman.ru/nashi/book/99343-24.html.

Kornev, S. "Stolknovenie pustot: Mozhet li postmodernizm byt' russkim i klassicheskim? Ob odnoi avantiure Viktora Pelevina." *Novoe literaturnoe obozrenie,* no. 28 (1997): 244–60.

Kornienko, Natal'ia. "Na kraiu sobstvennogo bezmolviia." *Novyi mir,* no. 9 (1991): 58–75.

———. "'Proletarskaia Moskva zhdet svoego khudozhnika' (K tvorcheskoi istorii romana)." In *"Strana filosofov" Andreia Platonova: Problemy tvorchestva,* vol. 3, ed. N. Kornienko, 357–71. Moscow: Nasledie, 1999.

Kostov, Heli. *Mifopoetika Andreia Platonova v romane Schastlivaia Moskva.* Helsinki: Helsinki University Press, 2000.

Krasnov, A. "Khudozhestvennye obrazy v proizvedeniiakh M. I. Makhaeva i S. I. Solov'eva i tvorchestvo A. N. Benua." *Niva,* no. 3 (2003): available online at http://magazines.russ.ru/neva/2003/3/krasnov-pr.html.

Kravtsov, N. I., and A. V. Kulagina, eds. *Slavianskii fol'klor: Teksty.* Moscow: Izdatel'stvo moskovskogo universiteta, 1987.

Kropywiansky, Lew. "Victor Pelevin by Lew Kropywiansky." *Bomb Magazine* (2004): available online at http://www.bombsite.com/pelevin/pelevin.html.

Kruk, I. T. "Blok i Gogol'." In *Russkaia literature,* no. 1 (1961): 85–104.

Kuritsyn, Viacheslav. "TELO TEKSTA: Ob odnoi sintagme, pripisyvaemoi V. G. Sorokinu." In *Poetik der Metadiskursivität: Zum postmodernen Prosa, Film- und Dramenwerk Sorokins,* ed. D. Burkhart, 61–65. Die Welt der Slaven 6. Munich: Otto Sagner, 1999.

———. "Zakliuchenie. K poniatiu postpostmodernizma." In *Russkii literaturnyi postmodernizm* (2004): available online at http://www.guelman .ru/slava/postmod/9.html.

———. "Zhizn' s kokainom." *Znamia,* no. 1 (1992): 212–19.

Kurz, Gerhard. *Metapher, Allegorie, Symbol.* Göttingen, Ger.: Vandenhoeck und Ruprecht, 1997.

Kuznetsov, Georgii. "Spiashchii krasavits" (2004): available online at http://www .snarky.com/Snarky/44Cols/C0000307.htm.

Kuznetsov, Iurii. *Izbrannoe: Stikhotvoreniia i poemy.* Moscow: Khudozhestvennaia literatura, 1990.

Kuznetsov, Sergei. "Postmodernism in Russia." In *International Postmodernism: Theory and Literary Practice,* ed. Hans Bertens and Douwe Fokkema, 451–63. Amsterdam: Benjamins, 1997.

Laird, Sally. *Voices of Russian Literature: Interviews with Ten Contemporary Writers.* Oxford: Oxford University Press, 1999.

Lamont, Rosette. "Yuri Zhivago's 'Fairy Tale': A Dream Poem." *World Literature Today,* vol. 51 (1977): 517–21.

Lanin, Boris. *Idei "otkrytogo obshchestva" v tvorchestve Vasiliia Grossmana.* Moscow: Magistr, 1997.

Layton, Susan. *Russian Literature and Empire: Conquest of the Caucasus from Pushkin to Tolstoy.* Cambridge, Eng.: Cambridge University Press, 1994.

Leerssen, Joep. "Imagology: History and Method." In *Imagology: The Cultural Construction and Literary Representation of National Characters: A Critical Survey,* ed. M. Beller and J. Leerssen, 17–33. Amsterdam: Rodopi, 2007.

Lesnaia, G. M. "Blokovskie traditsii v romane B. Pasternaka 'Doktor Zhivago.'" *Vestnik moskovskogo universiteta, Seriia 9, Filologiia,* no. 1 (1996): 104–13.

Levinton, G. A. "Zametki o fol'klorizme Bloka." In *Mif—Fol'klor—Literature,* ed. V. G. Bazanov, 171–86. Leningrad: Nauka, 1978.

Lipkin, S., ed. "'Istinnaia sila—Dobrota': Dva pis'ma Vasiliia Grossmana." *Voprosy literatury*, no. 1 (1997): 270–72.

Lipovetskii, Mark. "Mir kak tekst." *Literaturnoe obozrenie*, no. 6 (1990): 63–65.

Lipovetsky, Mark. *Russian Postmodernist Fiction: Dialogue with Chaos*. Armonk, N.Y.: Sharpe, 1999.

Litichevskii, Georgii. "Pesnia o Moskve." *Khudozhestvennyi zhurnal*, no. 34–35 (2001): available online at http://www.guelman.ru/xz/362/xx34/xx3430.htm.

Livers, Keith. "Bugs in the Body Politic: The Search for Self in Viktor Pelevin's *The Life of Insects*." *Slavic and East European Journal* 46, no. 1 (2002): 1–29.

———. *Constructing the Stalinist Body: Fictional Representations of Corporeality in the Stalinist 1930s*. Lanham, Md.: Lexington, 2004.

Livingstone, Angela. "Danger and Deliverance: Reading Andrei Platonov." *Slavonic and East European Review* 80, no. 3 (2002): 401–16.

———. "Gamlet: Dvanov: Zhivago." In *Tvorchestvo Andreia Platonova: Issledovaniia i materialy: Bibliografiia*, pt. 3, ed. E. I. Kolesnikova, 227–41. St. Petersburg: Nauka, 2004.

———, ed. *Pasternak on Art and Creativity*. Cambridge, Eng.: Cambridge University Press, 1985.

———. "Unexpected Affinities Between *Doktor Zhivago* and *Chevengur*." In *V krugu Zhivago: Pasternakovskii sbornik*, ed. Lazar Fleishman, 184–205. Stanford, Calif.: Department of Slavic Languages and Literatures, 2000.

Lomonosov, Mikhail. *Izbrannye proizvedeniia*. Moscow-Leningrad: Sovetskii pisatel', 1965.

Losev, A. F. *Vladimir Solov'ev i ego vremia*. Moscow: Molodaia gvardiia, 2000.

Lotman, Iurii. *Besedy o russkoi kul'ture: Byt i traditsii russkogo dvorianstva (XVIII–nachalo XIX veka)*. St. Petersburg: Iskusstvo-SPB, 1994.

———. "Siuzhetnoe prostranstvo v russkom romane XIX stoletiia." In *Izbrannye stat'i v trekh tomakh*, 3:91–106. Tallin: Aleksandra, 1993.

Lotman, Iurii, and Boris Uspenskii. "'Izgoi' i 'izgoinichestvo' kak sotsial'no-psikhologicheskaia pozitsiia v russkoi kul'ture preimushchestvenno dopetrovskogo vremeni ('Svoe' i 'chuzhoe' v istorii russkoi kul'tury)." In *Istoriia i tipologiia russkoi kul'tury*, ed. I. Lotman, 222–33. St. Petersburg: Iskusstvo-SPB, 2002.

Lysov, A. "'Schastlivaia Moskva' i 'Grad chelovechestva': O kontseptsii kul'tury v tvorchestve Platonova." In *"Strana filosofov" Andreia Platonova: Problemy tvorchestva*, vol. 3, ed. N. Kornienko, 131–43. Moscow: Nasledie, 1999.

Maiakovskii, Vladimir. *Sobranie sochinenii v dvenadtsati tomakh*. Vol. 11. Moscow: Pravda, 1978.

Maikov, Vasilii. *Izbrannye proizvedeniia*. Moscow-Leningrad: Sovetskii pisatel', 1966.

Makeeva, Kseniia Aleksandrovna. "Geroi V. Pelevina: V poiskakh svoego 'Ia.'"

Samizdat (2002): available online at http://www.teneta.rinet.ru/2002/kritika/BAK/14.html.

Makogonenko, G. P., and I. Z. Serman, eds. *Poety XVIII veka, V 2-x tomakh.* Leningrad: Sovetskii pisatel', 1972.

Makushinskii, Aleksei. "Otvergnutyi zhenikh, ili Osnovnoi mif russkoi literatury XIX veka." *Voprosy filosofii,* no. 7 (2003): 35–43.

Malečková, Jitka. "Nationalizing Women and Engendering the Nation: The Czech National Movement." In *Gendered Nations: Nationalisms and Gender Order in the Long Nineteenth Century,* ed. I. Blom, K. Hagemann, and C. Hall, 293–310. Oxford, Eng.: Berg, 2000.

Malia, Martin. "What Is the Intelligentsia?" In *The Russian Intelligentsia,* ed. R. Pipes, 1–19. New York: Columbia University Press, 1961.

Malygina, N. M. Andrei Platonov: Poetika "vozrashcheniia." Moscow: TEIS, 2005.

Mann, I. V. *V poiskakh zhivoi dushi: "Mertvye dushi": Pisatel'-kritika-chitatel'.* Moscow: Kniga, 1984.

Markish, Shimon. "Liubil li Rossiiu Vasilii Grossman?" *Russkaia mysl',* February 12, 1986: 12.

Markovich, V. M. "'Russkii evropeets' v proze Turgeneva 1850-kh godov." In *Ivan S. Turgenev: Leben, Werk und Dichtung: Beiträge der Internationalen Fachkonferenz aus Anlass des 175: Geburtstag an der Otto-Friedrich-Universität Bamberg,* ed. Peter Thiergen, 79–96. Munich: Otto Sagner, 1995.

Marsh, Cynthia. *M. A. Voloshin: Artist-Poet: A Study of the Synaesthetic Aspects of His Poetry.* Birmingham: University of Birmingham, 1982.

Marsh, Rosalind, ed. *Gender and Russian Literature: New Perspectives.* Cambridge, Eng.: Cambridge University Press, 1996.

———, ed. *Women and Russian Culture: Projections and Self-Perceptions.* New York: Berghahn, 1998.

Martin, Angela K. "Death of a Nation: Transnationalism, Bodies and Abortion in Late Twentieth-Century Ireland." In *Gender Ironies of Nationalism: Sexing the Nation,* ed. T. Mayer, 65–89. London: Routledge, 2000.

Masing-Delic, Irene. "The Mask Motif in A. Blok's Poetry." *Russian Literature,* vol. 5 (1973): 79–101.

Mathewson, Rufus W., Jr. *The Positive Hero in Russian Literature.* 2nd ed. Stanford, Calif.: Stanford University Press, 1975.

Matich, Olga. "Androgyny and the Russian Religious Renaissance." In *Western Philosophical Systems in Russian Literature,* ed. A. Mlikotin, 165–75. Los Angeles: University of Southern California Press, 1979.

Matveeva, I. "Simvolika obraza glavnoi geroini." In *"Strana filosofov" Andreia Platonova: Problemy tvorchestva,* vol. 3, ed. N. Kornienko, 312–20. Moscow: Nasledie, 1999.

Mayer, Tamar. "Gender Ironies of Nationalism: Setting the Stage." In *Gender*

Ironies of Nationalism: Sexing the Nation, ed. T. Mayer, 1–25. London: Routledge, 2000.

Mayo, Katherina. *Mother India.* Ann Arbor: University of Michigan Press, 2000.

Mazurana, Dyan, Angela Raven-Roberts, and Jane Parpart, eds. *Gender, Conflict, and Peacekeeping.* Lanham, Md.: Rowman and Littlefield, 2005.

McDermid, Jane. "The Influence of Western Ideas on the Development of the Woman Question in Nineteenth-Century Russian Thought." *Irish Slavonic Studies* 9 (1988). 21–36.

McVay, Gordon. *Isadora and Esenin.* Ann Arbor, Mich.: Ardis, 1980.

Medvedev, Pavel. *Dramy i poemy Al. Bloka: iz istorii ikh sozdaniia.* Leningrad: Izdatel'stvo pisatelei, 1928.

Meier, Andrew. "Obvenchavshiisia so svobodoi: Posleslovie." In *Russkaia krasavitsa,* by Viktor Erofeev, 219–23. Stavropol', Russia: Kavkazskii krai, 1992.

Meletinskii, E. M. *Ot mifa k literature.* Moscow: RGGU, 2000.

———. "Zhenit'ba v volshebnoi skazke (ee funktsiia i mesto v siuzhetnoi strukture)." In *Izbrannye stat'i, Vospominaniia,* 305–18. Moscow: RGGU, 1998.

Menzel, Birgit. *Bürgerkrieg um Worte: Die russische Literaturkritik der Perestrojka.* Cologne, Ger.: Böhlau, 2001.

Merezhkovskii, Dmitrii. *Antikhrist (Petr i Aleksei).* Moscow: Panorama, 1993.

———. *Atlantida-Evropa: Taina zapada.* Moscow: Russkaia kniga, 1992.

———. *Voskresshie bogi.* Moscow: Kniga, 1990.

Mickiewicz, Adam. *Dzieła poetyckie.* Vol. 2, *Powieści poetyckie: Księgi narodu polskiego i pielgrzymstwa polskiego.* Warsaw: Czytelnik, 1983.

Milner-Gulland, Robin. *The Russians.* Malden, Mass.: Blackwell, 1997.

Mints, Zara. *Aleksandr Blok i russkie pisateli.* St. Petersburg: Iskusstvo-SPB, 2000.

———. *Poetika Aleksandra Bloka.* St. Petersburg: Iskusstvo-SPB, 1999.

———. *Poetika russkogo simvolizma.* St. Petersburg: Iskusstvo-SPB, 2004.

Mochul'skii, Konstantin. "Vladimir Solov'ev: Zhizn' i uchenie." In *Vladimir Solov'ev: Pro et contra: Antologiia,* ed. V. F. Boiko, 556–830. St. Petersburg: RKhGI, 2000.

Mochulsky, Konstantin. *Andrei Bely: His Life and Works.* Ann Arbor, Mich.: Ardis, 1997.

Mogil'ner, Marina. *Mifologiia "Podpol'nogo cheloveka": Radikal'nyi mikrokosm v Rossii nachala XX veka kak predmet semioticheskogo analiza.* Moscow: Novoe literaturnoe obozrenie, 1999.

Mokeev, Gennadii. "Sud'ba zlatoglavoi sviashchennoi Moskvy: Moskva sviashchennaia, chast' tret'ia" (2004): available online at http://www.voskres.ru/architecture/moscow3.htm.

Morozov, I. A., ed. *Muzhskoi sbornik.* Vol. 1, *Muzhchina v traditsionnoi kul'ture.* Moscow: Labirint, 2001.

Moser, Charles. *Cambridge History of Russian Literature.* Cambridge, Eng.: Cambridge University Press, 1992.

Mosse, George L. *Nationalism and Sexuality: Respectability and Abnormal Sexuality in Modern Europe.* New York: Howard Fertig, 1985.

Mostov, Julie. "Sexing the Nation / Desexing the Body: Politics of National Identity in the Former Yugoslavia." In *Gender Ironies of Nationalism: Sexing the Nation,* ed. T. Mayer, 89–110. London: Routledge, 2000.

Mukhina, Ol'ga. *Iu* (1996): available online at http://www.theatre.ru:8080/drama/muhina/u.html.

Nabokov, Vladimir. *Mashen'ka.* Ann Arbor, Mich.: Ardis, 1974.

———. *Speak, Memory: An Autobiography Revisited.* London: Penguin, 2000.

Nadson, Semen. *Polnoe sobranie stikhotvorenii.* St. Petersburg: Akademicheskii proekt, 2001.

Naiman, Eric. "Communism and the Collective Toilet: Lexical Heroes in Happy Moscow." *Essays in Poetics,* vol. 26 (2001): 96–110.

———. "Historectomies: On the Metaphysics of Reproduction in a Utopian Age." In *Sexuality and the Body in Russian Culture,* ed. J. Costlow, S. Sandler, and J. Vowles, 255–76. Stanford, Calif.: Stanford University Press, 1993.

———. "Introduction." In *Happy Moscow,* by Andrey Platonov, xi–xxxvii. London: Harvill, 2001.

Najmabadi, Afsaneh. "The Erotic *Vatan* [Homeland] as Beloved and Mother: To Love, to Possess, and to Protect." *Comparative Studies in Society and History* 39, no. 3 (1997): 442–67.

Nekhoroshev, Grigorii. "Nastoiashchii Pelevin: Otryvki iz biografii kul'tovogo pisatelia." *Nezavisimaia gazeta,* September 29, 2001: available online at http://www.ng.ru/style/2001-08-29/8_pelevin.html.

Nekliudov, Sergei. "Telo Moskvy: K voprosu ob obraze 'zhenshchiny-goroda' v russkoi literature." In *Telo v russkoi kul'ture,* ed. G. Kabakova and F. Kont, 361–85. Moscow: Novoe literaturnoe obozrenie, 2005.

Nemirov, Miroslav. *Nekotorye stikhotvoreniia raspolozhennye po alfavity.* St. Petersburg: Krasnyi matros, 1999.

Nesterov, Mikhail. *Pis'ma: Izbrannoe.* Leningrad: Iskusstvo, 1988.

———. *Vospominaniia.* Moscow: Sovetskii khudozhnik, 1985.

Nietzsche, Friedrich. *Werke.* Berlin: Hanser, 1999.

Norris, Stephen M. *A War of Images: Russian Popular Prints, Wartime Culture, and National Identity 1812–1945.* DeKalb: Northern Illinois University Press, 2006.

Novalis. *Briefe und Werke.* Vol. 1. Berlin: Schneider, 1943.

Obermayr, Brigitte. "Russland: Konzept: Frau: Kulturtheoretische Anmerkungen zur Genderforschung in der Slawistik." In *Frauen in der Kultur: Tendenzen in Mittel- und Osteuropa nach der Wende,* ed. C. Engel and

R. Reck, 141–58. Innsbruck, Austria: Institut für Sprachen und Literaturen der Universität Innsbruck, 2000.

O'Brien, W. A. *Novalis: Signs of Revolution.* Durham, N.C.: Duke University Press, 1995.

Odesskii, M. P. "Ob 'otkrovennom' i 'prikrovennom': Sofiia v komediiakh V. I. Lukina." *Literaturnoe obozrenie,* no. 3–4 (1994): 82–87.

Odoevskii, Aleksandr. *Polnoe sobranie stikhotvorenii i pisem.* Moscow-Leningrad: Academia, 1934.

Olesha, Iurii. *Zavist'.* Oxford: Pergamon, 1966.

Onasch, Konrad. *Gross-Nowgorod: Aufstieg und Niedergang einer russischen Stadtrepublik.* Vienna: Schroll, 1969.

Openspace.ru. "Mozhet li ul'trapravyi pochvennik poluchit' premiiu Kandinskogo?" *Openspace.ru,* November 25, 2008: available online at http://www.openspace.ru/art/projects/160/details/6106/.

Orlov, Vladimir, ed. *Aleksandr Blok v portretakh, illiustratsiiakh i dokumentakh.* Leningrad: Prosveshchenie, 1972.

———. *O Rodine (A. A. Blok).* Moscow: Gosudarstvennoe izdatel'stvo khudozhestvennoi literatury, 1945.

Packalén, Anna Małgorzata. "The Polish Mother Figure on Trial: Some Preliminary Thoughts on Selected Works by Natasha Goerke and Olga Tokarczuk." In *The New Woman and the Aesthetic Opening: Unlocking Gender in Twentieth-Century Texts,* ed. E. Witt-Brattström, 205–15. Huddinge, Sweden: Södertörns högskola, 2004.

Paperno, Irina. *Semiotika povedeniia: Nikolai Chernyshevskii—Chelovek epokhi realizma.* Moscow: Novoe literaturnoe obozrenie, 1996.

Parthé, Kathleen F. *Russian Village Prose: The Radiant Past.* Princeton, N.J.: Princeton University Press, 1992.

Passage, Charles E. *Character Names in Dostoevsky's Fiction.* Ann Arbor, Mich.: Ardis, 1982.

Pasternak, Boris. *Doctor Zhivago,* trans. M. Hayward and M. Harari. London: Collins, 1961.

———. "K kharakteristike Bloka." In *Blokovskii sbornik II,* ed. Z. G. Mints, 450–54. Tartu, U.S.S.R.: Tartuskii gosudarstvennyi universitet, 1972.

———. *Sobranie sochinenii v piati tomakh.* Moscow: Khudozhestvennaia literatura, 1989–92.

———. *Sochineniia.* Vol. 2. Ann Arbor: University of Michigan Press, 1961.

———. *The Voice of Prose.* Vol. 1, trans. C. Barnes. Edinburgh: Polygon, 1986.

Pasternak, Evgenii. *Boris Pasternak: Biografiia.* Moscow: Tsitadel', 1987.

———. "Otrazhenie Blokovskoi poezii v lirike B. Pasternaka" and "Mir Bloka v romane Pasternaka 'Doktor Zhivago.'" In *Aleksandr Blok i mirovaia kul'tura,* ed. V. V. Musatov, 341–57. Velikii Novgorod, Russia: Novgorodskii gosudarstvennyi universitet, 2000.

Pasternak, Evgenii, and Elena Pasternak. *Zhizn' Borisa Pasternaka: Dokumental'noe povestvovanie.* St. Petersburg: Zvezda, 2004.

Payne, Robert. *The Three Worlds of Boris Pasternak.* London: Hale, 1962.

Pecherskii, Andrei. *V lesakh.* Moscow: Khudozhestvennaia literatura, 1977.

Pelevin, Viktor. *Chapaev i Pustota.* Moscow: Vagrius, 1998.

———. *Dialektika perekhodnogo perioda iz niotkuda v nikuda.* Moscow: Eksmo, 2004.

———. *Generation "P."* Moscow: Vagrius, 1999.

———. "Lev Kropyv'ianskii: Interv'iu s Viktorom Pelevinym." *Bomb Magazine,* November 19, 2004: available online at http://pelevin.nov.ru/interview/o-bomb/1.html, 19.11.04.

———. *Shlem uzhasa.* Moscow: Otkrytyi mir, 2005.

———. "Vdali ot kompleksnykh idei zhivesh', kak Rembo—Day by day." *Kommersant,* February 9, 2003: available online at http://pelevin.nov.ru/interview/o-komrs/1.html.

———. *Zhizn' nasekomykh.* Moscow: Vagrius, 1998.

Peppershtein, Pavel. *Dieta Starika: Teksty 1982–1997.* Vol. 3, *Eda.* Moscow: Ad Marginem, 1998.

Petrova, Aleksandra. *Vid na zhitel'stvo.* Moscow: Novoe literaturnoe obozrenie, 2000.

Pettman, Jan Jindy. *Worlding Women: A Feminist International Politics.* London: Routledge, 1996.

P'ianykh, M. F., ed. *Aleksandr Blok, Andrei Belyi: Dialog poetov o Rossii i revoliutsii.* Moscow: Vysshaia shkola, 1990.

Pipes, Richard, ed. *The Russian Intelligentsia.* New York: Columbia University Press, 1961.

Pisarev, Dmitrii. "Zhenskie tipy v romanakh i povestiakh Pisemskogo, Turgeneva i Goncharova." In *Literaturnaia kritika v trekh tomakh,* 1:179–229. Leningrad: Khudozhestvennaia literatura, 1981.

Platonov, Andrei. *Kotlovan: Tekst, materialy tvorcheskoi istorii.* St. Petersburg: Nauka, 2000.

———. *Schastlivaia Moskva.* In *"Strana filosofov" Andreia Platonova: Problemy tvorchestva,* vol. 3, ed. N. Kornienko. Moscow: Nasledie, 1999.

———. *Sobranie sochinenii v piati tomakh.* Vol. 1. Moscow: Informpechat', 1998.

Platonov, Andrey. *Happy Moscow,* trans. Robert Chandler et al. London: Harvill, 2001.

Pliukhanova, M. "Kompozitsiia Pokrova Bogoroditsy v politicheskom samosoznanii Moskovskogo tsarstva." In *Sbornik statei k 70-letiu prof. Iu. M. Lotmana,* ed. I. Lotman, A. Mal'ts, and V. Stolovits, 76–90. Tartu, Estonia: Tartuskii universitet, 1992.

———. *Kotlovan / The Foundation Pit.* Ann Arbor, Mich.: Ardis, 1973.

———. *Siuzhety i simvoly moskovskogo tsarstva.* St. Petersburg: Akropol', 1995.

Pogodin, Mikhail. *Istoricheskie aforizmy.* Moscow: V universitetskoi tipografii, 1836.

Polynskii, Andrei. "Vasnetsy s podvoria novgorodskogo." *Russkii dom,* May 2007: available online at http://www.russdom.ru/2006/200606/20060631.html.

Pomorska, Kristina. *Russian Formalist Theory and Its Poetic Ambiance.* The Hague: Mouton, 1968.

Popov, Oleg. "The Russian Oedipus." In *Idee w Rosji – Idei v Rossii – Ideas in Russia,* vol. 4, ed. A. Lazari, 591–99. Lodz, Poland: Ibidem, 2001.

Porter, Robert. *Russia's Alternative Prose.* Oxford: Berg, 1994.

Pravdina, I. S. "Iz istorii formirovaniia tsikla 'Rodina.'" In *Mir A. Bloka: Blokovskii sbornik,* ed. D. Maksimov and Z. Mints, 19–33. Tartu, U.S.S.R.: Tartuskii gosudarstvennyi universitet, 1984.

Prigov, Dmitrii. *Napisannoe s 1990 po 1994.* Moscow: Novoe literaturnoe obozrenie, 1998.

———. "Narod i vlast' sovmestno lepiat obraz novoi Rossii" (2003): available online at http://www.prigov.ru/action/performans.htp.

———. *Piat'desiat kapelek krovi.* Moscow: Tekst, 1993.

———. "Preduvedomlenie k sborniku *Novaia iskrennost'.*" In *Sbornik preduvedomlenii k raznoobraznym veshcham,* 171. Moscow: Ad Marginem, 1996.

———. *Sovetskie teksty.* St. Petersburg: Ivan Limbakh, 1997.

Propp, V. I. *Istoricheskie korni volshebnoi skazki.* Leningrad: Izdatel'stvo Leningradskogo universiteta, 1986.

Pryke, Sam. "Nationalism and Sexuality: What Are the Issues?" *Nations and Nationalism* 4, no. 4 (1998): 529–46.

Psaik. "A che za gundesh' . . . " (2004): available online at http://www.forum.msk.ru/files/guestbook-po020406.html.

Pushkin, A. S. *Polnoe sobranie sochinenii.* Moscow: Voskresenie, 1995–97.

Pyman, Avril. *The Life of Aleksandr Blok.* Vol. 1, *The Distant Thunder, 1880–1908.* Oxford: Oxford University Press, 1979.

———. *The Life of Aleksandr Blok.* Vol. 2, *The Release of Harmony, 1908–1921.* Oxford: Oxford University Press, 1980.

Rancour-Laferriere, Daniel. *Russian Nationalism from an Interdisciplinary Perspective.* Imagining Russia (Slavic Studies, vol. 5). Lewiston, N.Y.: Mellen, 2000.

Ratcliff, Carter. *Komar and Melamid.* New York: Abbeville, 1988.

Riabov, Oleg. *Matushka-Rus': Opyt gendernogo analiza poiskov natsional'noi identichnosti Rossii v otechestvennoi i zapadnoi istoriosofii.* Moscow: Ladomir, 2001.

———. *Russkaia filosofiia zhenstvennosti (XI–XX veka).* Ivanovo, Russia: Iunona, 1999.

Bibliography

————. *Zhenshchina i zhenstvennost' v filosofii Serebrianogo veka.* Ivanovo, Russia: Ivanovskii gosudarstvennyi universitet, 1997.

Riabova, Tat'iana. "Maskulinnost' kak faktor rossiiskogo politicheskogo diskursa." *Wiener Slawistischer Almanach: Sonderband 55: Gender-Forschung in der Slawistik,* ed. Jiřina van Leeuwen-Turnovcová et al. (2002): 441–51.

Riasanovsky, Nicholas. *A Parting of Ways: Government and Educated Public in Russia 1801–55.* Oxford: Clarendon, 1976.

Richards, Ivor. *The Philosophy of Rhetoric.* New York: Oxford University Press, 1965.

Rodina, T. M. *Aleksandr Blok i russkii teatr nachala XX veka.* Moscow: Nauka, 1972.

Rogger, Hans. *National Consciousness in Eighteenth-Century Russia.* Cambridge, Mass.: Harvard University Press, 1960.

Roll, Serafima. *Postmodernisty o postkul'ture: Interv'iu s sovremennymi pisateliami i krikitami.* Moscow: R. Elinin, 1996.

Rostopchina, Evdokiia. "Nasil'nyi brak." In *Poety 1840–50-x godov,* ed. B. I. Bukhshtab, 99–102, 477–78. Leningrad: Sovetskii pisatel', 1972.

Rowland, Mary, and Paul Rowland. *Pasternak's Doctor Zhivago.* Carbondale: Southern Illinois University Press, 1967.

Rozanov, Vasilii. *Mimoletnoe: 1915 god; Chernyi ogon': 1917 god; Apokalipsis nashego vremeni.* Moscow: Respublika, 1994.

————. *O pisatel'stve i pisateliakh.* Moscow: Respublika, 1995.

————. *Poslednie list'ia.* Moscow: Respublika, 2000.

————. *Russkaia gosudarstvennost' i obshchestvo: Stat'i 1906–1907 gg.* Moscow: Respublika, 2003.

————. *Sochineniia.* Moscow: Sovetskaia Rossiia, 1990.

————. "Zhenshchina pered velikoiu zadacheiu." In *Religiia: Filosofiia: Kul'tura,* 177–93. Moscow: Respublika, 1992.

Ruppert, W., ed. *"Deutschland, bleiche Mutter"—oder eine neue Lust an den nationalen Identität: Texte des Karl-Hofer-Symposions, 12–17.11.1990.* Berlin: Hochschule der Kunste, 1992.

Rutten, Ellen. "Kashchei the Immortal Versus the People: Viktor Vasnetsov and the Political Interpretation of Folk Tales in Russian Culture." In *Russian Legends, Folk Tales and Fairy Tales.* Exhibition catalogue, ed. P. Wageman, 50–60. Rotterdam: NAI, 2007.

————. "Mikhail Nesterov and Aleksandr Blok: Feminizing Russian Landscape Around 1900." *Slavonic and East European Review* 83, no. 2 (2006): 237–55.

————. "Ot 'dushi Ameriki' do 'molodoi Rossii': Delo Dunkan." In *Delo Avangarda: The Case of the Avant-Garde,* ed. W. Weststeijn, 489–501. Amsterdam: Pegasus, 2008.

————. "Where Postmodern Provocation Meets Social Strategy: *Deep into Russia.*" In *Provocation and Extravagance in Modern Russian Literature and*

Culture, ed. B. Dhooge, T. Langerak, and E. Metz, 163–79. Amsterdam: Pegasus, 2008.

Rylkova, Galina. *The Archeology of Anxiety: The Russian Silver Age and Its Legacy.* Pittsburgh, Pa.: University of Pittsburgh Press, 2007.

Sandomirskaia, Irina. *Kniga o rodine: Opyt analiza diskursivnykh praktik.* Vienna: Gesellschaft zur Förderung slawistischer Studien, 2001.

Sargeant, Lynn. "*Kashchei the Immortal:* Liberal Politics, Cultural Memory, and the Rimsky-Korsakov Scandal of 1905." *Russian Review* 64, no. 1 (2005): 22–43.

Savinova, E. "The Silver Age." In *Idee w Rosji = Idei v Rossii = Ideas in Russia,* vol. 5, ed. A. Lazari, 271–85. Lodz, Poland: Ibidem, 2003.

Savinova, E., and S. Zimina. "Kitezh." In *Idee w Rosji = Idei v Rossii = Ideas in Russia,* vol. 4, ed. A. Lazari, 279–83. Lodz, Poland: Ibidem, 2001.

Savkina, Irina, ed. *Gendernye issledovaniia,* no. 13 (*Gender po-russki: pregrady i predely*) (2005): available online at http://www.gender.univer.kharkov .ua/gurnal-013.shtml.

Schahadat, Schamma. *Intertextualität und Epochenpoetik in den Dramen Aleksandr Bloks.* Frankfurt am Main: Peter Lang, 1995.

Sedakova, Ol'ga. "Monolog o Venedikte Erofeeve." *Teatr,* no. 9 (1991): 98–102.

Seifert, Jaroslav. *The Plague Column.* London: Terra Nova, 1979.

Seifrid, Thomas. *Andrei Platonov: Uncertainties of Spirit.* Cambridge, Eng.: Cambridge University Press, 1992.

Senderovich, Savelii. *Georgii Pobedonosets v russkoi kul'ture.* Moscow: Agraf, 2002.

Seroff, Victor. *The Real Isadora.* New York: Hutchinson, 1971.

Severianin, Igor'. *Sochineniia v piati tomakh.* Vol. 4. St. Petersburg: Logos, 1995–96.

Shevchuk, Iurii. "Rodina" (2005): available online at http://www.lyricsworld .ru/lyrics/DDT-YUriy-SHevchuk/Rodina-11563.html.

———. "Rossiiane" (2005): available online at http://www.lyricsworld.ru/lyrics/ DDT-YUriy-SHevchuk/Rossiyane-37210.html.

Shevelev, Igor. "All of This Looks Like a Parable . . .: David Samoilov and His Diaries." *New Times,* December 2004: available online at http://www.new times.ru/eng/detail.asp?art_id=776.

Shkapskaia, Mariia. *Stikhi.* London: Overseas Publications Interchange, 1979.

Shklovskii, Viktor. *Sobranie sochinenii.* Vol. 1, *Povesti i rasskazy.* Moscow: Khudozhestvennaia literatura, 1973.

Shmel'kova, Natal'ia. *Poslednie dni Venedikta Erofeeva.* Moscow: Vagrius, 2002.

Sholokhov, Mikhail. *Sobranie sochinenii.* Vol. 6, *Podniataia tselina,* pt. 1. Moscow: Khudozhestvennaia literatura, 1966.

Shpet, Gustav. *Esteticheskie fragmenty.* Moscow: Pravda, 1989.

Siegel, Paul. *Revolution and the Twentieth-Century Novel.* New York: Monad, 1979.

Simpson, Pat. "Soviet Superwoman in the Landscape of Liberty: Aleksandr Deineka's *Razdol'e.*" In *Gendering Landscape Art,* ed. S. Adam and A. Gruetzner-Robins, 87–102. Manchester: Manchester University Press, 2000.

Siniavskii, A. "Nekotorye aspekty pozdnei prozy Pasternaka." In *Boris Pasternak and His Times: Selected Papers from the Second International Symposium on Pasternak,* ed. Lazar Fleishman, 359–72. Berkeley, Calif.: Berkeley Slavic Specialties, 1989.

Skoropanova, Irina. *Russkaia postmodernistskaia literatura.* Moscow: Flinta / Nauka, 1999.

Slobin, Greta. "Revolution Must Come First: Reading V. Aksenov's *Island of Crimea.*" In *Nationalisms and Sexualities,* ed. A. Parker et al., 246–63. London: Routledge, 1992.

Sluga, Genda. "Identity, Gender, and the History of European Nations and Nationalisms." *Nations and Nationalisms* 4, no. 1 (1998): 87–111.

Sokolov, Boris. "Russkii bog." *Druzhba narodov,* no. 12 (1996): 184–88.

Solntseva, Natal'ia. *Strannyi eros: Intimnye motivy poezii Nikolaia Kliueva.* Moscow: Ellis Lak, 2000.

Sologub, Fedor. *Sobranie sochinenii.* Vol. 8, *Stikhotvoreniia, rasskazy.* Moscow: NPK Interval, 2004.

Solov'ev, Sergei. *Istoriia Rossii s drevneishikh vremen,* pt. 4, vols. 7–8. Moscow: Mysl', 1989.

Solov'ev, Vladimir. *La Russie et l'église universelle.* Paris: Delamain, Boutelleau, 1922.

———. *Sochineniia v dvukh tomakh.* Moscow: Pravda, 1989.

———. *Sochineniia v dvukh tomakh.* Moscow: Mysl', 1990.

———. *Stikhotvoreniia: Shutochnye p'esy.* Munich: Fink, 1968.

———. *"Umom Rossiiu ne poniat' . . . " Satira: Iumor: Stikhi: Proza.* Rzhev, Russia: Rzhevskoe proizvodstvennoe poligraficheskoe predpriitie, 1998.

Solowjew, Wladimir. *Die nationale Frage in Russland: Deutsche Gesamtausgabe der Werke von Wladimir Solowjew.* Vol. 4. Munich: Wewel, 1972.

———. *Una Sancta: Schriften zur Vereinigung der Kirchen und zur Grundlegung der universalen Theokratie.* Vol. 2. Freiburg, Ger.: Wewel, 1954.

Solzhenitsyn, Aleksandr. *Rasskazy.* Moscow: Sovremennik, 1990.

———. "Sakharov i kritika 'Pis'ma vozhdiam.'" In *Publitsistika v trekh tomakh,* vol. 1. Iaroslavl', Russia: Verkhne-Volzhskoe knizhnoe izdatel'stvo, 1995.

Sorokin, Vladimir. "Mea Culpa?" *Nezavisimaia gazeta: Ex Libris,* April 14, 2005: available online at http://exlibris.ng.ru/tendenc/2005-04-14/5_culpa.html.

———. *Moskva.* Moscow: Ad Marginem, 2001.

———. "'Nasilie nad chelovekom—Eto fenomen, kotoryi menia vsegda pritiagival . . .' Interv'iu Tat'iany Voskovskoi s Vladimirom Sorokinym." *Russkii zhurnal,* April 3, 1998: available online at http://lib.ru/SOROKIN/interv01 .txt.

———. "Rossiia ostaetsia liubovnitsei." *Grani.ru,* March 23, 2005: available online at http://www.grani.ru/culture/theatre/m.86612.html.

———. *Sakharnyi Kreml'.* Moscow: AST, Astrel', 2008.

———. *Sbornik rasskazov.* Moscow: Russlit, 1992.

———. *Sobranie sochinenii v trekh tomakh.* Moscow: Ad Marginem, 2002.

———. "Tekst kak narkotik." Interview in *Sbornik rasskazov,* 110–27. Moscow: Russlit, 1992.

———. *Trilogiia.* Moscow: Zakharov, 2006.

Sorokin, Vladimir, and Oleg Kulik. *V glub' Rossii.* Moscow: Service, 1994.

Sorokin, Wladimir, and Alina Wituchnowskaja. "Nichts leichter, als ein Held zu sein: Wladimir Sorokin und Alina Wituchnowskaja im Gespräch." *Die Zeit,* November 9, 2000: 67–68.

Sosnina, N., and I. Shangina, eds. *Russkii traditsionnyi kostium: Illiustrirovannaia entsiklopediia.* St. Petersburg: Iskusstvo-SPB, 1998.

Spencer, Jerome. "'Soaked in *The Meaning of Love* and *The Kreutzer Sonata*': The Nature of Love in *Doctor Zhivago.*" In *Doctor Zhivago: A Critical Companion,* ed. E. Clowes, 76–89. Evanston, Ill.: Northwestern University Press, 1995.

Spieker, Sven. *Figures of Memory and Forgetting in Andrei Bitov's Prose: Postmodernism and the Quest for History.* Frankfurt am Main: Peter Lang, 1996.

Steussy, R. E. "The Myth Behind 'Dr. Zhivago.'" *Russian Review,* vol. 18 (1959): 184–98.

Stishova, Elena. "Zvuk lopnuvshei struny." *Nezavisimaia gazeta,* September 1, 2000: available online at http://www.guelman.ru/culture/reviews/2000-09 -01/010900ng/.

Struve, Gleb. *Russian Literature Under Lenin and Stalin, 1917–53.* Norman: University of Oklahoma Press, 1917.

Sukhareva, D., and I. Vizbor. "Aleksandra." In *Muzyki buket prekrasnyi: Populiarnye liricheskie pesni, romansy, muzykal'nye p'esy raznykh let,* ed. T. Kochura. Krasnodar, Russia: Izdatel', 1993.

Syrkin, A. *Spustit'sia, shtoby voznestis'.* Jerusalem: Ierusalimskii universitet, Tsentr po izucheniiu slavianskikh iazykov i literatur, 1993.

Taruskin, Richard. *Stravinsky and the Russian Traditions: A Biography of the Works Through Mavra.* Berkeley: University of California Press, 1996.

Tatarinov, V., ed. *Znakomye pesni: 100 Pesen sovetskikh poetov: Pesennik.* Moscow: Muzyka, 1964.

Tatishchev, S. S. *Imperator Aleksandr II: Ego zhizn' i tsarstvovanie.* Vol. 1. Second edition. St. Petersburg: A. S. Suvorina, 1903.

Tchaikovsky, Petr. *O Rossii i russkoi kul'ture*, ed. I. F. Kunin. Moscow: Gosudarstvennoe muzykal'noe izdatel'stvo, 1961.

Tengbergen, Maarten. *Klassieken van de Russische literatuur.* Utrecht, Neth.: Het Spectrum, 1991.

Terras, Victor. *Handbook of Russian Literature.* New Haven, Conn.: Yale University Press, 1985.

Tertz, Abram. *On Socialist Realism.* New York: Pantheon, 1960.

Thomson, Boris. *The Premature Revolution: Russian Literature and Society 1917–46.* London: Weidenfeld and Nicolson, 1972.

Timasheva, Marina. "'Kinotavr'—Debiuty i fil'my 'ne dlia zritelei.'" *Radio svoboda,* June 5, 2001: available online at http://www.svoboda.org/archive/ll_cult/0601/ll.060501-3.asp.

Timenchik, Roman. "Khram Premudrosti Boga: Stikhotvorenie Anny Akhmatovoi 'Shiroko raspakhnuty vorota . . .'" *Slavica Hierosolymitana,* vol. 5–6 (1981): 297–317.

Tiutchev, F. I. *Polnoe sobranie sochinenii v shesti tomakh.* Moscow: Klassika, 2002–.

Tokarev, Sergei, ed. *Mify narodov mira: Entsiklopediia v dvukh tomakh.* Vol. 2. Moscow: Sovetskaia entsiklopediia, 1982.

Tökés, Rudolf L., ed. *Dissent in the USSR.* Baltimore, Md.: John Hopkins University Press, 1975.

Tolstaia, Tat'iana. "Russkii chelovek na randevu." In *Den': Lichnoe,* 342–80. Moscow: Podkova, 2001.

Tolstaia-Segal, Elena. "Ideologicheskie konteksty Platonova." *Russian Literature* 9, no. 3 (1981): 231–80.

———. "Literaturnyi material o proze Andreia Platonova." In *Voz'mi na radost': To Honour Jeanne van der Eng-Liedmeier,* ed. A. van der Eng-Liedmeier, 193–207. Amsterdam: Slavic Seminar, 1980.

Tolstoy, Lev. *Polnoe sobranie sochinenii.* Moscow: Khudozhestvennaia literatura, 1928–64.

Tolz, Vera, and Stephenie Booth, eds. *Nation and Gender in Contemporary Europe.* Manchester: Manchester University Press, 2005.

Toporkov, A. "Materialy po slavianskomu iazychestvu (Kul't Materi-syroi zemli v der. Prisno)." In *Drevnerusskaia literatura: Istochnikovedenie,* 222–33. Leningrad: Nauka, 1984.

Toporov, V. N. *Sviatost' i sviatye v russkoi dukhovnoi kul'ture.* Vol. 1, *Pervyi vek khristianstva na Rusi.* Moscow: Gnozis, 1995.

Tornbjer, Charlotta. *Den nationella modern: Moderskap i konstruktioner av svensk nationell gemenskap under 1900-talets första hälft.* Lunds, Sweden: Lunds universitet, 2002.

Tret'iakova, V., ed. *Nashi liubimye pesni: Pesennik.* Moscow: Terra, 1996.

Trubetskoi, Evgenii. "Natsional'nyi Vopros, Konstantinopol' i Sviataia Sofiia." In *Smysl zhizni*, 355–70. Moscow: Respublika, 1994.

———. "Staryi i novyi natsional'nyi messianizm." In *Russkaia ideia*, ed. M. A. Maslin, 241–58. Moscow: Respublika, 1992.

Tucker, Robert. "The Image of Dual Russia." In *The Transformation of Russian Society: Aspects of Social Change Since 1861*, ed. C. Black, 587–605. Cambridge, Mass.: Harvard University Press, 1960.

Turgenev, Ivan. *Polnoe sobranie sochinenii i pisem v dvadtsati vos'mi tomakh.* Moscow-Leningrad: Nauka, 1960–68.

Ushakin, Sergei, ed. *O muzhe(N)stvennosti.* Moscow: Novoe literaturnoe obozrenie, 2002.

———. *Pole pola.* Moscow: Novoe literaturnoe obozrenie, 2007.

Ushakin, Sergei, and Mariia Litovskaia. "Muzhestvennost' v Rossii (Mezhdunarodnyi seminar 'Masculinities in Russia,' Illinoisskii universitet, Urbana-Shampein, SShA, 19–23 iunia 2003 g.)." *Novoe literaturnoe obozrenie*, no. 63 (2003): available online at http://magazines.russ.ru/nlo/2003/63/lit47.html.

Uspenskii, Boris. *Etiudy o russkoi istorii.* St. Petersburg: Azbuka, 2002.

Vadimov, Aleksandr. *Zhizn' Berdiaeva: Rossiia.* Oakland, Calif.: Berkeley Slavic Specialties, 1993.

Vaiskopf, Mikhail. *Siuzhet Gogolia: Morfologiia: Ideologiia: Kontekst.* Moscow: RGGU, 2002.

Valenius, Johanna. *Undressing the Maid: Gender, Sexuality and the Body in the Construction of the Finnish Nation.* Helsinki: Suomalaisen Kirjallisuuden Seura, 2004.

Van Baak, Joost. "Paradoks i psevdologika u Platonova (v chest' stoletiia so dnia ego rozhdeniia: 1899–1999)." In *Paradoksy russkoi literatury: Sbornik statei*, ed. V. Markovich and W. Schmid, 284–98. St. Petersburg: Inapress, 2001.

———. "Where Did Venička Live? Some Observations on the World of V. Erofeev's Poèma *Moscow–Petuški.*" *Russian Literature* 54, nos. 1–3 (2003): 43–65.

Van Leeuwen-Turnovcová, Jiřina, et al., eds. *Gender-Forschung in der Slawistik. Wiener Slawistischer Almanach Sonderband* 55. Vienna: Gesellschaft zur Förderung slawistischer Studien, 2002.

Vanchugov, Vasilii. *Moskvosofiia i peterburgologiia: Filosofiia goroda.* Moscow: ZAO Spetstekhnika, 1997.

Veeser, Aram, ed. *The New Historicism.* New York: Routledge, 1989.

Vekhi. Intelligentsiia v Rossii: Sborniki statei 1909–1910. Moscow: Molodaia gvardiia, 1991.

Velthues, Christoph. "Zur Evolution der russischen Literatur im 20. Jahrhundert." *Zeitschrift für Slavische Philologie* 56, no. 1 (1997): 1–31.

Vereecken, Jeannine. "Jaroslavna, de stem van de Russische aarde: Bijdrage tot de interpretatie van het *Igorlied*." 2008 (unpublished).

Verkhovtseva-Drubek, Natal'ia. "'Moskva-Petushki' kak parodia sacra." *Solo*, no. 8 (1973): 85–95.

Vitkovskii, Evgenii. *Pavel II* (2003): available online at http://books.rusf.ru/unzip/add-on/xussr_av/vitkoe01.htm?14/142.

V'iugin, V. "Poetika A. Platonova i simvolizm." In *"Strana filosofov" Andreia Platonova: Problemy tvorchestva,* vol. 3, ed. N. Kornienko, 267–73. Moscow: Nasledie, 1999.

Vladiv-Glover, Slobodanka. "Sorokin's Post-Avant-Garde Prose and Kant's Analytic of the Sublime." In *Poetik der Metadiskursivität: Zum postmodernen Prosa-, Film- und Dramenwerk Sorokins,* ed. D. Burkhart, 21–37. Die Welt der Slaven 6. Munich: Otto Sagner, 1999.

Vlasov, Eduard. "Bessmertnaia poema Venedikta Erofeeva 'Moskva–Petushki': Sputnik pisatelia." In *Moskva-Petushki,* ed. E. Vlasov, 121–559. Moscow: Vagrius, 2000.

Voloshin, Maksimilian. *Sobranie sochinenii.* Vol. 1, *Stikhotvoreniia i poemy 1899–1926.* Moscow: Ellis Lak, 2003.

———. *Stikhotvoreniia i poemy.* Moscow: Zvonnitsa-MG, 2000.

Von Plessen, Marie Louise, ed. *Marianne und Germania 1789–1889: Frankreich und Deutschland: Zwei Welten—Eine Revue: Katalog zur Ausstellung der Berliner FestspieleGmbH im Martin-Gropius-Bau.* Berlin: Argon, 1996.

Voronova et al., eds. *Knigi: Arkhivy: Avtografy: Obzory, soobshcheniia, publikatsii.* Moscow: Kniga, 1973.

Wachtel, Michael. *Russian Symbolism and Literary Tradition: Goethe, Novalis and the Poetics of Vyacheslav Ivanov.* Madison: University of Wisconsin Press, 1994.

Walker, Clint. "Journey from St. Petersburg to Moscow (and Back Again!): Petersburg Tropes in *Happy Moscow*." Paper presented at AATSEEL Conference, 2002.

———. "Unmasking the Myths and Metaphors of the Stalinist Utopia: Platonov's *Happy Moscow* Through the Lens of *The Bronze Horseman*." *Essays in Poetics,* vol. 26 (2001): 119–68.

Warner, Marina. *Monuments and Maidens: The Allegory of the Female Form.* London: Pan, 1987.

Wenke, Silke. "Gendered Representations of the Nation's Past and Future." In *Gendered Nations: Nationalisms and Gender Order in the Long Nineteenth Century,* ed. I. Blom, K. Hagemann, and C. Hall, 63–77. Oxford, Eng.: Berg, 2000.

Wessling, Robert. "Smert' Nadsona kak gibel' Pushkina: 'Obraztsovaia travma' i kanonizatsiia poeta 'bol'nogo pokoleniia.'" *Novoe literaturnoe obozrenie,* no. 75 (2005): available online at http://magazines.russ.ru/nlo/2005/75/ba7 .html.

Westphalen, Timothy C. *Lyric Incarnate: The Dramas of Aleksandr Blok.* Amsterdam: Harwood, 1998.

White, Hayden. *Metahistory: The Historical Imagination in Nineteenth-Century Europe.* Baltimore, Md.: John Hopkins University Press, 1973.

Wilson, Edmund. "Doctor Life and His Guardian Angel" and "Legend and Symbol in *Doctor Zhivago.*" In *The Bit Between My Teeth,* 420–47, 447–73. New York: Farrar, Straus and Giroux, 1965.

Wirtschafter, Elise Kimerling. *Social Identity in Imperial Russia.* DeKalb: Northern Illinois University Press, 1997.

Witt, Susanna. *Creating Creation: Readings of Pasternak's Doktor Živago.* Stockholm: Almqvist och Wiksell, 2000.

Yuval-Davis, Nira. *Gender and Nation.* London: Sage, 1997.

Zagoskin, M. N. "Dva kharaktera. Brat i sestra." In *Moskva-Peterburg: Pro et contra,* ed. D. K. Burlak, 127–32. St. Petersburg: RKhGI, 2000.

Zaitseva, Valentina. "National, Cultural, and Gender Identity in the Russian Language." In *Gender and National Identity in Twentieth-Century Russian Culture,* ed. H. Goscilo and A. Lanoux, 39–47. DeKalb: Northern Illinois University Press, 2006.

Zamiatin, Evgenii. "Moskva–Peterburg." *Nashe nasledie,* no. 1 (1989): 106–13.

Zamost'ianov, Arsenii. "Pristastrie k anekdotam s borodoi." *Znamia,* no. 6 (1996): 226–28.

Zander, L. A. "Filosofskie temy v romane Pasternaka 'Doktor Zhivago.'" *Vestnik russkogo studencheskogo khristianskogo dvizheniia,* no. 53 (1959): 37–48.

———. *Taina dobra (problema dobra v tvorchestve Dostoevskogo).* Frankfurt am Main: Posev, 1960.

Zazykin, V. I. "Zemlia kak zhenskoe nachalo i eroticheskie simvoly, sviazannye s nei." In *Natsional'nyi eros i kul'tura,* ed. G. D. Gachev and L. N. Titov, 39–88. Moscow: Ladomir, 2002.

Zen'kovskii, S. A. *Russkoe staroobriadchestvo: Dukhovnye dvizheniia semnadtsatogo veka.* Moscow: Tserkov', 1995.

Zhukovskii, V. A. *Sochineniia v trekh tomakh.* Vol. 2, *Ballady, poemy, povesti i stseny v stikhakh.* Moscow: Khudozhestvennaia literatura, 1980.

Zorin, Andrei. "Al'manakh—Vzgliad iz zala." In *Lichnoe delo No.: Literaturno-khudozhestvennyi al'manakh,* ed. L. Rubinshtein, 246–71. Moscow: Soiuzteatr, 1991.

———. "Opoznavatel'nyi znak." *Teatr,* no. 9 (1991): 119–22.

Zvereva, Galina. "Formy reprezentatsii russkoi istorii." In *Pol, gender, kul'tura: Sex, Gender, Kultur,* ed. Elizabeth Cheauré and Karolin Haider, 155–80. Moscow: RGGU, 1999.

Index

Page numbers in **bold** reference key passages about an entry.

Index

Index

Index

Index

About the Author

Ellen Rutten studied at the universities of Groningen and St. Petersburg and at the Humboldtuniversität in Berlin and has taught Russian culture and literature in Amsterdam, Leiden, and Cambridge. A cofounder and editor of *Digital Icons,* she is currently a postdoctoral fellow with the new-media research project The Future of Russian at the University of Bergen. Rutten has published on Russian literature, gender-nation stereotypes, and new media in *The Slavonic and East European Review, Osteuropa, kultura, Russian Literature,* and *Neprikosnovennyi Zapas,* among other journals. She is currently finishing a monograph on sincerity in post-Soviet culture. For updated information on Rutten's work and activities, see www.ellenrutten.nl.